Romans
The Divine Marriage
Volume 2 Chapters 9–16

A Biblical Theological Commentary

(Second Edition Revised 2020)

Tom Holland

COPYRIGHT

Romans: The Divine Marriage, A Biblical Theological Commentary, Volume 1 Chapters 1-8 and Volume 2 Chapters 9-16.

Copyright © 2011; Revised 2020 Tom Holland. All rights reserved. Except for brief quotations in critical publications or reviews, no part of this book may be reproduced in any manner without prior written permission from the publisher.

Write: Permissions, Apiary Publishing, Kemp House 152-160 City Road London EC4 2NX. Email: enquiries@apiarypublishing.com.

Scripture quotations are taken from the HOLY BIBLE, NEW INTERNATIONAL VERSION. Copyright © 1973, 1978, 1984, by International Bible Society. Used by permission of Hodder & Stoughton, a member of the Hodder Headline Group. All rights reserved. "NIV" is a trademark of International Bible Society. UK trademark number 1448790. [The NIV underwent a revision published in 2011. I regularly comment in this commentary on the bad choices that the translators had made in relation to the previous translations of Paul's use of *sarx* (flesh). Happily, in the new revision they have corrected most of these errors.

Volume 1 ISBN: 9781912445202

Volume 2 ISBN: 9781912445226

Cataloguing-in-Publication data:

Holland, Tom

Romans: The Divine Marriage: a biblical theological commentary / Tom Holland.

1. Bible. N.T. Romans—Commentaries. I. Title

BS2665.3 H75 2011

DEDICATION

Dedicated to
Eryl Davies,
a man of vision and grace,
and a Barnabas of our time.

ENDORSEMENTS

I. Howard Marshall described Tom Holland's ground-breaking *Contours of Pauline Theology* as a "remarkably fresh and creative study which makes one rethink familiar passages in new ways," while Anthony Thiselton remarked that "many of its arguments offer corrections to widespread misunderstandings of Paul."

Here in his new study the insights of Holland's former work, with its central "New Exodus" paradigm, impact radically upon earlier readings of Paul's Letter to the Romans, revealing that these readings were controlled by eclectic methodologies that have in varying measure obscured the message of the biblical text.

Those who have already encountered *Contours* will be eager to discover how a corporate reading of the Apostle Paul's greatest contribution to the New Testament unfolds, and how—to highlight but one issue—a forensic sense of justification is to be maintained in the light of a broader covenantal context.

Many readers will be amazed that yet another study of a biblical text that has been subjected to so many fingertip searches in the past can yield such fresh evidence. All in all, Tom Holland's new commentary will not only affect the way one reads Romans, it will change the that one looks at the Bible as a whole.

As the subtitle indicates, Tom Holland's Romans is truly both biblical and theological, as the letter is set firmly in its unfolding canonical context. Holland shows how Romans contributes to our understanding of God's covenant arrangement with humankind. The commentary digs deeply into current scholarship on the Old Testament roots of Paul's teaching, yet presents its conclusions in accessible language.
   Prof Douglas Moo, Wheaton College

This commentary on Romans develops many of the major themes explored in Dr Holland's useful and insightful book Contours of Pauline Theology. Tom Holland always remains alert to the influence and relevance of the Old Testament, and emphasises the impact of Paul's thought upon the Church as a community, and as well as on the individual as part of that community. Above all, Tom Holland deploys his scholarship to produce a very saline and practical commentary. The preacher will find here many practical applications, which will bring Paul's message to life for today. This is a clear and readable exposition, which well reflects Paul's pastoral concern for the community of the Church.

Anthony C. Thiselton, D.D., Professor of Christian Theology, University of Nottingham

This vigorously argued commentary seeks to allow Old Testament themes and thought patterns, not misguided scholarly conventions, to control Romans' message. Paul's ministry is seen rigorously in New Exodus terms; the church is the New Israel, Yahweh's people and (along with true Israel of old) figurative bride. Verses from the prophet Isaiah are particularly foundational. Organizationally Holland's treatment is strongly messianic in focus—every section of Romans is subordinated to "the Messiah King." Scholars of Romans will be stimulated by interaction with this canonically alert, creative, and frequently contrarian exposition and synthesis of a Pauline classic.

Robert W. Yarbrough, Covenant Theological Seminary, St. Louis, Missouri.

One of the greatest strengths of Romans: The Divine Marriage is that it compels readers to read Romans in light of the categories and covenants set forth in the OT. Whether or not one agrees entirely with Holland's reading, this work serves to remind us that the Scripture is a unified, not a fragmented, book with a single, coherent, and integrated message. And for that reminder we may be genuinely grateful.

Guy Prentiss Waters, Reformed Theological Seminary, Jackson, Mississippi, USA

I commended this well researched and well written book to the Church and believe that the reader will benefit from it as I have in my own reading. I trust and pray that the material will find a wide audience, for it is indeed most deserving of such attention. And it now takes its rightful place in that considerable library section on Romans, but stands out through both confession of true faith and courageous scholarship.

Michael A. Milton, Ph.D., Reformed Theological Seminary.

Holland's clearly stated exegetical conclusions will be of interest to those both within and outside of the perspectives of evangelical exegesis, particularly for his sustained corporate reading of Romans as well as his specific challenges to New Perspective arguments' .....Holland has 'very interesting perspectives to offer.

Prof Florence Morgan Gillman, University of San Diego.

Endorsements

Tom Holland's commentary on Paul's letter to the Romans is not just another commentary. He has a thesis to establish and he goes about his task with powerful argument, incisive exegesis and clear theology.
   Robert Strivens, Principal, London Theological Seminary

Tom Holland has written a thought-provoking book that will undoubtedly be fruitful for many teachers and preachers. More than any other commentator on Romans so far, he uncovers the Old Testament roots of the letter and shows the impact of Paul's thoughts upon the Christian church today.
   Dr Rob van Honwelingen, Theological University, Kampen, Netherlands

If you spend much time with Tom Holland, you're very likely to develop a far greater hunger for understanding the OT Scriptures! In this day, when the OT is so neglected in preaching and teaching, there is little doubt that Holland's work is potentially one of the instruments for change. Overall, I believe that this commentary should prove accessible and wonderfully impacting upon the thinking of those who choose to read it. May the Lord use this ground-breaking work as an instrument for good!
   M. Maxwell-Carr, posted on *Goodreads*

Holland not only shows that the main root of Paul's (Romans) theology is the Old Testament (especially Isaiah, the prophets and the theme of the new exodus), but he demonstrates more than any other commentary (through amazing and extended explanations of Paul's quotes and allusions to the OT) where Paul's thoughts are rooted. His contribution to the study of Romans is huge: he supplies us with a lot of "biblical theological insights".
   Laurent Dv, posted on *Goodreads*

Tom Holland's Romans is biblical and devotional in the best sense of those terms. His striking emphasis on the theological themes of the Old Testament is uncommon among New Testament specialists. Although New Testament scholars emphasize the history and world(s) of the first century, Holland focuses on theology within the context of Scripture. Leaving room for preachers and teachers to apply Paul's insight to their community today, Holland's Romans helps Christians enter into deeper communion with God and one another. This work is commendable not only for preachers wanting to offer insights into Paul's theology, it nicely disrupts current fads in Pauline scholarship. Romans: The Divine Marriage is a 'true' biblical theology influenced primarily by the witness of the Old Testament narrative, thankfully, without all the 'scholarly historic fiction' often produced by modern biblical scholars. All should 'take and read' in order to better understand the Bible's narrative.

'Tom', posted on *Goodreads*

CONTENTS VOLUME 2

Copyright	iii
Dedication	v
Endorsements	vii
Contents Volume 2	xi
Preface	xiii
Acknowledgments	xv
Abbreviations	xvii

Romans 9

The Messiah King and Israel's Hardening (9:1–33)	393
Excursus H: Election to Privilege and Service.	413
The Messiah and His Servants Hardening	427
Conclusion of Romans Chapter Nine	449

Romans 10

The Messiah King and His People's Recovery (10:1–21)	451
Conclusion of Romans Chapter Ten	482
Excursus J: The New Exodus Framework of Romans 9–11 and Other NT Passages.	483

Romans 11

The Messiah King and His New Covenant People (11:1–36)	493
Conclusion of Romans Chapter Eleven	526

Romans 12

The Messiah King and His Priestly People (12:1–8)	527
The Messiah King and His People's Character (12:9–21)	548
Conclusion of Romans Chapter Twelve	566

Romans 13

The Messiah King and His Delegated Representatives (13:1–14)	567
Conclusion of Romans Chapter Thirteen	581

Romans 14

The Messiah King and His People's Differences (14:1–23)	583
Conclusion of Romans chapter Fourteen	600

Romans 15

Romans: The Divine Marriage, Volume 2

    The Messiah King and His Servant's Work (15:1–33)   603
    Conclusion of Romans Chapter Fifteen   626

Romans 16

    The Messiah King and His People in Rome (16:1–27)   627
    Conclusion to Chapter Sixteen   645
    Excursus K: Concerning Methodology   647

Conclusion to the Letter

    Bibliography   673
    Index of Authors   701
    Index of Topics   709
    Index of Scriptures   729

PREFACE

Why subtitle a commentary on Romans *The Divine Marriage*? Mainly because the central message of the Bible has to do with the drama of God seeking out a people for himself. The Old Testament described Israel as God's bride because she was called to a unique, personal relationship with her God.

However, Paul's contention is that national Israel's exclusive claim to be the bride no longer stands. The apostle's message is that God has created a new covenant with those who believe in his Son, and that believing Jews and Gentiles have now become the true bride of God. The Jewish remnant and believing Gentiles both draw from the same divinely-appointed stock as they share the promises given by God to Abraham.

The theme of the divine marriage (which is the culmination of the New Exodus) shaped and guided the letters that Paul wrote. This is especially true for the letter to the Romans, the letter of the divine marriage.

ACKNOWLEDGMENTS

The writing of any commentary is far from a solitary task. Although authors hope that they bring a unique contribution to its understanding, all recognize that their thinking has been stimulated and aided by the writings of hundreds, if not thousands, of theologians they have read along the way. In the bibliography, I acknowledge those debating partners who have stimulated my thinking–and I do so with gratitude.

There have been others, whose aid has been as crucial as that of any debating partner. Their encouragement and support have made possible the long process of study and writing. Many individuals deserve mention, but I must limit myself to a few.

I gladly acknowledge the debt I owe to Dr Eryl Davies, the former principal of The Evangelical Theological College of Wales (now called Wales Evangelical School of Theology [WEST]). He appointed me to a teaching post in the school twenty years ago–a position I continue to hold. Eryl Davies is a Barnabas of our time. His patience, godly example, and support have been humbling to observe and experience. As he watched on, my research must have caused him much concern; but he allowed me the vital space to question and struggle with well-established interpretations of the text of Romans. His support and patience have been crucial to the completion of the research and the writing of this commentary.

I am also grateful to Jonathan Stephen, the present principal of WEST. He has encouraged me to persevere and has done everything possible to bring this book to publication.

I am also very thankful for a multitude of friends, who have kindly read sections of the text, making valuable suggestions as to how the reading experience could be improved. It is appropriate that I thank especially Colin Hammer, Howard Jones, Bernard Lewis, Anna Coplin, Elsie Marshall, Bill and Ann Weaver, Desmond Cartwright, Peter Wilkinson, Gareth Williams, Kevin Green, Iwan Rhys Jones, John Kendall, Tom Gledhill, and Barbara, my wife, for the time they gave to this task.

And, of course, how can I not acknowledge the patience and love of Barbara, who has allowed me to spend my life in the service of the Savior.

Tom Holland

ABBREVIATIONS

AffCr - Affirmation & Critique (Anaheim, Calif)
ALW - Archiv fur Liturgiewissenschaft (Regensburg)
AnaBib - Analecta Biblica
AnaBru - Analecta Bruxellensia
ATI - American Theological Inquiry
AusBR - Australian Biblical Review
Bib - Biblica
BibToday - Bible Today
BR - Biblical Research
BSac - Bibliotheca Sacra
BT - Bible Translator
BTB - Biblical Theological Bulletin
CBQ - Catholic Biblical Quarterly
Di - Dialog
DPL - Dictionary of Paul and his Letters
DS - Daughters of Sarah
EGT - Eglise er théologie
Enc - Encounter
EstBib - Estudios Biblicos
EvQ - Evangelical Quarterly
EvT - Evangelische Theologie
ExAud - Ex Auditu
ExpTim - Expository Times
HeyJ - Heythrop Journal
HTR - Harvard Theological Review
HvTSt - Hervormde Teologiese Studies
IBS - Irish Biblical Studies
Int - Interpretation
JBL - Journal of Biblical Literature
JETS - Journal of the Evangelical Theological Society
JJS - Journal of Jewish Studies
JPS - Journal of Pentecostal Studies
JSJ - Journal for the Study of Judaism
JSNT - Journal for the Study of the New Testament
JTS - Journal of Theological Studies
Jud - Judaica (Basil)

KEK - H. A. W. Meyer, Kritisch—exegetischer Kommentar über das Neue Tesament
Neot - Neotestamentica
NestTheolRev - Near East School of Theology Theological Review (Beirut)
NICNT - New International Commentary of the New Testament
NovT - Novum Testamentum
NTS - New Testament Studies
PCB - Peaks Commenatry on the Bible
RTR - Reformed Theological Review
ResQuart - Restoration Quarterly
RevExp - Review and Exposition
RBB - Revista biblica brasileira
SBET - Scottish Bulletin of Evangelical Theology
SBL - Society of Biblical Literature
SBLDS - SBL Dissertation Series
SBT - Studies in Biblical Theology
SE - Studia Evangelica
SID - Studies in Interreligious Dialogue
SJT - Scottish Journal of Theology
ST - Studia Theologica
TDNT - Theological Dictionary of the New Testament
Them - Themelios
TheolBeitr - Theologische Beiträge (Wuppertal)
TJ - Trinity Journal
TLZ - Theologische Literaturzeitung
TRu - Theologische Rundschau
TToday - Theology Today
TynBul - Tyndale Bulletin
USQR - Union Seminary Quarterly Review
VE - Verbum et Ecclesia
WTJ - Westminster Theological Journal
ZNW - Zeitschrift für die neutestamentliche Wissenschaft

Romans 9

THE MESSIAH KING AND ISRAEL'S HARDENING
(9:1–33)

I speak the truth in Christ—I am not lying, my conscience confirms it in the Holy Spirit—I have great sorrow and unceasing anguish in my heart. For I could wish that I myself were cursed and cut off from Christ for the sake of my brothers, those of my own race, the people of Israel. Theirs is the adoption as sons; theirs the divine glory, the covenants, the receiving of the law, the temple worship and the promises. Theirs are the patriarchs, and from them is traced the human ancestry of Christ, who is God over all, forever praised! Amen. It is not as though God's word had failed. For not all who are descended from Israel are Israel. Nor because they are his descendants are they all Abraham's children. On the contrary, "It is through Isaac that your offspring will be reckoned." In other words, it is not the natural children who are God's children, but it is the children of the promise who are regarded as Abraham's offspring. For this was how the promise was stated: "At the appointed time I will return, and Sarah will have a son." Not only that, but Rebekah's children had one and the same father, our father Isaac. Yet, before the twins were born or had done anything good or bad—in order that God's purpose in election might stand: not by works but by him who calls—she was told, "The older will serve the younger." Just as it is written: "Jacob I loved, but Esau I hated."

What then shall we say? Is God unjust? Not at all! For he says to Moses,

"I will have mercy on whom I have mercy, and I will have compassion on whom I have compassion."

It does not, therefore, depend on man's desire or effort, but on God's mercy. For the Scripture says to Pharaoh: "I raised you up for this very purpose, that I might display my power in you and that my name might be proclaimed in all the earth." Therefore God has mercy on whom he wants to have mercy, and he hardens whom he wants to harden.

One of you will say to me: "Then why does God still blame us? For who resists his will?" But who are you, O man, to talk back to God? Shall what is formed say to him who formed it, "Why did you make me like this?" Does not the potter have the right to make out of the same lump of clay some pottery for noble purposes and some for common use? What if God, choosing to show his wrath and make his power known, bore with great patience the objects of his wrath—prepared for destruction? What if he did this to make the riches of his glory known to the objects of his mercy, whom he prepared in advance for glory—even us, whom he also called, not only from the Jews but also from the Gentiles? As he says in Hosea:

"I will call them 'my people' who are not my people; and I will call her 'my loved one' who is not my loved one,"

and,

"It will happen that in the very place where it was said to them, 'You are not my people,' they will be called 'sons of the living God.'"

Isaiah cries out concerning Israel:

"Though the number of the Israelites be like the sand by the sea, only the remnant will be saved. For the Lord will carry out his sentence on earth with speed and finality."

It is just as Isaiah said previously:

"Unless the Lord Almighty had left us descendants, we would have become like Sodom, we would have been like Gomorrah."

What then shall we say? That the Gentiles, who did not pursue righteousness, have obtained it, a righteousness that is by faith; but Israel, who pursued a law of righteousness, has not attained it. Why not? Because they pursued it not by faith but as if it were by works. They stumbled over the "stumbling stone." As it is written:

"See, I lay in Zion a stone that causes men to stumble and a rock that makes them fall, and the one who trusts in him will never be put to shame." (Rom 9:1–33)

INTRODUCTION

Traditionally, chapters 9–11 have caused difficulty in understanding Paul's argument about election. Many scholars used to see the section as an intrusion into the letter, disrupting the argument that was being made; but, in recent decades, it has been appreciated as its heart.[477] In fact, the continuity of the argument is evident in that Rom 9:4–23 has a number of close parallels with Rom 3:1–7.[478]

Some Jewish believers were insisting that in order to be true members of the covenant people, Gentile believers had to keep the law and submit to circumcision. While such demands may have come from sincere attempts to apply the law, it is likely they were motivated by unspoken political concerns. The believing Jews must have been intimidated by the ever-increasing number of Gentiles who were professing faith in Jesus as Messiah and God's Son. At Paul's insistence, which was strengthened by the agreement he had won from the Jerusalem Council (Acts 15:12–35), the Gentiles were being admitted into the community of the Messiah on the same terms as the Jews. They were of little threat while their numbers remained relatively low. However, the blessing that accompanied their evangelization and the increasing resistance of the Jewish people to the message of the crucified Messiah meant that the Gentiles were speedily taking the reins of power in local believing communities by virtue of their numbers.

The problems produced by this growth were tearing the early church apart. A number of Jewish disciples came to believe that the only way to rein in the growing influence and power of the Gentile converts was to demand that they be circumcised. By controlling who was accorded full covenant membership, they could keep the upper hand. It was a simple, effective move, but one that Paul could not tolerate.

The danger with a divided community was that each faction would see the other as renegade. This was Paul's deepest fear as it would damage the gospel message incalculably. On the other hand, believing Jews and Gentiles living in harmony with each other would be a great demonstration of the power of God to restore relationships and overcome the evil of hatred and alienation.

Paul devotes the next section of his letter (chapters 9–11) to show that believing Jews and believing Gentiles are part of God's salvation purposes and

---

[477]Wright, *Messiah*, 166, says the theology in chapters 1–11 remains the same. Stendahl, "Introspective," 205, claims that chapters 9–11 are not an appendix but the climax of the letter. Räisänen, "Conversion," 410, says chapters 9–11 are about rejecting covenantal privilege. Gaston, "Enemies," 415, points out that the phrase "instruments of wrath" is based on Isa 53. This, once again, links the argument with the exile and New Exodus promises.

[478] See Williams, "Righteousness," 281.

how the rejection of one by the other is a denial of the Gospel. He shows that it is God's intention, as expressed in the Law and the Prophets, for Gentiles to be converted and for their successful evangelization to provoke unbelieving Jews to turn to the Messiah. Paul also wants the believing Gentiles to realize that they cannot exist, as far as God is concerned, without believing Jewish people—the remnant in Israel cannot be treated as having been cast off by God and, therefore, irrelevant.

However, Paul has to address another sensitive matter—the status of unbelieving Israel. In keeping with the corporate, covenantal framework he has been using throughout the letter, the text will be interpreted as a development of the New Exodus theme. Paul is concerned to show that Israel is in danger of being left outside of the covenant, which has been brought to fulfillment in Christ. Ironically, this is the very covenant made with Abraham, the father of the Jewish nation. We have seen the developing New Exodus theme in chapters 1–8; Rom 8:29–36 uses pilgrimage language to speak of opposition to the pilgrim community as it journeys to its inheritance. We also saw that Rom 7:1–4 summed up the argument of Rom 5:12–6:23. The issue at stake was how a people could be brought out of a relationship with Satan and into a new relationship with God. This relationship, in keeping with OT imagery and the expectation of a second exodus, was described using marital language. Israel was called to be Yahweh's bride, and she gloried in this privilege and status.

The question Paul must now answer is: where do the Jewish people fit into the New Exodus? Are they automatically included on the basis of having been the people of the Egyptian exodus? Do they bypass the conditions that are imposed on Gentiles who wish to be part of this community? Do they have a privileged status within it? Can they cast a deciding vote over who is included?

Paul fears that this new community–this new man–is in danger of self-destruction as Jews and Gentiles argue over their status before God. The Jews can, of course, appeal to their history and the promises given to their ancestor, Abraham. The Gentiles, however, can claim that the experience of the Jewish people *is* history, and that God has cast them aside in favor of blessing Gentiles. Their growing numbers and increasing dominance in the church must have seemed like undeniable evidence that this was so.

In chapter 9,[479] Paul begins his defense of Israel's status. Conscious of how crucial this issue is, he is concerned that the Gentile converts understand God's

---

[479] J.P. Martin, J.P., "Kerygma," 308, considers that chapters 9–11 recapitulate the argument of chapters 1–8.

purpose for his ancient people so that they can relate appropriately to them. However, behind Paul's argument is a further concern: "if God can cast off his ancient people who were bound to him by covenant, what security can there be for the new covenant community? Can God's promises be taken seriously if he was able to abandon his people when they failed him? Is God's commitment to the New Israel as frail as his commitment to her predecessor? If he chooses to disengage himself from his covenant promises to her, will not his reputation and the confidence of his people be at stake?" Paul reminds the Romans that the Jews have the birthright. They had received blessings from which the Gentiles were excluded. They had been privileged beyond any other nation on earth (Rom 9:1–5).

Paul goes on to show the principles of foreknowledge and election operating throughout salvation history. They were active when he called Jacob instead of Esau (Rom 9:6–17) and when he dealt with Pharaoh. God is at liberty to show mercy or to judge as he wills–and none can argue.[480] As the potter has freedom to mold clay however he wishes, so God has the right to express his will by exercising justice in the form of judgment (which all deserve) or mercy and forgiveness (which none deserve) (Rom 9:14–24).

It would be wrong to use these texts to support individual election.[481] In line with the argument of the whole Epistle, they are dealing with representative heads of communities. The freedom that a person has to enter or reject membership is a different matter. As this material applies primarily to states of solidarity, there are hermeneutical issues that need to be faced before truths are removed from their intended context and applied to the salvation of the individual. There are important overlapping concepts and principles in corporate and individual models, and these must be worked through and clarified before using them without reference to their original context and purpose.[482] In general, out of its great traditional concern for the salvation of the individual, Reformed theology has given insufficient emphasis to the corporate dimension of the argument being presented by Paul in this passage.

---

[480] Later, I will suggest that the argument is not principally about showing mercy in salvation (as is often understood) but more about grace in granting unmerited privilege, p. 402.

[481] For discussion on Rom 9 and individual election, see Schreiner, "Election," 25–40.

[482] See, for example, the discussion on justification in Excursus D: Justification in the Theology of Paul, p. 168.

However, while the corporate perspective must be kept to the fore, the argument in this section is presented in terms of individuals as Paul deals with heads of communities. This indicates that there must be individual significance in what is being said even though personal salvation is not the primary thrust of the passage.[483]

What is most significant is that Paul uses OT material that prophesies the Babylonian exile, bringing it into the developing New Exodus theme. He says that the final manifestation of Yahweh's righteousness is displayed in the fulfillment of the promise he made long ago to include the Gentile nations in the experience of the New Exodus salvation. This New Exodus is about bringing out the new covenant people of God from the domain of Sin. It does not deny the earlier covenants made with Israel–faith has always been the principle of initiation for sharing in the righteousness of God. Israel "after the flesh" was not being rejected, but invited into the new covenant. Many would refuse, preferring to misuse the law in a hopeless attempt to secure righteousness. Nevertheless, a remnant in Israel would be saved. This was a constant principle in the old covenant. A remnant had always stood against the Jewish community's popular mindset (2 Chr 34:21; Isa 10:20; 11:16; 37:32; Zeph 3:13). They would share in the faith of the Messiah as true people of God. This is in complete accord with the principle of election and is fundamental to all that the prophets had taught (Rom 9:25–33).

The New Exodus motif is further underlined as Paul considers Pharaoh. The hardening of his heart was prior to the Exodus (Rom 9:17–18) and, amazingly, Paul applies the same principle to his own kinsmen, unbelieving Israel (Rom 11:25)! By refusing to become part of the remnant, they have become the victims of the divine hardening and, as a result, have been excluded from the experience of the New Exodus. In this attitude of disobedience, they have done everything they could to deter their fellow countrymen from joining the people of the Way. In other words, unbelieving Israel in the New Exodus reflects Pharaoh in the Egyptian exodus. They both resist God and both have hardened hearts.

---

[483] The case parallels what we find in Rom 5:12ff. Adam, as the representative of his descendants, responds to God in such a way that they will know alienation and personal judgment. While the focus is Adam's sin, they are all involved because, collectively, they are "in Adam." Here, Pharaoh represents his people, who will come under judgment as a result of his decisions. If the corporate focus is taken away from either passage, a very different and inadequate reading will be produced.

We have already noted the extensive use that Paul makes of Isaiah. Here, in chapter 9, there are quotations from Isaiah in vv. 15, 27, 29 and 33. Each of these has been carefully chosen by Paul to support his ongoing argument, without doing injustice to their original contexts.[484]

9:1 I speak the truth in Christ—I am not lying, my conscience confirms it in the Holy Spirit.

Paul is concerned that he is not seen as rejecting his kinsfolk. He swears an oath, affirming that what he is about to say is a true reflection of his feelings for his kinsmen. Paul expresses grief over the state of unbelieving Israel. It was vital for the Roman Jewish believers to know that his grief was genuine as fabricated distress was a feature of their culture. The presence of professional mourners at the deathbed of Jairus's daughter in Capernaum is an example of such disingenuous sorrow, which turned so quickly to mocking laughter (Luke 8:51–53).

In the past, Paul's word had been doubted. Three years after his conversion, believing Jews in Jerusalem did not accept his story as true (Gal 1:18–20) and Barnabas had to speak, on his behalf, to the apostles (Acts 9:26–27). It was fourteen years later that Paul's testimony was believed in Jerusalem when he was accepted by the "pillars" of the church as an apostle to the Gentiles and given the right hand of fellowship (Gal 2:1–10).

No wonder Paul had such strong feelings about telling the truth and defending his trustworthiness—a matter he touched on in a number of his letters. He warned of untruthfulness in his letter to the Colossians (Col 3: 9–10), where, interestingly, he raised the issue in the context of church unity. When defending his ministry to the Corinthians, Paul wrote: "The God and Father of the Lord Jesus, who is to be praised forever, knows that I am not lying" (2 Cor 11:31).

Paul stressed that he is speaking the truth "in Christ." This is a solemn claim for him to make as he has written in chapter 8 about the one who "searches our hearts" (v. 27). In order to fully appreciate the corporate nature

---

[484] Aletti, "L'argumentation," 41–56, claims that Paul's argument in Rom 9 is concentric: A (vv. 6–9) and B (vv. 10–13): the divine choice, C (vv. 14–18) and C' (vv. 19–24): questions and answers concerning God and his justice, B' (vv. 25–26) and A' (vv. 27–29): the divine choice. Such an analysis reveals that Paul's emphasis in this chapter concerns the contrast between the elect and the non-elect. This observation suggests that chapter 9 is closely connected to chapter 8.

of his arguments, it is important to keep in mind that Paul normally applies the term "in Christ" to communities of believers rather than individuals. Some of the believing communities that he describes in this way are the Ephesian (Eph 2:13), Corinthian (1 Cor 15:18; 16:24), Philippians (Phil 1:1; 4:21), and Colossian (Col 1:2).

Paul writes that his conscience supports his claim of truthfulness and adds the phrase "in the Holy Spirit." This could be a reference to Rom 8:26, where he acknowledged the help given by the Holy Spirit to all believers, aiding them in areas of weakness.

9:2 I have great sorrow and unceasing anguish in my heart.

Paul's experience can only be understood by those who have been rejected by the people they love. He was not alone in having such an experience. David is considered by some to have composed Psalm 22 after fleeing from Jerusalem to escape the tyranny of his son, Absalom. He described the emotion of such rejection in this way: "I am poured out like water, all my bones are out of joint. My heart has turned to wax; it has melted away within me" (Ps 22:14).[485]

From his letters and the Acts of the Apostles, we learn of Paul's intense sufferings, including those he experienced at the hands of his fellow Jews. He was stoned in Lystra and left for dead (Acts 14:19), publicly misrepresented in Ephesus (Acts19:9), beaten in Jerusalem (Acts 21:27–32), and lashed on five occasions (2 Cor 11:24). In addition to physical sufferings, Paul writes these telling words in his letter to the Corinthians: "Besides everything else, I face daily the pressure of my concern for all the churches. Who is weak, and I do not feel weak? Who is led into sin, and I do not inwardly burn?" (2 Cor 11:28–29).

Such openness helps us to appreciate the man behind this statement in Rom 9:2; for, in addition to his immense concern for his kinsmen, he carried the memory of all that he had suffered at their hands as well as his daily concern for the churches. In spite of the ever repeating cycle in his heart of sorrow and

---

[485] The psalm is, of course, applied to Jesus, the Messiah, in the NT. As a Psalm of David, it best fits the circumstances of his flight from Jerusalem (2 Sam 15:13–31; 16:5–14), when his enemies divided his garments and he felt all strength drain from him as a result of the horror of his son's betrayal. Even the reference to the piercing of hands is poetic language, describing his utter helplessness. Of course, the psalm has a far more glorious fulfillment in the suffering of his descendant (Rom 1:3), whose hands were literally nailed and whose garments were divided.

anguish, Paul could not help but love his unbelieving brethren.[486] He felt this way because he knew the privileges that his kinsmen were rejecting, and of the judgment that faced them (Rom 9:25–29) if they lived and died rejecting the Savior whom God had sent (Rom 11:26).

9:3 For I could wish that I myself were cursed and cut off from Christ for the sake of my brothers, those of my own race, the people of Israel.

The intensity of Paul's love and concern is such that he would be willing to exchange his own position of blessing for the awful state of condemnation[487] if that would secure the salvation of his "brothers and fathers" in Israel. Scholars have noted the similarity between Paul's willingness to take the place of his people and the willingness of Moses to be cut off for the sake of the rebellious Israelites (Exod 32:32). Some have argued that Paul saw himself to be a new Moses.[488] This may be so, as in 2 Cor 3:7–18 Paul seems to compare his ministry with that of Moses. However, this latter point is disputed by some scholars.[489]

9:4 Theirs is the adoption as sons; theirs the divine glory, the covenants, the receiving of the law, the temple worship and the promises.

This verse lists the remarkable privileges the Jews[490] had as the covenant people of God.

They had been adopted as God's son(s) (Exod 4:22–23), had the Lord dwelling among them in his divine glory (Exod 40:34), and had been the only nation with whom God had entered into covenants. (Paul is probably referring to covenants with Abraham [Gen 15:1–21], Moses [though, in reality, he was the mediator of the covenant between God and Israel],and David [2 Sam 7:12–

---

[486] Contra Davies, W.D., *Jewish*, 137, and Campbell, W.S., "Freedom," 28, who suggest the emphasis is to answer those who have accused Paul of denying his heritage and national identity.

[487] The term is "anathema," which originally meant "devoted to destruction." In Paul's day, it had become a formula for excommunication.

[488] See Munck, *Israel*, 12ff., 29ff., who argues that Paul saw himself as a significant eschatological figure, parallel to Moses. Contra Siegert, *Argumentation*, 12.

[489] For further discussion, see Holland, *Paul, Israel's Law and God's Spirit*, forthcoming.

[490] Moo, *Application*, 292, notes that, when Jews speak about themselves and their special place in salvation history, they call themselves "Israelites."

16].) Furthermore they had received the law of God, which Paul sees as a privilege, even though he speaks elsewhere of it bringing condemnation.[491] They also had the temple in which the Creator God dwelt and his promise of blessing when he sent his Messiah into the world.

The significance of these privileges is difficult for Gentiles to appreciate; they define the Jewish people and their relationship with God. How could a nation be more blessed? However, despite all of these privileges, Paul describes unbelieving Jews as fallen olive branches (Rom 11:17–21), in desperate need of being grafted back into the tree. (This description of unbelieving Jews bears similarity to Jesus' words in John 15:1–11, a passage often used to challenge the fruitfulness and assurance of Christians. Such a reading fails to recognize that Jesus was speaking to the apostles who, as Jews, were still under the old covenant. He was warning them of apostasy within the nation, describing unredeemed Israel as unfruitful branches on the vine, which God, the divine gardener, cuts off. They wither and are cast into the fire. The fruit they failed to produce included truth, justice, righteousness, and purity. To preach the danger of Christians losing their salvation from John 15 misses the crucial meaning of the original context and wrongly identifies the subjects of the warning.)

So, Rom 9:4 is a reminder of the immense privileges afforded to Israel. It contains important information that will help us confirm the earlier claim that the letter should be read from an OT perspective, carefully considering the legitimacy of importing into it Greco-Roman cultural thought.

The first of the privileges was that the Jews had been adopted as sons. We have seen in Rom 8:17 that many scholars believe Paul's teaching on sonship to be modeled on the Roman practice of slave adoption, giving the slave the same legal status as natural siblings. Here, the word υἱοθεσία (*huiothesia*) "adoption" is used again, but it is clear that this has nothing to do with Roman adoption patterns.[492] The background is Israel's adoption as Yahweh's son, the nation coming under God's covenantal care (e.g., Exod 4:22; Deut 14:1; 32:6; Jer 31:9; Hos 1:10; 11:1). This model pre-dates adoption in the Roman legal system. Indeed, those who cite the Greco-Roman model often fail to note that

---

[491] See Holland, Paul, Israel's Law and God's Spirit, forthcoming.

[492] See Scott, *Sons of God*, 174. Wilder, *Echoes*, 77, (Contra Burke, *Adopted*) says that Scott's insights need to be pressed further, so that they might yield their full measure of corresponding reality and open up Paul's teaching regarding the law.

the practice was restricted to a very remote province. It is unlikely that the general public in Rome would have known of its existence.

However, Paul and the Roman believers did have a shared narrative context—the OT, This is attested to by the many OT quotations in the letter. Indeed, Paul builds his theology on the basis of these citations. It would seem reasonable to begin with these sacred texts to see if his doctrine of adoption reflects them.

The significance of this particular text (Rom 8:17) for Paul's doctrine of adoption is important. If he is following the OT understanding of sonship, it would confirm that, when he calls the believers *douloi* (which can be translated "slaves" or "servants"), he has "servants" in mind.[493] Israel was God's servant to the nations as well as being his son, and was commissioned to take the message of the knowledge of Yahweh to those in darkness. This is a task the nation was to perform as a son and not as a slave, serving the father willingly within the covenant. In this context, individual Jews were servants of Yahweh.

However, if we follow Paul's argument in the unfolding chapters, we will find him explaining how unredeemed Israel failed to fulfill this role. This is why the nation eventually lost the unmerited privileges that God graciously bestowed upon her when he elected Israel to be his servant.

Paul describes how the Gentiles are being grafted into the original stock as they take up the mantle of service. They draw nourishment from its root, as do the branches of the redeemed remnant of Israel. One assumes that, in Paul's mind, the stock is Abraham and the believers have become his true seed. Together, redeemed Gentiles and redeemed Jews fulfill the purposes of the covenant to the end that all the nations of the earth will be blessed.

The second privilege was that the Jewish people knew the presence of God in a way that no other nation did. The divine glory was exhibited at the Exodus when they were brought out of Egypt (Exod 15:11) and in the Second Exodus when they were brought out from exile in Babylon (Isa 40:5). The divine glory is the manifestation of God's presence and person. This is what Moses longed to see and of which he was granted a glimpse (Exod 33:18). The prophets looked forward to the day when, along with the nations, they would see the glory of God (Isa 66:18).

---

[493] See Holland, *Contours*, chapter 4; Thielman, *Story*, 185–89.

The third privilege was that, throughout OT history, God made a series of covenants with the Jewish people. He promised Adam that he would protect him and send a Redeemer from his family, Noah that he would not flood the world again, Abraham that he would establish him as the head of a nation that would represent him, and David, that one of his sons would always rule over the house of Judah. While these are the key covenants of the OT, God made many less significant covenants with individuals for various reasons. In all of these covenants, Yahweh was committing himself to his people. These unique, privileged agreements were focused on the people of Israel and were for their blessing.

The fourth privilege was that the Jewish people were blessed by the giving of the law. They esteemed it so highly that their teachers taught creation happened so that God could give his law to his people. The psalms express the delight that devout Jews had in the law, for it instructed them in Yahweh's ways and guided them in the paths of truth and righteousness. The commandments were not arid regulations that had to be observed but expressions of Yahweh's love for his people and, because of this, they were joyfully observed (Ps 1:2; 94:12; 119:29, 55–92; Isa 51:7). Of course, something went seriously wrong, for this same law became the means of Israel's condemnation.

Israel's sixth privilege concerned the Temple, the importance of which cannot be exaggerated. It was where Yahweh met with his people and where he dwelt. (Before King Solomon built the temple, God tabernacled with his people by dwelling in a temporary "tent.") However, Solomon's temple was razed to the ground when Nebuchadnezzar invaded Judah and destroyed Jerusalem. Removing this privilege from Israel symbolized the end of her covenantal relationship with God, and she was taken into exile in Babylon.

Seventy years later, a remnant returned to Jerusalem to rebuild the city, and its first priority was to rebuild the temple. According to promise, this would be achieved by a descendant of David. However, no such leader emerged, and the community decided to restore the building itself.

This building was eventually replaced by the temple that King Herod built. By means of this gesture, the Gentile king hoped to endear himself to the Jewish people; but his hope was in vain. It was in this edifice that Jesus declared: "destroy this temple and I will raise it again in three days" (John 2:19), confusing the Jews who did not realize that he was talking about his own body. As a result, the early church regarded Herod's temple as redundant because the living temple (the church), in which God dwelt by his Spirit, was raised to life in the death and resurrection of Jesus. The Jews, however, continued to see themselves as custodians of temple worship. They believed that they alone had access to the living God and that he was delighted to receive their praise and worship, which could only be offered in the appointed place. Of course, such confidence was severely shaken as a result of the war in 70 AD, when the Romans destroyed the temple.

Finally, the promises had been the unique property of the Jews. Eventually, however, they were given to bless the Gentiles. Different promises had been given at various points in Israel's history, all encouraging and looking forward to the nation's blessing and usefulness. The key promises have been considered in the introduction of this chapter.

9:5 Theirs are the patriarchs, and from them is traced the human ancestry of Christ, who is God over all, forever praised! Amen.

Paul has a theological understanding of history: "but when the time had fully come, God sent his Son, born of a woman, born under law, that we might receive the full rights of sons" (Gal 4:4). His understanding is like Matthew's (Matt 1:1–17) and Luke's (Luke 3:23–38)—both gospel writers being anxious to show the lineage of Jesus, the promised seed. Paul asserts that there was nothing haphazard about Jesus' line, for it came about through the purposes of God. He was the one whom Joseph predicted would be raised up to secure his brothers' welfare (Gen 49:10), the one about whom Nathan spoke (2 Sam 7:11–16), and the one anticipated by the prophets (Isa 9:2–7; Jer 23:5; 30:9; 33:17; Ezek 34:23; Rom 1:3).

The statement "who is God over all," is evidence that the early Christian community acknowledged the divinity of Jesus. The early church came to this conviction through her understanding of the OT Scriptures as well as from her experience and growing understanding of the salvation Jesus had secured. The NIV translates ὁ ὢν ἐπὶ πάντων θεὸς εὐλογητὸς εἰς τοὺς αἰῶνας (*ho ōn epi pantōn theos eulogētos eis tous aiōnas*)"who is God over all, forever praised." While such a reading is supported by the word order of the original Greek text, word order alone does not decide meaning. Punctuation must also be considered. Unfortunately, the punctuation of this text is not clear, for there is little or no punctuation in the earliest manuscripts.[494] The following are the possibilities that the Greek will bear:[495]

1. From them comes the Messiah according to the flesh, who is over all, God blessed forever, Amen. (Comma after "who is over all")

2. From them comes the Messiah according to the flesh, who is over all. God be blessed forever, Amen. (Full stop after "who is over all")

3. From them comes the Messiah according to the flesh. God who is over all be blessed forever, Amen.

The following considerations favor the meaning of the first possibility, with the consequence that Paul ascribes divinity to Christ. First, the grammatical argument heavily supports this interpretation. For such an expression of praise as "Amen" not to be linked to a word in the preceding sentence is exceptional in Paul's writings. Second, the confession in Rom 1:3–4 is widely considered to be programmatic for the letter. In that passage, Paul described Jesus as the "Son of God." In the light of this, a statement about Christ's deity in the body of the Epistle would be expected. (While the term "Son of God" in Rom 1:4 can be interpreted as a Messianic description and not a proof of divinity, Christ's status as being "over all" is repeatedly asserted in Paul's writings [Eph 1:22; 4:6; Col 2:10],[496] and these texts have high Christologies.) Third, the whole argument of Rom 9–11 moves towards the final affirmation of the universal sovereignty of Jesus as Messiah and Lord.

A key piece of evidence is found in Rom 10:4–13, where Paul calls Jesus Κυριος (*Kurios*) "Lord." This title is used in a section in which he quotes from the book of Joel 2:32 (3:5 [LXX]). There is no doubt that in the LXX, the title *kurios* stood for the tetragrammaton YHWH, the sacred name of Israel's God. Paul says: "For there is no difference between Jew and Gentile—the same Lord is Lord of all and richly blesses all who call on him, for, 'Everyone who calls on the name of the Lord will be saved'" (Rom 10:12–13). The inclusion of this passage from Joel 2:32 is telling. It determines the way Paul uses the term

---

[494] See Metzger, "Punctuation," 95–112; Harris, M.J., *Jesus*, 144–72; Turner, M., *Grammatical*, 13–17; Cullmann, *Christology*, 312–13; Moule, C.F.D., *Origin*, 137.

[495] As listed by Wright, "Romans."

[496] Of course, many scholars would not accept the Pauline authorship of these letters. I have argued that the evidence for rejecting Paul's authorship of the letter to the Colossians is methodologically flawed. See Holland, *Contours*, Ch. 12, etc. The arguments given are also applicable to the letter to the Ephesians.

kurios in the earlier part of the passage. He (the Lord) is the same LORD (Yahweh) who is spoken about by the prophet, and Paul says that he is Jesus.

Some scholars are understandably hesitant to embrace the statement as an expression of high Christology, believing this came much later in the understanding of the church. Also, they reason that trinitarianism was framed when the church confronted several challenges stemming from Greek philosophy in the second and third centuries. But the statement should not be seen as a flight into ontological theology. Its setting is that of salvation history. It asserts that Christ is the Redeemer of his people and, indeed, of creation itself. As the OT made abundantly clear, only Yahweh can redeem creation.[497] Therefore, it must follow, that if Jesus is the Redeemer, he must be Yahweh (God). Such a pathway to a high Christology is driven by the very doctrines of God, creation, and salvation, and is not dependent on any form of philosophical speculation or argument.[498]

9:6 It is not as though God's word had failed. For not all who are descended from Israel are Israel.

In human terms it appeared that the word of God had failed. When, from his "Christian" perspective, Paul considered the condition of Israel's unredeemed majority, it looked as though the promises given to his people had failed—indeed, that the word of God had failed. But, as the opening sentence in the verse states, his word had not failed! As the chapter unfolds, Paul quotes the prophet Isaiah, who stated that only a remnant of Israel would be saved while the majority would be condemned (Isa 10:27–28). He also quotes from the book of Hosea, in which God said of the Gentiles: "I will call them my people who are not my people" (Hos 2:23).

So Paul is saying that, despite the pain Israel's condemnation brings him, God's word is true, and he plays on the name "Israel" to explain how this is so. There are a number of ways of interpreting this verse. Paul could be saying that not all of the descendants of the nation of Israel are members of the true Israel. While he does not state the fate of Israelites who do not belong to the true Israel, we know from previous verses that he mourns their rejection and the fact they will be condemned should they fail to acknowledge Jesus as the Messiah. On the other hand, Paul could be saying that all who are descended from the patriarch Israel–Yahweh's name for Jacob (Gen 32:26–28) —are not members

---

[497] Isa 41:18–20; 42:5–17; 44:24–26; Jer 36:8–12.

[498] See Holland, *Contours*, chapter 12.

of the true Israel, i.e., the church (the body of redeemed people from all nations, including Israel). The implication of this is that the promises were not given to Abraham's natural descendants but to his sons of promise, such as Jacob. It is interesting that when Isaac blessed Jacob (Gen 28:3–4), he said: "May God . . . increase your numbers until you become a community of peoples" (Gen 28:3), the blessing being confirmed to Jacob by God in a dream (Gen 28:13–14).

At Pentecost, there was a tremendous wave of Jewish conversions (Acts 2:41; 4:4). To the disciples, it must have looked like God was bringing the nation to her Messiah. Sadly, this promising start did not continue, for many of those who came into the church in those early heady days[499] misunderstood the makeup of the new community. Their confusion is seen in the letter to the Hebrews and in the closing chapters of the Acts of the Apostles, where divisions between the Jewish believers became obvious as some sought to impose the law on Gentile converts.

This major disagreement about the Gentiles and the law almost ripped the church apart. Many of the Jewish converts found it impossible to move on from the security that the law had given them into total confidence in the completed work of redemption accomplished by Christ. They tried to straddle both camps, creating an ongoing problem for those who sought to welcome the uncircumcised Gentiles on an equal footing with the circumcised Jews.

So, in conclusion, it seemed that the promises of God to the patriarchs (including Abraham) had failed as the number of Jewish converts was declining rather than increasing. However, Paul refused to accept this as the true picture. The physical descendants of Abraham (and, therefore, of Jacob [or Israel]) are not his true children. His true descendants are those who share the same faith as Abraham. It was not correct to count the number of Jews coming into the church as a measure of the fulfillment of scripture. The Gentile converts were just as much the children of promise, and, in Paul's view, they must be taken into account when deciding whether the promises to the patriarch were being fulfilled.

---

[499]Even after a period of intense intimidation (Acts 5), Luke says: "So the word of God spread. The number of disciples in Jerusalem increased rapidly, and a large number of priests became obedient to the faith" (Acts 6:7). It is understandable why, at this time, the church would have thought that Israel was embracing her message and her Savior.

9:7 Nor because they are his descendants are they all Abraham's children. On the contrary, "It is through Isaac that your offspring will be reckoned."

Paul presses home the truth that being a physical descendant of Abraham does not mean automatic membership of the new covenant community. To show this, he points to the fact that the original promise was not given to all the physical descendants of Abraham such as Hagar's son, Ishmael, or the sons of his wife, Keturah (Gen 25:1–4), or of his concubines (Gen 25:6).

At the time when Abraham was promised he would father a son (Gen 15:2–6), he was not told the identity of the mother. So, many years later, when his old and barren wife, Sarah, insisted that he should father a family for her through her handmaid, he agreed.

His first child was born to Sarah's Egyptian handmaid, who came to be known as Hagar. When Hagar became pregnant, she was told by the angel of the LORD that her son, to be named Ishmael, would father numerous offspring (Gen 16:9–11). If Abraham had listened carefully to Hagar's account of the meeting, he would have realized that Ishmael was not to be the "son of promise" because the LORD had warned Hagar that Ishmael would live in hostility towards all his brothers. In contrast, Abraham's descendants, through his "son of promise," would be a blessing to the nations. Despite Ishmael being his firstborn son (and being circumcised with the patriarch), Abraham's "son of promise" had yet to be born.

When Ishmael was fourteen years old, Sarah gave birth to Isaac. Paul confirms that he was the child of promise through whom Abraham's offspring would be reckoned.

In Galatians, Paul goes even further, pointing out that the Scriptures say the nations would be blessed through Abraham's "seed"—not "his seeds" (Gal 3:16). He argues that the promise is directed to a specific descendant, i.e., Jesus, the Christ. The NIV has obscured this particular point that Jesus is the true seed of Abraham in Paul's letter to the Romans. It has translated σπέρμα (*sperma*) "seed" in Rom 9:7 as "offspring," hiding Paul's technical use of the term. Paul uses "seed" in this verse in the same way as he has used it in Galatians. The point he is making is that the promised seed is a particular descendant of Abraham's line. The term is not to be understood as encompassing all of Abraham's spiritual descendants.

In a parallel argument in Galatians, Paul appeals to the church to stay committed to the person of Christ. His argument presents him as the one true seed of Abraham and rejects all possible contenders for Jewish allegiance—

even such luminaries as Isaac, Jacob, Moses, Elijah, and David. Jesus alone is the true seed of Abraham, and it is through him that the covenant promises are fulfilled.

9:8 In other words, it is not the natural children who are God's children, but it is the children of the promise who are regarded as Abraham's offspring.

What Paul is arguing would have been bewildering for Jews in Rome. They regarded the fact that they were the physical descendants of Abraham and of Jacob ("Israel") as synonymous with being the children of the promise. Paul cuts right across this thinking—the same thinking he had once upheld. His claim that the Gentiles are equally, without reservation, children of Abraham through faith in Christ Jesus is the basis of his following argument. Indeed, their union with Christ, who is the true seed of Abraham, makes them not only the true seed, but also the remnant spoken so much about by the prophet Isaiah (Isa 10:20–22; 11:11–16; 28:5; 37:4, 31–32. See also, Jer 23:3; 31:7; 42:2; 43:5; 44:7; 50:20).

9:9 For this was how the promise was stated: "At the appointed time I will return, and Sarah will have a son."

Paul quotes from Gen 18, where the visit of the three men to Abraham is recorded: "Then the LORD said, 'I will surely return to you about this time next year, and Sarah your wife will have a son'" (Gen 18:10). It is of interest how, in Gal 4, Paul saw God's involvement in the birth of Isaac. When considering Ishmael and Isaac, he writes: "At that time the son born in the ordinary way persecuted the son born by the power of the Spirit" (Gal 4:29). The statement suggests that Sarah was enabled to conceive by the "power of the Spirit." This is a misleading translation of ἀλλ' ὥσπερ τότε ὁ κατὰ σάρκα γεννηθεὶς ἐδίωκεν τὸν κατὰ πνεῦμα, οὕτως καὶ νῦν. The NAS gives a better translation: "But as at that time he who was born according to the flesh persecuted him who was born according to the Spirit, so it is now also" (Gal 4:29 NAS). In other words, the birth of Isaac was the result of the divine promise and not the result of extraordinary faith as discussed in the Romans 4:18 commentary.

So, Paul's argument hangs on a correct understanding of the promise. The fact that Abraham and Sarah had to wait for the LORD's return in order for the promise to be fulfilled emphasizes that this birth was dependent on divine intervention. In human terms, God's appointed time for the couple was hardly their best time. They were both advanced in years (Abraham was one hundred and Sarah was ninety when Isaac was born) and the birth of a child, while joyous beyond measure, would usher in years of anxiety.

9:10–11 Not only that, but Rebekah's children had one and the same father, our father Isaac. Yet, before the twins were born or had done anything good or bad—in order that God's purpose in election might stand.

Again, Paul focuses on the descendants of the promised seed. Isaac's wife, Rebekah, experienced years of barrenness until God answered his prayer. His wife conceived and she bore non-identical twin boys. Paul makes the point that one was chosen and the other was not. This choice was not made after they were reared, when their developing personalities and characters could be assessed, but in the womb and before they were known to their parents.

How could there be anything to distinguish between the babies while they were still in the womb? From a human perspective, priority would be decided at the point of birth. The son who was born first—Isaac's firstborn—would be given the birthright and claim to the promised inheritance conferred on Abraham and his seed.

The point Paul is emphasizing is that human choice is not necessarily God's choice. He is not swayed by personality, talent, and achievement; or bound by "rights" and privileges of any kind. God alone makes his choices. These cannot be predicted because they are of a different order from those made by humans. Again, the emphasis is on the two boys having done nothing to determine the election of Yahweh. While they were still in the womb, God decreed that the firstborn would serve his younger brother. Paul is demonstrating that nothing can control the choices that God makes.[500] The one chosen will not be able to claim that this privilege was his right by birth or because of his works.

9:12 Not by works but by him who calls—she was told, "The older will serve the younger."

The phrase "not by works" recalls similar words in Eph 2:9: "not of works, so that no one can boast." This is the essence of the Gospel Paul proclaimed—absolutely no one can boast in his or her status before God (1 Cor 1:26–31). Nothing can be brought to God to convince him of human worth. Indeed, any such attempt to do so is grounds for rejection, as God will not share his glory

---

[500] Cranfield, *Romans*, 11, 480, says that if there is a hint of predestination here, it is strictly focused on the progress of God's saving activity within the process of history and not on individuals. Cf. Wilckens, *Römer*, 11, 196–97, and Käsemann, *Romans*, 265. That accepted, it still does not deflect from the sovereignty of God in making choices over individuals to achieve his purposes.

with another (Eph 2:9b). While it is valid to recall Eph 2:9, it must be realized that, in Rom 9:12, Paul is not dealing with how God chooses people for salvation but how people are chosen for privilege and responsibility. (We shall see that this perspective continues into chapter ten.) Indeed, when Eph 2:9 is examined, it is found to be saying a similar thing. Paul tells the Gentiles that they had been included into the covenant community solely because of God's grace and kindness. Therefore it is not in its intent a proof text for evangelism but a declaration of God's kindness to them. It is a corporate statement of the change of status afforded to all believing Gentiles—they have been included in the covenants of promise by God's grace and not by law observance. In that covenant, they share God's saving grace. Since they are saved from the judgment that will come upon the godless, the covenant speaks ultimately of salvation. Indeed, even though Paul's argument is about being elected for service, it moves on to salvation from judgment (v.27), i.e., the salvation of the believing community from the wrath it deserves. We shall see that Paul is insistent that this community is not exclusively Jewish or Gentile but made up of those who have faith in the redemptive purposes of God.

The detailed argument Paul has made prepares the believers in Rome for his claim that God has brought the Gentiles into the new community ahead of the Jews. He will go on to declare that God has set aside privilege, exalting those with none.

The term "works" in the phrase "not by works" has been interpreted by those favoring the "New Perspective" on Paul as referring to the law's requirements of rituals and practices. It is claimed that the term is not about keeping the moral or religious requirements of the law but about issues such as circumcision, diet, and Sabbath-keeping. While Paul does make use of this meaning for "works" in Rom 3:27 and Rom 9:4, there are other times when its meaning is much more than this. This meaning encompasses the keeping of the law's commands as a set of moral precepts as understood by the Reformers (Acts 13:38–39; Rom 3:19–20; 5:13, 20). What Paul is saying is that Jacob, the heir, was not chosen because he had attained a greater righteousness than Esau through his devoted obedience to the law.

9:13 Just as it is written. "Jacob I loved, but Esau I hated."

In saying that God hated Esau–the firstborn and natural inheritor of the promise—there is no intention to suggest there was malicious ill will towards him. The expression is a familiar Hebraism speaking of "loving less."[501] It does not necessarily imply that Esau had been rejected by God in terms of his love; it simply means that he was not chosen to be the bearer of the promise made to Abraham.[502] The same idiom is found in one of the sayings of Jesus. He said that unless a man hates his father, mother, and wife, he could not be his disciple (Luke 14:26). Jesus was not calling for his followers to hate their families but to love him more than them. In a similar way, the choice of Jacob did not mean God did not love Esau; it simply meant that he had chosen Jacob to continue the line through which his covenantal purposes would be fulfilled.

EXCURSUS H: ELECTION TO PRIVILEGE AND SERVICE.

Contrary to the claims of some scholars, there are a number of significant factors supporting the suggestion that, in Romans 9, Paul speaks about election for honor (privilege) and service rather than salvation.

First. As we have been discovering, the letter to the Romans makes better sense when interpreted as a document with the church's experience of God's saving work as its focus rather than that of the individual Christian. This corporate reading has resolved many of the difficulties presented by traditional individualistic readings.[503]

Second. In reference to Paul's statement that he is willing to be cut off from Christ for the sake of his brethren, some claim that he would not show this extreme distress over the loss of national privilege but that he would for

---

[501] Hodge, *Romans*, commenting on 2 Sam 12:11; 16:10 and Ps 105:25 says, "from these similar passages it is evident that it is a familiar scripture usage to ascribe to God effects which he allows in his wisdom to come to pass" (316).

[502] Heb 12:15–17 says: "See to it that no one comes short of the grace of God; that no root of bitterness springing up causes trouble, and by it many be defiled; that there be no immoral or godless person like Esau, who sold his own birthright for a single meal. For you know that even afterwards, when he desired to inherit the blessing, he was rejected, for he found no place for repentance, thought he sought for it with tears." This text does not challenge the reading offered above, for it speaks of a different event. The event in Rom 9:13 is about Esau being denied the role of Redeemer as a result of Yahweh's sovereign choice, whereas the Hebrews' text is about the bitterness that set into his heart as a result of losing his inheritance to his younger brother through selling his birthright. The point of the Hebrews text (written, of course, to Jews), is that they must strive not to lose their inheritance of the blessings that believers are entitled to. The discussion of both texts is about covenant privilege and responsibility, not salvation.

[503] For support of this corporate reading, see Thiselton, *Doctrine*, 187, 480.

the eternal salvation of individual Israelites.[504] This position, however, is not tenable. Most scholars acknowledge that, in his distress, Paul is identifying himself with Moses, who anguished over the judgment that was about to come upon Israel. Few, if any, would argue that Moses had an understanding of individual salvation. This was a doctrine that developed through succeeding generations, finally coming to its climax in the death and resurrection of Christ (2 Tim 1:10). If Paul keeps faithful to the original theological context and content (as many now recognize him to do), imposing a notion of individual salvation that was not in the original text needs to be justified. Furthermore, to see the loss of privilege and status as of little consequence is to fail to see the statement in its historical setting. The covenantal curses were spelt out in Deut 29–32, and among these curses, which were to fall on Judah in 586 BC, were conquest and deportation, It is significant that, when Moses prayed because he feared that as a result of the covenant being broken by the people's idolatry that Yahweh's wrath would come upon Israel, despite the judgment that the Levites had exercised (Exod 32:27–35).

In Paul's day, many were growing concerned about the increasing danger Israel was putting herself into as she provoked Rome by pressing her national aspirations.[505] The church must have been alarmed as she knew of Jesus' prediction that Jerusalem would be razed to the ground within the generation of those who heard him (Matt 24:1–2). To say that Paul would not know about this too, and, in response, would not wish himself accursed when he realized the inevitable outcome of Israel's hardening is to be theologically and historically naive.[506] It is natural that he would wish to be cut off for Israel's

---

[504] Schreiner, "Teach," 27; Moo, *Romans*, 559. This is also the argument of Piper, *Justification*, 156, who sees only an individualistic meaning in Rom 9:1–3. He acknowledges that this individualistic reading of Rom 9:1–4 is the key to his interpretation of Rom 9:18. Without it, his "election to judgment" reading of Rom 9:18 falls. However, he does not consider Israel's immediate 70 AD danger (see following). If the impending siege is the context of Paul's statement, his focus is not the individual Jew, and Piper's interpretation of Rom 9:18 collapses. He acknowledges this himself when he says: "Therefore the solution which Rom 9:6–13 develops in response to this problem *must* address the issue of individual eternal salvation," Piper, *Justification*, 64–65 (emphasis Piper's).

[505] See, for example, Wright, *Victory*.

[506] Wright, *Perspectives*, 142, sees 2 Thess 1:6–9 to refer to the fall of Jerusalem. The argument that Paul is not interested in the fate of his brethren other than their eschatological judgment asks us to accept that a deep concern held by Jesus and his disciples (Matt 24:1–2) had evaporated from the thinking of the early church. The possibility of the fall of Jerusalem is evident in texts throughout the NT. Heb 10:30–32

sake–he would not be a true son of Abraham if he did not. (Sadly, as feared, judgment was poured out in all of its destructive brutality when the Roman army laid siege to the city in 70 AD). In recognizing this to be the setting of Paul's anguish, what he says matches the theology of Moses' prayer perfectly.

Third. As noted above, those who argue for an individualistic reading of chapter 9 do so because they reason that Rom 9:1–5, which describes the benefits of Israel's election, is about Paul's concern for salvation of individual Israelites. It is argued that the passage is about the salvation of individual Jews rather than the loss of national privilege.

While Paul expresses deep grief for his brethren, who now stand under the curses of the covenant, the opening section of the chapter cannot be used to justify individualizing the verses that follow. In this introductory passage, Paul is saying that it is *as a nation* that the Jews have received the adoption, have known the divine glory, have partaken in the covenants, have received the law, have known temple worship and have received the promises. He writes: *"Theirs are the patriarchs"* (ὧν οἱ πατέρες Rom 9:5) and "out of *them* is the Christ" (ἐξ ὧν ὁ χριστὸς Rom 9:5). Clearly, none of these blessings belong to an individual Jew—it is the community that received them. What Paul is preparing to deal

---

and Luke 12:58–59 have these sorts of ideas behind them. The cry of Jesus over unrepentant Jerusalem (Luke 13:34–35) is a lament that pervades much of the NT. Following his reference to her as a city set on a hill, giving light to the world (Matt 5:14), Jesus warns of Jerusalem's future judgment if she does not build on the rock of his words (Matt 7:26–27). See also Matt 21:18–22:14 and parallels, especially Jesus' teaching on the significance of the curse of the fig tree. The same theme of Jerusalem's judgment is found in Revelation. Bauckham, *Climax*, xv, xvii., says: "The world created by the text is intended as an interpretation of the real world in which John and his readers live . . . In his symbolic vision of the past, present and future of the Roman empire, he brings together accurate references to the apparent contemporary realities of Roman power and prophetic perception of the hidden reality of divine power." See also, Hendriksen, *Conquerors*; Smolarz, *Marriage*. Regardless of the legitimacy of interpreting Revelation in the context of the church's future experience, the exegete's first task is to interpret it as it would have been understood by the intended readers. If this is valid, then it is clear that the fall of Jerusalem continued to be a vitally important topic for the church. Indeed, not to consider this context is a strange way of exegeting the teaching of the apostles, for if they had forgotten, or overlooked, Jesus' prophesy, how could they be trusted to communicate the rest of his teaching? Consequently, while Paul's main concern regarding salvation is eschatological, he is also deeply distressed over the impending judgment of his people. This said, as pointed out by Beale, *Revelation*, 45, the problem of limiting the judgment of Rev 13:7–8 to AD 70 is the need to: "provide an exegetical rationale both for exchanging a pagan nation with Israel as the primary object of Daniel's final judgment and for limiting the last judgment mainly to Israel and not applying it universally."

with is not individual salvation but how a people, who had been blessed above all others, could lose the privileges they once had. If this setting is not appreciated, alien issues will be imported into the case that Paul is making. As noted in our comments on v.4, while the benefits of the blessings are individually appropriated, they are corporately received.

Fourth. We have found throughout our exposition of Romans that Paul argues from OT models and texts. For this reason, it is important to guard against inadvertently introducing ways of thinking into Paul's perspective that are not supported by his firm grasp of OT theology. The fact is that there is no theology of individual election to salvation or damnation in the OT. The OT understanding of salvation is about God saving people from physical and moral danger. For example, Abraham and Lot were called to leave places saturated with ungodly practices, and when Yahweh rescued Israel from Egypt, her salvation was delivery from captivity and restoration to the role she was elected to fulfill. This is not to deny that a development of the doctrine of personal election took place in the NT. However, while I want to stand by the teaching that holds to God's electing grace toward the individual, I also want to assert that basing arguments for individual election on this particular passage confuses the discussion and misses some important issues that Paul is expounding.

Fifth. Immediately before the passage that speaks of God's judgment on Pharaoh, Paul recounts the principles of covenant theology, the essence of which is rooted in corporate representation (Rom 9:6–12). In v.7, he says: "It is the children of the promise who are regarded as Abraham's offspring." Because they are Abraham's seed, they have the blessings of the covenant that Yahweh made with Abraham. This is followed by a discussion concerning Esau. He was Isaac's firstborn, who forfeited his inheritance by giving it to Jacob in exchange for a pottage of meat. Although Jacob was an unworthy inheritor, through this transfer of privileges, the rights of the firstborn were bestowed upon him. In receiving this blessing, Jacob became the head of Abraham's family and, as a result, all his children became the inheritors of the promises that Yahweh had sworn to the patriarch.

Paul continues to explore the crucial issue of how Israel could lose her inheritance. This is the great theme that is thrashed out throughout the chapter, continuing on into chapters 10 and 11. It is clear that the metanarrative of these chapters is that Israel has lost all that she has been blessed with and that the believing Gentiles have been brought into the blessing promised to Abraham. (Gen 12:3). Thus, the examples that Paul draws upon to introduce his argument concerning Pharaoh's judgment are essentially about Jewish and Gentile election to privilege and service rather than to salvation. At no point in this prologue is there any suggestion that the discussion is about individual salvation.[507]

Sixth. Paul follows the discussion of Pharaoh's judgment with a citation from the book of Isaiah. There is some debate as to which passage he cites. The majority of scholars[508] identify Isa 29:16 as the source:

> You turn things upside down, as if the potter were thought to be like the clay! Shall what is formed say to him who formed it, "He did not make me"? Can the pot say of the potter, "He knows nothing"? (Isa 29:16)

However, while Isa 29:16 is found word for word in Rom 9:20, it lacks the question τι "why". The element τι is, however, found in another passage, which has a potter making a pot (Isa 45:9). In this passage, the clay challenges the potter as to why he has made it into the vessel it does not want to be. It is because of the presence of τι in Isa 45:9 that some believe Paul to have conflated the two texts, Isa 29:16 being augmented by the question of Isa 45:9.[509]

While scholars have highlighted their preference for the origin of the quote in Rom 9:20, those who recognize that Paul has introduced τί from Isa 45:9 fail to ask the fundamental question, "why has Paul done this?" Surely the answer is that Paul wants both passages to contribute and, in order to find out why, we need to consider their contexts.

---

[507] Contra Schreiner, *Romans*, 519, who says: "The strongest evidence that salvation is in view is the contextual flow of thought that informs Rom 9–11." As demonstrated above, the overall Paschal/New Exodus corporate argument of the letter along with the flow of the introduction to chapters 9–11 support a corporate argument. To shore up his argument concerning election to judgment, a topic that he can find no evidence for in any other text of scripture, Schreiner, op. cit. 521, has had to appeal to extra-biblical literature, saying: "Double predestination is also evident in Jewish sources, particularly Qumran." He also cites in support 1QS 3:15–16; 4:24–26; 1QH 7(15). 16–26, and then refers to Sir. 33:7–13, Apoc. and Abr. 22.1–5 (op cit. 522 n. 23). Schreiner dismisses the reading of Caird on the basis that: "he asserts mistakenly that the term 'vessels of destruction' does not relate to God's decree concerning the eternal destiny of individuals" (op cit. 522 n. 24). Schreiner's dismissal of Caird rests on what I seek to show is a misplaced confidence in his own exegesis. Basically, the essence of his argument is "because Caird does not agree with me, he is wrong."

[508] Os, "Isaiah," 75–78; Barrett, *Romans*, 188; Cranfield, *Romans*, 2:491; Piper, *Justification*, 195.

[509] Morris, *Romans*, 365; Dunn, *Romans*, 2:356; Fitzmyer, *Romans*, 369.

Isa 29:13–16 says:

> The Lord says: "These people come near to me with their mouth and honor me with their lips, but their hearts are far from me. Their worship of me is made up only of rules taught by men. Therefore once more I will astound these people with wonder upon wonder; the wisdom of the wise will perish, the intelligence of the intelligent will vanish." Woe to those who go to great depths to hide their plans from the LORD, who do their work in darkness and think, "Who sees us? Who will know?" You turn things upside down, as if the potter were thought to be like the clay! Shall what is formed say to him who formed it, "He did not make me"? Can the pot say of the potter, "He knows nothing"? (Isa 29:16)

What is interesting is that the illustration of the potter has Israel asserting that she has achieved her status by her self-effort. She thinks that her own wisdom has guided her through the dangers she has faced and that her own effort has elevated her.

But Yahweh warned, "the wisdom of the wise will perish, the intelligence of the intelligent will vanish" (Isa 29:14). Her leaders are told that they are foolish if they think they can do anything in secret, hiding their plans and guilt from God (Isa 29:15). They do not realize that Yahweh is totally different from them (Isa 29:16). They are arrogant, thinking that they are the designers and craftsmen of their own status and achievements. Indeed, they actually ask if Yahweh really is responsible for their achievements (Isa 29:16).

The picture is of Israel, boasting of her independence from Yahweh and refusing to credit anything to him. Her perception is that he had no hand in her development, it being the result of her own wisdom. Yahweh's accusation against Israel is upheld by his distress in Isa 28:18 that she had entered into a covenant with death (believed by many to refer to the Egyptian god of death, Môt).

The above picture of Israel and how Isaiah uses the potter illustration in Isa 29:16 is very different from the way it is used in Isa 45:9. This text, which was about the clay's complaint against the potter, is not coming from one who boasts of her achievements but from the nation, who complains to Yahweh for preferring Cyrus above herself and appointing him to be Yahweh's anointed. This is the very status that Israel forfeited through her disobedience. This Isaianic text is crucial for grasping the argument that Paul is making because, as previously noted, scholars are increasingly agreeing that he uses the OT with great respect, transferring texts along with their theological contexts. This key fact precludes us from using the quote to support an individualistic reading as it is *Israel* who is objecting to her God.[510] It is also crucial as Paul has taken the trouble to conflate the two texts, so that they make their own contributions to his case against Israel. Bringing the question from Isa 45:9 into such a brief extract from Isa 29:16 suggests that it is a vital part of his argument in the compiled citation. We would, therefore, be wise to pay close attention to what the question is focusing upon. Isaiah says:

> "This is what the LORD says to his anointed, to Cyrus, whose right hand I take hold of to subdue nations before him and to strip kings of their armor, to open doors before him so that gates will not be shut: I will go before you and will level the mountains; I will break down gates of bronze and cut through bars of iron. I will give you the treasures of darkness, riches stored in secret places, so that you may know that I am the LORD, the God of Israel, who summons you by name. For the sake of Jacob my servant, of Israel my chosen, I summon you by name and bestow on you a title of honor, though you do not acknowledge me. I am the LORD, and there is no other; apart from me there is no God. I will strengthen you, though you have not acknowledged me, so that from the rising of the sun to the place of its setting men may know there is none besides me. I am the LORD, and there is no other. I form the light and create darkness, I bring prosperity and create disaster; I, the LORD, do all these things.
>
> "You heavens above rain down righteousness; let the clouds shower it down. Let the earth open wide, let salvation spring up, let righteousness grow with it; I, the LORD, have created it.
>
> "Woe to him who quarrels with his Maker, to him who is but a potsherd among the potsherds on the ground. Does the clay say to the potter, 'What are you making?' Does your work say, 'He has no hands'? Woe to him who says to his father, 'What have you begotten?' or to his mother, 'What have you brought to birth?'" (Isa 45:1–10)

The context of the potter illustration in Isa 45:9 is very different from that of Isa 29:16. Here, the focus is not the arrogance of Israel but her confusion and frustration that another has been given the privilege of being the anointed (servant) of the Lord. Cyrus is not only given this most prestigious position, but all that had been said of Israel is now promised to him as he fulfills the ministry entrusted to him by Yahweh:

The Lord takes Cyrus's right hand (Isa 45:1). Nations are subdued before him and their might removed (Isa 45:1). All obstacles are removed that would hinder his progress (Isa 45:1–2). He is given an intimate knowledge of God and

---

[510] Implied by the designation "anointed."

an assurance as to his calling (Isa 45:3). The purpose and goal of his mission is made clear, it is to serve the people of God and act as their deliverer (Isa 45:4). His calling is totally of grace (Isa 45:5). The purpose of his calling is that Yahweh will be exalted among the nations (Isa 45:6). The LORD who has called Cyrus is sovereign (Isa 45:7–8).

All of these statements had been said of Israel, her mission, and her God. Now, they are addressed to Cyrus.

Unlike the potter's illustration in Isa 29:16 (which highlighted Israel's arrogance), this illustration highlights her confusion. She has learned that Yahweh has chosen Cyrus to be his servant (Isa 45:1). She cannot cope with this news, and asks him why she has been given a lower status, for she will be dependent upon Cyrus. This is at the heart of what Paul is about to argue. Believing Israel has to come to terms with the fact that the Lord has called the Gentile church to be his servant. Israel—even believing Israel—has no precedence over the new servant of the Lord.

Indeed, this is the very theme that Paul has raised in the opening of the chapter, where he laments the imminent judgment on Israel. Like her ancestors in Isaiah's time, she has abused her privilege and status, and is to be judged. If Paul was talking about individual salvation when considering God's dealings with Pharaoh, he has now introduced a theme that is completely against the flow of his earlier argument. The link between the judgments on Israel and Pharaoh is underlined by his statement that Israel has been hardened (Rom 11:7). If this is not the focus of his theme, it would mean that, as soon as Paul completes his discussion on Pharaoh's hardening (a hardening to eternal damnation, as is argued by those who support the double jeopardy reading), he jumps back to the theme of Israel's displacement in his citation of Isa 45:9, and then on into a further expansion of corporate election to honor and service (Rom 9:22–10:4). This construction has Paul wandering from subject to subject, without giving any clear pointers to the changing context of his ongoing argument and exposing him to the charge of inconsistency.

This proposed "election to honor" reading does not deny that the theme of individual salvation is raised in chapter 10 (Rom 10:9–11). However, introducing it into chapter 9 is contrary to the literary and theological controls of the passage, and cannot be justified. The proposed reading does not deny the doctrine of election to salvation; but it is on the evidence of other texts that it must be established.

Seventh. Most tellingly, as noted earlier, the proposed election to damnation reading of Rom 9:18 has support from no other biblical texts. Its proponents fail to present one piece of textual evidence to show that the doctrine has the support of the wider cannon.[511] The absence of this evidence causes them to go outside of the Christian Scriptures to draw support from the writings of other Jewish groups. This methodological issue has been discussed elsewhere,[512] but what is surprising is how scholars with a very high view of scripture are prepared to borrow from non-apostolic sources in order to create and support their case.

In addition to this lack of biblical support is the fact that when the potter imagery is used elsewhere in scripture, Isa 29:17; 45:7; 64:8; Jer 18:19; 19:11, the pottery is never an individual Israelite but always the nation of Israel. There have to be very good reasons for shifting from a corporate perspective to an individual one in the application of these passages, and none are given.

Eighth. The individual election argument assumes that Paul picks up the Exodus narrative where Moses addresses Pharaoh with the subsequent hardening of his heart and applies it to individual election.[513] Such a reading is common, because it has long been assumed that the hardening of Pharaoh happened after Moses delivered his declarations from Yahweh. It is therefore argued that the hardening followed the pronouncement and had nothing to do

---

[511] Piper cannot give one example of Isa 45:9 or Isa 29:15–26 being adapted in biblical literature to speak of individual judgment. Because of this (as Schreiner [*Romans*, 517]), Piper, *Justification*, 196, resorts to citing support from a text outside of the authoritative sources of the early church, i.e., the book of Wisdom. Indeed, Piper says of Wisdom 15:7—a text that is the bedrock of his case— "What is frustrating is that the meaning of Wis 15:7 has almost nothing in common with Paul's meaning." This hardly instils confidence for building an argument on this literature! Indeed, this is not an isolated case of such dependence. Piper cites five pages of NT texts in the index of his book *Justification*, half of which comes from Romans and approximately one third from the other NT letters. Surprisingly, approximately one quarter of the index comes from intertestamental literature. Such influences from sources that often taught the opposite of apostolic teaching is very concerning. It is only fair to say that not all of Piper's arguments rely on these quotations as crucial evidence, but a methodology that uses non-Christian texts as crucial evidence to defend arguments that lack supporting biblical evidence can hardly serve as a reliable foundation for a good Reformed biblical theology. As noted above,(), the same reliance on this literature applies to Schreiner, *Romans*, 522.

[512] See Holland, *Contours*, 51–68, and "new-perspective."

[513] So, Moo, *Romans*, 599: "Here, however, Paul is speaking about the work of God in individuals. And v. 22–23, where Paul expands on the idea of both God's mercy and his hardening, suggests that the division between those individuals who receive mercy and those who are hardened is basic and final."

with anything that Pharaoh had previously done. The election to judgment was therefore not based on works but Yahweh's sovereign decision.

We need to be careful that we don't allow often-valued traditions of interpretation to control the message of this passage. Allowing the text to have its own voice is an essential part of the Reformed tradition. We have seen in chapter 4 how traditional readings have missed important pointers regarding the significance of Paul's argument about justification, because details that were not present in his exposition have been unintentionally imported into the narrative. We found that the justification of Abraham did not take place at Isaac's birth but in his willingness to sacrifice his son as an act of obedience to Yahweh (Gen 22:10). I want to suggest that the same mistake is being made here.

Paul was of course fully aware of the narrative of Israel's deliverance from Egypt. We cannot follow his logic about Pharaoh unless we expose this shorter account (i.e., Rom 9:14–24) to the wider version of the Exodus narrative, allowing the latter to control how we interpret Paul's reasoning. It is clear that the text of Exodus makes it clear that Yahweh told Moses that Pharaoh's heart would be hardened after Moses made his declaration to the Egyptian ruler (Exod 4:21–23).

However, the message that Moses was instructed to deliver to Pharaoh suggests that this was not the first time Pharaoh had heard the demand to let the Israelites go into the desert to worship their God. This text is crucial, for it suggests that Pharaoh's hardening had begun *prior* to the time Moses delivered his message.[514] Indeed, this is clearly the case, for the Hebrew of Exod 4:22, 23 is about God having spoken in the past to Pharaoh regarding the release of Israel.

וְאָמַרְתָּ אֶל־פַּרְעֹה כֹּה אָמַר יְהוָה בְּנִי בְכֹרִי יִשְׂרָאֵל׃ 23 וָאֹמַר אֵלֶיךָ שַׁלַּח אֶת־בְּנִי

וְיַעַבְדֵנִי וַתְּמָאֵן לְשַׁלְּחוֹ הִנֵּה אָנֹכִי הֹרֵג אֶת־בִּנְךָ בְּכֹרֶךָ׃

(Exod 4:22–23 WTT)

---

[514] This earlier ongoing hardening of Pharaoh's heart is overlooked by Piper, *Justification*, 174: "not once in Exod 4–14 is the assertion of God's hardening of Pharaoh *grounded* in any attitude or act of Pharaoh. Instead, again and again the reason given for the hardening is God's purpose to demonstrate his power and magnify his name. Paul picks up precisely this theme in Rom 9:17. With this selection and adaptation of Exod 9:16 Paul indicates his understanding of the Exodus context: the action of God in Pharaoh's life is determined ultimately by the *purposes* of God, not Pharaoh's willing or running." (Emphasis Piper's)

This reading has been followed by several translations:

> And thou shalt say unto Pharaoh, Thus saith Jehovah, Israel is my son, my first-born: and I have said unto thee, Let my son go, that he may serve me; and thou hast refused to let him go: behold, I will slay thy son, thy first-born. (Exod 4:22–23 ASV)

> And thou shalt say unto Pharaoh, Thus saith the LORD, Israel is my son, my firstborn: and I have said unto thee, Let my son go, that he may serve me; and thou hast refused to let him go: behold, I will slay thy son, thy firstborn. (Exod 4:22–23 ERV)

> Then say to Pharaoh, 'This is what the LORD says: Israel is my firstborn son, and I told you, "Let my son go, so he may worship me." But you refused to let him go; so I will kill your firstborn son.'" (Exod 4:22–23 NIV)

Each of these translations observes the fact that the Hebrew speaks about a past event(s), when Yahweh demanded that Pharaoh let his people go to worship him. Even in the later stages of hardening, Yahweh offers mercy to Pharaoh.

If this is correct, then the hardening that followed Moses' message was an extension, possibly at a more significant pace, of what had already been going on. In the light of this, it is incorrect to argue that Yahweh's judgment was without reference to the works of Pharaoh.[515] We must also remind ourselves that this was not an eschatological judgment concerning Pharaoh's eternal salvation; rather, it was God's judgment upon a ruler and his people for challenging his will and purposes. Thus, the order of how the hardening progressed is, in reality, very different from the case made by those who see the passage dealing with election to individual hardening and damnation. The hardening had already begun when Yahweh offered a stay of execution to the increasingly reprobate ruler. Mercy had been shown long before Moses came on the scene; however, this "passing over" was coming to an end with the threatened slaying of the firstborn.

Ninth. God's willingness to stay judgment on a Gentile king/nation is found elsewhere in the OT. There is no difference between God's intention to judge Pharaoh and his intention to judge Nineveh. "When God saw what they did and how they turned from their evil ways, he had compassion and did not bring upon them the destruction he had threatened" (Jonah 3:10). This is in line

---

[515] Because I am not claiming that election in Rom 9:18 is to eternal salvation, the claim has no bearing on Paul's doctrine of salvation.

with other NT texts, such as: "This is good, and pleases God our Savior who wants all men to be saved and to come to knowledge of the truth" (1Tim 2:3–4). It is extremely serious to use a badly founded argument (such as election to damnation) to overturn such an important and unambiguous statement concerning the character of God. While there is general agreement over what 1 Tim 2:3–4 means, there is very real doubt over the syntax and, therefore, the meaning of Rom 9:17.[516] Furthermore, there are numerous verses that support 1 Tim 2:3–4,[517] while there are no biblical statements to support the reading of individual election to damnation. In dealing with other doctrines, strenuous efforts are made to harmonize the statements made with the rest of scripture and to ensure that the interpretation of a passage with justifiable concerns over its exegesis does not dominate others. The proposed reading of election to honor and service is supported by the whole of OT theology, whereas as we have seen earlier, nothing supports election to damnation.[518]

To demand the passage teaches that God elects individuals to damnation rather than to salvation from the judgment that reprobate humankind deserves, goes beyond biblical evidence. Those who propose this argument appeal to texts such as Rom 8:32–34; Eph 1:4 and 1 Thess 1:4.[519] However, they fail to note that these texts say nothing about election to damnation but are about a corporate calling to be God's people.[520] Not to notice these things is a serious failure. It can only suggest that such exegetes are so determined to uphold their understanding that they fail to notice the inappropriateness of their evidence is. Furthermore, the emphasis of scripture is that God is gracious and longsuffering; delighting in mercy and wanting all to come to the truth. While this may be difficult to reconcile with the doctrine that God elects some and not

---

[516] See Schreiner, *Romans*, 519, who acknowledges the complexity of the syntax and accepts that nothing can be based upon it.

[517] Matt 28:19; John 3:16; 5:34; 1 Thess 2:16. Of course, the matter of the election of individuals to salvation is a different issue altogether.

[518] As noted earlier neither Schiner, *Romans*, 522, nor Piper, *Justification*, 196, can offer one biblical text to support their arguments; both have had to seek support from intertestamental literature.

[519] So Piper, *Justification*, 58.

[520] Interestingly Schreiner, "Election," 39, acknowledges that these texts could be interpreted corporately and appeals to John 6:37, 44–45, 64–65; 10:26; Acts 13:48; 16:14. I have no hesitation in endorsing them as the correct source for a doctrine of election to salvation; however, they say nothing about an election to damnation.

others, we still have to recognize the overwhelming emphasis of scripture is that God is merciful and does not delight in the destruction of the wicked.

Tenth. The double jeopardy reading has failed to appreciate the servant theology that is operating in Rom 9–11. By citing a conflation of Isa 29:16 and Isa 45:7 (as discussed earlier), Paul is introducing, albeit indirectly, the figure of Cyrus. He was another pagan king appointed by Yahweh to achieve his purpose. In Isa 45:9, Israel complained that Cyrus had been appointed to be Yahweh's anointed (Isa 45:1). This interplay with another pagan king's calling to serve Yahweh's purposes supports the claim that Pharaoh's calling was to serve the historical, saving purposes of the living God. Pharaoh, like Cyrus, was appointed to be a savior-redeemer figure to Israel, as were all the examples given in Rom 9:6–13. Here, Isaac–though not Abraham's firstborn—is given the status of head of the people of promise and is, therefore, their redeemer figure. As such, he was chosen to care and provide for the promised seed. Similarly, Jacob—though not Isaac's firstborn—emerged as the appointed head. This servant theme is, therefore, at the heart of the argument that is being advanced. Consequently, this must be brought to the table when considering God's choice of his servant, Pharaoh. Central to this discussion is God's right to appoint people who have no natural claim to service—a role that bestows not only responsibility but gave honor. Within the story of Esau and Jacob, God takes the birthright from the one who, by order of descent, has a right to it and gives this blessing to another. This is the theme that drives Paul's discussion on the hardening of Pharaoh and Israel and the supplement of the calling of Cyrus in Rom 9:20.

The Pharaoh, who had been chosen as Yahweh's servant at the time of Joseph, had been a true shepherd of Israel. Exalting Joseph to a role that allowed him to welcome and provide for his family was clearly vital to the survival of the promised seed. However, when a later Pharaoh emerged who had not known Joseph, he abused his calling and sought to slaughter Israel's sons. Clearly, he was setting himself up to become a vessel of wrath. Later again, when Cyrus became Israel's shepherd, he provided the best resources for rebuilding the temple. Indeed, even King Nebuchadnezzar acted as a shepherd of Israel, exalting Daniel to a privileged position, which enabled him to care for the nation.

If the backgrounds regarding the role that the Pharaohs played in relation to the preservation of the seed of Abraham is not allowed to determine the interpretation of the hardening passage, then we will have failed to hear what Paul is arguing. This is given considerable support, as noted earlier, by the fact that Paul brings Cyrus into his argument by citing Israel's objection to his appointment.

Furthermore, this reading is demanded not only by the verses that immediately precede this passage but also by the ongoing argument, which runs into chapters 10 and 11. The whole thrust of the discussion is how Israel could lose her special status of being Yahweh's chosen servant. Because she failed to fulfill her divine appointment to be a light to the nations, she has been hardened and is under judgment. As a result, God has called the Gentiles to fulfill the role she has chosen to vacate. This concluding argument cannot be separated from what has gone on in the earlier chapter.

Significantly, the appointment of unworthy pagans to serve Yahweh by protecting his people is not limited to the above examples. Paul expands the theme in chapter 13 vv.1–7, when he argues that the ruling authorities have been established by God to do the Roman believers good, and that its servants are to be honored and obeyed.

Eleventh. The OT examples that Paul uses can only point in one direction—Paul is discussing the election of people to be Yahweh's servants.[521]

---

[521] This is a view that is supported by Herman Ridderbos, *Outline*, 345–46, who says: "The purport of Paul's argument is not to show that all that God does in history has been foreordained from eternity and therefore, so far as his mercy as well as his hardening is concerned, has an irresistible and inevitable issue. Rather, it is his intention to point out in the omnipotence of God's activity the real intention of his purpose. Everything is made subservient to the electing character of God's grace, not based on human merit or strength, and of the calling and formation of his people. So did God originally display it in Israel and to Israel, contrary to all human calculations, and contrary to all human resistance. And so does God maintain this sovereign electing character of his work of redemption over against Israel, when Israel misjudges this nature of its election as the people of God and has come to trust in its own righteousness, instead of in the righteousness of God (9:30ff.). Thus it can happen that Israel because of this misjudgment of its calling and election is placed next to Pharaoh as the exemplification of God's reprobation and hardening, and that what applied to Pharaoh holds for Israel as well, namely, that God by Israel's hardening and fall has chosen to make known the riches of his mercy (to the Gentiles) (Rom. 11:7–10, 12, 15). At the same time, however, it is evident that one may not identify the omnipotence and sovereignty of God's grace thus upheld on the one hand and of his reprobation and hardening on the other with irrevocable 'eternal' decrees, in which God would once and forever have predestined the salvation or ruin of man: for God has not only reprobated and hardened Israel in order to display his mercy to the Gentiles, but no less to provoke Israel itself to repentance and 'jealousy' (Rom. 11:11ff.). This concept of election denotes the omnipotence, not the deterministic character of God's work of grace and of the formation of his church. Election is an election of grace (*ekloge charitos*), that is to say: it does not take place on the ground of works (Rom. 11:5, 6). This contrast between

Indeed, the same language is used in 2 Tim 2:20–21, where we read: "In a large house there are articles not only of gold and silver, but also of wood and clay; some are for noble purposes and some for ignoble. If a man cleanses himself from the latter, he will be an instrument for noble purposes, made holy, useful to the Master and prepared to do any good work." The passage is clearly urging Timothy to ensure that he does not do anything that would damage his usefulness as a servant of the Lord, the very theme that I am arguing Rom 9:19–24 addresses. Pharaoh was disqualified from further use as a vessel of honor because of his disobedience. That led to the hardening of his heart. He was given over to the same hardening and ultimate destruction that Paul outlined in Rom 1:18–32.

THE MESSIAH AND HIS SERVANTS HARDENING

9:14 What then shall we say? Is God unjust? Not at all!

Paul responds to a possible charge that, by reversing the natural order of priority, God is being unjust. His point is this: because neither Jacob nor Esau deserved this honor, neither could claim merit. If they were to receive anything, it must be given by God out of his grace.

God has determined that those who are given this honor will not be able to claim it was theirs by right This is demonstrated by the twists and turns seen in the progressive succession of those who were selected to carry forth the covenantal promises given to Abraham. Scripture shows that God has regularly taken a surprising course, choosing the unexpected to be the bearer of the promises.[522] Yet, in doing this, he is always faithful to the covenant he swore with Abraham.

9:15 For he says to Moses, "I will have mercy on whom I have mercy, and I will have compassion on whom I have compassion."

To drive home his claim that election to honor and service is not based on merit or status, Paul again appeals to the Scriptures. The use of Exod 33:19 has particular relevance because of its context. Moses had asked Yahweh if he might see his glory, and, in reply, he was told: "I will cause all my goodness to pass in front of you, and I will proclaim my name, the LORD, in your

---

grace and works dominates the whole argument of Romans 9–11 with respect to the calling and election of the people of God."

[522] See, Levenson, *Death*.

presence." Yahweh then made the statement: "I will have mercy on whom I will have mercy, and I will have compassion on whom I will have compassion." The point is clear. God reveals himself to those who seek him, but not on the grounds of merit—his revelation is based solely on mercy. In this statement to Moses is echoed the divine name, which he revealed to him in Exod 3:14: "I AM WHO I AM" (or I WILL BE WHAT I WILL BE)—a name that speaks of God's refusal to be contained by a definition or expectation.

That God takes the initiative in salvation history has been demonstrated in the call of Abraham. The ancestor of the Jewish people was not chosen to be the conduit of God's blessings to all the families of the earth on the grounds of his merit but on the grounds of God's free electing grace. The same applies to the true descendants of Abraham—the sovereign God elects those who are allowed to see his glory. Our election to service and the privileges this brings is all of God's grace, prerogative, and initiative.

However, the case being argued is not for individual election but for that of peoples. God elected the Jewish people in their ancestor, Abraham. Now the Gentiles are part of his elect people and included in the covenant. As such, they are chosen by God to serve his purposes in redemptive history, i.e., they are included in the servant community that is appointed to take the good news of God's grace to the nations.

9:16 It does not, therefore, depend on man's desire or effort, but on God's mercy.

This is the only conclusion that can be reached from the texts considered. The Scriptures Paul selects are not taken out of context but faithfully portray the nature of God's sovereign choice. Being chosen to serve God's purposes springs from his mercy and has nothing to do with man's achievements or rights by birth (John 1:12).

9:17 For the Scripture says to Pharaoh: "I raised you up for this very purpose, that I might display my power in you and that my name might be proclaimed in all the earth."

We can easily miss the argument that Paul is making. We need to remind ourselves that Paul is discussing the judgment that has come on Israel. To illustrate this judgment, he considers God's dealings with Pharaoh. Many see this verse to be saying that God created Pharaoh in order to destroy him, so showing himself to be greater than the Egyptian ruler. But was Paul saying this? All that God would have achieved by such destruction would be a reputation that no person could get the better of him. However, the emphasis of this verse (and that of the Exodus narrative) is God's mercy. This message of how God's mercy triumphs over man's sinfulness will characterize Paul's conclusion to this entire section (Rom 11:33–36).

The text that Paul quotes must be considered in its original setting. Failure to contextualize the quotation and so grasp its intended meaning has frequently caused Paul's argument to be misunderstood. God was not going to destroy Pharaoh in order to display his power; he was, in fact, doing the very opposite. The power of God was demonstrated through his patience and kindness to a disobedient Pharaoh:

כִּי עַתָּה שָׁלַחְתִּי אֶת־יָדִי וָאַךְ אוֹתְךָ וְאֶת־עַמְּךָ בַּדָּבֶר וַתִּכָּחֵד מִן־הָאָרֶץ׃

וְאוּלָם בַּעֲבוּר זֹאת הֶעֱמַדְתִּיךָ בַּעֲבוּר הַרְאֹתְךָ אֶת־כֹּחִי וּלְמַעַן סַפֵּר שְׁמִי בְּכָל־הָאָרֶץ׃

Exod 9:15–16 WTT

> For by now I could have stretched out my hand and struck you and your people with a plague that would have wiped you off the earth. But I have raised you up for this very purpose, that I might show you my power and that my name might be proclaimed in all the earth. (Exod 9:15–16 NIV)

> For by now I could have put forth my hand and struck you and your people with pestilence, and you would have been cut off from the earth;[16] but for this purpose have I let you live, to show you my power, so that my name may be declared throughout all the earth. (Exod 9:15–16 RSV)

Examining the Exodus passage in its context[523] makes it clear that Yahweh's intention was not to glorify himself through the destruction of

---

[523] Piper, *Justification*, 64, considers that he has observed this method, i.e., of the context controlling his exegesis. He says: ". . . to understand Paul's intention in Rom 9:6–13 we must keep in view that these verses are an attempt to solve the problem raised in 9:1–5, namely that many within the elect nation of Israel are accursed and cut off from Christ. Many individual Israelites within the chosen people are not saved (cf. Rom 11:14). Paul is not moved to constant grief (9:2) because Israel has forfeited her non-salvific 'theocratic privileges' while another people (the church or the remnant) has taken over this 'historical role.' He is grieved because all the privileges of Israel listed in Rom 9:4,5 imply the eschatological, eternal salvation of his people . . . but many individual Israelites—his kinsmen according to the flesh—are damned in their unbelief . . . Therefore the solution which Rom 9:6–13 develops in response to this problem must address the issue of the individual, eternal salvation." But Piper's argument has several inherent weaknesses. First is that the blessings listed were not individual blessings, they were the blessings given to the community. Apart from community membership, these

Pharaoh but through his patient call to repentance. Indeed, although there is the warning of a future hardening, Pharaoh's heart had been hardened long before Moses addressed him.[524] He had sought to kill the newborn sons of the Hebrew families, and it is impossible to argue that he could do that without hardening himself towards Yahweh's word. When Moses stood before him, Pharaoh was already a hardened man to whom Yahweh, in his mercy, continued to give the opportunity to repent and thereby save his people from impending judgment. Even the consequence of Pharaoh's rejection of god's word did not impact only on him, every Egyptian family was judged! Thus, the order of progression of hardening is in reality very different from that which supporters of the election to divine hardening and damnation rely on. The hardening had already begun when Moses offered a stay of execution to the increasingly reprobate ruler. Mercy had been shown long before Moses came on the scene, but this was coming to an end with the threatened slaying of the firstborn. Inserting a

---

blessings could not be experienced. Also, Paul is clearly recalling Moses' request that Yahweh blot him out of the book of life if, by being judged, the people would be spared (Exod 32:32). It is widely recognized that the theology of the original OT passages cited in the NT are transferred with the citation (so, Dodd, *According*; Hays, *Echoes*; Beale, "Wrong Text") The concern of Paul, therefore, echoes the concern of Moses, and Moses was not concerned about individual Israelites but about the nation, and the fact that she was Yahweh's representative. If she is cast off, the nations would say that Yahweh was not a covenant-keeping God and his name would be dishonored. This is Moses' concern, and I would assert it is the nature of Paul's concern. Indeed, Rom 9–11 demonstrates this to be so. Piper refutes this, *Justification*, 155–6 and further justifies his individual reading (even though he acknowledges the corporate thrust of the overall text) by appealing to Rom 8:32, Eph 1:4, and 1Thess 1:4. These texts, however, are of no value to his case. Eph 1:13 shows that the "you" in Eph 1:4 refers to "you Gentiles." This is supported by the overall corporateness of the letter. (See Holland, *Contours*; Cozart, *Ephesians*) Again, the Thessalonian reference does not prove that Paul refers to the individual election of the believers for, as in Ephesians, it is a statement about the elect community–the church. I have shown how the letter to the Romans concerns the life and experience of the Roman church and not individuals. Rom 8:32 is about God's election of the church to be his people and of his faithfulness to the promises he had made to them. In the light of these facts, Piper has no grounds to impose an individualistic reading on Rom 9:17. This is not to deny that election of the individual to salvation is taught in the NT, but this teaching must be based on better exegesis than has been presented thus far. Indeed, Piper's own disciple Schreiner, "Exegetical," 38, notes the corporate setting of these texts. His argument is that, if the texts are corporate (dealing specifically with Eph 1:4), it still does not deny individual election. He says: "In fact individual election cannot be dismissed, since it is taught in too many texts (e.g., John 6:37, 44–45, 64–65; 10:26; Acts 13:48; 16:14)." I want to affirm Schreiner's correct identification of texts that support individual election, but to claim that they can be imported into Rom 9 to support an individualistic interpretation of the hardening of Pharaoh, and through this a doctrine of election to damnation, is not admissible.

discussion on election to damnation is not appropriate; indeed, it abuses the text.

Although God's show of power was demonstrated initially through his patience to Pharaoh, it became the grounds for God's judgment. In response to Pharaoh's willfulness, Yahweh began the process of divine hardening as distinct from the hardening that Pharaoh's guilt had produced. The Lord had had every reason to judge him, but he desisted in order that his power should be shown through his mercy. But because Pharaoh rejected his mercy and continued to harden his heart, Yahweh sealed his fate with his divine hardening. Yahweh had no other option but to bring judgment upon him.

However, this was not the reason for raising Pharaoh up. The statement made to Pharaoh (quoted by Paul) has nothing to do with God choosing him in order to harden his heart so that God could display his power in judgment. Granted, the judgment did display his power—but that is not the context of the quoted verse. God wanted to change the heart of Pharaoh through patience and kindness. He was urging Pharaoh to receive mercy through repentance and obedience. As noted, some scholars assume that Paul is discussing God's sovereignty in election—certain ones are chosen to receive mercy and eternal life and others are elected to damnation. This assumption is understandable in the light of Paul's consideration of the potter's right to make some pots for noble purposes and some for common use. Clearly, the illustration of the potter drives home God's right to make decisions about those he creates for noble purposes and those he creates for ordinary purposes. If the potter has this right, does not God have even more?

A number of reformed scholars believe the sovereignty of the potter points to the sovereignty of God in determining people's eternal destiny, but I would suggest this reasoning has abandoned the essential thrust of the argument. Paul has given examples of those who have been promoted (elected) to positions of authority and honor.[525] He has used Jacob as an example of someone who was chosen to receive the birthright, with all the privileges, responsibilities, and honor that such a position brings. By definition, Jacob became the family's

---

[525] Piper, *Justification*, 56, acknowledges the force of this argument when he says, "The clarifying question that must now be posed is this: If, as we have seen (p. 53), God's purpose is to perform his act of election freely without being determined by any human distinctives, what act of election is intended in Rom 9:11–13—an election which determines the eternal destiny of individuals, or an election which merely assigns to individuals and nations the roles they are to play in history? The question is contextually appropriate and theologically explosive."

redeemer. Paul is not discussing salvation issues but God's sovereignty in selecting people to be leaders of nations or communities. At this point, he is not arguing that people are chosen for eternal life or damnation, but is contending that positions of honor—as far as God is concerned—are not determined by nature or tradition but by his will. So, in regard to Esau, Isaac's firstborn, the birthright was taken from him and given to his younger twin, Jacob.[526]

In the case of Pharaoh, he had been chosen by God to rule, as had the Pharaoh who was ruling at the time of Joseph. In the closing chapters of Genesis, Joseph invites his father and his family to dwell in Egypt to escape famine. He could only do this with the consent of the Pharaoh ruling at that time, and, by granting Joseph's request, the Pharaoh acted as the Hebrews' benefactor, protecting them from danger. In the course of time, this benevolent relationship between Jacob's descendants and the Pharaoh changed. Rather than seeking to protect the Hebrews, a later Pharaoh sought to destroy them. He who had been appointed as a vessel of honor became a vessel fitted for destruction! This was a distressing development since he who had been given the privilege of acting as a redeemer figure to Jacob's descendants—a role that Cyrus would assume in the future—had not been elevated to be judged but to serve. We will find that Paul echoes the role of Cyrus as he deals with the protest of the vessel which the potter has made. This juxtaposition of pagans in the text is crucial. While no one would doubt the role that Cyrus was called to, most fail to see that it was also the role that the Pharaoh at the time of Moses was called to, and so filter out his calling from their discussion on the divine hardening.

The statement: "I could have stretched out my hand and struck you and your people with a plague that would have wiped you off the earth. But I have raised you up for this very purpose, that I might show you my power and that my name might be proclaimed in all the earth" (Exod 9:15–16) expresses God's focus was not one of salvation but of serving and honor. This is the central subject Paul continues to deal with when he turns to the story of Pharaoh. He is addressing the fact that Pharaoh's position had been given to him by God, but that he had abused it. He was created for honor but, by steadfastly rejecting God's word and purpose, his heart was hardened and, after exercising much patience, God judged him. Thus Pharaoh, who was chosen for honor, became a vessel prepared for destruction (v. 22). References to God telling Moses that he would harden Pharaoh's heart (Exod 4:21–23; 7:2–4; 14:4ff.) clearly speak

---

[526] For a study on how God chooses the outsider and not the one designated by the law, see Levenson, *Death*.

Romans 9

of what will happen when Pharaoh rejects Moses' message. Taking our hermeneutic from Paul's ongoing argument concerning men whom God raised up to bless and protect his people, Pharaoh is judged, i.e., hardened, because he refuses to be the servant he has been appointed to be. He failed to protect the promised seed.

We need to remind ourselves that Scripture has no difficulty in seeing pagan kings and leaders as "servants of God." God referred to Cyrus as his "anointed . . . whose right hand I take hold of" (Isa 45:1).[527] Cyrus was a pagan king who served his own deities; nevertheless, God said of him: "He is my shepherd and will accomplish all that I please" (Isa 44:28). Cyrus did what Pharaoh refused to do—he served as a shepherd for the promised seed. Of course, Paul will refer to this shortly (vv. 19–20). The example is part of the argument that he is making about God's sovereignty and, as we will see, vv. 19–20 is corporate and not about election to salvation.

Thus, if a pagan leader can be God's servant, chosen for noble purposes (i.e., a vessel of honor), then Pharaoh had the potential to be a vessel of honor too. Looking again at the context of Paul's quotation in Rom 9:17, Yahweh says to Pharaoh: "For by now I could have stretched out my hand and struck you and your people with a plague that would have wiped you off the earth" (Exod 9:15). By delaying the judgment of the Passover night, God exercised mercy by calling the ruler to humble himself in his presence (Exod 10:3). With this invitation, God was not playing a game of cat and mouse with Pharaoh; he was appealing to him from the same heart that, in future years, would ache and call to Israel, his firstborn servant, to turn from her sins and receive mercy.

Not all of Pharaoh's court agreed with the position their master took. As the plagues fell, some of the Egyptians responded in fear to God's display of power (Exod 8:19; 9:20). Many in the country thought highly of Moses and the Israelites (Exod 11:3), and, by implication, respected their God. Were these the first Gentile converts–the firstfruit from among the Gentiles? As many were familiar with the Hebrew people, did they hear about the coming plague on the firstborn? Did they avail themselves of the power of the blood of the Passover lamb?

The narrative of the pre-exodus events suggests an apparently repentant Pharaoh to whom God extends mercy and answers requests (Exod 8:8, 12–13, 28, 30–31; 9:27–28, 33; Exod 10:16–17 in particular). Yet, the moment he had

---

[527] KJV has servant.

relief from the plagues, Pharaoh's feelings of remorse were forgotten. He hardened his heart further (Exod 8:15, 19, 32; 9:12, 34; 10:20, 27–28) and any fear of the Lord was snatched away. Tragically, the seed of God's word had fallen on "thorny ground."

Pharaoh's rejection of God's mercy meant that "he sinned" (Exod 9:34). He and his officials hardened their hearts. This was expressed in Pharaoh's final venomous address to Moses: "Get out of my sight! Make sure you do not appear before me again! The day you see my face you will die!" (Exod 10:28). This hardening was the result of rejecting Yahweh's word. It was, therefore, the word of God that ultimately hardened Pharaoh.

Tragically and inevitably (Gen 15:13–14, where the covenant with Abraham promised blessing on those who dealt well with his descendants and wrath on those who sought their harm), Pharaoh's hardening was now to reap its just reward, and he was to become a vessel of wrath. Judgment, so long held back, was to visit him and all of the Egyptian people who disregarded God's word. Aaron and Moses did see Pharaoh again as, during the night of the Passover (after the death of the firstborn), they were summoned to the palace and granted freedom for themselves and their people. The one who had been chosen for noble purposes (v.21) had hardened his heart to the responsibilities his privileges demanded. He became, instead, a vessel of wrath. This new role manifested other aspects of God's power as righteousness and judgment were revealed.

The principle that noble "vessels of honor" can become "vessels of wrath" not only applies to Gentile rulers and the people they represent, but it also applies to Israel herself.

> "O house of Israel, can I not do with you as this potter does?" declares the LORD. "Like clay in the hand of the potter, so are you in my hand, O house of Israel. If at any time I announce that a nation or kingdom is to be uprooted, torn down and destroyed, and if that nation I warned repents of its evil, then I will relent and not inflict on it the disaster I had planned. And if at another time I announce that a nation or kingdom is to be built up and planted, and if it does evil in my sight and does not obey me, then I will reconsider the good I had intended to do for it.
>
> "Now therefore say to the people of Judah and those living in Jerusalem, 'This is what the LORD says: Look! I am preparing a disaster for you and devising a plan against you. So turn from your evil ways, each one of you, and reform your ways and your actions.' But they will reply, 'It's no use. We will continue with our own plans;

each of us will follow the stubbornness of his evil heart.' Therefore this is what the LORD says: 'Inquire among the nations: Who has ever heard anything like this? A most horrible thing has been done by Virgin Israel.'" (Jer 18:6–13)

Clearly, individual leaders and the nations they represent are not necessarily vessels of honor forever. God responds and acts in mercy when a people repent and turn to him. In addition we can note that the warning of Israel's destruction if she refuses to repent is clearly not at the level of annihilation, for Israel survived the exile. It thus speaks of God's judgment, whatever the form, as essentially removing privilege from those who had enjoyed it previously and exercising appropriate judgment. This observation supports the case being made that becoming a vessel of wrath, as a term used in Rom 9:22, is not about eternal damnation.

While we have noted that Paul is making a corporate argument, it is more significant to note that this was not a battle of wills with Yahweh triumphing over Pharaoh. Rather, the Exodus was a battle between Yahweh and Ra,[528] the Egyptian god. This god was seen to control the Egyptians and aliens (like the Hebrews) who lived within their borders. However, Yahweh had made a covenant with the Hebrews through their ancestors. If Ra triumphed over Yahweh, salvation history would be scuttled, Yahweh would be disgraced, his rule of creation and faithfulness to his covenant ended, and his reputation and character irreparably damaged.

In this drama, we see the outworking of the same principles that determined the destiny of the first man. Designed for honor and fellowship with God, and made to rule over God's creation as his vice-regent, Adam turned from his Creator and became a vessel of wrath. In the Garden, in one act of disobedience, man lost his honorable status and was prepared to be a vessel for destruction (Rom 1:18–32).

All of this supports the case that Paul's purpose in chapter nine is to discuss how God elects the people who are to serve him and to show that God can and does overturn privileges that he has given. "Now," says Paul, "Yahweh rejects the claims of the very people to whom he had previously committed himself—

---

[528] Dozeman, *War*, 3, says: "The destruction of the Egyptians is a story of holy war." For further details of God as a warrior, see Longman, *Warrior*, 31ff.

the Jews.[529] The firstborn nation (Exod 4:22), the nation with the divine calling and privilege, is to be replaced by a people who had no prior claims to his favor. The people who were 'no people' (Hos 2:23) are to be called 'the people of God' (Rom 9:25), just as Hosea had predicted." Further support for this position will unfold as we look further at specific verses. Thus, God is able to overturn the privilege of representation of those appointed through birth or even election, be it Esau, Pharaoh, Cyrus or Israel, and it is this theme that ties the section together. To depart, without any justification, into a discussion on people's eternal destinies and to use this passage as the key text is to miss what the passage is saying. There is a biblical doctrine, in my understanding, of individual election to salvation, but it should not in any way draw from this passage which is about something quite separate.

9:18 Therefore God has mercy on whom he wants to have mercy, and he hardens whom he wants to harden.

If the argument outlined above is correct and Pharaoh was a vessel of honor until he rejected Yahweh's word, then it changes the reading of the text significantly.[530] The emphasis is not that God has created people to be damned but that he created *all people* for dignity and service, i.e., to be vessels of honor.[531] In writing about salvation history and men who represent their respective nations, Paul focuses on communities, not individuals.[532] By addressing God's dealings with Moses and Pharaoh as representative heads, he

---

[529] Getty, "Salvation," 456–69, holds that several ideas in Rom 9–11 were probably written to check a trend of anti-Jewish sentiment within the church. She claims that this is evident in Paul's rebuke of the Gentiles for their anti-Jewish sentiment, their pride (Rom 11:20), their relative newness in the kingdom (Rom 11:24), and their status as grafted branches (Rom 11:17–18). For God's overturning of privilege, see Levenson, *Death*.

[530] Schreiner, *Romans*, 518, changes the meaning of the text by asserting: "the choice of one for eschatological honour and the other for judgment from the same lump indicates that those chosen had no special merits or distinctiveness that accounted for their being chosen." Thus, Schreiner has introduced the dimension of eschatological judgment when there is no mention of this in the text. Admittedly, once this has been introduced the case for election to judgment is stronger but the grounds for introducing the concept are not present.

[531] Clearly, at the socio-historic level there have always been leaders, (vessels of honor) but, in absolute terms, everyone is called to the service of God and have been created for honor and glory (Rom 3:23).

[532] See Wilckens, *Römer*, 2:196–97; Käsemann, *Romans*, 265; Hays, *Echoes*, 66.

shows how God chooses people groups to fulfill his purposes.[533] As Israel discovered, the fact that a people has been chosen does not mean that she is exempt from God's judgment. Indeed, it was because she had abused her privileged calling that God said to Israel: "You only have I chosen of all the families of the earth; therefore I will punish you for all your sins" (Amos 3:2). The promise of punishment was fulfilled in her conquest and exile. Thus, the proposed interpretation of this notoriously difficult section[534] is supported by the way Yahweh elected and then held Israel to account. She had been a vessel of honor, chosen to be the people through whom Yahweh would bless the nations (Gen 12:2; 17:16; 18:18; 26:4) but who, because of disobedience and the hardening of her heart, (Ps 95:8–11; Isa 63:17) was replaced by a people who "were no people" (Hos 1:10). This is the OT theme that is being thrashed out in Rom 9–11, and so the proposed reading stays firmly within the tradition of OT theology.

This divine principle of showing mercy to people groups can be seen throughout history. Nations and communities have experienced the mercy of God, with large numbers of their people turning to him in repentance. In Isa 34–35, the Gentile nations were warned of judgment but promised restoration and redemption if they sought the Lord. Yahweh even says to *Gentiles* who have come under judgment (Isa 34:1–17) but who call on him for mercy: "Be strong, do not fear; for your God will come with vengeance; with divine retribution he will come to save you" (Isa 35:4).[535]

Thus, blessing and salvation is never an end in itself, nor is judgment.[536] Any claim to having received God's blessing and mercy must be supported by evidence of service, exhibiting concern for others that they will become recipients of the same grace. For the Christian, the reality of blessing ultimately

---

[533] See Munck, *Israel*, 38, 42; Leenhardt, *Romans*, 249; Campbell, W.S., "Freedom," 29.

[534] Murray, *Romans*, 2:29, softens the example by saying that the hardening is the consequence of Yahweh not intervening to soften Pharaoh's heart. Hodge, *Romans*, 316, makes the case that: "Pharaoh was no worse than many other men who have obtained mercy, yet God, for his wise and benevolent reasons, withheld from him the saving influence of his grace." Both explanations are clearly pulling away from where their exegesis has led, i.e., Yahweh elected Pharaoh to be damned.

[535] For another example of God's mercy to the Gentiles, see Isa 19:19–25.

[536] Note Ridderbos, *Outline*, 112: "God's wrath places itself in the service of his love."

turns on a concern for people as they seek to reach them with the message of the Gospel of peace (Isa 42:1).

This principle also applies to local churches. All too often, when a time of revival recedes, the responsibility to witness to others wanes and energies become focused on divisive, peripheral issues. Believers within a church that has known blessing often become confused as non-essential features of its theology or cultural identity are seen as responsible for spawning the work of God. The congregation reasons that, in order to experience another visitation, its culture and values must be maintained.

When this stance is taken, the church unwittingly puts controls on God and exalts her own understanding. But God is never limited in this way. This was Israel's sin when she tried to impose non-essential practices on the Gentiles, idolizing her own status. When a church does this, her witness is often lost; her light goes out and her candlestick is removed (Rev 2:15). Even a church that has been richly blessed and used powerfully to advance the Gospel can become arrogant, proud, and hardened. If she falls into this state and rejects the call of her Lord (as did Pharaoh and Israel), she will become a vessel of dishonor and destruction (1 Cor 5:1–8; 10:1–13; Rev 2:4–6, 14–16, 21–23; 3:1–3).

9:19–20 One of you will say to me: "Then why does God still blame us? For who resists his will?" But who are you, O man, to talk back to God? Shall what is formed say to him who formed it, "Why did you make me like this?"

Paul again anticipates an objection: "If we are what we are because God has determined what we shall be, how can he judge us?" There is apparent substance to the complaint, but not when it is put into the context of God's sovereignty. Paul answers the anticipated objection by quoting what God said in response to a similar complaint made by Israel in Isaiah's prophecy.

The allegation of God's injustice is only possible because of the freedom he has given to the people he has made. The very fact that the creature can call the Creator to account is evidence that man has attempted to usurp God's authority. As the author of Lamentations wrote: "It is because of the LORD's unfailing mercies that we are not consumed" (Lam 3:22). Those who are embittered and who make a charge of injustice against God have been spared by his unfailing mercy, as God's justice without mercy requires that sentence be served forthwith. But they have been shown mercy, and the Day of Judgment is postponed.

To rain accusations upon the God who has shown such mercy, allowing opportunity for repentance, demonstrates man's sinful rebellion to overthrow his rule. However, if it had been God's will to withhold mercy so that swift judgment was meted out, what right did man have to challenge him?

We have seen that the letters to the churches had to be read corporately as they were not written to individuals but to congregations. Their arguments are concerned with God's ways throughout salvation history. As we have seen, rather than creating Pharaoh for destruction, he was created for honor. It was his refusal to hear and obey God's word that brought the hardening of heart and consequent judgment.

The narrative about people appointed to be vessels of honor continues in this passage. This time, however, Paul alludes to a passage that has in its background another world leader whom God raised up. Paul quotes from Isa 45:9: "Woe to him who quarrels with his Maker, to him who is but a potsherd among the potsherds on the ground. Does the clay say to the potter, 'What are you making?' Does your work say, 'He has no hands?'"

The passage is Israel's response on hearing that Cyrus had been raised up to serve Yahweh's purposes. Earlier, Isaiah recorded:

> "This is what the LORD says to his anointed, to Cyrus, whose right hand I take hold of to subdue nations before him and to strip kings of their armor, to open doors before him so that gates will not be shut" (Isa 45:1). After Israel complained about not having the status granted to Cyrus, God responds: "*I will* raise up Cyrus in my righteousness: *I will* make all his ways straight. He will rebuild my city and set my exiles free, but not for a price or reward, says the LORD Almighty" (Isa 45:13).[537]

We cannot separate the quoted text in Romans from its original OT context of Israel's complaint to God about decisions he had made. The theme of this passage in Rom 9 continues the argument about Pharaoh being raised up to display God's power. This is also the theme of Isa 45, from which Paul quotes the complaints that God anticipates Israel will make (Isa 45:9b). Rom 9–11 is about God's sovereignty in choosing people to fulfill his purposes, and Paul gives biblical evidence that he reserves the right to include Gentiles among those whom he uses. In the past, his choices included Pharaoh and Cyrus; now they include Gentile believers and the Jewish remnant. God has now chosen

---

[537] Emphasis added to show that Yahweh refuses to be controlled by the petty complaint of Israel.

these to serve him and, as in the past, the physical descendants of Abraham complain.[538]

9:21 Does not the potter have the right to make out of the same lump of clay some pottery for noble purposes and some for common use?

The imagery of the potter was well known to the Jews (Isa 29:16; 30:14; 45:9; 64:8; Jer 18:4–6). Here in v. 21, the potter takes clay and, pulling from it smaller pieces, he begins to work each piece. He forms different types of pots: some beautiful—skillfully turned for eating and drinking—and some roughly made for common use. The potter made different pots in different ways and for different purposes. The clay had no choice as to how it would be worked, and it was the choice of the potter as to what it would become. There had to be vessels made for noble purposes and there had to be vessels made for lesser purposes.

This was also the case with the families of man. Some nations were elected for what appeared to be noble tasks, while others, in comparison, had less significant functions. Paul's argument is that just as clay has no right to argue with the decisions of the potter, so man has no right to argue with the decisions of God. It is not that such decisions are fixed—if a beautiful drinking vessel leaks and no longer serves its purpose, it is destroyed. As we have seen, vessels of honor can (and do) come under judgment for turning away from God, and those that did not have honor can be promoted instead. As indicated in the earlier argument, this is how God has always dealt with men (Rom 9:6–13 [see also Hos 1:10]; 9:25–26).

---

[538] Yahweh's desire and determination to bless all the peoples of the earth –even in the face of Israel's complaint—is echoed in many parts of the scripture. The book of Jonah typifies this as do many other texts, such as: "In that day there will be an altar to the LORD in the heart of Egypt, and a monument to the LORD at its border. It will be a sign and witness to the LORD Almighty in the land of Egypt. When they cry out to the LORD because of their oppressors, he will send them a savior and defender, and he will rescue them. So the LORD will make himself known to the Egyptians, and in that day they will acknowledge the LORD. They will worship with sacrifices and grain offerings; they will make vows to the LORD and keep them. The LORD will strike Egypt with a plague; he will strike them and heal them. They will turn to the LORD, and he will respond to their pleas and heal them. In that day there will be a highway from Egypt to Assyria. The Assyrians will go to Egypt and the Egyptians to Assyria. The Egyptians and Assyrians will worship together. In that day Israel will be the third, along with Egypt and Assyria, a blessing on the earth. The LORD Almighty will bless them, saying, 'Blessed be Egypt my people, Assyria my handiwork, and Israel my inheritance'" (Isa 19:19–25).

In writing Rom 9:21, Paul may have had the Genesis creation story in mind. This narrative describes how man was made from the dust (or clay) of the earth. What God, the potter, decides regarding his creation is his own prerogative. In this argument, Paul is not saying that God is capricious, but that he does everything, at all times, according to truth and justice. He takes the fallen children of man (who, because of the hardening of their hearts through unbelief [Rom 1:18–32] were under judgment) and bestows honor and blessing upon them. Who can complain about God's dealings?

9:22 What if God, choosing to show his wrath and make his power known, bore with great patience the objects of his wrath—prepared for destruction?

Paul is writing to the believers in Rome to say that they must understand they cannot question God's actions and decisions. He asks the question: "What right do you have to challenge God if he chooses to show his wrath and display his power to rebellious people?" Paul reasons from what, at first, appears to be a hypothetical case. He focuses on the great patience of God, who keeps back his wrath from those who deserve judgment.[539]

Paul's argument emphasizes that the only thing that is not fair or just is that God has acted in mercy. Man's attempt to usurp the position and authority of his Creator (an attempt that eventually resulted in the death of God's Son) should have left him under the sentence of separation from God and eternal judgment. When Paul writes: "prepared for destruction," he does not necessarily mean that man was created for destruction but that, as a consequence of disobedience, he is prepared for destruction. Even though the line of demarcation has been crossed and man's heart has become hardened, Yahweh still pleads with the ones who disobey him to repent and avoid judgment. This is nothing new; it replicates his pleadings with Israel before they were cut off, in accordance with the covenantal curses. The ones who are put aside in terms of being instruments for achieving God's purposes continue to experience his patience and mercy until the very last moment. Of course, for those who fail to fulfill their assigned task and reject God, the consequence is not merely a loss of status; they also come under judgment for misrepresenting him and for the unrighteousness in which they took part. This is true for the Gentiles as much as it was for Israel.

---

[539] Schreiner, *Romans*, 519, acknowledges the complexity of syntax of vv. 22–23 and accepts that argument cannot be settled on this evidence. He concedes that it is the flow of the argument that is important for interpreting these verses.

9:23 What if he did this to make the riches of his glory known to the objects of his mercy, whom he prepared in advance for glory—

Another question is raised: "How are people prepared for glory?" Earlier, Paul discussed the redemption that is in Christ Jesus (Rom 3:21ff.) and his role in undoing the work of Adam (Rom 5:12ff.). The letter pivots around the exodus of the people of God from Egypt and then from Babylon. Both OT redemptive events show how God, having committed himself to his people in covenant, prepared for their deliverance. He made plans to bring them out of bondage, misery, and shame, in order that he might bring them into his glory (Isa 41:8–16). [540]

Using these powerful OT models, Paul is saying that God will be as glorified by his new covenant people's eschatological exile as he was when he made the ancient people a vessel of honor, delivering them first from captivity in Egypt and then from Babylon. The mercy that was extended to Israel has now been extended to nations that she considered to be "vessels of destruction." It is believing people from these Gentile people groups who, along with believing Jews, have been rescued from exile and brought into the kingdom of God (Col 1:13–14). Those who thought that they had divine rights to inclusion have been excluded.

9:24 Even us, whom he also called, not only from the Jews but also from the Gentiles?

God extended his mercy in order to bring about a single covenant community made up of believing Jews and believing Gentiles. The original argument against God having the right to reject or elect as he wished (v. 19) has not been fully developed. Now, Paul returns to his premise, spelling out the background to the calling of the Jews and their salvation history. Yahweh's purpose in choosing them was to bring to himself a people of Jews and Gentiles who would love him and display his grace and mercy to the whole of creation (Eph 2:8–18).

---

[540] Despite not interpreting the text corporately, Seifrid, "Romans," 647, notes: "Paul does not identify God with a hidden election of some to destruction and some to glory. Paul affirms that the Creator acts in sovereign freedom, but his response to the impertinent question of the human being does not rest with abstract assertion of the Creator's right; rather, he bears witness to the promise of the gospel, that the Creator's purpose is the restoration of his glory to those whom he is now preparing."

Romans 9

9:25 As he says in Hosea. "I will call them 'my people' who are not my people; and I will call her 'my loved one' who is not my loved one,"

Paul adapts the text of Hos 2:23. The original passage was from Hosea's life when, tragically, the prophet realized that the child his wife had borne was not his but her lover's. Yahweh uses the pain of Hosea to speak of his own anguish. He calls the northern kingdom of Israel "not my people." She had broken away from Judah and Benjamin (who stayed loyal to the line of David) and had played the harlot, setting up her own shrines to worship false gods (Hos 3:1; Ezek 16:23–34). Yahweh said that the children of Israel were not his, and separated himself from them by exiling them at the hand of the Assyrians (2 Kgs 18:11).

Paul now adapts the original passage to speak of the Gentiles, whom God has brought to himself. God honors them with the title "my people." The text was originally applied to a people who had forfeited their privilege by joining themselves to other gods—the very condition of man in Adam. God is going to accept the repentant children of Adam (believing Gentiles) back into his presence. The use of the quotation does not violate the original message given by the prophet but expands it.

9:26 And, "It will happen that in the very place where it was said to them, 'You are not my people,' they will be called 'sons of the living God.'"

Paul again quotes from Hosea 1:10. If he is deliberately emphasizing the place where the Gentiles will become part of the covenant community (Eph 2:11–15), he might have had in mind the prediction of the Gentiles going up to Jerusalem. The prophets saw Jerusalem as the place where the Gentiles would assemble when they sought Yahweh (Isa 2:1–4; 19:24–25). Some think this was the prophecy that motivated Paul to lead a deputation of Gentiles into Jerusalem with an offering for the believers who were suffering through extreme poverty (Rom 15:25; 1 Cor 16:1–3). Scholars reason this visit was a symbolic act on Paul's part, fulfilling the predictions of the prophets that the Gentile nations would come up to Jerusalem to worship the Lord.[541]

What is significant is the unquoted opening sentence of Hos 1:10: "Yet the Israelites will be like the sand on the seashore, which cannot be measured or counted." This is nothing less than a renewal of the Abrahamic covenant. It is a quote from Gen 22:17 and is not included in the earlier promises concerning

---

[541] See Munck, *Israel*.

the covenant (Gen 12:1–3; 15:5) or in the later promises given to Isaac and then Jacob. Just as Yahweh had given Isaac back to Abraham from the "dead" (Heb 11:19—later rabbinical writers interpreting the sacrifice of Isaac as atonement for Israel's sins), so now many sons (including Gentiles) are being brought from the "dead."

9:27 Isaiah cries out concerning Israel. "Though the number of the Israelites be like the sand by the sea, only the remnant will be saved.

Here we see a transition in Paul's argument. We have noted earlier in the chapter that the argument was not about election to salvation but to service. However, salvation terminology is introduced here, and Paul begins his discourse as to the condition of Israel in relation to God's saving activity. While the argument moves on to Israel's salvation rather than her call to service, the argument does, of course, continue to be corporate rather than individualistic. It is about Israel's salvation; not about individual salvation.[542]

We noted in the comment on the previous verse that the unquoted introductory sentence of Gen 22:17 in Hos 1:10 promised that Israel would be as "the sand on the seashore." Instead, Paul draws on the fuller statement from Isa 10:22: "Though your people, O Israel, be like the sand by the sea, only a remnant will return." The promise that Abraham would have a multitude of descendants was clearly important to the eighth century prophets. It must have sustained them, assuring them that Yahweh was bound by his own oath to save, at the very least, a remnant. If Yahweh allowed the extinction of Israel, his promise to Abraham could never be fulfilled.

Paul, of course, has demonstrated that the true children of Abraham—the children of the covenant—are those who share Abraham's faith in the God who keeps his promises to all who call upon him. In the original passage of Isaiah, there is an intended note of distress that only a remnant would be saved; but here, Paul writes out of hope. Despite the sinfulness of Israel, a remnant would still be saved. The emphasis is on the fact that even Israel's rebelliousness could not frustrate the sovereignty of God. This is the first direct mention that a remnant of Israel will be saved, although Paul has been implying it throughout the section since v.6.

---

[542] While that is the argument here, the preaching of the apostles stressed the importance of individual response in becoming members of the covenant community, so Acts 2:40; 3:19; 8:31–35; 10:32–34; 13:32–34; 13:47–48; 16:31–34; 17:16–17; 18:5–11; 19:8; 20:25–26; 28:20.

By incorporating Isa 10:22 into his evidence, Paul is able to show that Gentiles are included in the pilgrim community that returns from exile in Adam.

9:28 For the Lord will carry out his sentence on earth with speed and finality."

The final part of the Isa 10:22–23 passage makes it clear that God's judgments are final and that it is he who determines the time of their fulfillment. Throughout history, some have seen the longsuffering of God as a sign of weakness or non-existence. Both conclusions are foolish and dangerous. If his judgment could come on his covenant people with such devastation and ferocity that surrounding nations were aghast (Jer 22:8; 46:12–13; Ezek 5:15; 28:19), how foolish it would be to suggest that God would not bring judgment on all who rebel against him (1 Cor 10:1–11).

9:29 It is just as Isaiah said previously: "Unless the Lord Almighty had left us descendants, we would have become like Sodom, we would have been like Gomorrah."

The fall of Jerusalem at the hands of the Babylonians was so complete that it appeared to be the end of the covenant. It is true that Israel would survive in exile, but what sort of survival would it be? Without the temple and land, her people were disinherited. In ancient understanding, it was unthinkable for a people to be without their land and their god. Even in modern thinking, nationhood is often thought to be inseparable from homeland. This, sadly, is the reality for many millions of refugees at the beginning of the twenty-first century.

Those who survived the dreadful slaughter following the fall of Jerusalem were exiled to Babylon. Eventually, they came to terms with their new circumstances and started to make a life for their families. Many had worked successfully during the seventy years since their deportation and had been absorbed into Babylonian society. When Yahweh called them to return to their homeland, most chose to forsake their inheritance; they stayed in their new home, despite the promise that God would restore the nation after seventy years of exile (Jer 29:10–14). The return to the promised land was going to cost the Jews; they would have to endure great hardships, and, in so doing, deprive their families of the benefits they had as a community living in an advanced society. As a result, most rejected God's call to go back. The descendants referred to in Rom 9:29 must be the remnant who continued to believe Yahweh's promises given through the prophets. These people recognized that Yahweh would fulfill his word. He was a God who kept covenant with his people and who freely gave mercy. They knew that if this had not been so, Israel—like Sodom and Gomorrah—would have ceased to exist.

In mentioning these two notorious cities, Isaiah was acknowledging not merely the necessity for Jerusalem's judgment but her undoubted oblivion if God had not intervened. Jerusalem not only deserved a similar judgment to Sodom and Gomorrah but doubly deserved it (Gen 19:24–25, 28). These two cities had sinned in ignorance, but the people of Jerusalem had sinned in the face of all the warnings of the prophets and their appeals for them to turn from their sin. Israel's willful disobedience brought direct shame on Yahweh, whose servant she was supposed to be and whose honor she should have upheld. She was the one who had been called into covenant with Yahweh, and it was her rebellion, rather than the holiness of Yahweh (Lev 19:2), that the nations of the world had witnessed.

Paul skillfully uses the comparison with these two ancient cities to emphasize that no one can accuse God of being unjust for acting in judgment. Indeed, if God is to be accused of anything, it is that he has not given man the judgment he deserves. This has been delayed; and for those who believe, it has been averted at great cost—the cost of his own Son's death (Rom 8:32).

9:30 What then shall we say? That the Gentiles, who did not pursue righteousness, have obtained it, a righteousness that is by faith;

The irony is obvious. How could it be that those who sought to live according to the law have been rejected, while those who had such little concern have been accepted? To be told that neither good deeds nor religious activities earn God's salvation is still an unspeakable offense for many today. Such a claim, when referring to individual election, seems to make a monster out of God, as though he had lost his senses and ceased to uphold the moral law! From a strictly human perspective that would be right, for it is saying that man's efforts are worthless. But the argument that Paul is making is not about morality (how some define the "righteousness of God") but about how God does not choose a people to represent him, i.e., to be his servant, on the basis of works.[543] To read "righteousness" as another term for morality is to impose Hellenistic understanding on Paul's use of "righteousness," when what he is writing about is God's saving activity. The God of Scripture has revealed himself as the one who deals with all men on the same basis, that of his grace. Only in this way

---

[543] But of course election of people to salvation is a part of the gospel and it does offend many.

can they be released from their bondage to Sin and be brought into the covenant community.

For Paul, there is only one saving righteousness—one divine saving act—and that is what Christ's redeeming death is all about.[544] Thus, the term "righteous" is not limited to moral uprightness or vindication before the law. Paul uses the term with the meaning given by Isaiah within the context of redemptive history—it is God's saving activity (Isa 56:1 cf. Rom1:17). God has visited the Gentiles who had not sought him, and has brought representatives of all the nations into a covenant that binds them into the promises made to Abraham (Rom 2:25-29; 4:16-17). They have been redeemed from sin and condemnation, and brought into the kingdom of the Son he loves (Col 1:13-14).

9:31 But Israel, who pursued a law of righteousness, has not attained it.

The NIV rendering has been chosen out of a range of possibilities in an attempt to explain a difficult expression. Paul writes literally: "But Israel, did not catch up with the law." One suggestion is that Paul means Israel was pursuing uprightness through the law, but fell short.[545] Paul is not criticizing the Jews for pursuing the law; he simply laments that they have missed its purpose. The law was intended to be the nation's "schoolmaster/supervisor"[546] in order to bring the Jews to Christ (Gal 3:24), and not to be an end in itself.

9:32 Why not? Because they pursued it not by faith but as if it were by works. They stumbled over the "stumbling stone."

Paul's question: "Why not?" anticipates an objection to the above statement. Paul's answer is that man's way of righteousness is not the same as God's. It never has been and never will be. It has been argued by New Perspective theologians that Paul misrepresents the Jews[547] as they never were (certainly not in Paul's time, according to the rabbinical evidence) a people who thought that keeping the law earned them salvation. The New Perspective argument proposes that the Jews understood the law to be a gift from God and

---

[544] For further discussion on righteousness, see comments on Rom 4:3.

[545] See Fitzmyer, *Romans*, 578.

[546] These are the most widely accepted meanings of *paidagogos*. For an understanding that sees the law functioning as a "best man" preparing for a wedding, see Holland, *Contours*, 212 and *Paul, Law and Spirit*, forthcoming.

[547] See Sanders, *Palestinian*.

that this gift was bestowed upon them *after* he had accepted them as his covenant people. Their argument concludes with the question: "If this was their mindset, how is it that Paul could be interpreted as accusing the Jews of seeking righteousness by the law?" Of course, the question assumes this is how they did understand the law.

But for Paul, the issue was not how the Jews thought they were made right with God but how the Gentiles were to be made right with him. Their insistence that the Gentiles had to be circumcised was the acid test. If they really believed their relationship with Yahweh was without the law and that the law "merely" spelled out the covenantal obligations, what right did they have to require circumcision of the Gentiles? Their confidence and their understanding were flawed. Like Jonah, who feared that Yahweh would be merciful to Nineveh, they were demonstrating how far they were from the true meaning of the covenant. They wanted this grace solely for themselves and sought to protect their unique status by demanding that the Gentiles be circumcised. In other words, they taught that salvation could only be obtained within Judaism They had turned the grace of God into a set of legal requirements. Their understanding of what would save the Gentiles defined how they saw their own salvation; in other words, it was achieved by keeping the works of the law.[548]

9:33 As it is written: "See, I lay in Zion a stone that causes men to stumble and a rock that makes them fall, and the one who trusts in him will never be put to shame."

Paul cites the text that predicted the Jews would stumble. The NT understanding of Isa 28:16 speaks of those who reject the Messiah king. However, in its historical setting, Isa 28:16 spoke of the coming judgment on Judah and her subsequent exile. The whole section (Isa 28:11–16) is a key passage for NT theology. Isa 28:11 is quoted by Paul in 1 Cor 14:21 and Isa 28:16 (the stone text) is the most quoted OT verse in the entire NT. I will argue that Isa 28:15 is part of the background that informs Paul's understanding of what it means to be in Adam (see comments on Rom 10:11). Isaiah is saying that, rather than trusting in alliances with other nations for security—alliances made by the king that would cause the fall of Jerusalem—Yahweh would raise up a true Son of David. Those who put their trust in him would be brought out

---

[548] However, we must not forget that Judaism was not a homogeneous set of beliefs. A critique of a particular part of Judaism must not assume that the problem or misunderstanding being addressed was throughout the nation. See Holland, *Contours*, 202–3.

of the exile that had resulted from their forefather's sin. Again, we see Paul staying true to the original meaning of the Scriptures. The argument is that God has raised up the righteous Branch, who brings the sons of Adam out of the exile into which they had been sentenced as a result of the fall.

CONCLUSION OF ROMANS CHAPTER NINE

Paul shares the distress he experiences over the unbelief of his own people, the Jews. They had been privileged above all other nations, but they misunderstood their situation. In their minds, they would always be first in line for the blessings of God. To dispel this illusion, Paul highlights examples in Scripture. These show that God will not be bound to Israel's belief that Yahweh owes the nation privilege and protection. Even Pharaoh, Israel's great enemy, had been raised up by God (as had Cyrus) so that he could use him to achieve his sovereign purposes.

Paul answers the arrogance of his unbelieving kinsmen. Foolishly, Israel thinks she has a unique relationship with God that guarantees her privileged role. Paul answers from the Jewish Scriptures, and shows that what he says is no different from what the law has always said. He demonstrates that the promotion of the Gentiles above Israel for given periods of time had always been part of redemptive history.

The citations all come from texts that warn Israel of judgment and the calling of the Gentiles—themes that are part of the Second Exodus preaching of the prophets. The New Exodus was brought about so that Yahweh would have his bride, and Paul has made it clear that his bride would include Gentile believers.

Although this chapter is often used to support doctrines relating to individual election, that was never its purpose. It is about how God has, throughout history, chosen people and nations to be his servants. In being chosen, they are appointed to positions of honor. If they abuse their privilege, they are warned of the danger of judgment. If they continually resist God's appeals to repent, they are removed from their calling, become vessels of wrath, and are judged for resisting and seeking to overthrow God's purposes. This was, of course, the pattern of the fall of Adam—Yahweh's first servant.

Romans 10

THE MESSIAH KING AND HIS PEOPLE'S RECOVERY (10:1–21)

Brothers, my heart's desire and prayer to God for the Israelites is that they may be saved. For I can testify about them that they are zealous for God, but their zeal is not based on knowledge. Since they did not know the righteousness that comes from God and sought to establish their own, they did not submit to God's righteousness. Christ is the end of the law so that there may be righteousness for everyone who believes.

Moses describes in this way the righteousness that is by the law: "The man who does these things will live by them." But the righteousness that is by faith says: "Do not say in your heart, 'Who will ascend into heaven?'" (that is, to bring Christ down) "or 'Who will descend into the deep?'" (that is, to bring Christ up from the dead). But what does it say? "The word is near you; it is in your mouth and in your heart," that is, the word of faith we are proclaiming: That if you confess with your mouth, "Jesus is Lord," and believe in your heart that God raised him from the dead, you will be saved. For it is with your heart that you believe and are justified, and it is with your mouth that you confess and are saved. As the Scripture says, "Anyone who trusts in him will never be put to shame." For there is no difference between Jew and Gentile—the same Lord is Lord of all and richly blesses all who call on him, for, "Everyone who calls on the name of the Lord will be saved."

How, then, can they call on the one they have not believed in? And how can they believe in the one of whom they have not heard? And how can they hear without someone preaching to them? And how can they preach unless they are sent? As it is written, "How beautiful are the feet of those who bring good news!"

But not all the Israelites accepted the good news. For Isaiah says, "Lord, who has believed our message?" Consequently, faith comes from hearing the message, and the message is heard through the word of Christ. But I ask: Did they not hear? Of course they did:

"Their voice has gone out into all the earth, their words to the ends of the world." Again I ask: Did Israel not understand? First, Moses says, "I will make you envious by those who are not a nation; I will make you angry by a nation that has no understanding." And Isaiah boldly says, "I was found by those who did not seek me; I revealed myself to those who did not ask for me." But concerning Israel he says, "All day long I have held out my hands to a disobedient and obstinate people." (Rom 10:1–21)

INTRODUCTION

In chapter 10, Paul continues to express his deep longing for the salvation of his kinsmen (v. 1). He argues that, while the Jews think that they have been zealous for God, in reality they have been obstinate and disobedient, refusing to submit to the only righteousness that God can accept, i.e., the righteousness that is by faith in Jesus Christ (Rom 10:2–4). Their pride in being "people of the book" actually hindered them from discovering what the message of the book (the Torah) is all about. By quoting Deut 30:12–13 in Rom 10:6, Paul demonstrates that the law intended righteousness to be a gift given by faith.

Within this OT text, there are references to "ascending into heaven" and "descending into the deep." These phrases—familiar to Paul's Jewish readers—refer to the finding of the law. Paul applies them now to the finding of Christ. He can do this with great confidence because the law and the writings of the prophets point to Jesus, their decrees all being fulfilled in him who is the end, or goal, of the OT revelation.

Thus, Christ is to be found. He is not far off but is near to all who call upon him. Paul drives this lesson home by explaining how salvation is to be received: "If you confess with your mouth, 'Jesus is Lord,' and believe in your heart that God raised him from the dead, you will be saved" (Rom 10:9).

Paul highlights the vital importance of this message of faith by explaining that throughout history people have heard it. He stresses the necessity of it being told. He likens the witnessing NT believers to the exiles leaving Babylon. Using Second Exodus material (Isa 52:7), he writes that, just as the former exiles returned home announcing their message of salvation to all who would listen, so the NT believers, on their pilgrimage, announce that the Second Exodus of God's people has been accomplished. They declare that all those who hear and believe can share in the salvation and come out of their bondage to Sin. The summons to declare that Jesus Christ is Lord echoes Rom 1:4, where Jesus the Son of David, through the Spirit of holiness, was proclaimed to be the Son of God by his resurrection from the dead.

Paul uses the words of Isaiah to describe those who preach the Gospel (v. 15): "How beautiful are the feet of those who bring good news!" As already noted, the prophet was speaking about the Jews who, on returning to Jerusalem from Babylon, rejoiced that God had delivered them from their exile. As they journeyed towards Zion, they brought good news for the Jews who still lived there, that God would comfort, restore and exalt the ruined city. He would deliver her inhabitants from their shame—even raising up the promised Davidic prince who would bring the remnant into a glorious salvation. The NT constantly asserts that Jesus is this promised Davidic king. However, before sharing in His glory, the believing community must share in his sufferings (Rom 8:18).

The few who returned from the Babylonian exile joined the small number of Jews still living in the city. Together, they were the remnant through whom Yahweh would continue his purposes. Paul writes there is still a remnant of Jews who have heard God's call and obeyed, but the majority reject the call to join the redeemed community. He is distressed that his unbelieving kinsmen refuse to take their place in the eschatological community and to experience the salvation to which the Exodus had pointed (Rom 10:16–21).

10:1 Brothers, my heart's desire and prayer to God for the Israelites is that they may be saved.

The Jews considered themselves to be saved and in a right relationship with God because, in the time of Moses, Pharaoh had been overthrown and their ancestors had experienced the Exodus. Paul has made it clear in chapter 9 that in clinging to their history and privileges, the Jews are rejecting the eschatological reality to which their historical experiences point. Just as a wedding ceremony is prepared for by means of a rehearsal so that all in the bridal party can know their parts in the event, so the Exodus was a rehearsal for what Yahweh was to do for his people in the death of his Son. In ultimate terms, it was not intended to establish the relationship that was going to happen in the eschatological exodus, but the tragedy was that the Jews confused the rehearsal with the real event. They concentrated on the fact that they were redeemed from Egypt when they had not been redeemed from Sin. This redemption was to what the rehearsal had pointed.

Paul has written in chapter 9 of God's mercy in bringing the Gentiles into the covenant community. However, it must be remembered that in the Acts of the Apostles, Paul went to the Jews first with the good news. He visited their synagogues, proclaiming to worshippers that Jesus was the Messiah for whom they had been waiting. Indeed, earlier in the letter, he wrote that the Gospel is to the Jew first and also to the Greek (Rom 1:16).

In this verse, Paul pauses to share his constant burden. He knew the Jews had been blessed with many privileges and that nothing more could be done for them. Yet, despite their unique privileges, they, like the unbelieving Gentiles, were children of the kingdom of darkness. The realization of their condition caused Paul to cry to God.

Paul distinguishes between longing ("my heart's desire") and prayer. It is a fact that sometimes we pray because we know that we should rather than because we are driven by a burning desire. Paul probably knew the sort of praying that responded to duty rather than compassion. Here, however, he writes that whenever he thinks of his countrymen, he cannot but pray—his heart going out to God for them. The dynamism that drives such prayer is love, and Paul's affection and concern for his people result in deep distress over the dangerous condition they are in.

How easy it would have been for Paul to wash his hands of any responsibility for his fellow countrymen. They had done everything to silence him: they had planned his death (Acts 9:24), slandered him (Phil 1:17), and sought to ruin the work he had sacrificed everything to do (Gal 1:6–9). Yet, their eternal welfare was his primary concern. God blesses such a man who gives himself—regardless of the cost—to those who need to hear the good news of Jesus Christ.

10:2 *For I can testify about them that they are zealous for God, but their zeal is not based on knowledge.*

Paul is able to acknowledge the zeal that drives the Jews to silence him. It is the same zeal that had controlled him before his conversion (Acts 8:3). It now led them to go to incredible lengths in their attempts to assassinate him (Acts 23:12–15; 2 Cor 11:25). They belonged to the chosen nation, with privileges and blessings above all other nations.[549] How could they accept that a Galilean,

---

[549] Smiles, "Concept," 282–99, notes that "zeal" in Second Temple Judaism had to do with an impassioned defense of the covenant by observance of the law. Covenant and law were so bound together that they were essentially synonymous terms. Prior to becoming an apostle, Paul would have defended such a view. In this context, Gentiles were only important insofar as they affected Israel's capacity to be faithful to the covenant. Separatism was for the sake of obedience; the reverse was never true. Smiles argues that what Paul found wrong with the zeal of his opponents was the faulty understanding of their covenant which, in his judgment, made "works" its bedrock. For

Romans 10

crucified by the Romans, could possibly be the Messiah of God? It was this utter revulsion that drove them—as it had driven Paul—to persecute the Jewish followers of Jesus (Acts 22:3–5). While their rejection of Jesus seemed logical, their presuppositions were wrong. They interpreted the promises of God in terms of privilege and innocence, and not in terms of responsibility and guilt.

10:3 Since they did not know the righteousness that comes from God and sought to establish their own, they did not submit to God's righteousness.

In saying that they did not know the righteousness of God, Paul is not saying that the Jews were ignorant of God's requirements but that they had refused to accept what God had provided. This is what alarmed him for he had been like them at one time. He thought that he was pleasing God by his commitment to destroy the church, but, instead of pleasing God, he was actually fighting against him.

Before his conversion, Paul could not have accepted that God's righteousness had been made known and made available through the crucifixion of one at the hands of the Gentiles. To accept that the death of Jesus, sentenced as a common criminal, was part of the purposes of God was something Jews could not accept. They reasoned that nothing could transcend the events of their history. What could be greater than the revelation of God in saving his people from bondage in Egypt and in bringing them to Sinai, where he revealed himself in glory and majesty? What could be greater than the messages of the prophets and the deliverance from exile in Babylon? The answer to these questions was the resurrection of Jesus Christ from the dead. This alone was able to change Paul from persecutor to disciple and from destroyer to proclaimer. Until they faced this historic reality, which overshadowed all other demonstrations of God's power and presence, the Jews would continue to reject the message of the cross, preferring to embrace their own righteousness (that is, the experience of salvation through Moses) which actually held them captive to darkness.

Paul, it was essential to understand that the covenant was wholly a matter of grace (Rom 4:4, 16; 11:5–6).

10:4 Christ is the end of the law so that there may be righteousness for everyone who believes.

This has been a much discussed verse for obvious reasons.[550] Is Paul actually saying the law has no relevance because its life span is over? Such a suggestion would do nothing but terrify a devout Jew, for the law is an essential part of the covenant. In Jewish thinking, "no law" meant "no covenant." The end of the law would mean the end of the unique relationship between the Jewish people and Yahweh. This is a point that Paul is well aware of, and it is going to be the thrust of his argument in the next chapter. Here, he is specifically focusing on the law's role in achieving righteousness.[551] Paul is not rescinding the need for righteousness; he is redefining the scope of those who are its recipients, making it clear it is no longer limited to the Jews who alone had the law.

We need to remember that when Paul speaks of "righteousness," he uses it in the way that the OT prophets, especially Isaiah, used the term. In their writings, "righteousness" referred to the saving activity of God in delivering his people from exile in Babylon, so that they could return to their inheritance and appear in his presence. This is the argument Paul is making here. It is not only the Jews who are able to come into the presence of God as rescued and forgiven sinners; the Gentiles also are included in this act of salvation. It is not an act of redemption based on the OT acts of God and into which the Gentiles are invited to share (provided they convert to Judaism and come under the law). It is a salvation, or a righteousness, that has come through Christ's death and is available to all who believe. The old law is no longer applicable. There is a new

---

[550] For a summary of different understandings of Paul's attitude to the law, see Westerholm, *Law*, who argues that the law has no validity for the Christian. This was challenged by Cranfield, "Place," 50–64, saying that Paul continued to find the will of God in the law but in a new and distinctively Christian way. Schreiner, "View," 113–35, argues that the "end of the law" refers solely to the law as a means of salvation having come to an end. Further discussion on the various views on the law can be found in Strickland, *Law*.

[551] Hills, "Goal," 585–92, says Paul's meaning is that Christ was the goal of the law from the very beginning. He based this claim on the absence of a copula (i.e. a linking verb) between his use of τελος (*Telos*) and Χριστος (*Christos*). Thus Christ was, from the very beginning, the goal of the law. This is a similar understanding to that of Bechtler, "Telos," 288–308, who argues that the key to the meaning of Rom 10:4 is to be found in the relationship between Rom 9:30–33 and Rom 10:1–4, two paragraphs whose parallelism renders them mutually interpretative. The logic of the passage in chapter 9 demonstrates that Paul identified Christ not as the termination of the law but as the goal toward which God intended the law to lead Israel. In the logic of this argument, Jews who reject Christ reject the purpose and goal of the law.

covenant and, therefore, a new law—the law of Jesus, the new husband (Rom 7:1–6).

Paul is not saying the ethics of the law have no relevance to Christian living. His concern has to do with the law's role in establishing righteousness. Later in the letter, he says that love is the fulfillment of the law (Rom 13:8). For many Jews delivered from Egypt, it was the keeping of the law that demonstrated their gratitude to Yahweh. But the law, with its high principles, could only regulate outward behavior. Love regulates the whole life, the heart of man especially. For the new covenant, the law is inadequate and has to be replaced by the command: "Love." It is love for Christ that causes the believer to accept gladly the authoritative law of the new husband, the law of Christ.[552]

However, it is possible that Paul means that Christ is the end of the law in another way as well. We have noted the ongoing priestly theme of the letter. In Rom 8:34, Paul has written: "who is he that condemns? Jesus Christ who died—more than that, who was raised to life—is at the right hand of God and is also interceding for us." Such a strong statement concerning Christ's priesthood should not be overlooked. We have already noted that there are strong thematic links between the letter to the Romans and the letter to the Hebrews.[553] In the latter letter, the writer explained that the change of administration (i.e., the establishment of a new covenant), meant a change of priesthood and, with it, a change of law. If this is the background to the statement in Rom 10:4, then Christ is the end of the law because he is the end of the old administration. He is the High Priest of the new one and, in this new administration of grace, the law of Christ replaces the law of Moses and the priesthood he established. This suggestion makes good sense in the light of the argument that Paul is about to make for, as we shall see, the question: "'Who will ascend into heaven?' (that is, to bring Christ down)" (Rom 10:6), is better understood as a reference to Christ's ascension rather than to his incarnation. If the ascension reading is correct, then it links into the start of Christ's priestly which resulted from his ascension where he now intercedes for his people. Thus

---

[552] See comments on Rom 7:1–4.

[553] See Excursus B: The Influence of the Prophet Ezekiel in Paul's Theology. See also Moo, *Romans*, 246, who lists parallels between Ezekiel and Romans. However, Moo did not notice the absorption of the Day of Atonement sacrifices into the Passover as described in Ezek 45:25 and how this matches the merging of the Day of Atonement and Passover found in the letter to the Hebrews.

the law has come to an end because a better law has been established based on a new High Priest and a new covenant.

10:5 Moses describes in this way the righteousness that is by the law: "The man who does these things will live by them."

At first reading, this verse suggests that Paul is speaking about attaining righteousness by observing the law. This is an understandable interpretation, but it tends to exclude the OT's covenantal dimension of the term: "the righteousness of God." I have sought to show[554] that there are passages in his letters where Paul can be read against the background of covenantal nomism. This is the understanding that the law did not terrify the Jews but was seen as their greatest blessing and gift from a loving God to his covenant people. If this is so, then the "righteousness that is by the law" (v. 5), does not refer to salvation that is secured by its keeping for it had not been given for that purpose. Indeed, when we recall that righteousness in the OT is not essentially about character but about God's saving activity, we find that Paul is saying that the law does not secure this salvation. Indeed, in the Leviticus passage that Paul quotes (Lev 18:5), the thrust is not "keep the law and you will gain salvation" for the passage implies that the Israelites had already been saved: "You must not do as they do in Egypt, where you used to live" (Lev 18:3a). The passage continues: "and you must not do as they do in the land of Canaan, where I am bringing you" (Lev 18:3b). In other words, to know the fullness of the blessing of salvation, the Israelites now had to live according to the law of God.[555]

Thus, Paul's statement should be read in the same context as Moses' address to Israel: the saving activity of God is brought to completion by his people's response to the teaching of the law. The righteousness of God is initially established in the church (or the lives of believers) by the deliverance that comes through Christ's death. It is completed and finalized when those who have been redeemed are transformed at the appearing of Christ (Phil 3:21). It must be emphasized that this reading of righteousness, i.e., in a covenantal context rather than in a legal/forensic setting, still requires the free gift of God's forgiveness. This is because the covenant could not exist unless God was prepared to deal with man on the basis of grace rather than on his ability to fulfill the law. The passage is saying nothing different from Eph 2:4–10.

---

[554] See Holland, *Contours*, 183–236.

[555] For further discussion, see comments on Rom 4:2, and Holland, *Contours*, chapter 9.

The Greek text of Rom 10:5 begins with the word γαρ (*gar*) "for," which is omitted in the NIV. This word links vv.5–9 with the four opening verses of the chapter, where Israel's condition under the law and her attempt to use it to attain righteousness (salvation) have been discussed. Paul is explaining, therefore, how the law is fulfilled in a totally unexpected but, nevertheless, predicted way in Christ.

10:6 But the righteousness that is by faith says: "Do not say in your heart, 'Who will ascend into heaven?'" (that is, to bring Christ down)

Before attempting to unravel the meaning of the passage in its wider OT context (the source to which Paul and the Roman church unquestionably had access), we need to note that, once again, Paul demonstrates a high regard for the context of his OT quotations. The chapters preceding Deut 30 warned Israel of the danger of not keeping the covenant. If she lived according to its precepts, she would be richly blessed, but if she went after other gods, she would be uprooted from the land and given over to her enemies. While Deut 28–29 anticipated Israel's unfaithfulness and judgment resulting in her exile, the nation was also given a promise that she would be restored to her inheritance when she returned to Yahweh. As outlined in Deut 30, the process of turning back would be a national undertaking which required Israel's heartfelt repentance and call to God for mercy and deliverance.

Aware of the value his countrymen placed on the law, Paul sought to show them its limitations. To do this, he turned to another key statement of Moses in Deut 30:11–14. Paul used the Greek conjunction δὲ (*de*) "but" at the beginning of Rom 10:6 to turn the tide of Moses' statement to favor his own argument. While Moses taught the people to keep the law, Paul reasoned that Moses knew this could not be achieved and, because of this, told the people of another righteousness. Paul unpacks Moses' statement to show that this speaks of Christ.

Moses' question can be expressed as: "Who will ascend into heaven to get it (i.e., the book of the law) and proclaim it to us so we may obey it?" (Deut 30:12b). It was addressed to the Israelites before they entered the promised land and the question probably echoed their experience at Sinai when Moses, their leader, ascended the Mount for the final time. He carried in his hands the two stone replacement tablets upon which the Lord would inscribe the Ten Commandments—the words of the covenant. When Moses descended, he gave the Israelites all the commands the Lord had given him (Exod 34:1–32).

In Deut 30:11–12, 14, Moses told the Israelites not to look for anyone to ascend a mount again in order to receive a new revelation. They were to recognize that Yahweh had provided for them through the giving of the book of the law on Sinai. This would stand during their time in the promised land and after the return of their descendants from exile. That same word would always be near them—it was in their hearts and would be in the hearts of their descendants because it had been taught since the nation's inception. Moses pronounced that no new teaching or revelation would be needed for Israel— just willingness to obey what had already been given (Deut 30:10).

Paul chose to use Deut 30:11–14 as its Second Exodus context fitted his argument perfectly. He could bring the text over into his letter because it fitted its theological framework about God's salvation being accomplished through the New Exodus. (This suggested use of typological correspondence is also seen when Paul quotes Isa 52:7 later in the chapter [Rom 10:14–17]. This Isaianic passage recounts how the returning exiles entreated those residing along their route to join their pilgrimage to Jerusalem. They urged the people to become part of the returning community that was obeying the call to worship Yahweh in Zion.[556] It is clear that Paul transfers the Isaianic text to the church, for, in her pilgrimage to the heavenly Zion, she is also called to welcome all who will join her in seeking the Lord. Paul makes this link between the pilgrim communities without any explanation to the Roman believers—typological exegesis, evidently, did not need to be defended.[557]

---

[556] The setting of Deut 30:12 was the bringing down of a new law from Sinai (or heaven). When Moses originally went to receive the law, the Jews thought he had deserted them because of his delayed return. It may have struck the Roman believers that, while Moses was away forty days in the Mount, Jesus had been away from his people for many years. It would have been natural for them to have asked, "What must we do to bring him back among us?" This makes sense of Paul's answer: "He is already intimately with you. Faith will recognize that fact and rejoice in all of the blessing that the ascended Christ has poured upon you." Such a question certainly became part of a later period of Judaism for it was not uncommon for rabbis to argue that the Messianic kingdom would not come until the law had been kept perfectly, cf. Jewett, *Romans*, 626–27. Indeed, the letters to the Hebrews and the Colossians indicate that believers were tempted to return to the law—probably claiming that they would embrace it in a new way as a result of the coming of Christ. Regardless of this aspiration, they were subjecting themselves to the law and this was something that Paul could not tolerate. See Lincoln, *Ephesians*, 243. Kraus, *Psalms 60–150*, 53, links the ascension with the Exodus.

[557] See Goppelt, *Typos*; Friedbert, *Indicators*.

Romans 10

Before attempting to unravel the meaning of Rom 10:6, attention must be paid to the widespread understanding among scholars that Paul has constructed a wisdom Christology and that Rom 10:6 speaks of Christ's incarnation.

Moses' original statement urged the Israelites to stay faithful to the law. Scholars[558] have noted how Deut 30:12 was used by the writers of the Jewish pseudepigraphal works *4QMMT* and *Baruch 3*. In these texts, the theme of wisdom is linked with the quotation. This has led many scholars to hold that the intertestamental wisdom theme was the source of Paul's teaching about Jesus being the wisdom of God. They reason that, by using this material from the pseudepigraphal writings,[559] Paul has built a Christian doctrine which speaks of the incarnation of wisdom. However, while this suggestion has gained widespread acceptance, it poses insurmountable problems.

First, it relies on texts from Second Temple Judaism that do not have a homogeneous message. The construction of a doctrine from a set of texts requires that they all testify to the same thing—and this is something that the texts from Second Temple Judaism do not do. The fact is that the texts expressed many Jewish positions (often radically different) on any one theme, often using the same vocabulary to convey different meanings. As a result, constructing a reliable teaching of Second Temple Judaism becomes an unrealizable aspiration. Scholars who use these texts to explore Second Temple theology cannot possibly establish that it presented a unified perspective because there was not one but there were many theologies. In spite of this, having supposedly discovered the original fertile thought world of the NT, scholars often go on to impose their new found understanding on the NT texts they are attempting to exegete. However, their findings do not recover first century understanding but display twenty-first century methodological incompetence. It is akin to a scholar of contemporary Christian theology daring to use the teachings of Presbyterianism to understand the doctrines of Methodism. Such practice would never be countenanced, for the mixing of texts

---

[558] Bekken, *Near You*; Wright, "Romans," 662. See Jewett, *Romans*, 626, for an explanation of how Paul has altered the text so as not to follow the pseudepigraphal wisdom reading of Deut 30:12. Moo, *Romans*, 652–53, acknowledges the wisdom tradition but thinks it is not as widespread or important for Paul's Christology as some make it.

[559] Also found in other texts, such as *Sir* 24:8–12; *Wis* 9:9–10.

from different traditions does not lead to a greater understanding but an increased confusion.[560]

Second, reliance on Second Temple texts assumes that Paul knew them well enough to construct arguments from them and that his readers were sufficiently familiar with them to follow his reasoning. However, the likelihood that these texts were known and deliberately used by him to construct, in this case, a wisdom Christology and known well enough by the Roman believers to identify and decipher the relevance of allusions in his arguments is too remote for serious consideration. Alarmingly, this assumption is made by many respected scholars in their interpretation of numerous NT texts.

Third, the personification of wisdom in intertestamental literature has no links with a dying Messiah—yet this is clearly implied in Paul's statement: "God raised him from the dead" (Rom 10:9).[561] Moreover, this confession, which is at the end of the passage giving it the status of the purpose of its argument, focuses on the resurrection/ascension of Christ while saying nothing about his incarnation. This confession is the key to the use of Deut 30:12, for the argument that Paul has developed out of Moses' statement is part of the pathway to the confession of Christ's Lordship. The conclusion must control the reading of the preamble.

Fourth, there is no anticipation of an incarnate Messiah in the OT in any theology in Judaism or even in the pseudepigraphal writings. None of these sources saw someone ascending to heaven in order to escort the Messiah down to earth. Moreover, there is no suggestion of such an understanding in the NT. Nevertheless, despite an absence of evidence to support the interpretation, the incarnational meaning that relies on the Wisdom teaching of intertestamental literature is the one followed by most scholars.[562]

So, if evidence supporting the claim that Rom 10:6 speaks of Christ's incarnation is unreliable, is there an alternative reading worthy of serious consideration? I believe there is. It speaks of Christ's ascension into the Father's presence. I shall attempt to show that Deut 30:12 has become part of

---

[560] Holland, *Contours*, 51–68.

[561] Davies, W.D., *Rabbinic*, 155.

[562] The intertestamental Wisdom theme is not the same as that taught by John (Jn 1:1–3) nor should it be confused with the Wisdom theme that is rooted in the OT. For further discussion see Holland, *Contours*, 339–51.

an extensive ascension tradition in the OT[563] and that it is one of a number of passages taken over into the NT and used by Paul as a type of Christ's ascension.[564]

In Rom 10:6, Paul has brought Deut 30:12 into an argument saturated with quotations from the OT with Second Exodus themes pulsating within them. In this new setting, i.e., of the New Exodus that Paul is developing, the true Son of David has ascended into heaven from where he sends down the gift of himself to his people in the person of the Holy Spirit. Because of the descent of the Spirit of Christ, no one needs to go up into heaven in order to bring Christ down. He is already with his people by his Spirit.

The key for understanding Paul's fuller meaning of Deut 30:12 is the ongoing story of the New Exodus. While the prediction of a second exodus is the original setting of Moses' words, the New Exodus context of the letter is much more developed than the original promise of a return from exile. It is this New Exodus "flavor" that Paul's use of Deut 30:12 absorbs. Without appreciating this wider theological context, much is lost and logical consistency is impossible. Since Deut 30:12 is used by Paul to support an argument that brings his readers to the resurrection and ascension of Christ, I am persuaded that he has made the text refer to Christ's ascension and glorification.[565]

The difficulty with interpreting the statement: "Do not say in your heart, 'Who will ascend into heaven?' (that is, to bring Christ down)" (Rom 10:6) as a reference to the ascension of Christ is that the passage goes on to ask: "or 'Who will descend into the deep?' (that is, to bring Christ up from the dead)" (Rom 10:7). The difficulty with interpreting the statement in Romans 10: 6 "Do not say in your heart, 'Who will ascend into heaven?' (that is, to bring Christ

---

[563] Present in the coronation psalms (Ps 24; 47; 68; 110; 118). In the LXX, ascent language is used in Ps 24(25LXX):3; 47(48LXX):5; 68(69LXX):18.

[564] Nearly all NT writers testify to the ascension, although the Epistles (Rom 8:32; Eph 1:20–21; 4:8–11; Heb 6:20) assume rather than describe it. The Gospels focus on the physical aspects, whereas Paul, the theologian, emphasizes Christ's spiritual body. The Johannine periscopes do not mention the ascension but imply it on several occasions (John 8:14, 21; 13:3, 33; 14:4–5, 28; 16:5, 10, 17, 28). See Gulley, *Ascension*.

[565] Strictly speaking, the "going up" is not about the ascension of Christ but the challenge of someone ascending to bring Christ down. The point is that no one needs to ascend because Christ has already descended and is now amongst his people. This justifies focusing on an ascension reading of the passage. The ascension was the climax of Christ's saving work, and only because he was exalted to the Father's side was he able to fulfill the promise and send the Spirit. For the importance of the ascension in the NT, see Maile, "Ascension"; Donne, *Ascended*.

down)" as referring to the ascension of Christ is that the passage goes on to ask in verse seven, "or 'Who will descend into the deep?' (that is, to bring Christ up from the dead)." It is argued that the bringing of Christ up from the dead is a reference to his resurrection—the event preceding the ascension. The statement "who will ascend" cannot, therefore, refer to Christ's ascension. As a result, it is linked to his incarnation as an event that proceeds being brought up from the grave.

Evidence for this ascension tradition is found in Eph 4:8, where the writer cites Ps 68:18:

> This is why it says: "When he ascended on high, he led captives in his train and gave gifts to men." (What does "he ascended" mean except that he also descended to the lower, earthly regions? He who descended is the very one who ascended higher than all the heavens, in order to fill the whole universe.)

The ascension theme is implied in that Christ first descended to the lower earthly regions, a clear reference to his burial, and this defined the one who had ascended on high. With the passage of time, the original text in the Psalms has been loaded with an expanded meaning. The psalm originally spoke of Yahweh ascending Sinai after his conquest of the Egyptians. It was later interpreted as a reference to his ascent of Zion to rule Israel and then to the ascent of David to occupy the throne of Zion after the conquest of his enemies. This association of key OT texts had been made by the rabbinic writers who saw Ps 68:8 as speaking not only of the ascension of Yahweh and David but also of Moses.[566] In later history it was claimed by the church as evidence of the ascension of Christ to his heavenly throne from where he distributed the gifts "of war" to his people. With this Christian reinterpretation, a full circle has been turned. It now speaks of King David's greater Son (who is none other than Yahweh) taking his throne. In addition, significant textual editing has taken place so that the

---

[566] The Targum on the psalm has "You have ascended to heaven, that is Moses the prophet; you have taken captivity captive, you have learnt the words of the Torah; you have given it as a gift to men," cited by Lincoln, *Ephesians*, 242–43. Lincoln, op. cit., 243, goes on to say: "The 'Moses mysticism' with which this interpretation of the psalm is to be associated was widespread. It can be found elsewhere in the rabbinic writings (e.g., *Midr.Tĕhillîm* on Ps 24:1 and Ps 106:2; *b. Sabb.* 88b) and in Philo (e.g., *Quaest, Ex.* 2.40, 43; *Mos,* 1.158; *Poster,* 14; *Somn.* 1.186–88: cf. also, W. Meeks, *The Prophet-King* [Leiden: E.J. Brill, 1967], 122–25, 205–9)." According to the Targum, the gifts given in Ps 68 were the Torah and the heavenly secrets.

version used in the letter to the Ephesians, the psalm has "you received gifts from men" to "and gave gifts to me."[567]

What this reading of Eph 4:8 shows us is that there was a richly developed ascension tradition in the early church.[568] An examination of other NT texts suggests this tradition was extensive and formed a major part of the church's teaching.[569] If this is so, grounds are given to return to Rom 10:6 to see if, despite the apparent inappropriate word order, it reflects the same ascension tradition as found in Ephesians.

As has been stated, the only problem for an ascension reading of Rom 10:6 is its word order as following an ascension reading it puts ascension before resurrection. But if the word order can be resolved satisfactorily, a typological exegesis would be the most natural reading of Paul's use of Deut 30:12. The question has to be asked whether the word order is as crucial as is commonly understood or, indeed, has it been correctly interpreted?

What is clear from other Pauline passages is the way he utilizes OT texts. Paul is flexible, appearing comfortable with the way he adapts and applies the OT Scriptures in support of the cases he is making. So, for example, in Rom 11:26, he quotes from Isa 59:20–21 but does not quote the Hebrew or LXX text. Instead, Paul alters the text so that it serves his theological purpose. He identifies its original Second Exodus context and this gives him the freedom to

---

[567] There is a major change from the original LXX text of psalm 68 from "you receive" to "you give." This change is found in the Targum on the Psalms, and although the Targum is a late work, it is held that it has made use of an ancient rabbinical tradition. See Lincoln, *Ephesians*, 243. This suggests that the Christians have not had to create this tradition for themselves but may have received it from an established Jewish tradition.

[568] The descent theme in Eph 4:9–10 has three possible interpretations. First, it speaks of the descent of the pre-existent Christ in his incarnation. This reading is supported by Ernst, 352; Mitton 147–48; Schnackenburg, 18–81; Barth, 433–34 (listed by Lincoln) and Moo, *Romans*, 656. In its favor is the descent—exaltation Christology found elsewhere in the NT, especially in the Fourth Gospel (cf. John 3:13; 6:62) and in Paul (Phil 2:6–11). Second, it speaks of Christ's descent to the underworld following his death. This was popular among the patristics and has support from Robinson, 180; Dunn, 186f.; Arnold, 57 and Kreitzer; 127 (listed by Muddiman, *Ephesians*, 192–93). Third, some see it as referring to the descent of the exalted Christ in the Spirit (Supported by Caird, Descent, 73–75; Kirby, *Ephesians*, 187 n. 51; Harris. W.H., "Descent" 235–65 [listed by Lincoln, *Ephesians*]).

[569] See Maile, *Ascension*; Zwiep, *Ascension*.

make it serve the New Exodus model he is developing.[570] So, it is possible that Psalm 68 had undergone a refocusing on who ascended and gave gifts. Indeed, it is quite possible that the editing of Isa 59 in Rom 11:26 is evidence of the reshaping of a text to make it clear that no one had to ascend up to Jerusalem to meet with the Redeemer.[571]

But such textual adaptation was not even necessary in the case of Deut 30:12. It was abundantly clear that *Moses was a type of Christ* and that his ascent of the Mount represented the ascension of the leader of the eschatological New Exodus. As a result—if our reasoning is correct—Deut 30:12, as part of the ascension tradition found in the OT, did not require adaptation to make it fit the church's message.[572] All that was required for referencing Deut 30:12 in Rom 10:6–7 was a straightforward typological application and reading—a process that has been established as widely practiced by the early church.

Indeed, the difficult matter of the order of the terms "ascend" and "descend" may not be the problem that it first appears. Paul may be more careful in his use of the Deut 30:12 text than has been recognized. It is possible that he is reading back through redemption history and, as he looks back, the most recent event was the ascension and gift (or outpouring) of the Spirit (Rom 10:6), preceded by the death and resurrection of Christ (Rom 10:7). Viewed in this way, the statement is effectively saying that the Easter/Ascension and Pentecost events (death and resurrection/ascension and outpouring of the Spirit) have been accomplished, and it was these events that brought an end to the old covenant and the law that expressed it.[573] In comparison to other examples of textual adjustment, the practice of reading historical events retrospectively is easy to establish. It is something that Paul does on several occasions. Indeed, immediately following this instance he uses the same method of citation again: "How, then, can they call on the one they have not believed in? And how can they believe in the one of whom they have not heard?

---

[570] While the model was given by the prophets, then fulfilled and given new meaning by Christ, and was also used as the framework of his teaching ministry (see Wright, *Victory*),the apostles clearly developed themes within the context of the paradigm to make particular points.

[571] See comments on Rom 11:26.

[572] For a summary of this teaching, see Gulley, *Ascension*. For the ascension in Luke, see Zwiep, *Ascension*. The ascension has been described as the most neglected doctrine of the church. See Jansen, *Ascension*, 17.

[573] See comments on Rom 10:4.

Romans 10

And how can they hear without someone preaching to them? How will they preach unless commissioned? Just as it has been written: How lovely to see the feet of those announcing good news!" (Rom 10:14–15).

If Paul is looking back through the events of salvation history, the apparent "awkwardness" of his ascension reading of Deut 30:12 is resolved. He has no need to change the position of the events in the Deuteronomy text. He can leave them as they are for their existing order serves his purpose perfectly. He can begin with the climax of the covenant promise—the giving of the Spirit, which was secured by Christ's ascension. In reality it is more than this, for the ascension not only secured the outpouring of his Spirit on his people but also his exaltation as Lord, in whose presence every knee will eventually bow in submission. Indeed, it is by professing Jesus' Lordship that salvation is given before the Day of Judgment. The importance of this event is laid down in the confession of faith required in Rom 10:9 and this should control the earlier reading of Deut 30:12.

This proposed reading of Rom 10:6, i.e., the ascension of Christ and the giving of the Spirit (the descent of Christ to his people), parallels the reading of Eph 4:8 where the gift was the promised presence of Christ himself to the believing community (John 14:15–21; 15:26–27. Paul had written of this as the right of the church in Rom 8:10–17). This ascension and outpouring happened because God raised Jesus from the dead. As a result, there was no need for anyone to descend into the deep to bring Christ up, for it had been done and settled for all time.

Reading Rom 10:6 as referring to the ascension rather than the incarnation is supported by the fact that, throughout the letter to the Romans, Paul makes considerable use of Isaiah's writings—particularly his Second Exodus perspective. He uses these ancient texts to direct his readers to the Redeemer—the Son of David, on whom the prophets focused—as the bringer of deliverance.[574] As a result, Christ the Redeemer and Son of David, whose triumph was his ascension to his throne along with his delivered people (Rom 8:34), significantly informs Rom 9–11; and this section is, of course, the new context for Deut 30:12.[575] Thus, the teachings of other OT texts that form this

---

[574] Something of this is reflected in Acts 15:15–19; Gal 4:21–27; Heb 12:18–28. In each case, the progression of Moses to David and then to Jesus is evident.

[575] For a detailed examination of the influence of the Exodus theme in chapters 9–11, see Excursus J: The New Exodus Framework of Romans 9–11 and Other NT Passages, p. 485.

ascension tradition are echoed in the citation of Deut 30:12. These echoes support the exegesis that has been offered that the text is about the ascension of Christ (the son of David) and his giving of the Spirit, no one needing to go up "to bring Christ down."

Thus the typological argument guiding the reading of Deut 30:12 and the introduction of Moses into Psalm 68 found in the rabbinic traditions suggests there existed a willingness to replace Moses by David and vice versa. Thus the replacement of Moses by David in the NT (which had been in reverse in parts of second temple Judaism, Moses substituted for David) justifies the retrospective introduction of David into the Deuteronomy text. This was especially made possible because of its typological reading in which Moses anticipates Christ who was identified as the son of David. Thus for the early church, Deut 30:12 naturally referred to the ascension of Moses and to his New Exodus successor, David. Thus, the great son of David, who came down in the incarnation, has come down again in the person of the Spirit and now resides with his people as he had promised.

This reading is supported by the conclusion of the section. As noted earlier, this is what Paul's argument is working towards, which is why the quote from Deut 30:12 is at the heart of his preamble. Rom 10:6–7 leads to the declaration about how to become a member of the new covenant community in v.9: "if you confess with your mouth, 'Jesus is Lord,' and believe in your heart that God raised him from the dead, you will be saved." The resurrection of Christ is central to this confession; any reading of Rom 10:6–7 that fails to take this into account is more than likely to miss the point of Paul's discourse. The relation of Deut 30:12 to the confession is best appreciated when we read the text as a whole:

> But the righteousness that is by faith says: "Do not say in your heart, 'Who will ascend into heaven?'" (that is, to bring Christ down) "or 'Who will descend into the deep?' "(that is, to bring Christ up from the dead). But what does it say? "The word is near you; it is in your mouth and in your heart," that is, the word of faith we are proclaiming: That if you confess with your mouth, "Jesus is Lord," and believe in your heart that God raised him from the dead, you will be saved. For it is with your heart that you believe and are justified, and it is with your mouth that you confess and are saved. (Rom 10:6–10)

The relation between the statement of Moses and the confession that a seeker must make becomes evident and so the ascension reading of Rom 10:6 becomes much more secure.

In addition, Paul has prepared the Roman church for a Christological/ascension reading of Deut 30:12 by emphasizing at the opening of his letter that the resurrection of the Son of David declared him to be the Son of God (Rom 1:4). This resurrection/ascension emphasis is consistent with the importance Paul has given the resurrection throughout the letter (Rom 4:25; 6:1–4; 8:34). This emphasis on the death and exaltation of the Son of David, which leads to the outpouring of the Spirit, is found throughout the preaching of Acts (Acts 2:24–36; 3:21; 4:24–31; 5:29–34; 10:39–44; 13:22–52; 24:21; 26:23).

In conclusion, this reading of Deut 30:12 in Rom 10:6 directs the Roman church to the one who has replaced David and Moses in the New Exodus (Rom 6:4; 7:4–6; 8:31–39; 1 Cor 10:6–13; Col 1:13–14). His conquests have brought about the eschatological New Exodus event and with it the creation of a new covenant. With this new covenant, a new law (that is, the gift of the Spirit) has been given. Indeed, we saw in the introduction the massive transition in the Jewish prophetic tradition of the eighth century BC in which the future hope of Israel was no longer bound up with Moses but rather with the victory and, therefore, ascent of David's descendant (that is, Jesus Christ).[576]

Thus, the question, "Who shall ascend into heaven?" is understood to be about receiving the benefits of the work that the glorified Redeemer has achieved. It is not about receiving the law (as with Moses) but what the law pointed to, i.e., the fulfillment of the covenant and all of its blessings—not least, the gift of the Spirit. It is because of this that Christ is the end of the law for all who believe (Rom 10:4; cf. Gal 3:25; 5:18).

The argument that has been made for the meaning of Rom 10:6 has assumed a New Exodus setting of the text. That this is the correct setting can be further demonstrated when the wider context of the text is considered.[577]

10:7 "or 'Who will descend into the deep?'" (that is, to bring Christ up from the dead).

Paul considers the second obstacle that Moses said did not need to be overcome by the Israelite people. However, Paul changes the obstacle from the sea to the grave of the Messiah.

---

[576] See Strauss, *Davidic*.

[577] See Excursus J: The New Exodus Framework of Rom 9–11 and Other NT passages, p. 485.

Paul does not strictly follow Deut 30:13, which says: "who will cross the sea to get it [the book of the law] and proclaim it to us so that we may obey it?" Rather, he has:

"'Who will descend into the deep?' (that is, to bring Christ up from the dead)." We will consider this change in a moment.

In human terms, descending into the deep—the grave—is an impossible and hopeless situation. The most that could be hoped for would be that, in some way, the death of Jesus might inspire others to keep faith with what they believe, even to the point of death. But that was not God's intention. Jesus had not been abandoned in the grave by God, so man does not have to go searching for him in the terrifying arena of death. God has acted decisively by raising Jesus from the dead. Jesus is neither limited to heaven nor is he a prisoner of death. He is near to all who would call on him.[578]

The statement about going into the grave echoes Deut 30:13 (LXX). However, it is held by some scholars that Paul has used a translation of the text which is found in the Targums.[579] This echoes the wording of Ps 106:26 (LXX) (Ps 107:26, in most English translations). They consider that this source is preferred because the original text in Deut 30:13 has: "Nor is it beyond the sea, so that you do not have to ask, 'Who will cross the sea to get it and proclaim it to us so we may obey it?'" Those scholars who favor the Targum as Paul's source think it explains his revised text: "Who will descend into the deep?" The difficulty with this suggestion is this: how are the readers and hearers of the letter (particularly Gentiles) expected to know the Targum so as to understand the change that has been made to Deut 30:13? (As with other intertestamental literature, great care has to be exercised. Few seem to appreciate this need for care as the appropriate controls for the interpretation of texts are not being exercised.[580] Indeed, at this point in Israel's history, the Targums were still in oral form and only rabbinical scholars had access to them).

A more simple suggestion is that Paul made this connection between Deut 30:12 and Ps 107:26 and, as a result, produced the new reading. This hypothesis does not require the Roman believers to have had prior knowledge of rabbinic

---

[578] For a fuller discussion, see Humphrey, "Demonstration," 129–48, who argues that Paul is denying any need for visionary experience in order to hear and respond to the word of Christ. Paul's argument is that what is needed has been revealed in the Scriptures.

[579] See Jewett, *Romans*, 627.

[580] Controls such as those outlined by Hays, *Echoes*, 29–33.

sources as they had the same ability as Paul to reflect on internal echoes of Biblical texts.[581] This suggestion is reasonable because Ps 106 (LXX) (Ps 107 in the English Bible) recalls the experience of Israel in times of crisis and the subsequent mercy of Yahweh. There is widespread agreement that the psalm is a Second Exodus psalm about Jews returning from exile.[582] Indeed, the Jews used it in the Temple to celebrate Yahweh's faithfulness in rescuing the nation from Babylon. Through this liturgical use, it became well known and easy to recall.

So, the believing congregation in Rome could immediately see that Paul had legitimately embraced a typological application and that this had also been done with Deut 30:13, Paul inserting the Christological interpretation of Ps 68.[583] With David's approval (in that it could be argued David had written this paraphrase of Deut 30:13 in Ps 106 [LXX]), Paul had no need to defend his rendering!

The psalm lists four examples of Yahweh's saving activity toward Israel. What is especially interesting is that Ps 106:26 (LXX) has the phrase καταβαίνουσιν ἕως τῶν ἀβύσσων while Paul has Τίς καταβήσεται εἰς τὴν ἄβυσσον "Who will descend into the deep?" The passage in the psalm tells of how Jews on a journey out of exile faced death (v.26). They were caught in a terrifying storm at sea where waves lifted their boat up before throwing it down into a watery abyss. The craft was totally at the mercy of the wind, causing the waves to buffet the vessel. The similarity between the two texts (Rom 10:6 and Ps 106:26 [LXX]) persuades many to believe that Ps 106 reshapes the Deuteronomy text quoted in this verse (Rom 10:7), for Paul neither quotes the Masoretic text nor the LXX of Deut 30:13.

The interesting feature about Ps 106:26 (LXX) is that its theme of danger faced by the pilgrim community is echoed in Rom 10. Chapter 10 parallels Israel's pilgrimage as evidenced by the way that Isa 28:16 is quoted in v.11 and Isa 52:7 in v.15. The citation of Isa 53:1 in v. 15 ("Who has believed our message and to whom has the arm of the LORD been revealed?") brings to

---

[581] Again, so following the argument given by Hays, op cit.

[582] Allan, *Psalms, 101–150*, 88–89; Harman, *Psalms*, 354; Mays, *Psalms*, 346; Kraus, *Psalms, 60–150*, 330. Goulder, *Psalms*, 118ff., gives a detailed analysis of the psalm, showing how the imagery fits Israel's experiences in exile and during her journey from it.

[583] The psalm is, of course, post-exilic; but all of the psalms carry David's authority, for they are treated by the Jewish community as the "Psalms of David."

mind those in Babylon who refused to hear the message of the prophets concerning Yahweh's promise to save Israel from her captivity. As a result of their refusal to heed the prophets, they did not join the remnant community that returned to Jerusalem. The way Paul links Deut 32:21 and Isa 65:1 in vv. 20–21 serves to drive forward the theme of Israel's disobedience and the refusal of most of the exiles to hear the call to return to the promised land. The latter of the two citations warns unbelieving Israel that she will be replaced by the Gentiles. Ps 106 (LXX) describes four groups of people who were in danger, the psalmist telling how God delivered them. The important thing to note is that each of these groups cried to the Lord (vv. 6, 13, 19, 28) and he heard their cries and rescued them.[584] This fits Rom 10:13 where there is a quotation from Joel 2:32: "for everyone who calls on the name of the Lord will be saved."

There is a further reason for believing that Paul brought Ps 106 (LXX) into Deut 30:13. Ps106:26 (LXX) says: "They mounted up to the heavens and went down to the depths; in their peril their courage melted away." The mention of "going up to the heavens and going down into the depths" is an ideal paraphrase of Deut 30:13 and offers the opportunity to make it clear that Christ will not be brought from across the seas but from the depths of the abyss (the grave).[585] By this creative merger, Paul has given the words of Moses far greater significance. The one like unto Moses has not been brought from across the sea but up from the grave to speak Yahweh's decisive last word (Heb 1:1–4). Indeed, the one who has done this is none other than the Son of David (Rom 1:3), so it is appropriate that the words that bear his name (Ps 106 LXX) are used to instruct the church in Rome.

There could also be a subtle apologetic message in the transformation of the text so that it speaks of not having to cross the sea to meet with Christ. When we examine Rom 11:26, we shall see that Paul is not averse to making a fine adjustment to a text if it ensures that his readers understand its proper meaning in the light of the Christ event. This is especially important in situations like this where the unaltered text could lead to a false understanding

---

[584] The psalm is possibly the theological structure used by Luke in Luke 8. Here, the narrative records a series of saving events that Jesus performed. Each of the sub-narratives appears to correspond to one of the four saving activities found in Ps 106 (LXX). If this is true, it suggests the passage was read in the way that is proposed in the argument given above.

[585] The "abyss" is used elsewhere in the OT to speak of realms beneath the earth, so making it an ideal picture of the grave. See Deut 8:7; 33:13; Ps 71:20–21; 107:26. To change "sea" for "abyss" is not difficult for the Hebrew mind. Both are linked with the picture of the separation, both had the same connotation in spiritual terms.

of the role of Judaism and God's dealings with men. Could it be that, in his transformed text, Paul is directing the believers in Rome away from any thought that they needed to travel across the seas to meet with the Messiah? There was no need for them to make a pilgrimage to Jerusalem, and the following verse gives the reason why.

10:8 But what does it say? "The word is near you; it is in your mouth and in your heart," that is, the word of faith we are proclaiming:

Moses pronounced that the requirements of the law were clear to any who were truly seeking to know God's ways. When Moses said these words to the Israelites, he was about to leave them. They were soon to cross the Jordan under a new leader, Joshua. Moses assures them that, although he will not be with them to teach them, they know the message of truth for it is in their hearts. If they seek God with all of their hearts they will find him, for they have been taught his word.

Paul's reference to the word being in their mouths and in their hearts probably recalls Jer 31:33–34, where God declares that he will put his law into the minds and hearts of members of the new covenant community.

10:9 That if you confess with your mouth, "Jesus is Lord," and believe in your heart that God raised him from the dead, you will be saved.

Contrasting with the uncertainties of the legalistic use of the law and the inaccessibility of God is the ringing certainty, "you will be saved." But what is required of man to secure his release from Sin and bring him into the certainty and assurance for which his heart longs? It is the simplest thing that can be asked of any man: "confess . . . and believe."

However, confessing Jesus as Lord is no small thing. The Roman Christians knew it meant saying that the will of Jesus came before any claims that Caesar or any other being could make upon them. Life in Rome meant daily confrontations with claims for allegiance, and faith required that, into these situations, confessions of Christ's Lordship were spoken immediately. There was to be no hiding behind some indecisive gesture or turn of phrase that left onlookers uncertain as to what was being proclaimed. The confession had to be clear, unequivocal and absolute. It was not sufficient to say that Jesus was a lord or a great figure. To confess him as Lord was to say that there was no rival.

The Lord's will was for the early disciples to be committed to him, even if it cost them their lives. For many Roman Christians, this was exactly the price they paid. Just as a bridegroom and bride confess their acceptance of each other, regardless of the circumstances that will face them, so commitment to Jesus as Lord begins at the point of confession. Living with him and for him has to be worked out daily in every detail of life.

Surprisingly, the exhortation is not "believe and confess," but "confess . . . and believe." This was possibly the order required by the apostles as it followed the sequence given by Jesus to those who claimed allegiance: "Whoever acknowledges me before men, I will also acknowledge him before my Father in heaven" (Matt 10:32). This cuts through the danger of mere intellectual assent. Indeed, faith is born in the act of confession. In the indifferent West, the implications of this order can easily be missed. This is not so for those who live in hostile parts of the world, where to confess can be the most costly thing a person can do.

10:10 *For it is with your heart that you believe and are justified, and it is with your mouth that you confess and are saved.*

Paul spells out the way God saves people. It is with a simplicity that offends many because he demands no great feat from them. They presume the almighty sovereign Lord ought to be demanding great demonstrations of sacrifice and loyalty to his laws. Instead, Paul writes to the Romans that all he demands is confession of Jesus as Lord and obedience to him.

Paul is not bypassing the seriousness of sin. He has already spelled out the devastating consequences of it in the early chapters of the letter. He has shown how extremely serious sin is, and how dreadful it will be for any person to give an account before God. However, he has also explained that God has made a way of escape through the death of his Son.

In the first part of the verse, the NIV translators have interpreted the Greek noun δικαιοσύνην (*dikaiosunēn*) as "justified.". The passage literally reads: "for with the heart one believes into righteousness". The use of εἰς (*eis*) before the verb and noun gives: "you believed into righteousness" or "you believe, resulting in righteousness." Thus, they will be made right with God, their Creator, and restored to the relationship they were created for. The important difference between justified and righteousness is that the former is an event whereas the latter is a status. Righteousness leads to justification; they are not the same. In the justification and righteousness language of the prophets when used in relation to Israel, Yahweh acted in righteousness toward her—saving her from her oppressors. As a result, she was justified, i.e., brought back into the relationship she had lost with her God.

The statement reflects the confession that each of the converts were required to make. While I have argued for a corporate baptismal significance of Rom 6:1–4 and other Pauline baptismal texts[586] I do not deny the practice of the early church in baptizing those who came to faith (1 Cor 1:14,17), as evidenced throughout the book of Acts (Acts 2:38, 41, 47–48; 13:24; 19:5). The NT writers saw baptism as the natural way of confessing faith, i.e., acceptance of the Lordship of the Savior, Christ Jesus. Indeed, it was not only the natural way, it was what Jesus commanded (Matt 28:19).

10:11 As the Scripture says, "Anyone who trusts in him will never be put to shame."

Paul demonstrates that the principle of faith is not his invention. In quoting the prophecy of Isaiah (Isa 28:16), he is not making use of a text that is unrelated to his theme. The original context of the quotation is about Israel turning from God and entering into a covenant with Môt, the Egyptian god of death (Isa 28:15, 18). By means of this covenant, Israel sought protection from Yahweh's anger. Isaiah promised the people that Yahweh would protect those who returned to him; moreover, he would not put them to shame. If Môt, the god of death,[587] could be thought to offer protection to his subjects, how much more could Yahweh, the living God, secure his own from the onslaught of Satan?

This picture of Israel entering into a covenant with the enemy of Yahweh is the same picture that is used in the NT. Unredeemed humankind—including the Jews—is related to Satan in a similar way. Jesus told the Jews: "You are of your father, the devil" (John 8:44). While the Jews could accept this as a description of the Gentiles, this allegation of a relationship with Satan would have infuriated them. It was tantamount to saying they had no covenantal relationship with Yahweh and were children of darkness. Indeed, it was saying

---

[586] See Excursus E: Baptism into Christ, p.228.

[587] "Death" was a term the NT writers used as a pseudonym for "Satan" (1 Cor 15:26, 55; Rev 20:13). See also, Ps 49:14; 4 Ezra 8:53; Apoc Bar 21:23; Test. of *Levi*, 18, for evidence that the imagery was used elsewhere in Judaism.

they were in the same desperate plight as the Gentiles—people they despised and regarded as unclean.[588]

Paul seeks to make it clear that, while Jews and Gentiles are equally blessed in being offered salvation, they are also equally in danger if they reject God's offer of mercy. All unbelieving Jews and Gentiles are in covenant with Satan. This concern has been at the heart of Paul's Gospel exposition in chapters 5–7. While the Jews had been delivered from the dominance of the Egyptian gods (the covenant with Môt was abolished through the representative death of the lambs in place of the Hebrew firstborn), most in Israel had yet to be rescued from the reality that the Exodus pointed to, i.e., the cosmic bondage to Sin and Death. This is the condition of unredeemed humankind for all are caught up in this reality of bondage and exile and need deliverance.

The NIV translates καταισχυνθήσεται (*kataischunthēsetai*) as "put to shame." This rendering is too weak a translation. The meaning is "ashamed," and the opposite of "being ashamed" is "being saved." There are echoes of its use in Rom 1:16; 5:5; 9:33.

10:12–13 For there is no difference between Jew and Gentile—the same Lord is Lord of all and richly blesses all who call on him, for, "Everyone who calls on the name of the Lord will be saved."

Paul again turns to an OT prophet to support his argument. Joel 2:28 was directed to those who were in exile. The prophet predicted the coming of the Day of the Lord, when the Spirit would be poured out. His prophecy was fulfilled on the Day of Pentecost, when Peter, in his sermon, referred to the same text (Acts 2:21). The Day of the Lord was the Day when Yahweh raised up his servant, the descendant of David, to bring the captives out of exile (Isa 52:3–10). Paul, along with all of the NT writers, is saying that the Day of the Lord has come. Jesus, the Son of David, has delivered his people from exile.

Joel also declares that any who call on the name of the Lord will become part of the covenant community and experience deliverance. Again, the invitation is to all unredeemed Jews and Gentiles. The quotation naturally picks up on the use of Ps 106 (LXX) where those in exile and tribulation called upon the Lord and he answered them (see comments on v. 7). Paul stresses the universality of the Gospel; the Jews, as far as salvation is concerned, have no

---

[588] See Holland, *Contours*, chapter 10, for fuller discussion.

favored status. Their entrance into salvation is the same as that of Gentiles. They must call on the name of the Lord who is rich in mercy.

10:14–15 *How, then, can they call on the one they have not believed in? And how can they believe in the one of whom they have not heard? And how can they hear without someone preaching to them? And how can they preach unless they are sent? As it is written, "How beautiful are the feet of those who bring good news!"*

Paul asks a series of questions, drawing the Roman believers along his line of reasoning to the point where they recognize how important it is that the message of salvation is proclaimed. Paul's intention is not only to emphasize the need for the Gospel to be preached, but also to stress that it is part of the OT picture—it is the fulfillment of God's purposes. God's intention has always been to save through preaching the message of salvation.

The quotation is from Isa 52:7. It refers to the Jews returning from exile. As they journeyed through the wilderness, they announced to all they met that they were returning home because Yahweh had redeemed them. Isaiah described these returning exiles as having "beautiful feet." They announced that their exile was over, and invited all the Gentiles that they met to journey with them to Jerusalem where they could worship God together.[589] The returning remnant gave this invitation because the prophets had said that, once the exile had ended, the nations would come to Jerusalem to worship the Lord (Isa 56:6–8; 60:8–16).

This is how Paul envisages the ministry of the church in Rome. Having been delivered from the kingdom of darkness, she journeys towards her heavenly home. As she journeys, she tells everyone she meets—in and beyond the city—that her God has redeemed her. Everyone is invited to join her in her pilgrimage and become part of one of the witnessing redeemed communities at the heart of the Roman Empire.

10:16 *But not all the Israelites accepted the good news. For Isaiah says, "Lord, who has believed our message?"*

Isaiah was distressed because, as Jews in Babylon began their journey home, many refused to join the redeemed band (Isa 53:1). Their refusal was partly due to disbelief that deliverance really was at hand, but also to their

---

[589] Bornkamm, *Paul*, 165.

unwillingness to identify with the ministry of the Suffering Servant. Many declined to leave the security they had acquired in Babylon. They preferred to stay under the headship of the Babylonian king rather than return to a disgraced and troubled Jerusalem and to the service of Yahweh who had been the nation's judge. It was more comfortable to stay in Babylon than to undertake a demanding pilgrimage and the enormous task of rebuilding Jerusalem with all its attendant problems and deprivations.

This is obviously how Paul is using the text, for the first part of the verse is clearly linked with the ministry of the returning exiles in the previous verse. Paul removes Isa 53:1 from its OT context (i.e., the ministry of the Suffering Servant and the people's refusal to believe the prophets' message that Yahweh had redeemed them. The apostle then applies the passage to unbelieving Israel of his own day whose preference for the security of the old covenant over the suffering that the new covenant would bring gives a stark parallel.

In the original context, the description of the Suffering Servant applied to one who the kings of the earth could not speak about (Isa 52:15). This is an important clue for identifying the Servant. Aristocrats are rarely moved by the suffering of ordinary people, however, they are alarmed when one of their own suffers. We saw something of this when members of the Russian royal family were assassinated during the Bolshevik revolution. It sent shivers of fear throughout the royal families of Europe. They realized the same fate could be theirs, and mere mention of the tragedy distressed them.

This is what is happening in Isa 53. The Servant is Israel's king, and he is the one the nation had hoped would come in glory to deliver her from Babylon. Instead, she is told that he will be treated like a common criminal. Isaiah sees the Servant's death (that is, the king's death) as a sin offering for rebellious Israel. He goes on to say (Isa 55:3) that the suffering of the Servant brings the sure mercies of David to those who believe, confirming the royal significance of the Servant figure. While it is important to understand Isa 53 in its original context, it has become a key passage by which Christians interpret the death of Jesus—and rightly so. It is their king—the Jewish Messiah—who has died for their salvation.[590]

This ties in with the early proclamations made in Acts. Here, the Christological statements are almost entirely about Jesus being the promised Davidic King (Acts 2:25–36; 5:29–32; 13:32–39). The Christology of Acts and

---

[590] See Holland, *Contours*, 81–82, for a discussion on the use of this passage in the NT and why its atoning significance is not stressed in the way we might expect.

the Gospels is not at variance with Pauline Christology, despite what many scholars claim. Their Christologies are at one and stay firmly within the orbits of the OT and the testimony of Jesus. In his letter to the Roman believers, Paul says that the same rejection the Messiah suffered at the hands of his chosen people continues. They cannot accept that they are saved only through the death of God's representative, Yahweh's Messiah King.

10:17 Consequently, faith comes from hearing the message, and the message is heard through the word of Christ.

Paul takes the principles of the returning exiles' ministry and uses them to describe the ministry of the Christian community such as the one in Rome. However, the message the NT pilgrims carry is far more exalted because they are proclaiming Christ. He is not only the Son of David, leading his people to their inheritance, but he is the one who gave his life as the sacrifice which broke the power of Satan, delivering his people from bondage. Again, Paul emphasizes the importance of the Christian community emulating the example of the OT covenant people and fulfilling her role in a way that Israel had failed to do (Jer 5:11; 31:22; Ezek 39:23; Hos 4:12).

Since the message creates faith, Paul sees its telling to be crucial, even though its proclamation has put his life in danger. He was not so much threatened by the unbelieving pagan world but by the Jews, who were aghast at his betrayal of their heritage and the denial of their unique status as a result of election. Religious hatred like this can often spawn violence and injustice as communities defend their perceived purity and privileges. Paul will have none of this. All of these privileges are meaningless outside of Christ.

10:18 But I ask. Did they not hear? Of course they did. "Their voice has gone out into all the earth, their words to the ends of the world."

Paul anticipates that one of the Roman believers, listening to his letter being read, will suggest that perhaps the Jews had never heard the good news. He discounts this doubt by citing Ps 19:4, where the psalmist reasons how creation itself disperses the knowledge of God throughout the universe: "The heavens declare . . . the skies proclaim . . . Their voice goes out, etc." Paul argues that the creation displays the glory and knowledge of the Creator God. The psalm continues by extolling the Scriptures—the Jews will have known them from childhood and could be led by them in the way everlasting. According to the psalm, they are perfect, revitalizing, trustworthy, wise, right, joy-giving, radiant, enlightening, sure, righteous, precious, and sweet . . . and what is more, they are accessible to every Jew. So, because he had the witness of creation and the Scriptures, no Jew could excuse himself from seeking a right relationship with God.

However, despite the witness of creation, few responded to God. They silenced their consciences and persuaded themselves of their innocence before him (Rom 1:18–32). If men turn from the revelation of God in nature, how will they react when confronted with the actual preaching of the Gospel? The revelation contained in nature was, as it were, "testing the waters" for the reception of the declared word.[591] Paul's argument concerning the witness of nature applies especially to the Gentiles. It cannot apply in the same way to the Jews for they have the oracles of God (Rom 9:4) and are without excuse. The details of the immediate argument suggest that Paul's focus has moved away from unbelieving Israel to the unbelieving world. He will return to the specifics of unbelieving Israel in Rom 10:19.

While Paul argues that all have heard,[592] the dilemma remains that his fellow countrymen are outside of the true covenant that God has established through Christ. All other covenants have either been ended or have found their fulfillment in him, and there is no automatic transference from the old into the new. What is required is for unredeemed Israel to see that, by entering the kingdom of God, she would experience the vitally needed rebirth. Jesus expressed this to Nicodemus—a member of the Jewish ruling council—when he said to him: "you must be born again" (John 3:7).[593] In this phrase, the Greek for "you" is plural because Jesus was speaking about the nation that Nicodemus represented. Her rebirth would be as a result of the Spirit's activity. In the absence of national repentance, the individual must make his stand in the midst of unbelief and hostility.

---

[591] Contra Moo, *Application*, 344, who thinks the use of the psalm demonstrates the looseness with which Paul is able to use the OT—applying it in ways that were never intended. We have seen, however, that Paul always respects the context and meaning of the original quote and does not take liberties in using the quoted texts as dysfunctional proof texts (see Holland, *Contours*, chapter 2).

[592] Munck, *Christ*, 95–99, argues that "all" refers to representatives of all nations, so focusing on the concept of corporate solidarity.

[593] The words of Jesus spoken to Nicodemus are essentially about Israel's condition and need. While it is legitimate to apply them to individuals when urging the exercise of faith and repentance, it must not be forgotten that the thrust of the original conversation was not about the salvation of an individual.

10:19 Again I ask. Did Israel not understand? First, Moses says, "I will make you envious by those who are not a nation; I will make you angry by a nation that has no understanding."

What Paul is arguing for is not something new—certainly not something that should take his fellow countrymen by surprise. The apostle appeals to Moses, who was cherished by his countrymen above all other OT figures. Moses warned the Jews that Yahweh would make his people envious by giving his attention to the Gentiles (Deut 32:21). The blessings that God would pour upon them would provoke the Jews to envy.

Deut 32:21 is one of three citations from Deut 32 (the Song of Moses) in the letter. In Rom 12:19 Paul cites Deut 32:35, and in Rom 15:10 he cites Deut 32:43. It is clear that the Song of Moses was well known to Paul and to the believers in Rome. He expects them to identify with the original passages and their context. In the Song of Moses, Israel was warned about her rebelliousness (Deut 32:15–18) and threatened that God's judgments would come upon her (Deut 32:19–25). The warning is given in Deut 32:21. Because Israel had provoked God to anger by worshipping false gods, Yahweh would provoke Israel to jealousy by taking a people that were not his people in the place of those who had been his people.[594] Paul clearly sees this text as a prophecy of the calling of the Gentiles and continues this theme of jealousy into chapter 11.

10:20 And Isaiah boldly says, "I was found by those who did not seek me; I revealed myself to those who did not ask for me."

Paul demonstrates that the Jews ought to have realized that the nations would come into a special relationship with Yahweh. He quotes from Isa 65:2 in which the prophet warned the people that God would be found by those who had not sought him. The Gentiles would not have sought the Lord but for the fact that he revealed himself to them. This was tantamount to saying that Israel, who had been the recipient of this same divine self-disclosure, was no longer the sole benefactor of Yahweh's electing grace. Others whom the Jewish people despised were to come into the same privileges. No doubt this would cause violent protest from Paul's Jewish kinsmen, but he could respond by asking the question: "Don't you remember; this is the very same state that we were in when Yahweh elected us?" The Jews were also chosen when they were not a people and had no prior claims on Yahweh.

---

[594] See Ryan, "Fidelity," 89–93, for a discussion on Yahweh's faithfulness to Israel in electing gentiles.

10:21 But concerning Israel he says, "All day long I have held out my hands to a disobedient and obstinate people."

The same Scriptures are now used to warn Israel. Despite having the blessings of the covenants, she did not want the intrusion of Yahweh into her national life and would not respond when he made his rightful claims upon her. To emphasize his point, Paul cites Isa 65:2. Like Hosea, Isaiah depicted Yahweh as the husband and Israel as his bride. Yahweh had rescued Israel when no one else wanted her, and he secured her life. He nurtured her until she became strong and beautiful, and then took her as his wife. She committed adultery, however, turned to the gods of the surrounding nations, rejected Yahweh's love, and spurned his pleas (Ezek 16:15–29). This is a picture of Israel that all Jews are familiar with from the writings of the prophets.

The Jews of Paul's day could not see that they were doing exactly the same as their forefathers. Indeed, they were doing worse. For the love of God had been revealed in a way that was beyond anything the Jews of the OT period could have envisaged. Yahweh had sent his beloved Son to die as the Passover victim, to bring them out of their bondage to Sin, and to make them the new covenant community—the bride of Christ. The marriage theme is such a part of Jewish understanding that, at every Passover meal, the Song of Songs is read. It speaks of the love between a man and a woman, which points to a far greater love—the love of Yahweh for his people. The Passover celebrates the divine marriage, when Yahweh took Israel as his bride on the first Passover night.

Thus, Romans 10 pulls together the theme of the exhortation of Moses in Ps–13 with the instruction that, when the Israelites return from exile, they are not to search for someone who will represent them before God in the mountain as Moses had done. They are not to send emissaries overseas either to find someone of the caliber of Moses who was brought to the nation by Yahweh from beyond the Red Sea. There would be no "new revelation" from God. He would give his people all that they needed in the person of the prophet who would be raised up from among them. This prophet would be like Moses, and his words were to be obeyed. This is the exhortation which is accompanied with the powerful themes of pilgrimage and deliverance from exile—themes that resonate throughout Paul's letter to the Romans.

CONCLUSION OF ROMANS CHAPTER TEN

Paul continues his exposition of the condition of Israel. She has pursued God but not according to knowledge. Instead of focusing on faith, she has focused on works—seeing the law as a means of retaining a status that had, in fact, been lost at Sinai. Her unique status did not exist, and she had no grounds for boasting.

Paul takes his readers back to the Sinai event, and forcefully argues that the principle of faith was embedded in the giving of the law. Again, it is exodus-type material that floods into his mind as he makes his case against Israel's unbelief.

He stresses again that the Scriptures are full of warnings to Israel that her unbelief will exclude her from God's blessings—blessings that the Gentiles will be brought into ahead of her. The proof texts are all from passages that have to do with the original exodus or the promises that accompanied the Second Exodus preaching of the prophets. Paul quotes from Ps 19, which speaks of the word of God being like the sun. According to the psalm, the sun is like a bridegroom who runs a race (Prov 19:5; cf., Isa 61:10). In missing the true meaning of the Scripture, Israel has missed her encounter with the bridegroom! She is missing the immense purpose and privilege of the New Exodus and, because of this, the Gentiles have responded ahead of her.

EXCURSUS J: THE NEW EXODUS FRAMEWORK OF ROMANS 9–11 AND OTHER NT PASSAGES.

The following overview of the OT texts Paul used in Rom 9–11 supports the argument that Rom 10:6–7 refers to the victorious ascent of the Son of David. The OT citations all have Second Exodus roots and David is the center of the event. They act, therefore, as a catalyst for this new reading of Deut 30:12:[595]

> As the Scripture says, "Anyone who trusts in him will never be put to shame." (Rom 10:11, citing Isa 29:16)
>
> or, "Everyone who calls on the name of the Lord will be saved." (Rom 10:13, citing Joel 2:32)
>
> And how can they preach unless they are sent? As it is written, "How beautiful are the feet of those who bring good news!" (Rom 10:15, citing Isa 52:7)

---

[595] We need to remind ourselves that such "new readings" were given by the prophets. For example, Hosea's new reading concerning what happened at Sinai transformed the significance of the Exodus event from that given in the original exodus narrative. We shall find that Paul does this again in Rom 11:26.

> But I ask: Did they not hear? Of course they did: "Their voice has gone out into all the earth, their words to the ends of the world."[596] (Rom 10:18, citing Ps 19:4)
>
> Again I ask: Did Israel not understand? First, Moses says, "I will make you envious by those who are not a nation; I will make you angry by a nation that has no understanding." (Rom 10:19, citing Deut 32:21)
>
> And Isaiah boldly says, "I was found by those who did not seek me; I revealed myself to those who did not ask for me." (Rom 10:20, citing Isa 65:1)
>
> But concerning Israel he says, "All day long I have held out my hands to a disobedient and obstinate people." (Rom 10:21, citing Isa 65:2)

These eight OT texts in Rom 10 cannot but influence the way Deut 30:12 is read. Paul's use of it is controlled by the New Exodus context in which it is placed. This is not an abuse of the text, for Moses was saying that the Jews, who returned from exile following punishment for breaking the terms of the covenant, were not to abandon the revelation given to them at Sinai as "the word is in your mouth" (Deut 30:14). (In a short time the people would, indeed, have God's words in their mouths. Israel was to learn a hymn that God would recite to Moses and Joshua in order to stand as a witness to him against his people. The hymn would remind them of God's dealings in their past and warn them of such in the future, and Moses insisted that it must be passed down through the generations [Deut 31:19–32:47]).

This New Exodus framework is not a sudden introduction, for chapter 9 made similar use of these themes, supporting them with an array of OT texts. Paul lists the blessings his people have been given to prepare them for the coming of Christ, and writes:

> Theirs are the patriarchs, and from them is traced the human ancestry of Christ, who is God over all, forever praised! Amen. (Rom 9:5)

This designation of Christ as being "God over all" is a key to understanding the meaning of the phrase, "to bring Christ down."[597] The description clearly

---

[596] This unexpected text in a such a list of New Exodus allusions might be explained by the fact that the following verse says that the law of the Lord "is like a bridegroom coming forth from his pavilion, like a champion rejoicing to run his course" (Ps 19:5). It might be this bridegroom theme that Paul uses in support of his New Exodus understanding of Deut 30:12. In other words, the law—which represents Christ—is the Bridegroom who seeks his bride.

[597] See notes in the main body of the commentary on the possible meanings of Rom 9:5.

sees the Messiah to be exalted because he has fulfilled his Father's will. It is because salvation is through such a rejected servant that such offense is caused (Rom 9:33).

> Nor because they are his descendants are they all Abraham's children. On the contrary, "It is through Isaac that your offspring will be reckoned." (Rom 9:7, citing Gen 21:6)

> For this was how the promise was stated: "At the appointed time I will return, and Sarah will have a son." (Rom 9:9, citing Gen 18:10, 14)

> Just as it is written: "Jacob I loved, but Esau I hated." (Rom 9:13, citing Mal 1:23)

> What then shall we say? Is God unjust? Not at all! (Rom 9:14, citing Exod 33:19)

> For the Scripture says to Pharaoh: "I raised you up for this very purpose, that I might display my power in you and that my name might be proclaimed in all the earth." (Rom 9:17, citing Exod 9:16)

> But who are you, O man, to talk back to God? Shall what is formed say to him who formed it, "Why did you make me like this?" (Rom 9:20, citing Isa 29:16 or Isa 45:9)

> As he says in Hosea: "I will call them 'my people' who are not my people; and I will call her 'my loved one' who is not my loved one." (Rom 9:25, citing Hos 2:23)

> It will happen that in the very place where it was said to them, "You are not my people," they will be called "sons of the living God." (Rom 9:26, citing Hos 1:10)

> Isaiah cries out concerning Israel: "Though the number of the Israelites be like the sand by the sea, only the remnant will be saved." (Rom 9:27, citing Isa 10:22–23)

> For the Lord will carry out his sentence on earth with speed and finality. (Rom 9:28, citing Isa 10:22–23)

> It is just as Isaiah said previously: "Unless the Lord Almighty had left us descendants, we would have become like Sodom, we would have been like Gomorrah." (Rom 9:29, citing Isa 1:9)

> As it is written: "See, I lay in Zion a stone that causes men to stumble and a rock that makes them fall, and the one who trusts in him will never be put to shame." (Rom 9:33, citing Isa 28:16)

The linking of the original promise to Abraham with the promises of the New Exodus emphasizes that the latter have not superseded the former. Instead, the New Exodus is its rightful fulfillment. What is more, this concentration of interlinking thematic texts is not limited to chapters 9–10, for the same theme is continued in chapter 11:

> And David says: "May their table become a snare and a trap, a stumbling block and a retribution for them." (Rom 11:9, citing Ps 69:22)

> May their eyes be darkened so they cannot see, and their backs be bent forever. (Rom 11:10, citing Ps 69:23)

> And so all Israel will be saved, as it is written: "The deliverer will come from Zion; he will turn godlessness away from Jacob." (Rom 11:26, citing Isa 59:20)

> And this is my covenant with them when I take away their sins. (Rom 11:27, citing Jer 31:33–34)

> Who has known the mind of the Lord? Or who has been his counsellor? (Rom 11:34, citing Isa 40:13)

> Who has ever given to God, that God should repay him?" (Rom 11:35, citing Job 41:11)

This mass of OT Second Exodus material controls the theology of the section. It supports the claim that we should neither focus on the achievements of Moses nor on the parallels that are supposed to be in the NT, for, as we have seen, he is superseded by the Davidic king. This fulfillment becomes the springboard for examining the way Paul uses his OT texts. The predictions of Moses must be understood through the lens of David who is the type of his greater son, Jesus. We also need to remember the pervasive control that Isaiah's vision of a second exodus, under the leadership of the Son of David, the Servant of the Lord, has on the theology of the letter as a whole. This was identified by the way the quotes from Isaiah were carefully placed throughout Romans (see pages 16–18).

When this prophetic control of Deut 30:12 is appreciated, it becomes clear that the order within it is of little significance for Paul. He is happy to follow Deuteronomy's order. However, he does not commit himself to forcing the events of Jesus' incarnation into Moses' statement for they cannot fit—even with manipulation. There is no suggestion in Scripture that anyone brought Christ down for his incarnation; indeed, the statement of Moses in Deut 30:12 is never found to have a Messianic fulfillment in the literature of Judaism. In addition to these considerations, we have noted the presence of the priestly theme in Romans (Rom 1:1, 3; 5:2–3, 9; 6:10; 8:34; see also 12:1; 15:16) and how this matches the teaching found in the letter to the Hebrews. Here, the change of priest brings a change of law—the former law passing away with the displaced priesthood.[598]

> If perfection could have been attained through the Levitical priesthood (for on the basis of it the law was given to the people), why was there still need for another priest to come—one in the order of Melchizedek, not in the order of Aaron? For when there is a change of the priesthood, there must also be a change of the law. (Heb 7:11–12)

It is the priestly theme that prepares for the exposition of the new covenant in Heb 8. Again, the change of law is implied when the writer quotes from Jeremiah, saying:

> For if there had been nothing wrong with that first covenant, no place would have been sought for another. But God found fault with the people and said: "The time is coming," declares the Lord, "when I will make a new covenant with the house of Israel and with the house of Judah. It will not be like the covenant I made with their forefathers when I took them by the hand to lead them out of Egypt, because they did not remain faithful to my covenant, and I turned away from them," declares the Lord. "This is the covenant I will make with the house of Israel after that time," declares the Lord. "I will put my laws in their minds and write them on their hearts. I will be their God, and they will be my people. No longer will a man teach his neighbor, or a man his brother, saying, 'Know the Lord,' because they will all know me, from the least of them to the greatest. For I will forgive their wickedness and will remember their sins no more." By calling this covenant "New," he has made the first one obsolete; and what is obsolete and aging will soon disappear. (Heb 8:7–13)

Here we see the same themes as in Rom 10. With the inauguration of a new covenant, the Mosaic law is terminated (Rom 10:4; Heb 7:12).[599] The new law is established as the result of a priest-king ascending on high. In both letters, Jer 31:31–34 is quoted (Rom 11:27; Heb 8:8–12) and emphasis made that Christ, the priest-king, has ascended to heaven and will not appear again until he comes to complete his saving work (Rom 1:4; Heb 9:24–28). In addition, both letters say the law has been brought to an end because the promised new covenant, with its new priesthood, has been inaugurated. Thus, the proposed reading of Rom 10:4–10 as a reflection on the benefits of the resurrection has the support of the letter to the Hebrews, suggesting widespread

---

[598] See Rom 10:4.

[599] The New Exodus theme which lies behind Romans has been shown to lie behind the letter to the Hebrews also. See Shin, *Hebrews*.

familiarity with the themes identified. No extra-biblical documents have to be appealed to—only the OT Scriptures and those which formed part of the identifiable emerging cannon of the early church. The OT texts were not only available to the community but known by its members in considerable detail, evidenced by the way they were repeatedly used by Paul to sustain detailed and, at times, complex arguments.

Further support for this ascension reading of Ps 68 is a text that is used in Eph 4:7–13, where Paul[600] writes about the ascension: "This is why it says: 'When he ascended on high, he led captives in his train and gave gifts to men.'" The distribution of gifts by the ascended victorious Christ is a development of the original psalm in which Yahweh receives gifts from the spoil. In the Ephesian text, it is clear that the ascended Christ does not give a new law but spiritual gifts. The Spirit takes the place of the law, the Spirit of Christ being given as the new law (Rom 8:3–4). Christ, in the person of his Spirit, has come down, and no one else was needed to bring this about. He (the Spirit) came down because a fitting person ascended the hill of the Lord; the Lord God was pleased with his intercessions for his people and delighted to send his Spirit. His final self-disclosure was complete. It is of no small significance that Pentecost—celebrated by the early church as the sending of the Spirit—was the occasion of the giving of the law in the Jewish calendar.[601]

This reference to the exalted Christ in Eph 4:8 does not stand on its own. Earlier in the letter, Paul expanded on the same theme. In chapter 1, he wrote:

> He raised him from the dead and seated him at his right hand in the heavenly realms, far above all rule and authority, power and dominion, and every title that can be given, not only in the present age but also in the one to come. And God placed all things under his feet and appointed him to be head over everything for the church, which is his body, the fullness of him who fills everything in every way. (Eph 1:20–23)

Many scholars see this passage about Christ's exaltation to be a direct echo of Ps 110, which concerns the Davidic king's enthronement. In the second chapter of Ephesians, Paul describes the church's union with Christ in his death and resurrection, and goes on to say:

---

[600] I hold that, when Ephesians and Colossians are read corporately and through the lens of the Paschal New Exodus paradigm, there are no conflicts between these writings and the "officially recognized" letters of Paul. The supposed conflict is not in the documents but in the manner of their reading.

[601] See Kirby, *Ephesians*; Lincoln, *Ephesians*, 243.

By abolishing in his flesh the law with its commandments and regulations. His purpose was to create in himself one new man out of the two, thus making peace. (Eph 2:15)

He then writes:

In him the whole building is joined together and rises to become a holy temple in the Lord. (Eph 2:21. See also, Eph 1:13; 4:4)

So, again, we find that "the new law" which was promised to Israel in the OT has been given from heaven by the man Christ Jesus (i.e., through the death and resurrection of God's own Son). He continues to be present among his people by his Spirit. Such a natural interchange between God, the Spirit, and Christ has clear Trinitarian implications.

Thus, in Ephesians, we have what we found in Rom 10:6. As a result of the ascension, Christ has brought an end to the law and the division that existed between Jews and Gentiles. The new community that has been created from the two warring communities is the dwelling place of God's Spirit—it is the living temple made without hands.

The same themes of death, resurrection, ascension, and termination of the law are found in Colossians:

giving thanks to the Father, who has qualified you to share in the inheritance of the saints in the kingdom of light. For he has rescued us from the dominion of darkness and brought us into the kingdom of the Son he loves, in whom we have redemption, the forgiveness of sins.

He is the image of the invisible God, the firstborn over ("of" RSV) all creation. For by him all things were created: things in heaven and on earth, visible and invisible, whether thrones or powers or rulers or authorities; all things were created by him and for him.

He is before all things, and in him all things hold together.

And he is the head of the body, the church; he is the beginning and the firstborn from among the dead, so that in everything he might have the supremacy. For God was pleased to have all his fullness dwell in him, and through him to reconcile to himself all things, whether things on earth or things in heaven, by making peace through his blood, shed on the cross. Once you were alienated from God and were enemies in your minds because of your evil behavior. But now he has reconciled you by Christ's physical body through death to present you holy in his sight, without blemish and free from accusation. (Col 1:12–22)

The hymn has all the essential features we identified in our reading of Romans. The Davidic king (the firstborn from the dead), having died to secure his people's redemption as well as that of the rest of creation (he is the firstborn over all creation), has presented his people perfect before his father. Christ is not merely the Jewish Messiah but is the Creator of all things. It is because of this cosmic redemption and reconciliation that the church has been released from the law and brought into a totally new relationship with God. This relationship is not achieved through law-righteousness but through the redeeming work of Christ.

This salvation has changed the very nature of the Jewish law. What it required has been fulfilled in a completely different way from what its adherents expected, but in a way that is in complete harmony with its original intentions.

> In him you were also circumcised, in the putting off of the sinful nature (Gr *sarx*, flesh), not with a circumcision done by the hands of men but with the circumcision done by Christ. (Col 2:11)

As we have seen elsewhere—but especially in Rom 10:4—the law has been brought to an end through the death of Christ:

> having cancelled the written code, with its regulations, that was against us and that stood opposed to us; he took it away, nailing it to the cross. (Col 2:14)

The Colossian community, having died with Christ, has received the gift of the Spirit from the ascended Lord. We know this because Paul commends her members for their love in the Spirit (Col 1:8). Thus, as in Hebrews and Ephesians, Jesus—having died for his people and having brought the law to an end through the establishment of a new Melchizedek priesthood and a new covenant—has given his people his Spirit. This teaching is also the basis of Paul's argument:

> You, however, are controlled not by the sinful nature but by the Spirit, if the Spirit of God lives in you. And if anyone does not have the Spirit of Christ, he does not belong to Christ. (Rom 8:9)

The whole idea that Christ is among the believers (i.e., the Spirit of Christ, who is the Spirit of God) confirms that the paradigm fits the evidence and the argument. Furthermore, the death and resurrection of the Davidic king is at the heart of Paul's message to the Roman church (Rom 1:3–4; 3:21–27; 5:8).

So, through the gift of the Spirit, the promised eternal presence of God among his people has become a reality. God is no longer far off but near to all who call on him. Paul has called the Spirit, "the Spirit of God" and "the Spirit of Christ" (Rom 8:9). He is the Spirit of truth and he leads his people. There is no further revelation to be given. All has been given in the gift of the Spirit. He is the gift of the ascended Son to his bride.

From this exploration of Rom 10:6, we see that it is all too easy to lose the flow of the argument and finish up with a different story from what Paul and the other NT writers were telling. This is more likely to happen when we appeal to extra-biblical texts to construct the argument—a practice that has determined the meaning of this text for many modern scholars. It is not because these sources are not "Scripture," but because they are not the story of the Christian community—a story that is fundamentally different from those of other Jewish communities. Because the pseudepigraphal texts are narratives of different communities within Judaism, they should not be merged with the Christian story in an attempt to give a common account.[602] Such a method leaves the reader with elements of narrative reconstruction that do not belong to each other and do not match the Christian story. The proposed readings of these non-canonical texts introduce understanding into apostolic teaching that seriously disfigures the message it proclaims.

So, to be faithful to the narrative, someone must go up to heaven. Like Moses who ascended Sinai, Christ ascended into heaven following his resurrection. Because of his ascent, a new high priest has been inaugurated and the church given a new law—the law of the Spirit. This resulted in the outpouring of the Spirit who is the gift of Christ to his people. Thus, Paul writes: "Christ is the end of the law so that there may be righteousness for everyone who believes" (Rom 10:4). While no new law came down from heaven, the Holy Spirit did! It is the law of the Spirit that is life in Christ Jesus. Paul writes: "through Christ Jesus the law of the Spirit of life set me free from the law of sin and death" (Rom 8:2). The gift of the Spirit has been given, and his coming is the direct consequence of Christ's ascension. Thus, someone has ascended to heaven and, as a result, the new revelation—the law of the Spirit—has been given to the church.

---

[602] It is obvious that the Pharisees and Sadducees read the history of redemption differently than the disciples of Jesus and from those residing at Qumran. Each community's story must be kept separate as an amalgamation is not the story of any community.

Romans 11

THE MESSIAH KING AND HIS NEW COVENANT PEOPLE (11:1–36)

I ask then: Did God reject his people? By no means! I am an Israelite myself, a descendant of Abraham, from the tribe of Benjamin. God did not reject his people, whom he foreknew. Don't you know what the Scripture says in the passage about Elijah—how he appealed to God against Israel: "Lord, they have killed your prophets and torn down your altars; I am the only one left, and they are trying to kill me"? And what was God's answer to him? "I have reserved for myself seven thousand who have not bowed the knee to Baal." So too, at the present time there is a remnant chosen by grace. And if by grace, then it is no longer by works; if it were, grace would no longer be grace.

What then? What Israel sought so earnestly it did not obtain, but the elect did. The others were hardened, as it is written: "God gave them a spirit of stupor, eyes so that they could not see and ears so that they could not hear, to this very day." And David says: "May their table become a snare and a trap, a stumbling block and a retribution for them. May their eyes be darkened so they cannot see, and their backs be bent forever."

Again I ask: Did they stumble so as to fall beyond recovery? Not at all! Rather, because of their transgression, salvation has come to the Gentiles to make Israel envious. But if their transgression means riches for the world, and their loss means riches for the Gentiles, how much greater riches will their fullness bring!

I am talking to you Gentiles. Inasmuch as I am the apostle to the Gentiles, I make much of my ministry in the hope that I may somehow arouse my own people to envy and save some of them. For if their rejection is the reconciliation of the world, what will their acceptance be but life from the dead? If the part of the dough offered as firstfruits is holy, then the whole batch is holy; if the root is holy, so are the branches.

If some of the branches have been broken off, and you, though a wild olive shoot, have been grafted in among the others and now share in the nourishing sap from the olive root, do not boast over those branches. If you do, consider this: You do not support the root, but the root supports you. You will say then, "Branches were broken off so that I could be grafted in." Granted. But they were broken off because of unbelief, and you stand by faith. Do not be arrogant, but be afraid. For if God did not spare the natural branches, he will not spare you either.

Consider therefore the kindness and sternness of God: sternness to those who fell, but kindness to you, provided that you continue in his kindness. Otherwise, you also will be cut off. And if they do not persist in unbelief, they will be grafted in, for God is able to graft them in again. After all, if you were cut out of an olive tree that is wild by nature, and contrary to nature were grafted into a cultivated olive tree, how much more readily will these, the natural branches, be grafted into their own olive tree!

I do not want you to be ignorant of this mystery, brothers, so that you may not be conceited: Israel has experienced a hardening in part until the full number of the Gentiles has come in. And so all Israel will be saved, as it is written: "The deliverer will come from Zion; he will turn godlessness away from Jacob. And this is my covenant with them when I take away their sins."

As far as the gospel is concerned, they are enemies on your account; but as far as election is concerned, they are loved on account of the patriarchs, for God's gifts and his call are irrevocable. Just as you who were at one time disobedient to God have now received mercy as a result of their disobedience, so they too have now become disobedient in order that they too may now receive mercy as a result of God's mercy to you. For God has bound all men over to disobedience so that he may have mercy on them all.

Oh, the depth of the riches of the wisdom and knowledge of God! How unsearchable his judgments, and his paths beyond tracing out! "Who has known the mind of the Lord? Or who has been his counselor?" "Who has ever given to God, that God should repay him?" For from him and through him and to him are all things. To him be the glory forever! Amen. (Romans 11:1–36)

INTRODUCTION

In the eleventh chapter,[603] Paul continues to express his concern about the present state of Israel. He shows that the principle of the "remnant" is not new but has been part of God's purpose and Israel's history throughout the ages (Rom 11:1–6), as demonstrated by the Scriptures (Rom 11:7–10). Paul explains that the rejection of Israel is not final, but temporary and partial (Rom 11:11–12), and he makes reference to the firstfruits offering (Rom 11:16) and the grafting of olive branches (Rom 11:17–21) to illustrate his argument.

These two illustrations are significant as they are both images from exodus material. Instructions for the firstfruit offering of bread were given at Sinai in Lev 23:17, when the children of Israel were at the beginning of their journey to the promised land. Reference to the olive tree was made in Jer 11:16–17 and in Hosea 14:4–6 where a promise of blessing was given for those who would be brought out of the predicted exile in Babylon.

Thus, the New Exodus motif emerges once again in Paul's argument. His reasoning is at two levels. First, he wishes to show that a New Exodus has taken place of which the church is the firstfruit, creation itself sharing in this eschatological event. Second, he wants to demonstrate continuity. There has not been a total break with the purposes of God as revealed in the OT. The original, cultivated olive tree, which was not yielding the fruit it should have done,[604] has now been pruned of most of its branches and has new branches (albeit from wild stock) grafted in amongst the remaining old ones. This second picture was given to illustrate that Gentiles from many nations have been brought into the community of faith to receive the blessings promised to Abraham alongside the believing Jewish remnant. These Gentiles are also now Abraham's children by virtue of sharing his faith (Gal 3:6–9, 26–29). Paul writes to the Jewish and Gentile believers in Rome that originality (the creation of a new covenant people) and continuity (the fulfillment of the OT promises) are distinguishing features of the purposes of God (Rom 11:22–24).

In the conclusion of the section, Paul insists that unbelieving Jews could still have a place in these purposes. However, they will be accepted on the same terms as all other people. Israel's salvation is conditional (as is that of the

---

[603] See Johnson, D.G., "Structure," 91–103, for discussion on the structure of Rom 11.

[604] Isa 5:1–7 makes the same point about Israel's unfruitfulness but Isaiah bases his illustration on the vineyard.

Gentiles) on recognition of need and reception of saving mercy (Rom 11:25–32). This will happen when the deliverer comes from Zion.

The reference to the "deliverer" coming "from Zion" (Rom 11:26) is a distinctively Pauline adaptation. The prediction is based on Isa 59:20: "The Redeemer will come to Zion, to those in Jacob who repent of their sins." Paul's use of the quotation involves significant alterations. He does not appear to think that the term "Redeemer" is appropriate when writing about Christ's future saving of Israel. He chooses to use the title "deliverer."

The conclusion of this theological section of the letter is a doxology in which the wisdom of God in his saving purposes is proclaimed, reinforcing the claim made earlier that wisdom is not ontological for Paul but rather the origin of salvation.[605]

11:1 I ask then. Did God reject his people? By no means! I am an Israelite myself, a descendant of Abraham, from the tribe of Benjamin.

Because he had quoted from the prophets who speak about Yahweh bringing Gentiles into a special covenant relationship (e.g., Isa 10:20), Paul feared that some of the Gentile believers in Rome might think they had replaced the Jews as the covenant community. He is careful to show this is not the case.[606] If Yahweh could abandon his covenant with the Jewish people, he could not be trusted–and Christian confidence in him would be undermined. After all, if Yahweh had given up the Jews, could he not also abandon the Gentile believers in Rome?

Paul begins his response to the claim that God had abandoned the Jewish people by outlining his own Jewish pedigree. Paul always held that he had not compromised his Jewish heritage even though he now valued it differently. Before he met the risen Lord when he was on the way to Damascus to arrest followers of Jesus, he hated everything about what he knew concerning the new sect known as the Way (Acts 19:23). His encounter with the Living Lord changed everything. Paul came to see that Jesus did not destroy his Jewish faith, he fulfilled it. Elsewhere Paul used his personal testimony as a corrective to possible error, so for example, when writing to the Philippian church to warn

---

[605] See Holland, *Contours*, 339–51, for further discussion.

[606] See Given, "Restoring," 89–96, who makes a case for restoring "the inheritance" to the text of Rom 11:1. Given seeks to demonstrate the superiority of the marginal reading through a combination of text-critical and intertextual arguments.

the believers about the teaching of Judaizers who were pressing for Gentiles to be circumcision (Phil 3:2–14).

11:2–3 *God did not reject his people, whom he foreknew. Don't you know what the Scripture says in the passage about Elijah—how he appealed to God against Israel: "Lord, they have killed your prophets and torn down your altars; I am the only one left, and they are trying to kill me"?*

By asking if God has rejected "his people," Paul uses the Greek word σπέρμα (*sperma*) "seed." He has used this term in Rom 9:7–8, and the expression clearly has important theological significance. It refers to the promised descendants of Abraham.[607] The point that Paul repeatedly makes is that descent from Abraham is no guarantee of covenant membership—at least, not of the covenant that ultimately matters.

Paul continues his argument by appealing to the Scriptures. This time he considers the era of Elijah (1 Kgs 19:10, 14), reminding his readers that the prophet thought all had forsaken Yahweh. Evidence supporting Elijah's despair was all around him: the Israelite people, now following Baal, had torn down the altars where Yahweh was worshipped and were seeking the prophet's life. It was no idle threat. They had already killed many of Yahweh's prophets. It seemed to Elijah that the covenant had been rescinded—Israel's sin finally brought her relationship with God to an end.

11:4 *And what was God's answer to him? "I have reserved for myself seven thousand who have not bowed the knee to Baal."*

Yahweh told Elijah that even though he could see no obvious evidence to support the LORD's answer, the situation was not hopeless. (1 Kgs 19:18). He was not alone as other prophets had also stayed true to Yahweh and been preserved. They were the remnant and the object of Yahweh's concern. Who could harm them when under the protection of the living God?

The point Paul is making is that even during one of the worst periods of apostasy in Israel's history, Yahweh had still preserved a remnant for himself who remained faithful to Him and His covenant. It was a time of famine, so the pressure for the Israelites to worship Baal—the god of fertility—must have been immense. Yet despite that it had not rained for three and a half years,

---

[607] See Gal 3:16–29, where Paul applies *sperma* to Christ (the true descendent of Abraham according to the seed of promise) and to believers (the community that are the offspring of Abraham according to faith).

seven thousand refused to bow the knee to Baal. The drought was Yahweh's judgment on the sinfulness of Israel, and only when she responded in repentance was the judgment lifted (1 Kgs 18:39, 45).

11:5 So too, at the present time there is a remnant chosen by grace.

Although it appeared that God's purpose for Israel was thwarted, there was no possibility of this happening as, through his saving grace, Yahweh had preserved a remnant for Himself. Paul writes that the same thing is true in his day.

That Paul reasoned in this way is evidence of a massive change in expectation from the immediate post-Pentecost days when Jews, in their thousands, were entering the kingdom of Christ (Acts 2:36–41; 6:1–7). In those heady days, it must have seemed as though Israel's acceptance of Jesus as her Messiah was imminent.[608] How quickly this optimism changed, and how difficult it was for Jewish believers to accept that Gentiles were coming into the kingdom ahead of their kinsmen. These types of misplaced expectations, leading to disappointment, have characterized the church over the centuries. As a result of misinterpreting certain texts, God's people have often been mistaken when it comes to the timing and the way that Scriptures will be fulfilled. Such exegesis has resulted in optimism and expectation that have conflicted with fundamental biblical truths, causing confusion and harm to the people of God.

In seeing the Jews who believed in Jesus as a remnant, Paul makes a comparison with the remnant that refused to worship Baal. The logical conclusion of Paul's argument is that he considers Judaism to be a pagan religion akin to Baal worship—a concept that would have horrified the orthodox Jews. It was pagan because it sought to demand allegiance from the Jewish people in the face of the claims of their Messiah. It has been suggested that Paul uses this ploy in his letter to the Colossians.[609] In that letter his argument follows the same line of thought—Judaism is a religious system that has rejected the Messiah. In so doing she has become nothing less than pagan.

---

[608] Despite these comments, it must be noted that Paul's argument is one of optimism. God has not abandoned his promises to Abraham. There will be a future ingathering of the Jewish remnant and it will acknowledge Jesus as the true Messiah King.

[609] Wright, *Colossians*.

11:6 And if by grace, then it is no longer by works; if it were, grace would no longer be grace.

The believers were not in relationship with God as a result of their own work. Paul introduces the word "grace" into the argument despite the fact there is no mention of it in the original OT incident involving Elijah. Paul legitimately embellishes the story by the addition of the word "grace" because the remnant has received far more than those of Elijah's day for they have now been brought into the Messiah's kingdom! Yahweh's incredible mercy could only be summed up by the term "grace"–total and absolute unmerited favor. The contrast is clear. While it was God who kept the remnant in Elijah's day safe, because they had remained faithful, so it could be claimed they were rewarded for faithfulness or works. In the New Exodus however, the Jews were not present because of their commitment to Yahweh, but because of His commitment to them as fallen and defiled sinners. This is why Paul wrote to the Ephesians: "For it is by grace you have been saved, through faith—and this not from yourselves, it is the gift of God—not by works, so that no one can boast" (Eph 2:8–9).

11:7 What then? What Israel sought so earnestly it did not obtain, but the elect did. The others were hardened.

What is tragic in this analysis of Israel's history is that although driven in her pursuit to please God, she fell far short of the target. This is a shocking claim for any Jew to consider. Paul argues that those whom the Jews despise—who have not followed their path of works—have received that which they had never sought: a right relationship with God.

The tragedy of unbelieving Israel is that she has been hardened. This was the description of the condition of Pharaoh's heart (Exod 8:32; 9:12) as he sought to stop the Jews from leaving Egypt for the promised land. Paul is in effect saying that in the early years of the Christian church's pilgrimage, the one who now plays the role of Pharaoh is unredeemed Israel. She is seeking to prevent the people of God from leaving the kingdom of darkness to follow the Davidic Messiah on his triumphant march to the promised land. To suggest such a startling reversal of roles would have left any orthodox Jew appalled.

11:8 As it is written: "God gave them a spirit of stupor, eyes so that they could not see and ears so that they could not hear, to this very day."

Paul appeals to the writings of Isaiah (Isa 29:9–10), in which he warned Jerusalem of her forthcoming judgment. He also appeals to Moses (Deut 29), who summoned the Israelites to renew their covenant with God.

Isaiah warned Jerusalem not to be complacent because her situation was immensely dangerous. The reason for the Jews' ill-judged perception of security was because Yahweh had given them a spirit of stupor. It was as if they were dazed and unable to reason. God had turned against his own people because they continually rejected his word.

In Deut 29, Moses said a similar thing to the Israelites. Despite all that he had done in delivering them from Egypt and in keeping them during forty years of wanderings in the desert, they still had a warped understanding of God. Moses said the Lord had blinded their eyes and stopped up their ears (v.4), effectively causing them to stumble as if their senses were withdrawn.

Paul is making the point that the present hardening of heart his kinsmen were experiencing was not a unique event—God had acted in judgment against his own covenant people throughout the OT. While the Jews thought the covenant protected them from Yahweh's chastening, the Scriptures made it clear that, because they were the covenant people of Yahweh, they would be chastised ahead of the Gentiles (Amos 3:2).

11:9–10 And David says: "May their table become a snare and a trap, a stumbling block and a retribution for them. May their eyes be darkened so they cannot see, and their backs be bent forever."

Now, to add insult to injury, Paul brings the words of their own Messianic king to witness against his unbelieving subjects (Ps 69:22–23). David's prayer was for Yahweh to exact vengeance on his enemies, but Paul applies it to the Jews. Paul does not misuse the passage as those who sought to overthrow David were members of his own family.

There is another reason why Paul uses David's psalm. Paul has been describing how the Gospel is the fulfillment of the promises made to David and Abraham. To reject Jesus, therefore, is to reject David and the covenant made with him (2 Sam 7:5–16). It is entirely appropriate to apply David's cry in Ps 69:22–28 to the Jews of Paul's day, for they persecuted their own countrymen who had turned to the Son of David for salvation.

The mention of the "table" in David's psalm may have a significance that is not immediately obvious. The term was used by Paul in 1 Cor 10:21: "You cannot drink the cup of the Lord and the cup of demons too; you cannot have a part in both the Lord's Table and the table of demons." This possible link suggests that the term has a cultic significance for Paul. He may be suggesting through the use of "their table" that the Jewish sacrificial system has become a snare and a trap, preventing the Jews from seeing their need for Christ's death.[610] This is also the thrust of the argument in the letter to the Hebrews. If this suggestion is correct, Paul is saying that David's psalm predicted the obsolescence of the sacrificial system as a means of getting right with God.

11:11 *Again I ask. Did they stumble so as to fall beyond recovery? Not at all! Rather, because of their transgression, salvation has come to the Gentiles to make Israel envious.*

In responding to his own question concerning the permanence of Israel's fall, Paul answers an emphatic: "Not at all!" He explains that the very purpose of the Gentiles being brought into the covenant was to provoke Israel to envy. It is doubtful if Paul intended the Roman believers to think this was the only reason for the salvation of the Gentiles because the rest of Scripture presents a much higher motive—the glory of God himself (Eph 2:10; 3:10–11). The provocation of Israel to envy is with the intention that Jews will seek Yahweh and so bring him more glory.[611]

11:12 *But if their transgression means riches for the world, and their loss means riches for the Gentiles, how much greater riches will their fullness bring!*

The method of argument in this verse was well known in Judaism. If negative events bring positive results, then positive events would bring positive results of a greater magnitude. A modern equivalent would be the question: "If a sick child can make so many people happy, how much more joy will he bring when made well?"

Paul asks the church in Rome a similar question about his kinsmen: "if their sin, with its consequential loss of blessing, is the cause of the Gentiles coming into blessing, how much more blessing will overflow to the Gentiles

---

[610] See Käsemann, *Romans*, 302.

[611] Paul has already introduced the Gentiles' provocation of the Jews in Rom 10:19–20.

("salvation has come to the Gentiles" [Rom 11:11]) when God graciously, out of his mercy, restores the Jews to their forfeited place in the covenant?"[612]

In writing about Israel's "transgression" παράπτωμα (*paraptōma*), Paul uses the same term he used in Rom 5:15: "But the gift is not like the trespass. For if the many died by the trespass of the one man, how much more did God's grace and the gift that came by the grace of the one man, Jesus Christ, overflow to the many!" Again, in Rom 5:20 we read: "The law was added so that the trespass might increase. But where sin increased, grace increased all the more." This suggests that not only Israel's historic national failure (the focus of the discussion), but also her inclusion in Adam's sin is the transgression which brought the Gentiles blessing. In chapter 5, Paul made it clear that all humanity is in Adam, and in Adam all have sinned and come short of the glory of God (Rom 3:23).

Of course, the greatest sin Paul's people have been guilty of is rejecting their Messiah and their part in his death (Acts 7:51–53). This is certainly the transgression that has brought riches to the world. It reflects man's rejection of Yahweh in the garden and its tragic consequences. The parallel between the two events has been drawn by Paul in Rom 5:15–21, and is likely therefore to be behind the repetition of the term here in chapter 11.

What exactly is Paul referring to when he writes about "their gain"? The immediate reference to "their loss" must refer to expulsion from the Garden or from the land. Both themes are fundamental for the understanding of what the death of Christ achieves. He undid what Adam had done and liberated his people from the enslavement Adam produced. In light of this comparison, "their fullness" must be their restoration to covenantal relationship and blessing—becoming part of the new covenant people of God. Paul seems to anticipate future blessing for his kinsmen: "how much greater riches will their fullness bring!" Such blessing will lead to even greater blessing for the Gentiles, not the sidelining of them because of the blessing of the Jews.

---

[612] See Donaldson, "Riches," 81–98, who argues that the logic in Paul's statement is not the spatial logic of displacement but the temporal logic of delay. Donaldson says that Israel's failure to respond to the gospel makes possible the "riches for the Gentiles" by opening up time, not space.

Romans 11

11:13 I am talking to you Gentiles. Inasmuch as I am the apostle to the Gentiles, I make much of my ministry.

Paul addresses the Gentiles in the congregation and reminds them of his status. He is the apostle who has been called specifically to minister to them (Acts 9:15–16; Rom 1:5). His calling gives him the right to speak with authority. Paul's instruction is not from an academic, detached position; it is the exhortation of a man who is investing his life in bringing the good news to those who were estranged from the covenants of God (Eph 2:11–13).

While it would be understandable for the Gentiles in Rome to resent intrusion from an outsider, Paul states his credentials ("*the* apostle to the Gentiles" [emphasis added]) and his life's commitment to reaching them with the Gospel. With these come his right to correct any behavior that is unbecoming of those who have been "brought near."

11:14 In the hope that I may somehow arouse my own people to envy and save some of them.

Paul says that part of his ministry to the Gentiles is directed towards his own countrymen.[613] This is a fascinating insight into his mind, and an example of how it has been shaped by the Scriptures. This same desire to jolt Israel out of her sinfulness by showing that the Gentiles are preferred before her is also in the heart of God (Isa 19:23–25).

The use of the term τινας (*tinas*) "some" is telling. Paul is not expecting that the entire nation of Israel will be saved through his ministry. He understands the promise to Abraham was there will always be a true and saved seed, and his argument flows from this expectation that a remnant—bearing witness to Yahweh's faithfulness—will be preserved. These are the Jews that Paul is longing to reach!

11:15 For if their rejection is the reconciliation of the world, what will their acceptance be but life from the dead?

Paul reasons in the manner of many rabbis, i.e., from the lesser case to the greater. He tells the Roman Gentiles they must not cast the Jewish people off

---

[613] The Greek term that the NIV translates as "countrymen" is *sapξ*, "flesh." This picks up other uses of *flesh* in relation to Israel's status; see also chapters 7–8; 9:3. The implication is that Paul is deliberately placing Israel in the same sphere as Adam.

as though they had no further purpose in the plans of God.[614] Indeed, he reasons that the real blessing of mankind through the Jewish people is yet to happen. If her casting off brought salvation to the Gentiles, what will her return bring? Paul says it would be wrong and foolish to discount the Jewish people with the assumption that they no longer had any place in the purposes of God.

The expression of "life from the dead" echoes Ezek 37, the vision of the valley of dry bones where Israel was resurrected. It spoke, of course, of her return from exile. Its significance for our discussion on Israel's future is that only the remnant came back from the dead. The majority of the nation remained in exile and continued to suffer the consequences of the covenantal curses—they remained cut off from fellowship with God, for sadly, they chose to remain in a foreign land rather than to be faithful to their calling and the claims of Yahweh.

In saying that believing "Israel" would be part of redemptive history (not lording it over Gentile believers but sharing with them as co-heirs of the covenants of promise [Isa 19:19–25; Eph 2:19]), Paul is not saying that her acceptance is a future event which will happen before the resurrection of the dead. He is saying the resurrection of the Jewish people has taken place, or is taking place (1 Cor 15:52; cf. Hos 13:14). The imagery of resurrection was used to describe Israel's return from exile (Hos 13:14 [cited in 1 Cor 15:55]; Ezek 37:1–14; Dan 12:2).[615] If this is the imagery Paul is alluding to, he writes that in turning to the Messiah, Israel is being resurrected from spiritual death. She comes from exile, returning to God to worship him.[616] The fact that his is a present reality is evidenced by the growing community of Jews who, as a result of Yahweh's faithfulness to the covenant he made with Abraham, are now coming to Christ.

What a glorious finale to human history! The promises of God are completely fulfilled so the whole of creation can be in no doubt that he is to be worshipped as the covenant-keeping God.

---

[614] Chilton, "Dialogue," 27–37, says that although Paul's argument demands reinterpretation of Judaism and its Scriptures, it prohibits a supersessionist view of Israel.

[615] While normally seen as referring to the resurrection at the end of the ages, Daniel shares the same hope as Hosea and Ezekiel of a return from exile that is likened to the resurrection of the nation. The text, like the prophecies of Ezekiel and Hosea, has a more immediate application as well as eschatological hope. I owe this insight to Dr. Piotr Lokre.

[616] By this observation, I do not deny the general resurrection as a future hope.

11:16 If the part of the dough offered as firstfruits is holy, then the whole batch is holy; if the root is holy, so are the branches.

The previous suggestion of the eschatological ingathering of Israel just prior to the resurrection is born out in the reference to the "firstfruits." Paul used the term in 1 Cor 15:20 with distinct reference to the resurrection: "But Christ has indeed been raised from the dead, the firstfruits of those who have fallen asleep."

In Lev 23:9–15 (v.11 especially), we find that the firstfruits were offered three days after the offering of the Passover sacrifice.[617] In 1 Cor 15:3, Paul writes that Jesus rose from the dead on "the third day according to the scriptures," and then adds that he is the "firstfruit of those who sleep" (v. 20).[618] It is clear Paul places the death of Jesus in the context of the Passover (1 Cor 5:7), as did the Gospel writers, and he interprets its significance from that setting.

In the Jewish practice of offering firstfruits at the harvest, the first of the gathered fruit (or grain) was offered to God to indicate that the rest of the harvest belonged to him. Paul applies this concept to the Jews. He writes in effect, that because Abraham was the firstfruit, the rest of the nation is not only offered to God but is also holy. This has nothing to do with her achievements, any more than the Gentiles could claim it was their achievements that saved them. God accepted them out of his grace in order to stay faithful to the covenant he had made with Abraham.

Paul now brings to the Gentile believers' attention the image of the olive tree, a long established symbol of Israel (Jer 11:16–17; Hos 14:6; Zech 4:3, 12–14). He has already written about Abraham being the father of all who believe within Judaism and within the nations of the world (Rom 4:16–17). In making use of the picture of the olive tree, it seems probable that Paul saw its root to represent the promises made to Abraham and its branches to represent his spiritual offspring—believing Jews and Gentiles who are justified and made holy by the same faith as their "father."

> So then, he (Abraham) is the father of all who believe but have not been circumcised, in order that righteousness might be credited to

---

[617] See Bruce, *Corinthians*, 140.

[618] It must be noted that, while the ideas of firstborn and firstfruits are related (being Paschal themes), the firstborn has a particular redemptive/propitiatory role that the firstfruits do not have. See comments on Rom 3:21–26; Holland, *Contours*, 237–73.

them. And he is also the father of the circumcised who not only are circumcised but who also walk in the footsteps of the faith that our father had before he was circumcised. (Rom 4:11b–12)

By arguing in this way, Paul begins to prepare his hearers to view soberly their inclusion in the new covenant community.

11:17 *If some of the branches have been broken off, and you, though a wild olive shoot, have been grafted in among the others and now share in the nourishing sap from the olive root.*

Paul now asks the Christians in Rome to imagine a situation where some of the branches of the olive tree have been broken off. It seems likely that Paul had Jeremiah's description in mind by which he warned the houses of Israel and Judah: "The Lord called you a thriving olive tree with fruit beautiful in form. But with the roar of a mighty storm he will set it on fire, and its branches will be broken. The Lord Almighty, who planted you, has decreed disaster for you, because the house of Israel and the house of Judah have done evil and provoked me to anger by burning incense to Baal" (Jer 11:16–17).

Paul will go on to say that the branches were broken off because of unbelief, but at this point in his argument he is more concerned to illustrate the picture of the Gentiles' inclusion in the covenant community, and he uses his readers' knowledge of grafting to achieve this.

Paul asks the Roman Gentiles to imagine the situation where an olive grower would break off the many unproductive branches from a cultivated olive tree and, having cut a branch from a wild olive tree, graft it into the cultivated stock among the few remaining productive branches. This picture alone will have made an uncomfortable point for many of his hearers. How foolish for an olive grower to invest time and effort in grafting a wild branch into a cultivated stock. How limited his harvest will be!

Nevertheless, this is what the grower has decided to do, and the success of his grafting (however limited) will depend upon an ongoing supply of water and minerals being drawn up from the ground by the cultivated root. Paul's point is clear: the very inclusion of the Gentiles in the covenant community is by grace. They are dependent upon the continuance of God's purposes for his ancient people because the root, which transports the nourishing sap, is their "father" Abraham. They must remember that the covenant made with Abraham, as well as the promises given to the patriarchs and reiterated by the prophets, allow the Gentiles into the grace they now enjoy. Any temptation to reject their believing Jewish brothers and sisters would be a rejection of Abraham himself–the root upon which they depend.

While the salvation of the Gentiles has not replaced the salvation of the Jews[619] (the grafted shoot is sharing the same rising sap as the remaining, original branches), the prophets promised their conversion as the consequence of Israel coming into her own inheritance (Isa 42:1–7). It is interesting that the order expected by the reforming prophets was not fulfilled, because the Gentiles came into the new covenant ahead of the majority of Jewish people.[620] However, their inclusion is still dependent upon the promises Yahweh made to Abraham and his descendants.

This rearrangement of key redemptive, historical events takes place elsewhere in the NT. For example, the Gentiles were brought into the covenant without circumcision (Acts 10:44–48; 15:14–21). Also, the Spirit, who was expected to be poured out when Israel was restored to her promised glory, is poured out on the church who has shared in the death of her Savior. Yahweh had returned to his temple as promised, but it was no longer a building made with hands, it was, as it had always been intended, his people (Ps 114:2; John 2:18–21; 1 Cor 6:19–20; Eph 2:18–20;1 Pet 2:4–6; Rev 21:22–26).

Here in Romans, the prophetic predictions about the Gentiles' acceptance have been rearranged so that it happened *during* redemptive history rather than at its end. In Jewish expectation, this event was to be the climax of history. Isa 19:19–25, which looks forward to this occasion, is one of the most remarkable passages in the OT relating to the in-gathering of the Gentiles. There we read they will be accepted as nations in their own right, with no suggestion that they will be required to convert to Judaism.

Paul has not only rearranged the order of key OT redemptive expectations, he has also, as has been hinted, changed the order of the illustration. Normally, branches grafted into a stock have superior, desirable features. The old stock,

---

[619] Of course, it was Jews who first entered the new covenant community (Acts 2).

[620] Note Paul's statement to the Ephesians. Speaking to the Gentiles he says, "In him we were also chosen, having been predestined according to the plan of him who works out everything in conformity with the purpose of his will, in order that we, who were the first to hope in Christ, might be for the praise of his glory. And you also were included in Christ when you heard the word of truth, the gospel of your salvation" (Eph 1:11–13). The "we" is likely to refer to the Jewish believers and the "you" to the Gentile believers. If so, Paul's order implies that the conversion of Jews by their acceptance of Christ leads to the blessing of Gentiles.

while hardy, is merely used to support and nourish each scion. Paul reverses this situation in his illustration as the root is superior to the grafted branch. It is quite possible that Paul has done this deliberately in order to emphasize, as he has stated earlier, that the Gentiles are dependent on the promises made by Yahweh to the Jews. It never is, or was, the other way around.[621]

11:18 Do not boast over those branches. If you do, consider this: You do not support the root, but the root supports you.

Paul's concern is to stress to the Gentiles that they must not become arrogant towards the believing Jews in the congregation. At the heart of his concern is that the Gentile believers were beginning to look at their Jewish brothers and sisters with disdain, and their arrogance offended him deeply.

He had to warn them their conceit was dangerous. Indeed, esteeming themselves over the Jews in the church would reverberate back down through the generations to Abraham, the Jews' natural ancestor. Paul is concerned for the Gentiles respect the patriarch. He was the one with whom God made His covenant to the eternal benefit of the Gentile nations.

Paul has already written about the patriarch in his letter (Rom 4:1–3, 12, 13, 16, 18; see also Gal 3:6, 8, 9, 14, 16; 4:22), and now reminds the Gentiles that as a branch of the olive tree, they do not support Abraham, the root. On the contrary, the Gentiles are totally dependent on the covenant which God entered into with Abraham and the promises made to him, because "Abraham believed the Lord, and he credited it to him as righteousness" (Gen 15:6). The Lord said to him, "I will make you into a great nation . . . and all peoples on earth will be blessed through you" (Gen 12:2–3) and, "As for me, this is my covenant with you: You will be the father of many nations . . . I will establish my covenant as an everlasting covenant between me and you and your descendants after you for the generations to come, to be your God and the God of your descendants after you" (Gen 17:4, 7). Paul's words to the Jews in Rom 3 seem just as appropriate for the Gentiles: "Where, then, is boasting? It is excluded" (Rom 3:27).

Paul continues to use this fitting illustration of the olive tree, developing and applying it as the passage unfolds (see v.24).[622]

---

[621] See Esler, "Differentiation," 103–24, for a fuller discussion.

[622] Baxter & Ziesler, "Arboriculture," 25–32, note that Paul's use of the grafting picture produces problems for various commentators but they argue the point of the

11:19 You will say then, "Branches were broken off so that I could be grafted in."

Paul moves away from the main thrust of his argument so that he can deal with the response he anticipates his Gentile readers will make. He expects them to say something like: "God has put almost all of the Jews out of the covenant community and we have replaced them. We were chosen, and grafted into the tree in their place. We are the privileged people and they, the removed branches, have been abandoned." This was the very attitude of pride which took over the hearts of the Jews in the OT and led to their ultimate downfall (Isa 25:11).

It is vital for Paul to warn the Gentiles about their attitude as they must not be under any illusion regarding their spiritual security now that they are covenant people. God can treat them in exactly the same way as he treated the Jews–chastening them for their pride and arrogance. The same hand of correction that had fallen on the covenant people of the OT could just as easily fall on them.(Exod 32:1–35; Jer 11:1–17; 1 Cor 10:1–22).

11:20 Granted. But they were broken off because of unbelief, and you stand by faith. Do not be arrogant, but be afraid.

Paul grants the claim of the Gentile believers concerning their status and also that of the unbelieving Jewish community as far as the new covenant blessings are concerned. However, he warns them of the danger of arrogance and of not being fearful of the living God, lest they become like the unbelieving Jews and fall under judgment.

The reason Israel was brought under judgment was more than the term "unbelief" implies–a term which can suggest a period of grave doubt. The term Paul uses is ἀπιστία (*apistia*). Surprisingly, it is not found in any of the OT writings and is used only five times in the NT (Mk 9:24; Rom 3:3; 4:20; 11:20, 23; 1 Tim 1:13). The term can mean "unfaithfulness," making Israel's removal from the covenant community understandable. She did not merely have a lapse of confidence in God but displayed a rebellious and determined turning-away.

The same imagery of branches being lost is used by Jesus in John 15:1–4, where the Lord refers to vine branches being cut off. However, in Romans 11 the branches were "broken off" from the olive tree–not a technique used in tree

---

grafting in Rom 11 was the rejuvenation of the tree and that the illustration was used primarily to stress God's intention to save Israel.

management. Perhaps Paul envisaged them as being diseased and blown off in a storm: "The Lord called you a thriving olive tree with fruit beautiful in form. But with the roar of a mighty storm he will set it on fire, and its branches will be broken. The Lord Almighty, who planted you, has decreed disaster for you, because the house of Israel and the house of Judah have done evil and provoked me to anger by burning incense to Baal" (Jer11:16–17).

In Jesus' analogy, the divine gardener cut the branches that did not bear fruit, but in Paul's illustration the gardener only came into view when he chose to graft in the wild branch. Why was this? Perhaps the answer lies in the term ἁπιεστια (*apiestia*) which as has been noted can be translated "unfaithfulness." In the quotation from the book of Jeremiah, Jews had been unfaithful to Yahweh, the nation's "husband," and had "turned to the right and to the left" in their worship of false gods. As a result, they had died to Him. They had broken covenant with him and could no longer be part of his covenant community. This awful "break" of the covenant led to an appalling consequence—the branches fell. The Jews who were removed from the covenant had, in essence, removed themselves.

It should be noted that when Jesus spoke of branches being removed (John 15:1–8), he used the imagery of the vine. This plant was another well-known description of Israel (Ps 80:8–18). By means of this imagery, Jesus was effectively saying: "I am the true son of God. Unlike most of Abraham's descendants, I am the one whose disciples will bear fruit pleasing to the Divine Gardener." It was a powerful image but not appropriate for Paul's argument as Jesus was speaking to, and about, Jews. Paul needed a horticultural example where grafting was a common practice because he wanted to illustrate how God was bringing in the Gentiles and joining them to the covenant community. Grafting into a vine, though possible, was infrequently done. The image of Israel as an olive tree (a tree with which the technique of grafting into old stock was practiced) was well known in the ancient world, and it provided Paul with the picture he needed. Thus, the unfruitful branches were broken off and the Gentiles grafted in.

(As a side note, the illustration of the vine and branches used by Jesus in John 15, and which, at first glance seems to be related to Paul's example in this passage, is often misunderstood, The imagery used by Jesus in John 15 has been seen by many to challenge the doctrine of eternal security. This is not the case. In this passage, Jesus was speaking to the Jewish people and not to the church, which his death and resurrection had yet to bring to birth. He speaks at two levels: to the nation of Israel and to the individual Jew. The cutting off and burning of the branches specifically applies to the nation[623] albeit that individuals make up its identity.

In the first exodus, such "breaking off and burning" took place when the wilderness generation came under judgment and could not enter the land of promise. It also happened in the Second Exodus when the nation was delivered up to the Babylonians and the Jews were deported–cut off from the blessings of the covenant [Ezek 19:10–14]. In John 15, Jesus warned his disciples they were members of another generation that was in danger of such judgment. It soon happened, for Rome destroyed Jerusalem and drove the nation from the land.

Thus, we must not read Jesus' words as a direct warning to the individual Christian about his fruitfulness. They are about Jewish apostasy and its consequences.)

Paul has already told the Gentiles in Rome not to boast to their Jewish brethren. Now he tells them, "Do not be arrogant," because he fears this attitude may lead to their own judgment. Paul and the Gentiles would have been familiar with many examples of such arrogance in the OT and of the Lord God's attitude towards it: "'Surely the day is coming; it will burn like a furnace. All the arrogant and every evil doer will be stubble, and that day that is coming will set them on fire,' says the Lord Almighty. 'Not a root or a branch will be left to them'"(Mal 4:1). When writing to the church in Corinth, Paul was concerned about the attitudes of the believers there also. He warned them in 1 Cor 10:12: "So, if you think you are standing firm, be careful that you don't fall!"

However, Paul's warning to the Gentiles in Rome was not that they would lose their salvation but that they would experience the Lord's discipline. This would be exercised with the intention of bringing them back to him in repentance and renewal.[624] Paul has already implied that not all of the broken branches (the Jews) were discarded or consumed. The gardener (God) clearly preserved them so that he could, if he wished (i.e., when the Jews did "not persist in unbelief" but turned back to God in repentance) graft them in again to the olive tree (the covenant community), so re-establishing his covenant with them.

---

[623] Ps 80:16: "Your vine is cut down, it is burned with fire; at your rebuke your people perish." See also Ps 80:8–18.

[624] Paul deals with this theme in 1 Cor 5–6. See Holland, chapter 6.

Finally, in this verse Paul instructs the Gentiles to "be afraid." He fears that unless they revere the Lord, their attitude may bring the Lord's chastisement: "'Should you not fear me?' declares the Lord. 'Should you not tremble in my presence?'"(Jer 5:22–25). "I tell you my friends, do not be afraid of those who kill the body and after that can do no more . . . Fear him who, after the killing of the body has power to throw you into hell. Yes, I tell you, fear him" (Luke 12: 4–5). "Now all has been heard; here is the conclusion of the matter. Fear God and keep his commandments, for this is the whole duty of man. For God will bring every deed into judgment, including every hidden thing, whether it is good or evil" (Eccl 12:13–14).

11:21 For if God did not spare the natural branches, he will not spare you either.

Paul presents the inevitable logic of his reasoning with clarity and force. What right has the Gentile believing community to think that it will survive if the natural branches suffered chastisement for the same sin of arrogance? It is too easy for the Gentiles to think they are a special, privileged case whom God will excuse. Once they begin to think in such a way, they are in grave danger of being cast out of the covenant community as a consequence of the Lord's discipline.

11:22 Consider therefore the kindness and sternness of God. Sternness to those who fell, but kindness to you, provided that you continue in his kindness. Otherwise, you also will be cut off.

It is disturbingly easy to take the grace of God for granted; but Paul reminds his Gentile readers that the character of God has not changed. He is both stern (the term can mean "severe" and is never applied to God or any person elsewhere in the Scriptures) and kind. He is kind to those who feel their need and turn to him in humble repentance. On such he pours his love and forgiveness without measure (Rom 2:4). But to those who are proud or arrogant, he sets himself against them in judgment. He has always been such a God. Paul urges the Gentiles to remember this and not presume they have a relationship with a God who changes his character.

Paul's warning still applies today. When Christians become inflated with pride and self-satisfaction, they are in danger of losing the sense of God's graciousness and of falling into a deepening abyss of conceit and obstinacy. The judgment of God on his people is a theme all too rarely heard from the pulpits of twenty-first century Christendom. The modern message focuses on the certainty of forgiveness. In some respects, this is right, but if salvation loses its transforming effect as a result of indifference to what God has done in giving up his own Son to death, there is real danger of his new covenant people coming under a discipline no less severe than the Jewish people experienced and of which the Gentile Christians in Rome were warned. Hence, the awfulness of the warning: "you also will be cut off."

This warning is not addressed to individuals regarding the loss of their salvation but to Christian communities, whose behavior may cause them to come under discipline with the subsequent removal of their witness (Rev 2:5). Similar language was addressed to Israel when she was warned of being cut off by being sent into exile (Deut 29:18–29). There, she was chastened until she repented and accepted the call from God to return to her inheritance.

11:23 And if they do not persist in unbelief, they will be grafted in, for God is able to graft them in again.

Far from God having closed the door to the Jews, Paul asserts they also can come into the blessings of the new covenant—not on the basis of merit or ancestry but on the same basis as Abraham, i.e., by faith. It is unbelief (unfaithfulness) which has caused the Jews to be cut off from their glorious destiny; but this destiny will be restored to them as soon as they exercise the same faith as their illustrious ancestor.

11:24 After all, if you were cut out of an olive tree that is wild by nature, and contrary to nature were grafted into a cultivated olive tree, how much more readily will these, the natural branches, be grafted into their own olive tree!

Paul now brings his illustration of the olive tree to an end. His closing point is a further warning to the Gentile believers. It is as easy for God to reverse the position they are boasting about as it is for him to restore believing Jews to their former place within the covenant community. This would not be difficult for God to do. Even in horticulture, it would be more fruitful, reliable and easy to graft a previously cultivated branch back into its old cultivated tree than to graft in a branch from a wild tree. The latter process is notoriously unfruitful. Yet, this is what God did when he introduced the Gentiles into the new covenant community of faith. Paul must have left his Gentile hearers in no doubt that their inclusion in the community was purely of grace. He had, indeed, chosen a very effective and telling illustration!

11:25 I do not want you to be ignorant of this mystery, brothers, so that you may not be conceited: Israel has experienced a hardening in part until the full number of the Gentiles has come in.

Paul calls the inclusion of the Jews back into the covenant community a "mystery."[625] This term is used elsewhere to describe the inclusion of the Gentiles (Eph 3:4–6). A "mystery" in biblical terms is not a puzzle. It is used to speak of something that could never be known unless God revealed it.[626] As an expression of his grace and according to his own wishes, he reveals his mystery and purposes to all sorts of people, regardless of their intelligence or station in life..

Too often, wrong attitudes emerge in the lives of Christian people because they fail to see God's greater plan. When the picture of God's saving purposes is out of focus, spiritual life can be damaged. Theological distortions are of grave concern as, instead of believers developing attributes that reflect the character of God, they are spiritually "defaced" and exhibit characteristics that are more like their former father, the devil (John 8:39–44). The tragedy of this truth litters the pages of history. For this reason, Paul does not want his hearers to be ignorant of this mystery.

In speaking of Israel's salvation as being dependent on the in-gathering of the Gentiles, Paul has reversed Jewish expectation. The OT clearly shows (Isa 42:1; 49:6; 49:22; 56:7; 62:2; 66:12; Ezek 38:23; Mic 4:2; Mal 1:11) that the blessings of the new covenant will come to the Gentiles following the in-gathering of the Jewish people. Paul says they have come in ahead of the Jews because Israel has rejected the Messiah. Consequently, the Jews must now wait for the blessing of the Gentiles to be completed before the nation can enter into the promises made to Abraham.

---

[625] Kim, "Mystery," 412–29, claims the concept of mystery came from a very early interpretation of Paul's Damascus revelation in which he reflected on the significance of Isa 6:49 for his apostolic ministry.

[626] Glancy, "Israel," 191–203, claims that Paul's situation overcame him, causing his logic to fail. She understands Paul to be arguing that Israel suffers in her loss of identity. This means that Israel, by this suffering, is symmorphic with Christ. This vicarious suffering offers Gentiles an opportunity to also become symmorphic with Christ. Israel will be resurrected in her eschatological encounter with the Redeemer from Zion. While Glancy's position probably reflects the tension that is in Paul regarding his kinsmen, to say his logic has failed places the blame for inconsistency on the apostle's mindset rather than on the reader's. Accusations such as Glancy's litter Pauline commentaries.

No wonder the Jewish community had great difficulty in coping with Paul. Not only did he insist that the Gentiles should not be made to undergo circumcision, he also taught they were now the conduit for Israel's blessing!

11:26 And so all Israel will be saved, as it is written: "The deliverer will come from Zion; he will turn godlessness away from Jacob.

The first question the text raises is whether "and so" is a correct translation of οὕτως (*houtōs*). It has been suggested it should be translated "only then" or "in this way."[627] The second question is: "who is Israel in this passage?" Is Paul still thinking of spiritual Israel as discussed in Rom 2:28–29 and in Rom 4:11–12, i.e., Jews and Gentiles who share the same faith as Abraham? If so, then he refers only to those who believe and are the true sons of Abraham.[628] Or is Paul using the term with its national historical meaning, i.e., the nation of Israel?[629]

It is difficult to avoid the conclusion that Paul meant the latter because of what he goes on to write in Rom 11:28—how can the members of spiritual Israel, the true sons of Abraham, be described as "enemies" in relation to the Gospel?

However, if this is accepted as the meaning another question is raised: "Is Paul saying that *all* of the nation of Israel will be saved?" This question is difficult to answer, but it could be resolved if the term "all" is intended to convey all believers in Christ in the nation. However, in accepting this meaning, we still have to resolve the problem that all believing Jews are described as "enemies."[630]

---

[627] Van der Horst, "Meaning," 521–25, argues that while most translators and commentators take *outws* in Rom 11:26 in a moda —"and so [or 'thus'] all Israel will be saved"—he presents evidence from Greek authors as well as Jewish and Christian writings to show that a temporal sense of *outws*—"and then [or 'only then' or 'thereafter'] all Israel will be saved"—is more widespread than is commonly assumed.

[628] See Calvin, *Romans*, 440; Wright, "Romans," 691, and *Climax*, 246–51.

[629] See Käsemann, *Romans*, 307; Ziesler, *Romans*, 285; Carbone, "Israele" 139–70; Cranfield, *Shorter*, 282; Moo, *Romans*, 722; Wright, "Romans," 689.

[630] Interestingly, Calvin, *Romans*, 440, who favors reading "Israel" as the church, has nothing to say about Paul describing her as an enemy. Neither does Wright, op cit. The normal argument is the preceding discussion determines that Israel refers to the church. Murray, *Romans*, 96, says: "It is exegetically impossible to give 'Israel' in this verse any other denotation than that which belongs to the term throughout this chapter."

In seeking to understand the scope of "all Israel," it is helpful to recognize that the term in the OT does not include every Jew but a large number of representative Jews (1 Sam 18:16; 28:4; 2 Sam 3:21).

This section concerning Israel's calling is notoriously difficult to unravel, so, it will be helpful to give careful attention to Paul's use of Isaiah 59. Resolving Paul's meaning here might assist in unravelling the meaning of the rest of the passage. Unfortunately, Paul's use of the quotation is complicated by the fact that he follows neither the Hebrew nor the Greek text of the LXX. Clearly, Paul's alteration of the Isaianic text requires attention.

First, we should note that the Hebrew text speaks of the "Redeemer coming to Zion."[631] "'The Redeemer will come to Zion, to those in Jacob who repent of their sins,' declares the Lord" (Isa 59:20). However, Paul alters the text, writing: "The *deliverer* will come *from* Zion; he will turn godlessness away from Jacob" (emphasis added). Paul alters the text in two significant ways: he calls Isaiah's Redeemer "the deliverer" and writes that he comes "from Zion" rather than "to Zion." Why has he made these changes?

It may be he wants to emphasize that the salvation which the deliverer will bring is not a salvation for the Jews alone. Paul may be writing, in effect, that the deliverer is more than a national figure. He is the Savior of all men; so he does not come "to Zion" but "from Zion," i.e., he is the Jewish Messiah coming to the remnant to save his people including those in the Gentile world. This fits in perfectly with what we have noted and with contemporary scholarship. Paul did not abandon his Jewish heritage but stayed within its boundaries as he expounded the Gospel for the Gentile world.[632]

But there is another possibility. In writing that the deliverer will come "from Zion," it could be Paul is implying that he is coming to those who do not make Zion their hope, leaving behind those who stress that Zion is the place of salvation. In other words, Paul writes that salvation is not found "in Zion" but

---

[631] Johnson, B.C., "Tongues," 102, points out that the reference to the Redeemer coming out of Zion in Rom 11:26b is based on an amended text of the LXX of Isa 59:20. This has ἕνεκεν Σιων. Johnson says there is no sure way of knowing whether ὁ ρ υομενος 'the Redeemer' refers to Jesus Christ or to God. See also Davies, W.D., "People," 25, who further says it is most natural to assume it refers to Yahweh. See also, Stuhlmacher, *Reconciliation*, 178.

[632] See Dunn, *Theology*; Hays, *Echoes*; Wright, *Climax*.

comes "from Zion" to those who know that there is no salvation in the institutions of Judah.[633]

The image of the Messiah coming to the Israelite people of faith who are nonetheless outside of Zion (that is, not depending on its institutions), fits the picture drawn in the letter. These people are the believing Jews who wait for the return from exile, i.e., the eschatological exodus of the people of God. They recognize there is another Jerusalem (see Gal 4:24–27; Heb 12:22; Rev 21:1–2) to which they must come and have no confidence in national achievement or historical privilege. Indeed, they recognize they are outside of Zion (their heavenly home) as they make their pilgrimage, and it is from there (the heavenly Zion) that the deliverer comes.[634] The argument is about the salvation of the Jews. It suggests they share the same faith as the Gentile believers among whom they dwell, for they also await the coming of the deliverer. If this is the perspective of Paul's argument, he is saying that "all Israel" is "believing Israel" who, with all believing Gentiles, comprise the true seed of Abraham, i.e., the ones who will be saved.[635] Although the argument Paul makes in this passage has nothing to do with Gentiles believers, we know that he sees them to be part of spiritual Israel by what he has already written in the letter (Rom 2; 4; 9:6).

This line of exegesis is supported by Paul's use of Isa 52:7 in Rom10:15. The original setting of the Isaianic passage was the return of the exiles when they proclaimed to all who wanted to hear that Yahweh had redeemed them from bondage. The task of the remnant was to encourage the Gentiles to join them on their pilgrimage. This task has been transferred to the church, which is made up of the remnant of Jews and Gentiles. It is her task, while on her eschatological pilgrimage, to encourage others to join her and experience the grace of God's redeeming love. If this is a correct understanding of the way that Paul has adapted the OT scripture, it suggests that the true people of God are still to enter Zion and that Paul's alteration of the OT is intended to point to this fact. Moreover, Paul goes on to quote from Jer 31:33 (Rom 11:27). This is,

---

[633] Contra Seifrid, "Romans" 674–75, who see the reference to coming from Zion be intended to say that the Redeemer comes to confront the threatening nations; i.e., to defend Israel.

[634] The reference can, of course, be to the Redeemer's first coming or to his second coming. As Paul's discussion is about Israel's future salvation, it suggests that he is focusing on the Redeemer's second coming.

[635] See Calvin, *Romans*, 437.

of course, a promise regarding the new covenant, suggesting that his argument is not about the *parousia* but the coming of the Gospel.

Whoever is the intended focus of the adjusted prophecy's fulfillment, it is clear that the deliverer will transform the lives of those he has come to—"he will turn godlessness away from Jacob" (see conclusion of Rom 11). From the quote borrowed from Isaiah, the Roman Gentiles would have known that "godlessness" (a term only used by Paul) would have been "turned away from Jacob" when those in Jacob repented of their sins (Isa 59:20).

Before moving on to Rom 11:27, we need to note that Paul—in keeping with the rest of the NT–has avoided calling Jesus "the Redeemer." This is especially significant here for it would have been natural to follow the Hebrew text. Instead, Paul chooses the term "deliverer." This is in keeping with his Paschal theology where the term "Redeemer" has been dropped in preference for the more definitive title: "Firstborn."[636] Paul, as do the other NT writers, keeps in step with this Paschal theology.

From this discussion, it appears that Paul cannot bring himself to say national Israel has been abandoned but that the conditions of her acceptance are the same as the Gentiles. She will only be restored through the salvation that Christ has made possible through his death and resurrection. "All Israel," therefore has two meanings. First, it refers to all believing Jews; second, to all the sons of Abraham, i.e., Jewish and Gentile believers. Paul, it would seem, is quite fluid in the way he uses the term. What it does not refer to is the nation of Israel.

11:27 *"And this is my covenant with them when I take away their sins."*

Paul continues to make use of the Isaianic quote by combining the first phrase of Isa 59:21 with the sense of Isa 59:20b.

The above suggestion that the "Israel" who will be saved refers to those in spiritual exile from Zion,[637] fits the theme of the New Exodus around which, some suggest, the letter to the Romans was constructed. We have repeatedly heard echoes of the fulfillment of prophecy in connection with the homecoming of Israel from exile under the leadership of a Messiah of Davidic descent. For

---

[636] See Holland, *Contours,* chapter 10.

[637] Contra Sanders. He says Jews will be saved by covenant and sinners by Christ. This is rejected by Allison, "Jesus," 66; Davies, W.D., "People," 39, says: "to argue that God saves Israel apart from Christ rests on silence and some improbable interpretations of Rom 11:25–27."

the eighth century prophets, the "return from exile" was the forgiveness of sins.[638] We have seen that many of the Scriptures Paul uses are from this period in Israel's history when the prophets were comforting the nation that it had not been cast off forever. Paul supplements this eighth century material by drawing upon aspects of the Passover, the central event of the first exodus.[639] This indicates forgiveness is not without the shedding of blood but is based on the fact that "Christ our Passover has been sacrificed for us" (1 Cor 5:7).

It is clear that Paul instinctively looks to the prophecy (Jer 31:33–34) of a new covenant, which promised that Israel's sins would be forgiven. This is significant, for this promise was made to the Jews in exile. If Paul is exercising his usual respect for the original context of the passage he quotes, the application has to be to those who are exiled from Zion. Indeed, the promise originally made by Jeremiah was not to all the Jews. Most stayed in Babylon, refusing to respond to the call to return to Zion. Such people excluded themselves from this new covenant. The promise was not for those who refused the hardships of the return but for those who responded in faith and went back to their homeland—despite those hardships—in order to serve and worship their God.

It does not take much imagination to see the NT parallel. The "exile" is not separation from the earthly Zion but from the heavenly one. Those living in the earthly Zion are the ones who refuse the call to faith and the challenge to leave behind all that is precious to them. Those to whom the deliverer comes are the ones who find no comfort in Zion with its nationalism and hardness of heart. They wait for their deliverer to appear and lead them to the heavenly Zion for which their hearts long.

The above exegesis suggests that the reference to "all Israel" in v.26 includes the physical descendants of Abraham who share his faith and look for a country that has not yet been given to them.[640] It would be unwise to go beyond this by saying that "all" refers to all of Abraham's physical offspring. This glorious conclusion is available to all Israel, but it will only be a reality

---

[638] See Wright, *Victory*.

[639] See comments on Rom 3:21–25.

[640] See Calvin, *Romans*, 441, who says: "Paul maintains that the purposes of God stand firm and immovable, by which he had once deigned to choose them for himself as a peculiar nation. Since then, it cannot possibly be that the Lord will depart from that covenant which he made with Abraham, 'I will be the God of thy seed,' (Gen XVii.7). It is evident that he has not wholly turned away his kindness from the Jewish nation."

for an individual Jew if he rejects what once he had gloried in and embraces what once he had despised. The statement: "I will forgive their sins" was equivalent to: "I will bring them out of exile," for it was because of their sins that they had been cut off from their inheritance.

11:28 As far as the gospel is concerned, they are enemies on your account; but as far as election is concerned, they are loved on account of the patriarchs.

Paul has already used the term "enemies" ἐχθροί (*echthroi*) in his letter. Indeed, he included himself in the term when describing God's saving activity on behalf of his people in Rom 5:10. He wrote: "For if, when we were God's enemies, we were reconciled to him through the death of his Son, how much more, having been reconciled, shall we be saved through his life!" In Rom 5, Paul writes that God's enemies are people who have not been reconciled to him, and this seems to be the sense of the term in Rom 11. He uses the term "enemies" in a number of his letters.[641] In Phil 3:18–19, Paul elaborates, with tears, on the lifestyle and destiny of people who live in enmity to the Gospel: "I have often told you before and now say it again even with tears, many live as enemies of the cross of Christ. Their destiny is destruction, their god is their stomach, and their glory is in their shame. Their mind is on earthly things."

Paul is not intending to convey the sense that the Jews are hated as far as the Gospel is concerned but, at this point in their history, they are loved less (or, to use a better term, "behind")[642] the believing Gentiles, who have been reconciled to God and brought into the kingdom ahead of them.

Yet, even though this is so, it is only temporary. The Jews are loved on account of the patriarchs and their election has not been put aside. Paul has been at pains to stress how the new covenant has redefined Israel, and this redefinition has not reneged on the promises made to the ones with whom God had made the preparatory covenant. It is the fulfillment of these ancient covenants (those made with Abraham [Rom 4:1–25] and David [Rom 1:3]) that brings blessing to the Gentiles and for which they should be eternally grateful.

11:29 For God's gifts and his call are irrevocable.

Regardless of what the Roman Gentile believers think about his explanation of the Jews' standing, Paul reminds them that ultimately their status

---

[641] Rom 12:20; 1 Cor 15:26; Gal 4:16; Phil 3:18; 2 Thess 3:15.

[642] See the meaning of "hated" in Luke 14:26.

is not dependent on the consent of men. It is settled by a sovereign God whose decisions cannot be challenged. This is true of God's right to bestow gifts to men and his right to exercise his prerogative in choosing who he will save and in what order.

We need to keep in focus the fact that Paul is not discussing individual election but that of people groups, namely Jews and Gentiles. This does not alter the fact that, elsewhere, the same principle is applied to individuals.[643]

11:30 Just as you who were at one time disobedient to God have now received mercy as a result of their disobedience.

Upon hearing Paul's letter read to the gathered church, the Gentile believers in Rome were reminded there was a time when they also were disobedient to God and enemies of the cross of Christ. Indeed, at the opening of his letter, Paul exposed the fact that he knew of the depraved behavior and ongoing disobedience among some of the believers. Rom 2:1–16 must have made very uncomfortable listening for some.

But, despite their disobedience, the Gentiles had received mercy when they responded in repentance to the Gospel which was extended to them as a result of God's grace. Paul writes: "Through him and for his name's sake, we received grace and apostleship to call people from among all the Gentiles to the obedience that comes from faith. And you also are among those who are called to belong to Jesus Christ" (Rom 1:5–6).

Had the Gentiles in the congregation been listening carefully to the letter as it was being read to them, they would have known their call came about because of the disobedience of the Jews. Paul had already reminded them of the words of the prophet Hosea (Hos 2:23) in Rom 9:24–26 that God would call them "my people" who were not his people and "my loved one" who was not his loved one.

11:31 So they too have now become disobedient in order that they too may now receive mercy as a result of God's mercy to you.

Paul clearly sees that responsibility accompanies the mercy which has been extended to the Gentiles. They are obliged by divine grace to bear witness to

---

[643] Acts 13:48.

the unbelieving Jews so that they too may hear the good news of God's saving activity in Christ, repent, and be reconciled to the God of their fathers.

It might seem strange that Paul says the Jews will receive mercy because of the mercy that the Gentiles have received, but this is not so strange when it is appreciated that, once again, his frame of reference is the prophetic word of the OT. The prophets had said the Gentiles would be brought into the covenant community, and that God would provoke the Jews to jealousy by calling a people he had not formerly known to be his people (Rom 9:25). The Gentiles were actually being used to provoke the Jews—to make them realize that their unbelief was denying them the blessing of fellowship with God.

Of course, arguments alone from the believing Gentiles would not win the Jews to Jesus the Messiah—they would do that through their lives. They had to demonstrate to the Jews that they had turned from their sin and disobedience to serve the living God in the very way that the Jews had been called, but had failed, to do. Rather than being the cause of boasting, the calling of the Gentiles gave them a great and awesome responsibility to live as the servants of God.

11:32 For God has bound all men over to disobedience so that he may have mercy on them all.

There is no limit to the "all" in this statement. All the children of Adam—whether descendants of Abraham or not—who actively disobey the command of Yahweh (i.e., those who are outside of Christ) are under judgment (Rom 3:22–24). It can no longer be said that Yahweh gives Israel privileges over the Gentiles. Indeed, all her privileges have come to an end in terms of her special relationship with him. She is now in the same position of danger as the Gentiles. She must turn to her God in repentance and, like them, seek the same kindness and mercy.

11:33 Oh, the depth of the riches of the wisdom and knowledge of God! How unsearchable his judgments, and his paths beyond tracing out!

Paul has come to the end of his presentation on the equality of Jews and Gentiles before God. The first eleven chapters of his letter have argued for this equality on theological grounds—the next section will argue for it in practice.

At this point of transition, Paul pauses. He is not able to conclude his argument without reflecting on the wonder of what he has been presenting. His heart rings with praise and thanksgiving to God, and he writes the longest doxology that appears in any of his extant writings.[644] This brief, concluding section is possibly a key passage in an unexpected way. It shows us that the man God used not only knew his theology but was overwhelmed by its message and the God about whom it spoke. Paul is a powerful example to those of us who love theology that a passion for academics can never be a substitute for loving God himself. May we not be like some of the Pharisees and Scribes who pursued theology as an intellectual exercise but, rather, like the Apostle Paul who was moved by its truths.

He begins his eulogy by dwelling on the "depth of the riches of the wisdom of God." Both Jews and Gentiles have challenged God's decisions and callings throughout history, seeing them—at times—as arbitrary, ruthless and cruel. When tempted by adverse crushing circumstances to doubt God in such a way, we need to ask if such judgments reflect the character of the God who gave his own Son up to death for the salvation of those who hated and abused him. How can such evil be charged to such a God? We can only conclude that any evidence which suggests that God is ruthless and merciless is unreliable and untrue. This does not deny that he will judge—sometimes in this life—but it does warn us of the danger of attributing characteristics to him that befit the prince of lies.

Paul declares the depth of the richness of God's knowledge. The term "depth" is used throughout the Scriptures to denote those areas that are beyond the inspection of man (e.g., Prov 18:4; 1 Cor 2:10; Phil 1:9). In his letter, Paul has argued for God's right to make decisions that man may not approve. He would not be God if he had to seek the endorsement of man for his decisions and actions. Because he is uniquely omniscient no one should challenge his wisdom. How dare we, in our foolishness, question the judgments and decisions of the Lord God! "How unsearchable his judgments, and his paths beyond tracing out!" God's judgments are at a depth that man cannot fathom, and his actions, therefore, are always going to be beyond what man can comprehend.

11:34 "Who has known the mind of the Lord? Or who has been his counsellor?"

While there is an echo of Job 15:8 in this verse, Paul clearly relies on Isa 40:13, which he also uses in 1 Cor 2:16: "Who has understood the mind of the Lord, or instructed him as his counselor?"[645] The questions are rhetorical, and

---

[644] Or hymn. See Jewett, *Romans*, 716.

[645] See Holland, Paul, Israel's Law and God's Spirit, forthcoming.

asked not because Paul was expecting an answer (for he and his hearers knew that the answer was "No one") but because he intended that their very asking would remove any complacency.

The original text in Isa 40 celebrated the wonder of Yahweh who announced that he would deliver his people from exile in Babylon. The declaration by Isaiah was to answer those who challenged the prophet's message by claiming there was no possibility that God would bring Israel back home to Zion. No one would have advised God to act in this way as it was contrary to all that the nation deserved. However, instead of casting her off forever, God was working to redeem her and re-establish the relationship she had rejected. Of course, what Isaiah declared about God redeeming his people from bondage in Babylon pales into insignificance when we recall the length to which God went to redeem his people from bondage to Satan. He did this so that he could bring his people home to the heavenly Jerusalem.

I have argued the letter is set within a New Exodus framework, and here, in the closing section of the theological discussion, Paul again uses the words of Isaiah. The presence of Isaiah's oracles is a clear reminder of the importance of this eighth century prophet's perspective and the many predictions and comforts he brought to Israel in that crucial period of her history. Paul's use of the prophet of the Second Exodus, underlines the continuity of these great themes and promises that have, and are, being fulfilled in Christ.

Paul asserts the impossibility of any man being able to instruct God: "who has been his counselor?" To think that we can manage, understand, and advise God in a way that satisfies our puny, fallen, darkened minds is ridiculous. Such arrogance is ludicrous, and beyond comprehension. God is not beholden to man. He does not have to seek man's approval for his decisions and goals. He is the Creator who answers to no man, thing, or being. He is not a capricious God. He is the God who redeems and saves those who call on him. The sufferings of creation are not the result of his affliction but the consequence of humankind's fall. Into this sin-cursed existence, God has come in the person of Jesus, to bring life and immortality by means of the Gospel (2 Tim 1:10). His judgments are unsearchable and his paths beyond finding out.

This has been the thrust of Paul's argument throughout his letter to the Romans. Man has given himself over to Sin (Satan). As a result of this covenant relationship with Satan, man is in exile; there is nothing he is can do to annul this relationship and reverse its consequences. The quotation from Isaiah is a comment on the theology of the letter over which the previous verse has burst into gratitude and praise. The attention of such a God to the wellbeing and deliverance of his people is a source of unspeakable comfort (Isa 40:1).

11:35 "Who has ever given to God, that God should repay him?"

The quote is difficult to identify with any certainty, but it is possibly based on Job 41:11.[646] This section of Job concludes a long, searching debate between Job and his "comforters," finally ending with God's challenge to Job as to his authority to question his Creator. Job responds with a hymn of intense praise, which glorifies Yahweh for his wisdom, power, and might.

The point Paul is making is that no man can understand God's ways; it is only as Yahweh reveals himself that man can possibly begin to understand his own insignificance and frailty. There is nothing man can give to God; he needs to receive everything from him. The relationship is not one of equals, and yet, incredibly, God desires to treat man as though he was an equal. In the light of God's perfection, majesty, and power, the redemption of man is beyond anything that could have been contemplated. "Where," asks Paul, "has this salvation come from?" He answers: "From the heart of God himself."

11:36 For from him and through him and to him are all things. To him be the glory forever! Amen.

There is no praise for man. He deserves nothing but judgment and condemnation, as he is guilty and totally helpless.

All of God's gracious dealings with redeemed men and women, Jew or Gentile, are because God has purposed to do "all things" for them: "And we know that in *all things* God works for the good of those who love him, who have been *called* according to his purpose. For those God *foreknew* he also *predestined* to be *conformed* to the likeness of his Son, that he might be the firstborn among many brothers. And those he predestined, he also called; those he called, he also *justified*; those he justified, he also *glorified*" (Rom 8:28–30, emphasis added). Thus the "all things" are those things that pertain to salvation.[647] Paul can only respond: "To him be the glory forever! Amen."

---

[646] Jewett, *Romans*, 718, thinks that Paul has carefully selected Job 41:3, along with the earlier use of Isa 40:3, so as to construct a chiastic development of the riches, wisdom, and knowledge of God referred to in Rom 11:33.

[647] See also Peter's argument in 2 Pet 1:3.

CONCLUSION OF ROMANS CHAPTER ELEVEN

Paul puts Israel's unbelief in context. He shows that it has been the pattern of her history throughout the OT. How different her story would have been if she had truly believed and repented!

Yet, in spite of this unbelief, Paul insists the purposes of God still stand—he is living evidence that a believing remnant still exists, just as it has existed throughout Israel's history.

He fears that some Gentile believers in Rome are in danger of falling into Israel's sin of pride and unbelief (disobedience). He urges them not to boast that they have replaced Israel, showing them that the Jews are the "natural, cultivated, fallen branches of the olive tree," and that it would not be difficult for God to bring them back into the blessings promised to Abraham. After all, God had grafted the Gentiles into the tree as wild branches, so why could he not restore the natural branches to the site where they once grew?

He concludes with an affirmation that all of believing Israel will be grafted back into the tree. The spiritual Israel will be saved in the fullness of time when the Gentiles have been brought in as predicted by the prophets. This argument is brought to its climax with the declaration from the prophet Isaiah that the deliverer (Hebrew גָּאַל "redeemer") would come from Zion. The culmination of his coming is found in Isa 61:10, where Isaiah testifies: "he has clothed me with garments of salvation and arrayed me with a robe of righteousness, as a bridegroom adorns his head like a priest, and as a bride adorns herself with jewels." Believing Israel will, at last, be joined with the Gentiles to form the bride in the divine marriage.

Romans 12

THE MESSIAH KING AND HIS PRIESTLY PEOPLE (12:1–8)

Therefore, I urge you, brothers, in view of God's mercy, to offer your bodies as living sacrifices, holy and pleasing to God—this is your spiritual act of worship. Do not conform any longer to the pattern of this world, but be transformed by the renewing of your mind. Then you will be able to test and approve what God's will is—his good, pleasing and perfect will.

For by the grace given me I say to every one of you: Do not think of yourself more highly than you ought, but rather think of yourself with sober judgment, in accordance with the measure of faith God has given you. Just as each of us has one body with many members, and these members do not all have the same function, so in Christ we who are many form one body, and each member belongs to all the others. We have different gifts, according to the grace given us. If a man's gift is prophesying, let him use it in proportion to his faith. If it is serving, let him serve; if it is teaching, let him teach; if it is encouraging, let him encourage; if it is contributing to the needs of others, let him give generously; if it is leadership, let him govern diligently; if it is showing mercy, let him do it cheerfully. (Romans 12:1–8)

INTRODUCTION

Paul has now concluded the theological section of his letter in which hugely important issues have been patiently yet decisively presented. However, Christian living is not only about understanding theology but also about living it out, and it is to this that Paul now turns.

God saved his people to serve him in truth and holiness, qualities which Israel tragically failed to display. Living as faithful servants is obligatory, for we have been saved from the awful judgment that awaits those who are not in Christ. Like the Jews in the Exodus who benefitted from the death of the lamb, the church is saved as a result of the death of its Paschal sacrifice, Jesus the Firstborn and Redeemer. Because of this, "there is now no condemnation for those who are in Christ Jesus" (Rom 8:1).

As a result of Israel's exodus from Egypt she was called to be a priestly people, and this, Paul says, is now the calling on the church.

12:1 Therefore, I urge you, brothers, in view of God's mercy, to offer your bodies as living sacrifices, holy and pleasing to God—this is your spiritual act of worship.

In using the adverb "therefore," Paul is effectively saying: "In light of what I've written, this is how you should respond." It does not refer to the material of chapter 11 alone (where Paul explained the role of the Jews in the purposes of God) but to the argument that has gone on from the beginning of the letter.

Throughout the letter, Paul has focused on the history of God's saving activity, showing the believers that Jesus, the Son of David, has fulfilled all the predictions of the OT prophets, bringing salvation to those who looked to the living God. Despite Israel's rebellious history, God's many promises and the examples of how he acted in history show that he would continue to have compassion on them and be merciful to them (Isa 63:9; Neh 9:31). It is into this mercy that the Gentiles have now been brought, sharing with those in Israel who have true faith.[648]

By appreciating that the first eleven chapters of the letter provide the backcloth of the exhortation of chapter 12, we can understand more clearly what motivated Paul's appeal. The prophets had, albeit implicitly, anticipated the death of Jesus.[649] His death was nothing other than the great eschatological Passover. Paul discussed this is Rom 3:21–26, and the ramifications of this awful event overshadow the rest of the letter.

In the original Passover, the Jewish firstborn sons were spared death because lambs were slain on their behalf. These firstborn sons were then claimed by God as priests, and were set apart to represent the nation in worship (Exod 13:2; 22:29b). God then provided an alternative arrangement, allowing the Jewish families to keep their firstborn sons by substituting the tribe of Levi for them (Num 3:12–13). The Levites acted in their place as the priesthood of the nation. Regardless of this arrangement, God named those who had been

---

[648] Campbell, W.S., "Rule," 278, stresses that Paul seeks to create a community ethos in Rome so that there can be unity within diversity: one church made up of Jews and Gentiles.

[649] See comments on Rom 3:21–26.

spared (indeed the whole nation) his "firstborn," calling them all to a ministry of priestly service (Exod 4:22–23; 19:6).[650]

This is Paul's argument. He has explained how through the death of Jesus—God's beloved son and firstborn of all creation—believers have been spared. No spotless lamb was killed in their place but, as with the Egyptian families, the victim of judgment was their elder brother (Rom 8:3–4, 29). Note the theme of redemption throughout chapter 8 in which the life of the firstborn was surrendered as God, through Christ, became his people's Redeemer.[651]

The death of Jesus means that believers have been set free—released from bondage and impending judgment. Just as those Jews who were spared the judgment of the first Passover were claimed by God as priests, so, in the great Passover when Christ died, God claimed those he had spared as his priestly people. All the redeemed of the Lord were henceforth called to be a holy nation and a royal priesthood (1 Pet 2:5, 9).[652]

The priestly theme is part of the Exodus, Second Exodus and the New Exodus. Not only was Israel redeemed to be Yahweh's bride but also his priestly people. Isa 61:10 describes the condition of restored Israel not only in terms of being the bride of Yahweh but also his priesthood: "I delight greatly in the Lord; my soul rejoices in my God. For he has clothed me with garments of salvation and arrayed me in a robe of righteousness, as a bridegroom adorns his head like a priest, and as a bride adorns herself with her jewels."

This is the background of Paul's appeal to the believers of the Roman church that they offer themselves as a living sacrifice. That was precisely what the priesthood was meant to be in the OT—the people were to be a living

---

[650] According to rabbinic tradition, the firstborn had been the servants of the sanctuary but had lost the office owing to the worship of the golden calf. The honor went to the Levites (Ginzberg, *Legends*, 3:211). The Levites were substituted for the firstborn, the tribe having the responsibility of atoning for the sin of the firstborn among the children of Israel (*Legends*, 3:226). This connection of the priesthood of believers with the Paschal theme is supported by other parts of the NT, suggesting that the Paschal paradigm was the origin of the believers' priestly ministry. See Holland, *Contours*, chapter 10.

[651] See Holland, *Contours*, 237–73, for discussion on the firstborn in redemptive history.

[652] Commenting on Rom 12:1, Campbell, D.A., *Deliverance*, 651, notes the cultic setting and comments on the presence of cultic imagery throughout Romans saying: "All this material is just too pronounced to ignore. Christ, the Spirit, Paul himself, and the Christian community all receive overtly cultic coding at certain points in Romans."

sacrifice. This is the basis of Christian living for all believing people. It is not a calling for special classes of Christians such as "full-time" and "cross-cultural workers." Such distinctions were never suggested in the NT. All Christians are "full-time" because they have been fully redeemed, and the implications of this are far reaching for the way they live their lives. What we expect from certain "categories" of Christians is no different from what God expects of all his people. As priests of the living God, believers are called to minister in intercession as well as instruction, for the priests of the OT formed a teaching community (2 Kgs 17:27; 2 Chr 15:3; 17:7; Ezek 44:21–23). The NT knows nothing of a division between laity and ordained as all believers are "priests unto God" (Rom 15:16; 1 Pet 2:5; Rev 1:6). All are called to serve by making Christ known, being totally committed to this task because they have been redeemed and are not their own.[653]

When Paul urges the Roman believers to yield their bodies, he is not limiting his appeal to the dedication of their physical bodies. His appeal includes the whole of their persons, and could legitimately be translated as "yield yourselves" (Rom 6:13–14). This is not playing with words, for scholars who have studied the way the ancient Jews used the term "body" (*soma),* have shown that it was used differently by the Greeks for whom it mostly meant "physical body."[654] However, for the Jews it was a term that embraced the whole of the person—it encompassed mind, emotions, will, and physical being.

Thus, Paul's appeal is for the Roman believers to be totally and completely dedicated to God, recognizing that they belong to the one who has given his Son for their forgiveness and salvation. If, when listening to the letter being read to them, they grasped the enormity of what God had done for them in Christ, Paul's appeal for dedication would have been met with ready assent from the assembled congregation.

The NIV translation of this verse reads: "Therefore, I urge you, brothers, in view of God's mercy, to offer your bodies as living sacrifices, holy and pleasing to God—this is your spiritual act of worship." It is understandable for this exhortation to be seen as an individualistic, introspective appeal to all the

---

[653] Stuhlmacher, *Theme*, 341, comments that "Rom 12–16 belongs inextricably to the letter . . . because the apostle nowhere (and certainly not in Romans) expounds abstract theology, but always only concrete exhortation. Whether the Romans really believe in Christ as their redeemer and Lord will be evident, according to Paul, by how they (as Gentile and Jewish Christians) deal with one another and how they resolve the tensions among one another in Rome."

[654] Holland, *Contours*, chapter 6.

Romans 12

believers in Rome to live holy lives which can be offered to God as individual living sacrifices. The picture this conjures up is of Roman believers striving to live holy lives in the context of their families and social responsibilities within the city. They come together to be strengthened and helped through the teaching of the Scriptures and the celebration of the Lord's Supper so that they are prepared for the more important task of living their independent, sacrificial lives in the days ahead.

However, Paul is saying more than this. The fuller picture is hidden by the translators' lack of respect for the use Paul makes of individual and corporate vocabulary. As the believers listened to the letter being read, they would have heard the appeal more like this: τὰ σώματα ὑμῶν θυσίαν ζῶσαν (*ta sōmata humōn thusian zōsav*) "offer yourselves (pl.) as *a living sacrifice* (sing.), *holy* and *pleasing* to God—this is your (pl.) *reasonable service*." Paul had already addressed them corporately in Rom 6:12: Μὴ οὖν βασιλευέτω ἡ ἁμαρτία ἐν τῷ θνητῷ ὑμῶν σώματι (*mē oun basileuetō hē amartia en tō thnētō humōn sōmati*) "do not let sin reign in your (pl.) mortal body (sing.)."

I think what Paul is saying to the believers in Rome is something like this: "Remember how I told you earlier in the letter that God rescued you from bondage to Sin through the death of his Son and gave you life through his Spirit? In response to his mercy and grace that has given you these things, I urge you to offer yourselves to him as a corporate sacrifice. You are all equally part of Christ's church. You are all children of Abraham, and despite the differences that have divided you in the past and made you suspicious of each other (I hope you now know that these must stop), you are to recognize that God has accepted you all. So, you are *all* called to priestly service, Jew and Gentile alike, and you are all to offer yourselves in order to make the *church* in Rome a living sacrifice. And I want this offering to be a sacrifice that God can accept. In other words, the church must be spotless and without blemish. This means that you all must be holy—conformed to the image of his Son—and you must be united. If, as a church, you make an offering to God of this quality (and, after all the things that he has done for you, this is surely not too much to ask), you will bring him great pleasure and be effective in his service."

Since sacrifices were offered in the temple by priests, Rom 12:1 suggests that Paul saw priestly ministry as continuing in the NT church. This is indeed how the early church saw her service, for when they chose seven of their number to serve as "deacons," the apostles prayed and laid hands on them (Acts 6:6). When Barnabas and Saul were set apart to do their missionary work among the Gentiles (Acts 13), the elders also laid hands on them in the manner of setting priests apart.⁶⁵⁵ Later in this letter (Rom 15:15–16), Paul writes: ". . . . because of the grace God gave me to be a minister of Christ Jesus to the Gentiles with the priestly duty of proclaiming the Gospel of God, so that the Gentiles might become an offering acceptable to God, sanctified by the Holy Spirit." Paul is clearly saying that as a NT priest his responsibility is to make the Gospel known to the Gentiles. It is through his proclamation that Gentiles will believe and become proclaiming priests in turn, so becoming part of the "offering acceptable to God." Of course, while the priesthood of the NT draws from imagery from the OT institution, it is unlike that order, for it is not about offering physical sacrifices but rather spiritual ones. Also, unlike the OT priesthood which was exclusive, the NT priesthood is all inclusive. Every believer, regardless of ethnicity and no matter position in society or gifting in the church, is a priest.

As I have noted, Paul did not use the term πνευματικος *pneumatikos* "spiritual" but λογικος *logikos* "logical" or "reasonable," and so he writes: "This is your reasonable (or logical) service."⁶⁵⁶ So Paul writes that in light of God's faithfulness, the gift of the Spirit, and the taking of the church as his bride "your (pl.) reasonable (sing.) service (sing.)" is to be a living sacrifice. Again, there is a corporate dimension to this phrase—all the believers contributing to the single, united, acceptable, holy offering to God that is the redeemed community, i.e., the church in Rome. All the believers are to see that, as a church, their priestly act of service was the reasonable response to God's undeserved mercy and that all are responsible for maintaining the church's integrity as a holy and pleasing sacrifice. This interpretation is supported by what Paul says in Rom 15:16 where he speaks of his own calling: "to be a minister of Christ Jesus to the Gentiles with the priestly duty of proclaiming the gospel of God, so that the Gentiles might become an offering acceptable to God, sanctified by the Holy Spirit."

12:2 Do not conform any longer to the pattern of this world, but be transformed by the renewing of your mind. Then you will be able to test and approve what God's will is—his good, pleasing and perfect will.

Another way of saying "do not conform to the pattern of the world," is to say, "do not let the world mold you." The Roman church had two options. It

---

⁶⁵⁵ Kidner, "Metaphors," 119ff., points out that in Num 8:10ff., the Levites had hands laid on them and were offered as living sacrifices to the Lord.

⁶⁵⁶ Bruce holds that there is a contrast here between "the externalities of Israel's temple cult." Cited by Morris, *Romans*, 434.

could either allow God to mold it (by submitting to the Spirit, to God's word as revealed in the OT, and to its leaders [including Paul] as they interpreted and taught the Scriptures) or the church could allow Roman society to shape it as it had the believers before they were converted.

The tragedy is that this molding of lives often takes place unnoticed. Values are disseminated throughout popular culture, being expressed through media, science, and non-Christian families, friends and work colleagues. They change people imperceptibly. Regardless of how noble our societies may appear, Paul would urge: "Brothers and sisters, do not conform any longer." The values believers embrace are to be based on those of another kingdom— the one that Christ rules.

In saying this, Paul is not urging believers to be less than human. Culture is an expression of man's creativity. It is a gift from God and part of the enriching experience of life. His concern for the Roman Christians is that the city's prevailing culture can be anti-God and an instrument by which he can be deposed from the throne of the church's heart and mind. He wants the believers to control its influence. In Phil 4:16, he writes "Whatever is true, whatever is noble, whatever is pure, whatever is lovely, whatever is admirable—if anything is excellent or praiseworthy—think about such things." We are to reject what is base, crude, false, and unkind as part of our refusal to be molded by the world (Rom 6:13–14).

When Paul uses the term "world" in the phrase "Do not conform any longer to the pattern of this world," it has a particular meaning. It speaks of the activities of people from which God is excluded. (This is the way that the Apostle John used the term when he wrote "Do not love the world or anything in the world. If anyone loves the world, the love of the father is not in him" [1 John 2:15]. The usual meaning of the term "world" in his gospel is "humankind," e.g., John 3:16.)[657] Paul's use of αἴων (*aiōn*) "age," links into one of the meanings of a common term encountered throughout the letter: σαρχ (*sarx*) "flesh." To be conformed to (or molded by) the world is to live "in the flesh" (Rom 8:13).[658]

The condition of unredeemed humanity, i.e. "being in the flesh," is a result of Adam's disobedience to God's commands. The Scriptures say that there is a

---

[657] There could also be a literal element to "the world," creation being redeemed through the death of Christ by the God who loves it. See Rom 8:18–25.

[658] For Paul's use of "flesh," see F: Sin in the Theology of Paul, p/273.

spiritual war raging between God and Satan into which man, through Adam, has been drawn. His decision to reject God's offer of mercy leaves him bound in covenant to Satan and the life he lives "in the flesh" reflects the character of the federal head he has chosen.

For those who embrace God's mercy, the death of Christ—their "firstborn"—breaks this covenantal binding, setting them free to enter into covenant with Christ (Rom 7:1–4). However, Christ's redeemed people on earth are still living in the world, interacting with many who are "in the flesh" and feeling the pull of their old allegiance to it. Their minds need to be constantly renewed, and this can only be achieved when they take the message of Scripture seriously and evaluate everything in its light. Only when they do this will they see the significance of issues that face them. Paul urges the church in Rome to seek such a Christ-centered worldview.

Paul urges the church to be "transformed by the renewing of your (pl.) mind (sing)." He continues to be concerned for its corporate identity and witness (see also Eph 2:16; 4:17–32; Col 3:5–17), urging a renewal that comes from submission to the word of God. A renewed mind will enable the church to test and evaluate the issues it faces in Roman society as well as discern God's will. No promises are made that the church would be given direct revelation of God's will in the way Paul had experienced. The believers would discover the sort of life that God wanted them to live as they listened to the Scriptures being explained when they met together under the ministry of gifts given to the church.

It is likely that Paul speaks of the renewing of the church's mind in contrast to what he has said in Rom 1:28 about those living "in the flesh": "since they did not think it worthwhile to retain the knowledge of God, he gave them over to *a depraved mind*, to do what ought not to be done."[659] The renewing of the church's mind, therefore, is a rediscovering of God's perspective by a community of people who value the retention of his word and values. The effectiveness of a church that is renewed in this way is described by Paul in his letter to the Philippian church: "Do everything without complaining and arguing, so that you may become blameless and pure, children of God without fault in a crooked and depraved generation, in which you shine like stars in the universe as you hold out the word of life" (Phil 2:14–16a).

Paul describes God's will as "good, pleasing and perfect." Some see this statement to speak of Paul's conviction that there is a perfect, unique plan for

---

[659] See Peterson, D., "Worship," 271–88.

Romans 12

the life of every Christian. If Paul believed this, supporting texts would be needed to confirm this view. However in this statement he is addressing the church. This is clearly indicated by his urging of the Roman believers to σώματα ὑμῶν (*sōmata humōn*) "offer themselves" ("your bodies"). By doing this, the *church* will come to know God's perfect will.

I would question whether there is an individual plan for a believer's life. Verses that are usually appealed to in support of such a conviction are not normally about the experience of the individual but of the church. The "plan" is for the people of God collectively, and it is the responsibility of each Christian to strive to fulfill his part in it. God's will is that the community will fulfill its role as a servant of the Lord, bringing knowledge of him to those who are in darkness.[660]

Statements which indicate that the will of God may be known are found elsewhere in Paul's writings (1 Thess 5:18; Eph 5:17; Col 3:15). When it is remembered that these letters are addressed to churches and not individuals, "his will" is found to have a corporate perspective. The letters speak of the churches' corporate experience of the peace of God as evidence of his will being revealed. (We have already noted that this corporate experience is reflected in λατρείαν ὑ'μῶν' [*latreian humōn*] "your reasonable [or logical] service," where "your" is plural and "reasonable service" is singular). In other words, it is a corporate act of worship.[661]

The plan is for the people of God as a whole, and it is the responsibility of each Christian to seek to fulfill his part in the corporate plan so that the community will be a faithful servant of the Lord, bringing the knowledge of God to those who are in darkness, under the control of Satan, and living in the flesh. Just as God spoke to Moses "Speak to the entire assembly of Israel and say unto them: 'Be holy because I, the LORD your God, am holy'" (Lev 19:2), so Paul speaks to the Roman church. Just as all the children of Israel were asked to be holy, so every member of the Roman congregation had to put the teaching into action and live out the challenge before the pagan world.

The question must be asked: "How does the church know God's will?" First, his will can be known from the Scriptures (Ps 119:7–112; Prov 3:5; Rom 15:4). The Scriptures make clear what God's plan is for his people and it is in

---

[660] See Friesen and Maxson, *Decision*, for an excellent discussion.

[661] The corporate dimension of the argument is noted by Witherington, *Romans*, 297–98. He rightly says that the ethics that follow are about the community's behavior.

them that we find how the church was led in its mission in the early years. Although Paul says that Christ is the end of the law for those who believe (Rom 10:4), it is clear that he constantly referred to the OT and used it as an inspired tool as he taught the early church. Second, his will can be known through the Holy Spirit who guides and prompts the church to fulfill her mission (Acts 13:2; 16:7). In addition to these foundational means of knowing God's will, there is the counsel of mature believers who are able to give advice in the light of Scripture and their knowledge of the leadings of the Holy Spirit in similar circumstances. However, these "secondary means" are subjective in nature and can easily be misinterpreted. Because of this, secondary means must never be contrary to the clear message of Scripture.

12:3 For by the grace given me I say to every one of you: Do not think of yourself more highly than you ought, but rather think of yourself with sober judgment, in accordance with the measure of faith God has given you.

The direction of the appeal changes in this verse, for Paul now addresses the individual believers using his apostolic status: "For by the grace given me I say . . ."

In his appeal to the believers, Paul is effectively saying: "If apostles are called not to become conceited, then so are you." Elsewhere, Paul highlights the danger of people having over-inflated opinions of themselves. Such people are :"arrogant and boastful . . . they know God's righteous decree that those who do such things deserve death" (Rom 1:30, 32) and he also says that an overseer: "must not be a recent convert, or he may become conceited and fall under the same judgment as the devil" (1 Tim 3:6). Conceit is a serious sin. It was the root of Satan's rebellion, for in aspiring to be like God, pride entered his heart.

Exercising an over-inflated self-opinion is a sin that is all too easy to commit and Paul felt obligated to write to the congregation about this sensitive matter. Seducing Christians to seek their own advancement at the expense of others is one of Satan's most effective ploys. When writing to the church in Philippi, Paul urged the believers: "Do nothing out of selfish ambition or vain conceit, but in humility consider others better than yourselves. . . . Your attitude should be the same as that of Christ Jesus" (Phil 2:3, 5).

God is not as concerned about our gifts as about his grace being manifest in our lives. Conceited Christians can so easily become Absaloms in their local churches (2 Sam 15:1–4), despising and passing judgment on church leaders. Often this sort of criticism comes from hearts that have failed to think of themselves with sober judgment and where the interests of others are subjugated to their own. Perhaps Paul had heard reports about such believers in the church in Rome and was concerned about the damage that they could do to its witness (Rom 14:10). Perhaps he had in mind the bringing together of the Jews and Gentiles in the birth of the Roman church and was appealing to the two communities not to think more highly of themselves than they should. He goes on in the letter to say: "Live in harmony with one another. Do not be proud, but be willing to associate with people of low position. Do not be conceited" (Rom 12:16). Certainly, this understanding maintains the corporate dimension of the letter.

The reference to "the measure of faith" could be understood in one of three possible ways. First, the measure of faith could refer to the amount of faith or trust that a person has. If this is what Paul meant, he is in danger of driving vulnerable believers to continual self-analysis and deprecation, particularly in the presence of those with faith to "move mountains."

Second, the measure of faith could refer to the degree of faithfulness that the believers have, for that is how faith is evident. If this is correct, then Paul is writing that the believers ought to assess themselves in light of their commitment to Jesus Christ. Without such commitment, their gifts might prove to be a liability leading to boastfulness and conceit. This sort of meaning is behind Paul's warning to Timothy not to appoint a young, unproved convert— no matter how talented—to the role of overseer or elder as he may become conceited and fall under judgment (1 Tim 3:6). Sadly, history is strewn with examples of those who once ran well as young Christians but who were "promoted" within their churches too early. This was something that Paul feared could even happen to himself (1 Cor 9:27).

Third, the measure of faith could refer to zeal for the Gospel. Paul uses it in this way in his second letter to the Corinthians, where he says:

> We do not dare to classify or compare ourselves with some who commend themselves. When they measure themselves by themselves and compare themselves with themselves, they are not wise. We, however, will not boast beyond proper limits, but will confine our boasting to the field God has assigned to us, a field that reaches even to you. We are not going too far in our boasting, as would be the case if we had not come to you, for we did get as far as you with the gospel of Christ. Neither do we go beyond our limits by boasting of work done by others. Our hope is that, as your faith continues to grow, our area of activity among you will greatly expand, so that we can preach the gospel in the regions beyond you. For we do not want to boast

about work already done in another man's territory. But, "Let him who boasts boast in the Lord." For it is not the one who commends himself who is approved, but the one whom the Lord commends. (2 Corinthians 10:12–18)

If this is the correct meaning, Paul is encouraging the believers to measure themselves in the light of the sacrifice they have made for the sake of the Gospel. Such people know, of course, that the sacrifice is never adequate when compared to the one made to save them from sin. But lest there be any who might boast about his opportunities for service, Paul goes on to expand his teaching on the body, its gifts, and the honor given to its members. He does this to put every form of Christian service into its right perspective.

12:4 Just as each of us has one body with many members, and these members do not all have the same function.

Paul now prepares to tell the Roman believers how they can make sober judgments of themselves. He is going to remind them of the gifts God has given them. It will be through their ministry that the church will know how to renew her mind. Once again, he draws their attention to the corporate reality of their situation. No gift is given for the recipient's sake but for the benefit of the believing community.

Paul has used the imagery of the body to describe the church in his first letter to the Corinthians (1 Cor 12, 14). "Body of Christ" imagery comes naturally from the concept of the divine marriage, which—as we have seen—is threaded throughout the argument of the letter to the Romans. The church is the "bride of Christ." Just as the body of a bride belongs to her husband, the church (the new covenant community) becomes the body of Christ. Note that the same language is used in Eph 5:25, the background of which is clearly marital and New Exodus.

Paul not only applies this imagery to the worldwide church but also to the local church. He sees each believing community to be the witnessing "body of Christ" in its particular locality (1 Cor 1:2; 1 Thess 1:1). In preparation for using "body of Christ" imagery, Paul reminds the believers of the makeup of the human body. He will soon use this analogy to illustrate the corporate body, the church—to which they belong.

Paul's initial point is that there is diversity among the members of the human body, each member having a particular role in its healthy functioning. It is obvious to all that the body will be impeded in health and vitality if certain of the observable members fail—eyes no longer seeing, ears no longer hearing, tongue no longer speaking, etc.

12:5 So in Christ we who are many form one body, and each member belongs to all the others.

Paul then applies this simple illustration to the church, which is comprised of many believers to form one body, and just as in the human body, there is diversity among its members. This diversity is fundamental to the understanding of the status and dignity of individual believers. In 1 Cor 12 and 14, Paul argues this principle more fully, his main thrust being that hidden parts of the body are often the most important while obvious parts, despite attracting the greatest attention, are of less consequence for its on-going maintenance. It is more disastrous if the brain malfunctions than if an eye is lost.

Paul stresses the unity of the local body of Christ. He does not write that each member belongs to Christ, which they obviously do by virtue of being "in Christ," but that "each member belongs to all the others." This is a beautiful way of expressing a church's interdependence and unity. Gifts are given for the building up of the local body of Christ. Although given to individuals, they are not for their blessing but for the benefit of the whole body.

Many believers think that they have been denied gifts; but this is not so. All gifts given to the church are for the sake of all. They are given in order that everyone can be built up so that, corporately, believers can progress in an understanding of God's purposes and love to the end that he will be glorified in the church.

A believer's transformation—making him more like Christ—is not an individualistic matter anymore than it was an individualistic concern for the Jew to make the pilgrimage from exile back to the promised land. His return was only achievable when he was part of the pilgrim community. Individually, it was highly unlikely that his return from Babylon could be achieved, but corporately it was possible.

So this transformation is experienced in the individual believer as he recognizes that he goes on a pilgrimage to the heavenly home with other believers in the church. Together they encourage each other as they benefit from the gifts God has given them. In Paul's thinking, being renewed in the image of Christ is a corporate concept of the church becoming like its savior (Eph 4:20–24; Col 3:10).

12:6 We have different gifts, according to the grace given us. If a man's gift is prophesying, let him use it in proportion to his faith.

In v. 3, Paul spoke of the grace that had been given to him. Now he applies the giving of grace to the Roman church. He is clearly concerned that the believers grasp the truth that there are different gifts bestowed on believers in the church through God's grace. A failure to appreciate this can lead to divisions as a result of petty jealousies and rivalries.

Many Christian fellowships have been divided over gifts because of pride, jealousy, and hurt. The danger of division is avoided when it is understood that God has given gifts according to his will. They are not inherited talents whose distribution among men is governed by genetic makeup. However, despite these gifts having a divine origin, churches often select leaders on the basis of talent, personality, status, and family, seeing these as indicative of divine gifting. Such appointments may place churches in danger of damage from pride and ambition.

Paul begins to specify gifts that are given by the Spirit. He does not mention that these gifts are the gifts of the Spirit as he does in his first letter to the Corinthians (1 Cor 12:8–11). Here, the gifts are simply the gifts that God has bestowed. This is an indication of Paul's "Trinitarian" understanding—a term that he, of course, does not use. He often attributes OT descriptions of God to either Christ or the Spirit (e.g., 1 Cor 8:6; 2 Cor 13:14. See also Phil 2:10–12, where the quotation from Isa 45:23b originally applied to Yahweh).

When Paul encourages the gift of prophecy, he qualifies its use by saying "let him use it in proportion to his faith." This exhortation is unlikely to refer to the confidence the recipient has in his powers of oratory as that would promote self-confidence, leading to arrogance. The term "faith" is likely to mean "faithfulness," as discussed earlier. A church should only encourage the gifts of its members when it sees them living in faithfulness to Christ. The exercising of gifts without the appropriate grace leads a church into a spiritual minefield.

Prophesying was clearly a common ministry in the early church. The NT prophets' responsibility was to apply the word of God. This had been the function of the prophets in the OT. They did not bring a new revelation to Israel but constantly reminded them of the covenant of which they were part. That is not to deny that they occasionally predicted the future or that they developed themes that had previously been known only in part. However, their main task was to remind the people that because of the covenant, Yahweh made claims upon them. Their preaching was essentially a reiteration of the promises and warnings of the covenant in which Israel was urged to walk obediently (Isa 40:1–5; Jer 34:1–10; Hos 14:1–3; Amos 5:4–5).

This was no less the function of the NT prophets. Their gift was to direct the church to the OT Scriptures, which spoke prophetically about the coming age. They were able to draw from those Scriptures the obligations of the new covenant and to urge the church to fulfill them. In this, God would be glorified; and, in turn, he would respond in blessing. Although the church was given teachers (v.7), the prophets' ministry also included teaching. It is possible that the prophet spoke with more authority—the Spirit of God empowering his message. Because of this, the word of God came to the people with a sense of "the Holy Spirit says" (Acts 13:2; 21:11).

It is clear from the first Corinthian letter that Paul thought highly of the gift of prophecy—a gift which he said was for believers (1 Cor 14:22): "But everyone who prophesies speaks to men for their strengthening, encouragement and comfort . . . he who prophesies edifies the church" (1 Cor 14:4).

12:7 If it is serving, let him serve; if it is teaching, let him teach.

The gift of serving is the next gift listed by Paul. While it is difficult to know exactly what he had in mind regarding this gift (and in 1 Cor 12:5 he states that there are different kinds of service), it is of interest that Paul placed serving between prophesying and teaching, suggesting that its place in church life was of great importance.

It has often been thought that "serving" refers to the meeting of practical needs within the local church and amongst needy believers in other churches. When he wrote the letter, Paul was on his way to Jerusalem with a gift for those who were suffering from poverty and he describes his anticipated visit as being "in the service of the saints" (Rom 15:25). In his first letter to the Corinthians, Paul commended to them the household of Stephanas because of their "service to the saints" (1 Cor 16:15–17).

The role of deacons in the early church has often been linked with the gift of "serving" (1 Tim 3:10, 13) as has the general expression of concern that believers show for one another within a fellowship (Rom 12:9–11; Gal 5:13). In his letter to the Ephesians, Paul says that apostles, prophets, evangelists, pastors, and teachers have been given to the church "to prepare God's people for works of service, so that the body of Christ may be built up" (Eph 4:12). While we shall consider the outworking of "works of service" later in the chapter, an alternative understanding of the gift of "serving" may be of interest.

At the opening of his letter, Paul assured the believers of his prayers by writing these words: "God, whom I serve with my whole heart in preaching the gospel of his Son, is my witness how constantly I remember you in my prayers" (Rom 1:9–10). Moreover, in Rom 15 he wrote: "I am a minister of Christ Jesus to the Gentiles with the priestly duty of proclaiming the gospel of God . . . Therefore I glory in Christ Jesus in my service to God" (Rom 15:16–17). It is, therefore, possible that Paul saw the gift of serving—the second gift in his Romans list—to be the proclamation of the gospel, i.e., the gift of evangelism (Eph 4:11–12).

Support for this view is found in the letter to the Corinthians. Paul—who sees his work as priestly ("serving at the altar" rather than at tables)—wrote that those who preach the Gospel should receive their living by it (1 Cor 9:13–14). In his second letter to the church, he reminded the Corinthians that he had served them by "preaching the gospel of God" (2 Cor 11:7–8). Finally, the letter to Timothy states: The glorious gospel of the blessed God was entrusted to me. I thank Christ Jesus our Lord, who has given me strength, that he considered me faithful, appointing me to his service" (1 Tim 1:11–12).

It is clear that those who did the work of evangelism exercised other gifts in the church. Philip—one of the seven deacons in Acts 6:1–6—became known as "Philip the evangelist" in his town of Caesarea (Acts 21:8–9) and Timothy—who was urged to devote himself to preaching and teaching in Ephesus (1 Tim 4:13–14)—was encouraged to "do the work of an evangelist" (2 Tim 4:5). Thus, if the gift of service is evangelism, Paul sees the proclamation of the gospel to be one of the foundational gifts to the church because of its prominent position in his list—a position not so suitable for its traditional meaning.

Teaching is the next gift to be mentioned. It may refer to the catechizing of new converts, enabling their understanding of basic Christian truths, or to its more public ministry to the gathered church. Whatever the form of teaching received by the Roman church, Paul commends the believers' whole-hearted obedience to it. As a result of teaching, they had been set free from sin and had become servants to righteousness (Rom 6:17–18). Paul appreciated how vital teaching was for the health of the church. It would prepare the congregation for service, building its members up in the knowledge of God and bringing them to maturity (Eph 4:11–14).

Teaching was a gift that the apostles exercised when they taught the young church in the days following Pentecost (Acts 2:42). Indeed, they recognized the danger of neglecting the gift when the practical needs of the infant church pressed in upon them. So, after the church had chosen seven wise, spirit-filled men from the congregation and the apostles had set them apart to ensure that the social needs of the believers were not overlooked, they gave themselves to prayer and teaching. The results were remarkable! (Acts 6:1–7).

Like the apostles, many Christian leaders feel the pressure of being expected to do a wide range of tasks in their congregations to the neglect of their teaching ministries. The consequence of yielding to such pressure is that believers are not well taught and are left exposed to false teachings. As a consequence, the word does not spread in the locality and the leaders are left exhausted. Even the Roman congregation, with its obedient assent to the teaching it received, had to be warned against its exposure to false teaching (Rom 16:17–19).

Men who have responsibility for teaching in a church need mentors like Jethro, who, on drawing alongside Moses, saw the pressure he was under and suggested the appointment of officials to lighten his load. Moses was then free to teach decrees and laws to the people as well as to settle major disputes (Exod 18:17–26). The NT shows that church leaders need to be part of a leadership team, which provides a forum for mutual support and understanding within the church. So we find Paul urging Titus to appoint elders in every town (Titus 1:5). Such men, like the apostles, corporately bore the load, each contributing his particular gift(s) to the building up of the church for which they were responsible. The support, understanding, and mutual encouragement necessary in church leadership cannot be provided by inter-church fraternalism alone, however valuable they may be. The NT does not recognize the "one-man ministry" that characterizes many churches. The "minister" is the church—the people of God—and it is their collective gifts that make Christian service possible. The church, of course, requires leadership to oversee the ministry in which the believing community is engaged, but this leadership is the community's servant rather that its dictator.

Timothy was told not to neglect his gifts of preaching and teaching but to be diligent in their use. He was also told to watch his life and doctrine closely. It is clear that "the knife can be blunted" through sin and laziness, to the detriment of the preacher/teacher and the congregation he serves.

12:8 If it is encouraging, let him encourage; if it is contributing to the needs of others, let him give generously; if it is leadership, let him govern diligently; if it is showing mercy, let him do it cheerfully.

Paul now urges those in the congregation with a gift of encouragement to exercise their gift. The Greek noun παρακλήσει (*paraklēsis*) allows for this to mean "bringing comfort," and this was how the term was used in some NT passages (Acts 15:22–31; Eph 6:21–22). It is the same term that Jesus used when he described the ministry of the Holy Spirit: ἄλλον παράκλητον δώσει ὑμῖν (*allon paraklēton dōsei humin*) "He will give you another Counselor" (John 14:16).

Paul himself benefited from encouragement. Barnabas whose name means "the son of encouragement," befriended Paul as a new convert, introducing him to the leadership of the church in Jerusalem (Acts 9:27). Moreover, he was Paul's co-worker on his first missionary journey during their time in Antioch (Acts 11:26). In his second letter to the Corinthian church, Paul told the believers that he and Timothy had been "comforted" by Titus and the church in Corinth at a very difficult time in their ministry (2 Cor 7:5–7), and, in a sensitive letter to Philemon, he expressed his gratitude for the encouragement he had received from Philemon's love for the saints (Phlm 4–7).

But is this encouragement and comfort what Paul had in mind when writing about the gift of encouragement? It is possible that the gift of encouragement was more a gift of exhortation: "he who exhorts, in exhortation" (Rom 12:8 NKJ), the Greek allowing for this meaning of the term. This would fit neatly into Paul's list as it is the gift that follows prophesying, serving (evangelizing), and teaching—all gifts concerned with the ministry of the word.

Encouraging by means of exhortation can be done by members of the congregation. For example, the believers in Thessalonica were urged to "encourage each other" about the coming of the Lord (1 Thess 4:13–18; 5:11). However, it is probable that the gift refers to a more public ministry of encouragement (Acts 13:14–52; 14:21–22; 1 Cor 14:3; 1 Thess 2:1–3, where "appeal" [NIV] is "encouragement" or "exhortation;" 2 Tim 4:2; Titus 1:7–9). The following is written to Timothy: "Until I come, devote yourself to the public reading of Scripture, to preaching and to teaching" (1 Tim 4:13). In this NIV translation, "preaching" (παρακλήσει *paraklēsis* "comfort") would be better translated "encouraging" or "exhorting. "To conclude, if the gift of encouragement is a public ministry, its exercising in a congregation would reflect the ministry of the Godhead to his people—God encouraging them through the Scriptures he has given for their edification (Rom 15: 4–5).

The next gift in the list—"contributing to the poor"—is usually seen to refer to the support of needy believers. Paul's desire is that this gift be exercised "generously." The Greek carrying the idea of giving without reservation. The idea is of a bountiful generosity that springs from a desire to help those in need. Paul uses the verb μεταδίδωμι (*metadidōmi*)—which can be translated "impart," "share," or "give"—on three other occasions in his letters. On one occasion, he uses the sense as translated by the NIV: "He who has been stealing must steal no longer, but must work, doing something useful with his own hands, that he may have something to share with those in need" (Eph 4:28).

However, in 1 Thessalonians and Romans, the term is used differently: "We loved you so much that we were delighted to share with you not only the gospel of God but our lives as well, because you had become so dear to us . . . For you know that we dealt with each of you as a father deals with his children, encouraging, comforting and urging you to live lives worthy of God" (1 Thess 2:8, 11–12). Here, Paul uses the term "share" to describe the proclamation of Christ as well as the giving of himself and his co-workers.

He uses the term at the beginning of his letter to the Romans where the NIV translates it as "impart": "I long to see you so that I may impart to you some spiritual gift to make you strong—that is, that you and I may be mutually encouraged by each other's faith . . . That is why I am so eager to μεταδιδωμι (*metadidōmi*) "share/preach the Gospel . . ." also to you who are at Rome" (Rom 1:11–12, 15). Paul seems to be using the term to speak of his *personal* imparting of the good news, to the end that he and the believers would be encouraged in their faith.

The term translated "to make strong" in Rom 1:11 στηριδω (*stērizō*) can be translated "to establish" and it is used by Paul at the close of his letter: "Now to him who is able to *establish* you by my Gospel and the proclamation of Jesus Christ " (Rom 16:25a). This verse together with Rom 1:11 suggests that it was Paul's desire that the Roman believers would be *encouraged* and *established* by God in their faith when they received Paul's spiritual gift, that is, his *ministry of the word,* which he would *impart* to them or *share* with them when he came to visit them *personally.*

So, the phrase under consideration in Rom 12:8 would perhaps be better understood as "he who imparts or shares the things of God and himself, with the result that believers are encouraged and established in their faith." This understanding reflects the ministry of Jesus to his disciples. He shared with them the good news and gave himself for their blessing and establishment.

Paul says in Rom 12:8 that this gift of "imparting," "sharing" or "contributing to the needs of others" must be done "generously." This term ἁπλότητι (*aplotēti*) also means (with) singleness, simplicity, sincerity, and frankness. It richly describes aspects of effective ministry to believers and personal work among them. In conclusion, it seems possible that the gift of "contributing to the needs of others" is pastoral ministry (Eph 4:12), and a believer gifted with this spiritual gift to the church is a pastor. Elsewhere Paul has written:

> It was he who gave some to be apostles, some to be prophets, some to be pastors and teachers, to prepare God's people for works of service, so that the body of Christ may be built up until we all reach unity in the faith and in the knowledge of the Son of God and become mature, attaining to the whole measure of the fullness of Christ. (Eph 4:11–13)

Next Paul addresses himself to the leaders of the congregation, writing to them that, if leadership is their gift, they must "govern diligently." It is no surprise that leadership is listed with gifts that benefit the work of the Gospel in the local church. Its diligent exercise is crucial, as ineffective leadership results in an undisciplined church where lives are damaged. Extreme outcomes of bad leadership were on display in Corinth where there was toleration of incest (1 Cor 5:1–2),[662] an involvement in occult practices (1 Cor 10:21–22), a lack of propriety in worship (1 Cor 11:2–16; 14:33b–35), unresolved divisions (1 Cor 11:18), disrespect for the Lord's Supper (1 Cor 11:17–34), and disorderly worship. Crucially, there was a denial of the resurrection (1 Cor 15:12–18). Understandably, these issues necessitated Paul's detailed instructions to correct (1 Cor 14:26–33).

The leadership of a local church was the province of elders who were set apart for the task (Titus 1:5;). Their appointment was not to be made in haste as the scrutiny of their lives was essential (1 Tim 3:1–7; 5:22; Titus 1:6–9). Their work was extremely demanding. In writing to the Thessalonian believers, Paul urged them to "respect those who work hard among you . . . Hold them in the highest regard in love because of their work" (1 Thess 5:12–13). It was demanding because their ministry involved preaching and teaching—with all of the resulting pastoral needs of people seeking to apply what they had heard—as well as the oversight of the church's affairs (1 Tim 5:17; Titus 1:9). In addition to these demands, all their dealings had to be conducted with a godly attitude (1 Pet 5:1–3).

The comments I cited from Paul's Corinthian letter give some insight into a church's oversight. When the congregation gathered for worship its meetings had to be ordered and organized, the practicing of spiritual gifts had to be controlled—and the presence of gossiping women had to be managed. The

---

[662] Taking a stepmother (as the verse implies) is a prohibited relationship but is not strictly incest. Incest legally applies to one's own birth mother.

Lord's Supper had to be celebrated in a worthy fashion and ungodly believers had to be warned and disciplined. In addition to all this, elders had to vigorously refute those who opposed sound doctrine (Titus 1:9, 11, 13) while carrying, at the same time, the worry of potential accusation (1 Tim 5:19).

The term that Paul uses for "leader" (Rom 12:8), προϊστάμενος (*proistamenos*), can also be translated "being over," "superintending," and "presiding"—and it was God's household over which the elders had to exercise leadership (1 Tim 3:15). The same term that is applied to an overseer's and deacon's management of their homes and families in 1 Tim 3:4,12.

As Paul appreciated from the situation in the Corinthian church, leadership could be of poor quality. So he urges the leaders in the church in Rome to exercise their gift "diligently" (NIV). The term translated "diligently" can be translated "eagerly," "enthusiastically," and "zealously." It can also be translated "speedily" and "hastily." Perhaps in choosing this term, Paul had in mind the re-building of the temple in Jerusalem during Ezra's time: "The work is being carried on with diligence and is making rapid progress" (Ezra 5:8). Paul would have loved to have heard a similar report from the leaders of all the churches because he would then know that the lives of believers and the churches to which they belonged were being built up.

Finally, in the Romans verse under consideration Paul writes to the believers "if it is showing mercy, let him do it cheerfully." It is difficult to be certain who Paul is referring to as recipients of mercy, what the gift entailed, and who exercised it.

The term translated "showing mercy" can also mean "has or shows mercy or pity." Paul used this term when speaking of the Lord's mercy in 1 Cor 7:25, and in Phil 2:27 when speaking of God's mercy to the sick Epaphroditus. The Romans text is Paul's only reference to mercy being extended by and to a believer.

The same term is used in Matt 5:7 when Jesus promises that God will show mercy to the merciful, and in Matt 18:33 when the wicked servant in the parable was rebuked for not showing mercy, Jesus equating mercy with "forgiving your brother from the heart." In addition, Jesus spoke of the rich man, in torment in hell, asking Abraham to show mercy to him (v.24).

The Phil 2 text cited above, however, informs us that mercy was shown by God to Epaphroditus and to Paul without the context of forgiveness. God took pity on Paul's very sick companion who had travelled on behalf of the Philippian church to meet the apostle's needs. In doing this God had also shown mercy to Paul, who would have been heartbroken, had Epaphroditus died. Clearly in this case the showing of mercy was not about God forgiving the two men but caring for them in their frailty.

So, while the term can be used to speak of forgiveness, it is also used to speak of compassion to the needy and it is likely that this meaning is the context for "showing mercy" in Rom 12:8. This gift would have been exercised, at the very least, by deacons in the church—men who were set apart for the task of dealing with pressing social concerns in the fellowship so that the prophets, evangelists, teachers, pastors, and elders could give full attention to exercising their gifts (Acts 6:1–6; 1 Tim 3:8–13). Perhaps Paul had the deacons in mind when he wrote this to the church in Rome.

He urged that the gift of showing mercy be carried out with "cheerfulness." This reflects the wisdom of the book of Proverbs, which says: "a cheerful heart is good medicine, but a crushed spirit dries up the bones" (Prov 17:22). The term "cheerfully" ἱλαρότητι (*hilaroteti*) means "with gladness," "with graciousness," "without reluctance," and even "with hilarity"—qualities and attitudes that would be invaluable to deacons carrying out their role of "showing mercy" to the needy!

In conclusion, it is possible that in Rom 12:6–8 Paul encourages the prophets, evangelists, teachers, preachers, pastors, elders, and deacons to exercise their gifts in the church in Rome. Like Timothy, they would probably exercise more than one gift, fulfilling their calling so that together they would "prepare God's people for works of service, so that the body of Christ may be built up until all reach unity in the faith and in the knowledge of the Son of God" (Eph 4:12–13) What a powerful, public display of a living sacrifice to God in Rome that would be!

THE MESSIAH KING AND HIS PEOPLE'S CHARACTER (12:9–21)

Love must be sincere. Hate what is evil; cling to what is good. Be devoted to one another in brotherly love. Honor one another above yourselves. Never be lacking in zeal, but keep your spiritual fervor, serving the Lord. Be joyful in hope, patient in affliction, faithful in prayer. Share with God's people who are in need. Practice hospitality.

Bless those who persecute you; bless and do not curse. Rejoice with those who rejoice; mourn with those who mourn. Live in harmony with one another. Do not be proud, but be willing to associate with people of low position.

Do not be conceited. Do not repay anyone evil for evil. Be careful to do what is right in the eyes of everybody. If it is possible, as far as it depends on you, live at peace with everyone. Do not take revenge, my friends, but leave room for God's wrath, for it is written: "It is mine to avenge; I will repay," says the Lord. On the contrary: "If your enemy is hungry, feed him; if he is thirsty, give him something to drink. In doing this, you will heap burning coals on his head." Do not be overcome by evil, but overcome evil with good. (Romans 12:9–21)

In Rom 12:9–21, Paul returns to his concern that the believers in Rome live holy lives as priests of the living God (v.1), so that they can offer to him a church that is "a living sacrifice, holy and pleasing." He has urged all of the believers to evaluate their lives seriously and honestly (Rom 12:3; Matt 7:1–5), reminding them of the gifts that God has given the church (Rom 12:6–8). As they benefit from these, Paul hopes that the corporate body of believers will rise to the challenge to renew its mind.

In the passage we are now considering, Paul begins to tell the church how it can stop conforming to the world and become a transformed, renewed, believing community. His appeal echoes the teaching of Jesus in his Sermon on the Mount (Matt 5–7).[663] Indeed, it seems possible that Paul applied the teaching of Jesus to his disciples to the context of the local church (Matt 7:24–27; Eph 2:22).

The following table compares the parallel themes found in the Gospel and the letter.

Romans 12:9–21	Matthew 5–7
Theme: "Love must be sincere" or "Sincere Love."	Theme: "Love you neighbor as yourself"

---

[663] See, Fitzmyer, *Romans*, 652. Barrett, *Romans*, 240, considers Paul to be using a Semitic source. This probably originated in the very early church because of the presence of participles instead of imperatives. Further support for dependence on Matthew is being provided by Stuart Laurer, a PhD student. His case is that the Gospel of Matthew was a standard text in the early church. It was used by the apostles and left with the churches they established as an authoritative reference source. Laurer's work focuses on the saying in 1 Cor 4:6: "Do not go beyond what is written." His conclusions suggest that Matthew's Gospel was distributed widely throughout the apostolic ministry.

Romans 12:9–21	**Matthew 5–7**
v. 10 Hate what is evil; cling to what is good.	If your right hand causes you to sin. Blessed are the pure in heart 5:8; 5:29–30; 6:19–21, 24.
v. 10 Be devoted to one another in brotherly love.	You are the salt of the earth (salt being a symbol of lasting concord) (5:13; 7:12)
v. 11 Honor one another above yourselves.	Blessed are the poor in spirit (5:3)
v. 12 Never be lacking in zeal, but keep your spiritual fervor, serving the Lord.	Blessed are those who hunger and thirst after righteousness (5:6; 6:33)
v. 12 Be joyful in hope,	Rejoice and be glad because great is your reward in heaven (5:12)
v.12 patient in affliction,	Blessed are you when people insult you (5:10–12, 38–42)
v. 12 faithful in prayer.	And when you pray, do not be like the hypocrites (6:5–15)
v. 13 Share with God's people who are in need. Practice hospitality.	Blessed are the merciful (5:7; 6:1–4)
v. 14 Bless those who persecute you; bless and do not curse.	Pray for those who persecute you (5:44)
v.16 Rejoice with those who rejoice; mourn (weep) with those who mourn (weep).	Blessed are those who mourn (5:4)
v. 16 Live in harmony with one another.	Anyone who is angry with his brother will be subject to judgment (5:21–26)
v. 16 Do not be proud, but be willing to associate with people of low position. Do not be conceited	Blessed are the meek (5:5, 22b)
v. 17 Do not repay anyone evil for evil	Do not resist (5:39)
v. 17 Be careful to do what is right in the eyes of everybody	You are the light of the world (5:14–16)
v. 18–19 If it is possible, as far as it depends on you, live at peace with everyone. Do not take	Blessed are the peacemakers (or peace-lovers 5:7, 23–24) Every tree

Romans 12:9–21	Matthew 5–7
revenge, my friends, but leave room for God's wrath, for it is written: "It is mine to avenge; I will repay," says the Lord.	that does not bear good fruit is cut down and thrown into the fire (7:17)
v. 20 On the contrary: "If your enemy is hungry, feed him; if he is thirsty, give him something to drink. In doing this, you will heap burning coals on his head."	Love your enemies and pray for those who persecute you (5:44, 40–42)
v. 21 Do not be overcome by evil, but overcome evil with good.	If you forgive men when they sin against you (6:14)

Paul begins his exhortation by introducing its theme—"Sincere Love." His desire is that the greatest fruit of the Spirit will be demonstrated in the believers' lives. This will transform the church in Rome, affecting those within the fellowship and those outside in the wider community.

When the believers heard this passage read, they would have taken from it a challenging pattern for individual living. While Paul's exhortation in chapter 12 is to individuals in the congregation, it must be remembered that his emphasis throughout the letter has been *the church*—the body of believers. Although his desire was that the lives of the individual believers would be built up (Rom 15:2; 1 Thess 5:11), his greatest desire was that the local church would be built up to become a "dwelling in which God lives by his Spirit" (Eph 2:22).

12:9 Love what is sincere. Hate what is evil; cling to what is good. As previously mentioned,

Paul begins his exhortation with what seems to be its theme: "Sincere Love." The adjective "sincere" ἀνυπόκριτος (*anupokritos*) "without hypocrisy," is related to the verb ὑποκρινεσθαι (*hypokrinesthai*) "to answer." It was used to speak of the reply an actor gave on stage and was associated with the pretense of the performer in his role. Affection that is a pretense of friendship is odious (1 John 4:20–21). It is the very opposite of Christian love, which must be the expression of genuine concern.

In his letter to the Galatians, Paul wrote that love ἀγάπη (*agapē*) was one of the fruits of the Spirit (Gal 5:22), and in his first letter to the Corinthians, he described the transformed attitudes of people who display this love (1 Cor 13:4–8a). In 1 Cor 13:13, he says that it is the greatest spiritual fruit that we can exhibit, reflecting the love that God has for his people (Rom 5:8). Indeed, it is the essence of God himself, for he is its source (Rom 5:8; 1 John 4:7–19). So, how do the believers in Rome love in sincerity? Paul cuts straight to the chase by telling them to engage their wills. They are to "hate what is evil."

God's standard is clear—he hates evil (Amos 5:14–15; Ps 97:10). Those who would have fellowship with him must share his concern and values. Despite the values of those around, the Roman believers must be concerned about pleasing God alone (Rom 12:21). This is the only time that Paul—or any NT writer—tells believers to "hate" evil, ἀποστυγοῦντες (*apostugountes*) being better translated "abhor." As mentioned, it is a position that God himself takes and which he wants to see his people follow. After bringing the children of Israel out of Egypt, God comforted them with these words: "I will not abhor you ... you will be my people" (Lev 26:11–12). However, they broke covenant with him and his abhorrence of them returned (Lev 26:14–17, 30; Amos 6:8). It is also an attitude that King David displayed. In the psalms, he wrote that he "hated and abhorred falsehood" and he expressed his abhorrence for men who actively rebelled against God (Ps 119:163; Ps 139:19–22).

The believers in Rome were told to abhor evil—the objects of David's abhorrence being examples of the evils they should abhor. Jesus said that men are "unclean" because of the evils that come from within, such as "evil thoughts, sexual immorality, theft, murder, adultery, greed, malice, deceit, lewdness, envy, slander, arrogance and folly" (Mark 7:20–23; Luke 6:45). He also said that his disciples would be the recipients of evil because of their allegiance to him (Matt 5:11).

The Christians in Rome were to abhor evil within their hearts and any expression of it in society. If the church had access to the Gospel of Matthew (as has been suggested), the believers would know from Jesus' Sermon on the Mount that in being recipients of evil as a result of their allegiance to Christ, they must not hate the evil-doers but take encouragement from the fact that persecution will bring blessing.

While hating what is evil, the believers were told to "cling to what is good." The phrase suggests a desperate situation, like a drowning man in a storm clinging to a beam of wood, and feeling so weak that he does not know how he can survive. All he must do is keep on clinging! The problem is that this understanding places all the responsibility on the believer to keep hold of what is good, despite all the pressures that buffet him.

The word translated "cling" can be translated "join oneself to," "join closely together," or "unite." It is the same term used by Paul in 1 Corinthians, where he writes: "Do you not know that he who unites himself with a prostitute is one with her in body? For it is said, 'The two will become one flesh.' But he who unites himself with the Lord is one with him in Spirit" (1 Cor 6:16–17). In light of this usage, perhaps Paul is writing that the Roman believers must abhor evil by changing their allegiance and uniting to what is good. The union is an act of their wills, reflecting the covenant of marriage. The believers are to commit themselves to the Lord and his people.

12:10 Be devoted to one another in brotherly love. Honor one another above yourselves.

The exhortation to be devoted to one another in brotherly love is an outworking of sincere love (v. 9). Paul uses φιλαδελφία (*philadelphia*) "brotherly love" in one other letter: "Now about brotherly love we do not need to write to you, for you yourselves have been taught by God to love each other. And in fact you do love all the brothers throughout Macedonia. Yet we urge you, brothers, to do so more and more" (1 Thess 4:9–10).

In his letter to the Romans, Paul's instruction is clearer than the "more and more" of 1 Thess 4:10. He tells the believers to be "devoted" in brotherly love—taking this love to a deeper, more personal, and committed level. The term translated "devoted" is used nowhere else in the Scriptures.

Peter, when writing to the scattered believers, also urged a deepening of love for each other. He recognized the sincerity of their brotherly love but urged them to love "fervently" or "intently" (1 Pet 1:22). His appeal is consistent with Paul's that the believers in Rome, benefiting from the ministry of the Scriptures, make devoted brotherly love a hallmark of the church.

Being devoted to one another is not a directive to accept everything that a fellow Christian does. Such mindless acceptance will not bring glory to God but will be an opportunity for Satan to exploit. God was devoted to the Jewish people throughout the long history of the OT—but that commitment resulted in tough action. He not only spoke against them when they were breaking his commandments but also warned them that he would use the armies of mighty Babylon to wield the sword when they repeatedly refused to hear and obey his word. So, being devoted to one another may mean the leaders of the church exercising "tough love" in situations where the word of God is being rejected or ignored. Such "tough love" was prescribed by Paul for the church in Corinth when it refused to deal with the case of incest (1 Cor 5–6), and is seen in the warnings that Jesus gave the churches in the book of Revelation (Rev 2:1–3:22).

Paul now tells the believers to "honor one another above yourselves." Honoring one another would have been hard enough for the Jewish and uncircumcised Gentile believers in Rome, but honoring each other above themselves would have seemed well-nigh impossible. Another challenge for the believers would have been the honoring of disadvantaged brethren in the congregation. This would have been particularly challenging for those in leadership positions. However, in his letter to the Corinthians, Paul leaves us in no doubt as to God's wishes in this matter (1 Cor 12:22–26).

It would have been a crushing command for the believers but for the fact that God had sent his Spirit into their hearts (Rom 8:15), bringing with him a different set of values from the ones they had lived by (Rom 8:9, 12–13; Gal 5:16–26). Later, when writing to the church at Philippi, Paul referred to a very early Christian hymn. It shows how the infant church dwelt on the example of Christ's death and how believers drew inspiration to consider others better than themselves. The hymn has an introduction:

> Do nothing out of selfish ambition or vain conceit, but in humility consider others better than yourselves. Each of you should look not only to your own interests, but also to the interests of others. Your attitude should be the same as that of Christ Jesus.

The hymn follows, focusing on the example of Christ:

> Who, being in the very nature God, did not consider equality with God something to be grasped, but made himself nothing, taking the very nature of a servant, being made in human likeness, And being found in appearance as a man, he humbled himself and became obedient to death—even death on a cross! Therefore God exalted him to the highest place and gave him the name that is above every name, that at the name of Jesus every knee should bow, in heaven and on earth and under the earth, and every tongue confess that Jesus Christ is Lord, to the glory of God the Father. (Phil 2:6–11)

12:11 Never be lacking in zeal, but keep your spiritual fervor, serving the Lord.

Paul has just exhorted the believers to be devoted to each other in brotherly love and to honor each other above themselves. He now exhorts them to maintain their zeal.

A believer's first rush of excitement on discovering the glorious reality of God's love can easily become fossilized. An improvement in living standards (resulting from a more disciplined lifestyle) can become the purpose of life and an intellectualization of new-found faith can replace the warmth of first love.

The zeal of loving and serving Christ can disappear like the morning dew—it happened to Israel's love for Yahweh (Hos 13:3) and sadly it happens to Christians' love for Christ (Gal 1:6; 2 Tim 4:10; Rev 2:4).

The NIV translation of this verse gives the impression that Paul is exhorting the church to be "zealous."[664] Certainly, being zealous was a characteristic of his people, the Jews. In Rom 10, Paul testifies that the Jews display ζῆλος (*zēlos*) "zeal" in the defense of their faith (v.2), and in his letter to the Philippians he writes retrospectively of himself, "as for zeal ζῆλος (*zēlos*) persecuting the church" (Phil 3:6). However, he uses a term here which means "diligence" or "earnestness," ζέοντες (*zeontes*) translating literally as "boiling in spirit." So, the opening phrase of v.11 would be better translated "never be lacking in *diligence* or *earnestness*." Paul uses this term again when writing his second letter to the Corinthians (2 Cor 7:11; 8:7–8) and in all cases it is translated "earnestness" by the NIV translators.

Perhaps Paul is referring to what he has just written—urging the believers to be diligent, with no hint of laziness, in their devoted love and preference for each other. The writer to the Hebrews exhorted the Christians to "keep on loving each other as brothers" (Heb 13:1), having previously written: "God is not unjust; he will not forget your work and the love you have shown him as you have helped his people and continue to help them. We want each of you to show this same diligence to the very end, in order to make your hope sure. We do not want you to become lazy, but to imitate those who through faith and patience inherit what has been promised" (Heb 6:10–12).

As the believers in Rome heard the letter read to them, they heard an exhortation to be "fervent in spirit, serving the Lord" (NKJ—a better translation than NIV). The term fervor ζέοντες (*zeontes*) can be translated "hot." It is a

---

[664] The Zealot movement, which emerged out of the Maccabean revolt (167–160 BC), takes its name from this term. Its adherents drew their inspiration from the story of Phinehas, the priest. Burdened with the dishonor brought to God by Israel's idolatry, he slew an Israelite man and a Midianite woman in their blatant act of immorality, thereby staying the wrath of God from destroying Israel: "The LORD said to Moses, 'Phinehas son of Eleazar, the son of Aaron, the priest, has turned my anger away from the Israelites; for he was as zealous as I am for my honour among them, so that in my zeal I did not put an end to them'" (Num 25:10–11). As this story was well-known in Judaism and in the early church, Paul's appeal to be zealous would be heard by many in light of it. Of course, the believers were not to execute judgment in their zeal but to direct people to the one who turned God's wrath away from sinners by his propitiatory death (Rom 3:25–26).

term that implies passion. The RSV translates it "aglow" in an attempt to portray the passion of the term.

But how can the believers maintain fervor? Paul has given the answer in the earlier part of his letter. By reflecting on who Christ is and what God has done for them through his death their hearts will be moved (Rom 8:1–3). This means that the believers must put themselves under the authority of the Scriptures, for these were written for their instruction (Rom 10:14b;17;15:4).

The call to serve the Lord has a textual variant. Some MSS[665] have δουλευοντες τυ καίρω (*douleuntes tu kairō*) "serve the hour" instead of κυρίω (*kyriō*) "Lord." The latter is possibly the result of a copyist's confusion of an abbreviation where *Kō* has been read as *Krō*.[666]

12:12 Be joyful in hope, patient in affliction, faithful in prayer.

Paul writes to the believers in Rome telling them that they should be "joyful in hope." He has already written sublimely about this theme in the opening verses of chapter 5. Having described the extraordinary access that the believers have to God through Christ (vv. 1–2a), he then explains the hope that galvanizes Christians. He does not exhort the believers *to* hope, but tells them of the sure and certain hope they have of sharing in the glory of God (Rom5:2b).

Having explained the sufferings that the church is called to endure as she bears witness to the one who has called her, Paul writes "and hope does not disappoint us because God has poured out his love into our hearts by the Holy Spirit, whom he has given us" (Rom 5:5). Clearly, this hope sustains and empowers the church—it is a hope that is founded in God's love for his people.

Paul will reaffirm the importance of the Scriptures in chapter 15, when he will writes "For everything that was written in the past was written to teach us, so that through endurance and the encouragement of the Scriptures we might have hope" (Rom 15:4). At the close of the chapter, Paul will describe God as being the God of hope who fills the believers with all joy and peace so that they will overflow with hope by the power of the Holy Spirit (Rom 15:13).

In other words, the future for the Roman Christians is so glorious that joy ought to characterize their lives. No matter what happens—and appalling persecution was soon to come—their hope remains a sure certainty. Loss of status, health, wealth, friends, etc. could not affect their certainty, for their

---

[665] D and G.

[666] See, Metzger, *Text*, 187.

inheritance is laid up in heaven (1 Cor 2:9; 1 Pet 1:4–5). Only the Christians in Rome could rejoice in what lay ahead. For everyone else, death would be the entrance into God's presence where they will be judged. For the Christians, it will be altogether different. Instead of this frightening scenario, death will be their glorious entrance into the Lord's presence and into joy unspeakable. The Christians' hope should permeate their lives so that they are characterized by joy (Ps 16:11; John 16:20; Rom 14:17; 15:13; 1 John 1:4).

Paul writes that they should be "patient in affliction." The term "affliction" θλίψις (*thlipsis*) should be translated "tribulation," which has a more serious tone. He had written to them in chapter 5: ". . . we also rejoice in our sufferings (tribulations), because we know that suffering (tribulation) produces perseverance; perseverance, character; and character, hope" (Rom 5:3–4).

Should any of the believers be experiencing tribulation, much of Paul's letter would prove to be an enormous comfort and encouragement. As Paul says earlier in the letter:

> "I consider that our present sufferings (tribulations) are not worth comparing with the glory that will be revealed in us. . . . We ourselves, who have the firstfruits of the Spirit, groan inwardly as we wait eagerly for our adoption as sons, the redemption of our bodies. . . . If we hope for what we do not have, we wait for it patiently. . . . Who shall separate us from the love of Christ? Shall trouble or hardship or persecution or famine or nakedness or danger or sword? . . . No, in all these things we are more than conquerors through him who loved us . . ." (Rom 8:18–39).

The patience in tribulation that Paul desired the church to have is rooted in her hope in the Lord Jesus Christ. This hope marked out the believers in Thessalonica.. Paul wrote to the church there, commending the believers for their patience in tribulation (1 Thess 1:3b; 2 Thess 1:4).

Being faithful in prayer was essential if the believers were to be patient in tribulation and joyful in hope. Prayer is about committing ourselves and the things that concern us into the hands of God. When we are confident that our lives are in his hands we can know the sort of confidence that these verses speak about. When we are confident in the unchanging dependability of God's covenant love, we are empowered to face the problems of life (Rom 5:1ff; Jas 1:2–8; 1 Pet 4:12–16). It is then that we can share in the psalmist's experience that we shall not fear what men will do to us (Ps 27:1–3).

Prayer is the natural expression of spiritual life. When Paul was conquered by the realization that Jesus was the Christ and had been raised from the dead, spiritual life flowed through his soul. When Ananias was told by the angel to go to Paul and pray for the restoration of Paul's sight, Ananias was told "he is praying" (Acts 9:11). Spiritual life begins with prayer, and prayer upholds it. The Acts of the Apostles demonstrates that just as prayer was vital to Jesus (cf. Matt 14:23; 14:23; 26:36; Luke 3:21; 5:16; 6:12; 9:28), so it was to the church he left behind (Acts 1:14; 2:42; 3:1; 6:4; 12:5; 16:13–16).

If the believers in Rome are not faithful in prayer, there will be no possibility of them living lives that will corporately make their church a living sacrifice, and no possibility that they will patiently bear the awful tribulations yet to come.

12:13 Share with God's people who are in need. Practice hospitality.

One of the characteristics of the early church that made an impact on the unconverted was their care for one another (Acts 2:44–45; 4:32–35; 6:1–4). This sprang from their brotherly love and was expressed in many ways. Here, Paul identifies a specific aspect of care—that of sharing with those in need. This was a ministry that he benefited from himself when the church at Philippi met his needs while in chains (Phil 4:10, 14–16, 18). How staggering it must have been for the people of Rome to see wealthy Christians being concerned for those Christians who had very little—if anything—of this world's goods.

The Gospel abolishes all sorts of barriers. The removal of social distinctions is because believers are loved and valued by the God who has made them in his own image. They know that only the death of Jesus was sufficient to redeem them from the kingdom of darkness and the guilt of sin, and that the cost of this redemption underscored the value God placed on them all.

This injunction to care for one another regularly appears in the NT (Acts 24:23; Gal 6:10; Eph 4:28; Phil 2:25; 1 Tim 6:18; Heb 13:16). The apostle clearly could not conceive of a believing community not giving care towards those who were in need as his letters to the Corinthians make abundantly clear (1 Cor 16:1–4; 2 Cor 8–9). It is thought by some that there is the possibility of a veiled hint that the Roman church was providing for the destitute members of the impoverished Jerusalem church.[667]

Paul's comments to Timothy are interesting in this regard. Paul is quite specific on who qualifies for help in the church in Ephesus: "Give proper recognition to those widows who are really in need" (1 Tim 5:3). "No widow

---

[667] So Fitzmyer, *Romans*, 655.

may be put on the list of widows unless she is over sixty, has been faithful to her husband, and is well known for her good deeds . . ." (1 Tim 5:9–10). However, "If any woman who is a believer has widows in her family, she should help them and not let the church be burdened with them, so that the church can help those who are really in need" (1 Tim 5:16; 5:4,8). There are few things more disgraceful than Christians who neglect the needs of elderly parents, preferring to invest their time and gifts into the life of their local church while leaving others to make up for their lack of care. Jesus spoke against those Jews who avoided family obligations. By saying that all they had was "Corban," devoted to God (Mark 7:11) they were able to claim that their money was not theirs to use—it was God's! Such a "tax haven" was abhorrent to Jesus. Christian duty is to provide for our families (1 Tim 5:8), especially needy parents!

Hospitality was an important demonstration of the Gospel in the days of the early church (3 John 3–8). As Christian workers moved around the empire, there were few places where they could stay safely. The inns were not the most desirable of places and would expose itinerant preachers (such as Tychicus, Eph 6:21–22) to physical and moral danger. The *Didache*—a second century document of basic Christian teaching—instructed the believers to extend hospitality for no more than three nights. If the one being entertained was a true servant of Christ, he would not want to stay longer, being anxious to move on in order to fulfill his ministry. The implication is that the early church discovered how easy it was for some unscrupulous people to present themselves as dedicated servants of Christ in order to take advantage of hospitality in the homes of caring Christians.

When writing his letter, Paul tells the believers about the hospitality that he had received in the home of Gaius (Rom 16:23) and commends Phoebe to them for their help and hospitality when she arrives (Rom 16:1–2). When writing to Timothy about the eligibility of widows for church help, the author says that one of the conditions was their giving of hospitality (1 Tim 5:10, and John commends Gaius for his hospitality to fellow workers in the Gospel (3 John 5–8).

From the above citations it is possible to get the impression that hospitality was merely given to itinerant preachers and visitors from afar, but Peter encourages the practice of willing hospitality within the local church (1 Pet 4:9).

12:14 Bless those who persecute you; bless and do not curse.

Paul extends the principles of Christian living to the area of personal persecution.[668]

At first sight, it seems that v.14 should be relocated before v.17, a verse which introduces a section concerning the pressure from hostile relationships. Sadly, it appears that Paul sees the need to advise faithful believers in Rome on their response to persecution within the church (Rom 2:1; 14:10–13).

Paul was writing out of experience as he had enemies within the wider church. Some of his greatest opponents were "believing" Jews who saw him as a betrayer of all that was eternally true, i.e., a betrayer of what God had given to Moses. These "believing" Jews—including circumcised Gentiles—would have applauded Paul if he had led the Gentiles into the fold of Judaism through their submission to circumcision. The hatred that his non-compliance generated is difficult to appreciate but is evident throughout his letters and the Acts of the Apostles (Gal 6:12; 1 Thess 2:13–16; Acts 21:20–22; 23:12–22).

In urging the believers to bless those who persecute them, Paul was not asking them to abandon principles of justice. In Rom 13:1ff., he will explain the God-appointed role of rulers for maintaining justice, and in 1 Cor 6:1–8 he urges believers to seek settlement of their disputes from the church leadership. There is no suggestion that we have to abandon justice within the church in order to bless. Indeed, a characteristic of the early church was its anxiety to uphold the laws of the state. By asking the Roman believers to bless their enemies, Paul was effectively saying that they should pray for them—not seeking their humiliation or destruction (Matt 5:44).

The object of all discipline must be that the offender is restored to fellowship and welcomed back with all the forgiveness that God gives to repentant sinners. The Scriptures do not ask us to do anything more than what God would do himself. He forgives only when there is genuine repentance, and when he has to punish never delights in its implementation. Likewise, Christians can only forgive those who have wronged them when there is genuine repentance. Where there is no repentance, there can be no forgiveness, and the resulting pain can be hard to bear for the Christian who has been

---

[668] Braaten, "Romans," 12:14–21, 291–29, considers the genre of the passage to be a moral discourse with a wisdom flavor that has parallels in other religions. However, Paul's ethic is rooted in the love of God, which is displayed in the giving up his Son to death (Rom 5:8). In that sense, there is no comparison between this and the texts of other faiths.

wronged. Clearly the Christian should always want reconciliation and be ready to forgive. If the law has been broken and due process, as described by Paul in 1 Corinthians 6, has failed to resolve the issue, a Christian must feel empowered to seek legal advice.[669] However, in the pursuit of justice, he must pray for his brother and not delight in his downfall.[670]

12:15 *Rejoice with those who rejoice; mourn with those who mourn.*

It may be that Paul is referring to the normal events in life when he invites the believers to rejoice with fellow believers, events such as births and marriages within the church. However, he usually uses the term "rejoice" in the context of suffering and hope—suffering for Christ and hoping in him (cf. Phil 2:17–18; 4:4–7; Col 1:24). This reflects the teaching that Jesus gave to his disciples in the Sermon on the Mount (Matt 5:10–12; Luke 6:22–23) and is in agreement with Peter's teaching (1 Pet 1:6–9; 4:12–16 where Peter uses a term meaning "rejoice/exult").

When writing to the Philippians, Paul contemplated the possibility of martyrdom and invited the believers to rejoice with him: ". . . I am glad and rejoice with all of you. So you too should be glad and rejoice with me" (Phil 2:17b–18). This passage reflects his exhortation to the believers in Rome to rejoice with each other.

How could this work out in practice in the local church? Perhaps Paul was exhorting the Christians to rejoice with those who, despite the sufferings that they were experiencing, were rejoicing in the Lord. The believers are not being advised to draw alongside those who are suffering as "Job's comforters" but as encouragers, pointing the sufferers to the great hope that awaits them all. "Let us rejoice and be glad and give him glory! For the wedding of the Lamb has come, and his bride has made herself ready" (Rev 19:7).

Paul then writes that the believers should "weep" κλαιω (*klaiō*) with those who weep. This is a true mark of sincere love for a fellow believer. The tears

---

[669] 1 Cor 6: 1–11 deals with injustice that is done by a believer against another believer. The good of the witness of the community has to be seriously considered.

[670] Yinger, "Nonretaliation," 74–96, argues that while Rom 12:9–13 is commonly understood to speak of congregational insiders, Rom 12:14–21 speaks of outsiders. More likely, the persecutors (Rom 12:14) and the enemy (Rom 12:20) are hostile insiders (as in Jewish community-literature contemporary to Paul). Yinger claims that this interpretation provides a stronger theological backdrop for Paul's pointed admonitions in Rom 14:1–15:13.

are not the fabricated ones of the mourners in the home of Jairus's daughter in Luke 8, or of the professional mourners who followed Jesus to Golgotha (Luke 23:27–31). They come from a spirit that has been deeply troubled and moved at the suffering of another (John 11:33–36, 38).

In today's culture, weeping as an expression of emotion was not often witnessed until recently. There have been incidents covered by TV news and other media that have shown men weeping over events ranging from tragedies in their families to the failure of their football team to succeed in the competition they had thought would be theirs. Paul was unashamed at showing his emotions (2 Cor 2:4; Phil 3:18). He recalls the tears he had shed while with the church in Ephesus (Acts 20:17–19, 31). On bidding the elders of the church a final goodbye before going to Jerusalem, he and the elders wept (Acts 20:36–38). When writing to Timothy, the author recalled Timothy's tears (2 Tim 1:4), and the writer to the Hebrews records the tears that Jesus shed throughout his life as he prayed (Heb 5:7).

What Paul asks of the believers in Rome is that they do not rush to comfort and encourage the broken-hearted with words alone, but that they show their deep sorrow by entering into the pain of their fellow believers. Then, words such as Isaiah 61:1–3 can have their place.

12:16 Live in harmony with one another. Do not be proud, but be willing to associate with people of low position. Do not be conceited.

The NIV translation "live in harmony with each other" leads us to assume that Paul is commenting on the previous verse. Unfortunately, this is a misleading translation of φρονοῦντες (*phronountes*). It means "be of the same mind"(literally, 'think the same thing') as one another." This appeal underscores the importance of the believers meeting together to hear the Scriptures explained.

The related term "being of one mind" φρονεομι (*phroneomai*) has identical roots with φρονοῦντες noted above, "mind" and "mindset" appearing often in Scripture. Paul has already written in his letter about the importance of a right mind. He has mentioned the "depraved mind" of unredeemed humanity (Rom 1:28–32; 8:6–7) and has reflected on his pre-conversion experience (Rom 7:21–25). Elsewhere, he has written about having the mind of the Spirit (Rom 8:6). Matthew records the rebuke of Peter by Jesus who discerned that Peter did not, at this that stage, have in mind the things of God (Matt 16:23).

However, it appears that after conversion the renewed mind can become corrupt again, especially when exposed to false teachings. So Paul warns the church in Ephesus about some of its community with unspiritual minds wreaking havoc in the church (Acts 20:28–31).

The sanctification of the mind in this way is not an option for believers. In replying to a question posed by a Pharisee, Jesus answered: "'Love the Lord your God with all your heart and with all your soul and with all your mind.' This is the first and greatest commandment" (Matt 22:37–38).

Paul then addresses the matter of pride and conceit in the church. There was clearly much evidence of this—Jews looking down on uncircumcised Gentiles, circumcised Gentiles (who called themselves Jews) looking down on uncircumcised Gentiles, and believing Gentiles looking down on unconverted Jews as discarded branches of the olive tree. The mind of Christ was not much in evidence, and the issues of pride and conceit had to be addressed if the church was to be a light to the nations.

These two sins do more to damage the fellowship of God's people than almost any other. The tragedy is that those who commit them are often unaware of the damage that they are doing, and when approached are deeply offended. The proud and conceited have normally achieved success in life and feel it is their right to pass judgment on others, especially when they perceive them to be hindering the progress of the work into which they themselves invest resources and time (3 John 9–10). In other words, pride and conceit is a particular danger to those who have been promoted to leadership within the Christian community. How dangerous this is. The very ones who should be examples of the grace of Christ can so easily be the cause of offence to new, struggling believers.

12:17 Do not repay anyone evil for evil. Be careful to do what is right in the eyes of everybody.

Paul is emphatic in excluding revengeful acts of evil within the church in Rome. He encourages following OT commands where God demanded that the welfare of enemies had to be upheld. The law of Moses commanded that if someone found his neighbor's animal out of its confines and in danger of getting hurt, the animal had to be delivered safely back to its owner even though he might have previously harmed the one who found the animal (Deut 22:1–3). The Scriptures are realistic in recognizing how feuding—which results from taking revenge—incalculably damages the parties involved as well as other members of the community.

Paul urges the Roman believers to appreciate the danger of doing things that are lawful but that give a wrong impression. In saying that they must do what is right in the eyes of everyone, he is effectively saying that their actions must be open to scrutiny. Paul is not so naive as to suggest that we can please everyone or do what everyone considers right. After all, he was criticized by many for what they saw as his radical acceptance of uncircumcised Gentiles.

Many of the world's leading social reformers have had to stand against what their societies considered right because of the flaws they discerned. If we find ourselves in conflict with prevailing values that are morally wrong, we must make sure that we are not open to the accusation of doing wrong to achieve right. For Paul—and the other NT writers—the end never justifies the means. The means we employ to take our stand have to be ones that God himself would own.

12:18 If it is possible, as far as it depends on you, live at peace with everyone.

Strain in relationships—even between believers—is recognized in this verse. Paul knows that despite all of his exhortations, tensions do occur within the Christian community as well as outside (Phil 4:2–3). Here, he urges his readers to do all they can to ensure that they are not responsible for the breakdown of peace.

12:19 Do not take revenge, my friends, but leave room for God's wrath, for it is written: "It is mine to avenge; I will repay," says the Lord.

The danger in being wronged is of becoming a double victim. If we respond by taking revenge we have taken our case out of the hands of God in order to exercise our own authority. While it is a natural instinct, it is one that must be brought into subjection to Christ. He was wronged more than any, yet did not take matters into his own hands. He committed himself to his Father and suffered the just for the unjust. Once we take matters into our own hands, we cease to be God's servants and people through whom he can reveal himself. His power is never revealed through his people's sin but through his people's weakness.

Paul writes to the believers in Rome that they are to leave revenge to God. He quotes "It is mine to avenge; I will repay, says the Lord" from Deut 32:35 (see also Lev 19:18). The Roman Christians can be confident in the knowledge that the judge of all the earth will do justly. Before God acts on their behalf, he will offer the same mercy to those who offended them as he did to the believers before they responded to his mercy. If this mercy is rejected, he will act in judgment at the time of his choosing (Rom 2:5, 8; 1 Thess 1:10).[671]

12:20 On the contrary: "If your enemy is hungry, feed him; if he is thirsty, give him something to drink. In doing this, you will heap burning coals on his head."

The believers are not only to leave their case in the hands of God (who will avenge and repay as he sees fit) but are to do good to those who do evil to them. While responding in like manner justifies the behavior of those who have done wrong, acts of kindness disarm them, leaving them confused and vulnerable. For such people, this is more painful than revenge. The quotation is from Prov 25:21ff. (LXX).

Some find conflict in Paul's teaching. He urges the Romans not to take revenge into their own hands, and yet says that by doing good to their enemies burning coals are heaped on their heads. There need not be any conflict. If Paul means that their kindness will make their enemies extremely uncomfortable, the same meaning is upheld. In other words, Paul is counseling the believers to recognize that revenge will only confirm the attitude and not change the character. By kindness, their enemies can be made so uncomfortable that they can no longer bear it.

However, there is a possible alternative meaning within this text and that echoes the OT. Live coals are a symbol of purging (Isa 6:6–7), and were part of Isaiah's preparation for the service God was calling him to. Perhaps there is an echo of this purging in the passage. It is possible that Paul is saying the outcome of the kindness of the believers is the salvation of their enemies who will then be brought into God's service and counted among his redeemed.

12:21 Do not be overcome by evil, but overcome evil with good.

Paul's concern is that the church's testimony is not lost. The church is to overcome evil with good. This is the way God has conquered us and disarmed our hostility toward him.[672]

---

[671] The same ideas are found in the DSS. See 1QS, 10:17ff.; CD, 9:2–3.

[672] Johnson, L.T., *Reading*, 196, summarizes the prevailing view of the ancient worlds of Judaism and Hellenism regarding the validity of taking revenge against those who harm loved ones.

CONCLUSION OF ROMANS CHAPTER TWELVE

Just as Moses urged Israel to live out her calling as a priestly people, so Paul exhorts the church. She is to live to please her great high priest to whom she is betrothed by living a priestly life, making her God known to the nations. The emphasis is not about obeying the Torah but fulfilling the law of love by encouraging others and being patient in the face of hostility.

Romans 13

THE MESSIAH KING AND HIS DELEGATED REPRESENTATIVES (13:1–14)

Everyone must submit himself to the governing authorities, for there is no authority except that which God has established. The authorities that exist have been established by God. Consequently, he who rebels against the authority is rebelling against what God has instituted, and those who do so will bring judgment on themselves. For rulers hold no terror for those who do right, but for those who do wrong. Do you want to be free from fear of the one in authority? Then do what is right and he will commend you.

For he is God's servant to do you good. But if you do wrong, be afraid, for he does not bear the sword for nothing. He is God's servant, an agent of wrath to bring punishment on the wrongdoer.

Therefore, it is necessary to submit to the authorities, not only because of possible punishment but also because of conscience.

This is also why you pay taxes, for the authorities are God's servants, who give their full time to governing. Give everyone what you owe him: If you owe taxes, pay taxes; if revenue, then revenue; if respect, then respect; if honor, then honor. Let no debt remain outstanding, except the continuing debt to love one another, for he who loves his fellow-man has fulfilled the law. The commandments, "Do not commit adultery," "Do not murder," "Do not steal," "Do not covet," and whatever other commandment there may be, are summed up in this one rule: "Love your neighbor as yourself." Love does no harm to its neighbor. Therefore love is the fulfillment of the law. And do this, understanding the present time. The hour has come for you to wake up from your slumber, because our salvation is nearer now than when we first believed. The night is nearly over; the day is almost here. So let us put aside the deeds of darkness and put on the armor of light. Let us behave decently, as in the daytime, not in orgies and drunkenness, not in sexual immorality and debauchery, not in dissension and jealousy. Rather, clothe yourselves with the Lord Jesus Christ, and do not think about how to gratify the desires of the sinful nature. (Romans 13:1–14)

Romans: The Divine Marriage, Volume 2

INTRODUCTION

Having instructed the Romans in the preceding section about their priestly calling (Rom 12:1–2) and the need to maintain their zeal (Rom 12:11), Paul turns to the issue of earthly rule. There has always been a tendency throughout the church's history to claim authority for herself that exceeds what God intends her to have. Here Paul, clearly aware of the danger, instructs the church in Rome regarding her duties to assist the servants of the state in their God-given calling to promote the good of the people of the empire and to maintain law and order.

Despite the trend to see Paul, and indeed, Jesus himself as political activists, this key passage shows us that Paul never had such ambitions. In fact Paul valued his own Roman citizenship and used the privileges it gave him to ensure that he had a fair trial by appealing to Caesar (Acts 25:10–11). No doubt there were other motives in operation when he made his appeal to Caesar than solely his own survival. He had been told (Acts 9:15) that he was to carry Christ's name "before the Gentiles and their kings," and this knowledge was clearly a driving force for his whole ministry.

Paul not only calls the Roman believers to respect the state and its servants, but to live pure and good lives that mark them out as the people of Christ in a dark and failing society.

13:1 Everyone must submit himself to the governing authorities, for there is no authority except that which God has established. The authorities that exist have been established by God.

In saying that "everyone must submit," πασα ψυχη (*pasa pauxē*), Paul emphasizes the importance of willing acceptance of the rulers' claim to authority over the Roman believers. The authorities are not to be obeyed because they have the power to punish but because their authority has been conferred on them by God. They are his appointed agents to govern.

Paul uses the term "authority/ies" in different ways in his writings. He applies it to men such as the chief priests (Acts 26:12; 1 Cor 9:12 [translated "right of support"]; 2 Cor 10:8) and to spiritual powers (Acts 26:18 [translated "power"]; Eph 1:21; 2:2 [translated "kingdom"] 3:10; 6:12; Col 1:13 [translated "dominion"]; 2:10; 2:15).While Paul rarely applies the term to the state, this is generally accepted to be his application in Rom 13, the authorities being civil rulers who hold the sword on God's behalf.[673]

If we accept that "authority/ies" in Rom 13 refers to such rulers, we can assume that Paul draws his understanding from the OT Scriptures. It was Yahweh who appointed Saul (1 Sam 9:16) and David (1 Sam 16:1) as Israel's kings. Indeed, the coronation psalms show that the king was the servant (son) of God (Ps 2:7). Importantly, it was not only the Jewish kings who were seen to be Yahweh's agents but also pagan kings. Cyrus, the Persian king, was referred to as "his anointed" and his "chosen," whom God summoned, exalted, and strengthened (Isa 45:1–5). Paul would thus be staying within the OT perspective that, no matter how evil the world, Yahweh controls the nations.[674]

This OT background would provide the reason for Paul's appeal to Christians to recognize that a regime soaked in paganism and violence (with ensuing moral consequences) was, nevertheless, the God-appointed government in Rome. When its laws did not conflict with their calling as Christians, the Roman believers were to give it due honor and homage.[675]

Recently, an alternative understanding of "authority/ies" in Rom 13 has been put forward. It is argued that local churches did not always separate from the local synagogues perhaps because they afforded protection to the believers, and that this was the situation in Rome. This meant that Jewish worshippers and Jewish believers in Jesus mixed with each other when they came to the synagogues for worship.[676] Such a situation was not unknown in Judaism as Jews themselves embraced different messiahs and actively sought to persuade their countrymen of the credentials of their chosen "anointed" ones. This relative openness witnesses to the diversity of the Jewish synagogue system as does the fact that visitors were encouraged to share with the congregation messages of exhortation, of news, or some other matter (Acts 13:5, 15; 14:1; 17:10–12; 18:4; 19:8).

---

[673] See Cullmann, *State*.

[674] Wright, *Romans*, 721–22, notes: "being" able to respect the office while at least reserving judgment about the holder is part of social and civic maturity."

[675] Denova, "Romans 13:1–7," 201–29, claims that an analysis of the authorship, the religious/political context, and the content of early Christian moral teaching shows that this passage is not a systematic political theory nor a Christian blueprint for the state. It is merely an attempt to help Gentile Christians adjust to their new circumstances. For a discussion on the authorship of the section, see Witherington, *Romans*, 304.

[676] See Nanos, *Mystery*.

However, a major cause of friction in many synagogues was that the followers of Jesus were bringing the message of a crucified Messiah to the congregations. In addition, they were introducing uncircumcised Gentiles as men with equal rights as the orthodox Jews. Indeed, not only did these Jewish followers of Jesus argue for the inclusion of uncircumcised Gentiles into the covenant community, they argued that, unless law-observing Jews believed in Jesus, *they* were excluded from the covenant community! This historical setting has been used to argue that the "governing authorities" of v. 1 are not representatives of the Roman state but of the synagogue.[677]

This recently argued understanding has Paul pleading for the Gentile believers to accept the authority of the Jewish leadership of the synagogue because God has appointed it. If this is the setting of the exhortation, the problem is no longer how the believers relate to the state but to the religious leadership. Paul is appealing for respect, but not at the cost of compromise.[678]

13:2 Consequently, he who rebels against the authority is rebelling against what God has instituted, and those who do so will bring judgment on themselves.

The outcome of Paul's reasoning is predictable. If the governments (civil or religious) are the appointed agents of God, to rebel against them is to rebel against the God who appointed them. This is a remarkable position to take if Paul is referring to civil authorities, as many of the believers in Rome were slaves. Their distressing conditions were often due to the greed, ambition and ruthlessness of the mighty Roman Empire, so it would be more than understandable if some of them bitterly resented their masters. As with the earlier exhortation not to take revenge (Rom 12:19), this exhortation would have cut right across their instincts for justice.

---

[677] There are some points that support this position of Nanos, but the main difficulty is that Paul describes the authorities as bearing the sword. This description is too severe a portrayal of the legal authority that the Roman Empire allowed the synagogue to wield. Any capital punishment had to be ordered by the state, as is evident in the sentence carried out on Jesus. Rome would not tolerate anything that challenged her right to order the death penalty. It was a matter of Roman law and order. The reference to paying taxes to the authority in v.6 is thought by most to refer to state taxes–a tax most Jews resented. Nanos claims that it is a reference to synagogue taxes

[678] Talbert, *Romans*, 296, comments: "All that is asked of the believers is that they 'do good,' 'pay taxes,' and 'honor and respect those in power.' What is legitimately ascribed to the authorities is the punishment of evil and the reward of good. This limited homage is far from an enthusiastic endorsement of the empire."

Paul is as clear on this issue as he was about revenge: Rebellion would leave the believers open to judgment. Such judgment might be meted out by the authority using its might and power in suppression, or it might be meted out by God for rejecting the authority he had ordained. While this latter suggestion is a possibility, the argument that follows suggests that Paul has the judgment of the former in mind.

13:3 For rulers hold no terror for those who do right, but for those who do wrong. Do you want to be free from fear of the one in authority? Then do what is right and he will commend you.

Paul was not idealizing rulers as men who always acted with the purest of motives. He was not naive. He knew the intrigues of political maneuvering in the synagogue and in the state, and how the innocent were often victims of miscarriages of justice, suffering because their legitimate grievances were ignored. How should the Roman Christians respond should these be the prevailing circumstances? While Paul does not address this here, it is hard to believe that he would urge his readers to give blind obedience. On such occasions, they will have to take a stand that may prove very costly.

The questions must be asked: "When a ruling authority is corrupt, does it cease to be God's instrument? Moreover, do Christians have a responsibility to join with others to bring such a tyranny to an end?" These are questions that Paul does not address and their answers must be sought by examining Scripture to see what principles it provides. Paul had the same attitude to these matters as Jesus. We are to "give to Caesar what is Caesar's and to God what is God's."(Mark 12:17, cf. Rom 13:6).

13:4 For he is God's servant to do you good. But if you do wrong, be afraid, for he does not bear the sword for nothing. He is God's servant, an agent of wrath to bring punishment on the wrongdoer.

The one in authority—be he the leader of the synagogue or the head of the state—is God's servant; and his responsibility is to seek the good of the citizens in his care. Of course, authorities should not only punish wrongdoers in order to protect the weak, but should commend and nurture those who do good.[679]

---

[679] Winter, *Welfare*, 26–38, suggests that Paul is exhorting his readers to become benefactors who will receive recognition from the state. By this, they will promote the cause of the Gospel as unbelievers watch on.

If Paul had the Roman civil authorities in mind, then the believers who lived within their jurisdiction ought to be grateful for how much Rome (God's servant) had bequeathed on them in terms of legal and religious privilege. However, they had to be aware that any civil authority could also punish wrongdoing. Paul warns his readers that if they do wrong they must not think that they will be exempt from punishment.[680]

If Paul meant that the synagogue rulers were God's servant, then he would have in mind the good done by them in, for example, religious, moral, legal and educational matters. The reference to the synagogue ruler bearing the sword is not a problem in this context as the synagogue was the legal center of the Jewish community and the place where punishment was meted out on those who violated its laws. Paul himself had represented such a ruling authority, brandishing the sword on behalf of the high priest (Acts 9:1–2; Gal 1:13–14). Indeed, after his conversion on the Damascus road he became the recipient of its judgment; however such an interpretation is not likely to be correct if it sees the synagogue eldership as having the right to take life as discussed above.

The reference to the sword is possibly from Deut 32:41, where Yahweh threatens to take his sword and wreak vengeance on his adversaries. This is supported by the fact that Paul has already quoted from the chapter. He quotes Deut 32:21 in Rom 10:19 and v.35 in Rom 12:19. The threat of Yahweh taking the sword against his enemies suggests that Paul sees that the danger of those who profess faith and disobey is that they are enemies of the Lord. This is not a new perception for Paul—he has spoken of Israel as a nation of unbelievers and having become, effectively, Yahweh's enemy and suffering judgment by his hand. He warned the Corinthians of this danger of coming under their Lord's discipline in 1 Cor 10:1–10, and threatened it in 1 Cor 5–6.[681]

---

[680] Furnish, *Moral*, 115–41, understands the "sword" to refer to that of the tax police who use it to protect tax collectors. The weakness of this view is that vv. 3–5 clearly refers to higher officials than tax collectors.

[681] See Holland, *Contours*, chapter 6.

13:5 Therefore, it is necessary to submit to the authorities, not only because of possible punishment but also because of conscience.

Paul underlines two reasons for obeying the authorities. The first is the fear of punishment and the second is because conscience, or religious duty requires it (Exod 22:28; Acts 23:5).[682]

It might seem strange that Paul mentions fear as a motive. Indeed, he not only lists it but puts it before conscience. We live in an age when psychologists tell us never to use fear as a motive. The fact is that society, having yielded to such advice, is returning to the dark ages in terms of much social behavior. Scripture has no hesitation in spelling things out as they are; and for most, including Christians, fear of punishment in this life and the next affects them deeply. We should not be afraid of an emotion that is part of human experience and which can save us from harm.

13:6 This is also why you pay taxes, for the authorities are God's servants, who give their full time to governing.

As has been mentioned, Paul asserts the principle taught by Jesus: "Give to Caesar what is Caesar's and to God what is God's" (Matt 22:21b). Because the authorities are God's servants, he has ordained that people should support them.[683] If Paul sees the authorities as the state, then those who work full time in the upholding of social order should be provided for by means of taxation. Paying taxes would then be as much an act of giving to God as paying "tithes." The former would be for the administration of society's needs, the latter for the administration of the Gospel.

Paul sees nothing wrong in officials being paid fairly for the work they do–theirs is a high calling, ensuring the smooth and just running of affairs. They should be paid appropriately to avoid corruption. Poorly paid officials might be

---

[682] Rancine, " Romains," 187–205, argues that the use of συνείδηεις *(suneidēsis)* "conscience" and ὑποτάσσεσθαι *(upotassesthai)* "to be in subjection" suggest that Paul was promoting an intelligent and critical respect for the social order. They contributed to the church's faith rather than to a blind obedience towards the civil authorities.

[683] Kroger, "Authorities," 344–66, argues against those who claim that vv. 1–7 are a non-Pauline interpolation. He thinks that Paul was aware that taxation was a vexing issue for the Roman Christians. He says that Paul counters the problems this could cause by urging them to adopt a practical attitude of obedience and submission to the governing authorities.

tempted to accept bribes to supplement their wages if their families' needs could not be met.

13:7 Give everyone what you owe him: If you owe taxes, pay taxes; if revenue, then revenue; if respect, then respect; if honor, then honor.

Paul extends the principle of what is owed to governing officials to what is owed to those in daily life.[684] He tells the Romans that they are to settle all their debts–no matter to whom they are indebted.

Debt can cripple the conscience. Moreover, when left unpaid it can cause devastation to those who depend on its repayment. All too often, those who live in abundance hold on to what is not theirs, leaving the ones who are owed with the problem of coping with the unpaid debts. While it is not right at a commercial level, it is especially inappropriate for Christians not to settle debts (Jas 5:4–5). The OT has much to say about this (Deut 24:10–13; Job 24:3; Prov 20:16; Ezek 33:15), and there is no doubt that it is from this source that Paul draws his ethical principles.[685]

Debts are owed by the Roman believers in monetary and non-monetary terms. Paul writes to them that they are to pay appropriate debts of respect and honor to all in authority. If those who have been given responsibilities by God fulfill them in a way honoring to him, they deserve due recognition. Paul would expect the Roman believers to apply this principle to their civil, synagogue, and church lives, recognizing and respecting the work done in the latter by its prophets, evangelists, teachers, pastors, elders and deacons (1 Tim 3:8; Titus 1:7 & 3:2; Heb 13:7, 17; 1 Pet 5:5).

This debt of gratitude owed by the Roman believers to their officialdom could be usefully heeded by churches today. We live in an age of criticism and cynicism, where expression of gratitude is of less importance than demand to entitlement. Many churches would be transformed if members of their congregations took to heart Paul's exhortation to the believers in Rome and

---

[684] Coleman, "Binding," 307–27, discusses the terms "tribute," " tax," "reverence," and "honor" in relation to the Greco-Roman semantic field of political obligation. He divides them into the categories of tangible and intangible obligations. He also examines Rom 13:7 in light of the social context of the Neronian era in which there was an increasing burden of taxation and the introduction of legal penalties for failure to show due reverence and honor to those in authority.

[685] See Rosner, *Scripture*.

paid debts of gratitude to those who, often voluntarily, seek to care for their souls.

13:8 Let no debt remain outstanding, except the continuing debt to love one another, for he who loves his fellow-man has fulfilled the law.

The exception to the rule regarding the repayment of debts is the debt of love, which can never be settled. The mention of love is probably a reference to the love of God about which Paul has spoken movingly in Rom 5:8. In saying "he who loves his fellow-man has fulfilled the law," Paul is not suggesting that we can keep the law. Indeed, this is his point. This debt cannot be met because we can never satisfy the law's demands. It is a debt that only Christ has met.

13:9 The commandments, "Do not commit adultery," "Do not murder," "Do not steal," "Do not covet," and whatever other commandment there may be, are summed up in this one rule: "Love your neighbor as yourself."

Paul reminds the believers of the commandments that relate to the treatment of others, reinforcing the permanence of these laws. They express the bottom line for behavior. If a believer loves someone, he cannot sin against that person in ways the commandments forbid. Love is a higher principle than law. What the law commands is the beginning of the expression of love, not its limit.

The commandment "Do not commit adultery" continues to be the key to every stable marriage. While the world treats sexual morality as a private affair, it recognizes that the betrayal of a partner is inexcusable and the immediate grounds for divorce. In this case, natural justice reflects divine justice. Adultery not only sins against God and the partner, but the extended family (especially the children). Scripture is uncompromising in speaking out against sexual immorality because it destroys the fabric of lives. It robs families of security, trust, and dignity, and casts them into a darkness with which little can compare.

Jesus extended this commandment to attitudes of the heart. He warned that whoever looked upon a woman and lusted after her had already committed adultery with her as far as God was concerned (Matt 5:27–28). Such high standards are not out of touch with the pain that women feel when they see their husbands' lingering glances at other women. Such glances attack their security and self-worth.

Murder is another act that is universally recognized as wrong. Many will argue their right to steal and covet, but few would argue that murder is acceptable. While there are grounds for a state taking a life to protect its population against an aggressor, reason can become warped, justifying executions for the wrong cause. The Jesuits, in their South American mission, put people to death on the pretext that their souls would be saved. The Crusaders did the same thing in the Islamic states during the Middle Ages. Jesus gave the commandment against murder a spiritual dimension (Matt 5:21–22). He said that hating a person is as bad as physically harming him. Peoples, characters, and reputations can be put to death just as much as the body can, and Jesus justly applied the commandment beyond the limits of the Mosaic law.

The command "Do not steal" is clear. We are not to take from individuals, companies, or governments. Stealing does not only involve tangible things. It can be taking time from an employer as well as stealing a man's good reputation through gossip and slander.

Coveting is the desire to have what belongs to someone else. This does not mean that we are forbidden to admire a possession of another person and resolve to acquire the same through legitimate means. It means that jealousy—the twin sister of covetousness—must never be in our hearts. We ought to be glad that others have been blessed with possessions that we are not able to own. This is not a hopelessly impossible ideal. Its attainment begins with valuing spiritual blessings above material ones.

Paul writes that these and other commandments are summed up in the principle of loving our neighbor as ourselves. It is one of the great commandments that Jesus gave in response to the scribes' attempt to catch him out. The other is that we love God with all our hearts (Mark 12:29–30). While Paul cites the command to love from Lev 19:18b (a command relating specifically to loving fellow Jews), he is not restricting his command to ethnic Israel. For Paul, as for Jesus, his neighbor is all humanity.

13:10 Love does no harm to its neighbor. Therefore love is the fulfillment of the law.

When Paul writes that "love does no harm to its neighbor,"[686] it seems that anything causing pain or sadness cannot spring from love. However, Paul often said offensive and hurtful things (2 Cor 6:14–18; Gal 2:14; Phil 3:2), indicating that there are times when keeping quiet harms a person more than the initial distress caused by speaking out. In other words, there are times when we have

---

[686] See the discussion in Witherington, *Romans*, 316, for the meaning of "neighbor." He demonstrates that while it can refer to members of the same community, it can apply to a "fellow human being."

to see the long term good of our neighbor and act with that in mind. There can be no greater good than a person's acceptance into heaven. Incalculable harm can be done by believers keeping silent on the remedy for sin for fear of causing their neighbors any distress.

The same principle applies when someone steals from us, attacks our property, or violates us in any way. Paul is not saying that we should disregard the law's support or protection. Indeed, a Christian should hope that the moral welfare of the guilty party will be served by facing the seriousness of what he has done. In other words, Paul's injunction not to harm a neighbor is about dealing justly with him. There should be no thought of stealing from him, slandering, or hurting him in any way. Regardless of his color, creed, or status, he is to be treated with respect and dignity at all times. This concern for equality and justice comes from the OT, where Israel was told to protect the vulnerable. They not only included orphans and widows but strangers (immigrants) and economic casualties (Exod 22:21–27). They were to be accepted as those made in the image of God and those for whom the Lord would plead the cause if they were violated.

This sort of reasoning can be extended to other areas of Christian living. The principle Paul is emphasizing is that we have no right to judge one whom God has accepted. The moment we think that we are more acceptable to God is the moment we cease to appreciate his free grace. To grade Christians in terms of favor is to fall into serious error. We are all accepted on exactly the same grounds, i.e., God's free grace and mercy.

The purposes of the law are that people give to God the love and honor he deserves and that they give to others—who are made in God's image—the love and respect they deserve. Love means dealing with others in the way that God deals with us. This is the fulfillment of the law.

13:11 *And do this, understanding the present time. The hour has come for you to wake up from your slumber, because our salvation is nearer now than when we first believed.*

By writing "And do this," Paul emphasizes that faith in Christ is not only expressed in ideals and doctrines but in the life the Roman believers lead (Rom 12:1–21; 13:9–10). Jesus often stressed what men had to *do*. Faith in him does not take away the Roman believers' personal responsibility but provides them with the resources for living the Christian life (Gal 5:16–26).

Their actions must flow from an understanding of their current situation in Rome. They must not be content with comfort but alert to the fact that others in the city are in mortal danger and in need of rescuing from God's coming judgment. Paul urges the believers to wake from slumber and buy up the opportunities of serving Christ in the city (cf. Eph 5:8–20). The call to "wake up from slumber" is a direct quote from Isa 60:1, where the people were told that Yahweh was coming to bring them salvation. It is, of course, a text that has New Exodus significance. The original context was Yahweh's call to Israel to prepare herself for her return pilgrimage to Jerusalem.[687]

Peter speaks of the coming of Christ as the new dawn (2 Pet 1:19). Until that breaks, unredeemed humanity dwells in darkness; but it is a condition from which he can be rescued. As Christ will come in judgment, those who have declined to be rescued will be left in the darkness they have preferred (Matt 6:23; Eph 5:8; Col 1:13; 1 Pet 2:9) and will be sent into an eternal outer darkness (Matt 8:12; 22:13). It is imperative that the believers in Rome spread the knowledge of God so that it shines in the hearts of those in the city who will believe, bringing them forgiveness and salvation (Acts 26:18). This task demands that they put aside "deeds of darkness" (v. 12) as unbelievers will take the Gospel seriously when they see it being lived out with integrity by the believers.

13:12 *The night is nearly over; the day is almost here. So let us put aside the deeds of darkness and put on the armor of light.*

Elsewhere, Paul has written that the Christian needs to put on the full armor of God in order to bear a good witness (Eph 6:11). This is an echo of Isa 59:16–17 where Isaiah records the coming of the Redeemer to Zion, fully armed and equipped for his saving work. Because of this divine intervention, the remnant was released to make its journey to the promised inheritance—the city of Zion.

The OT citations (and especially Isa 60:1, which was considered in Rom 13:11) suggest that Paul sees believers to be involved in a pilgrimage (see also Rom 5:1ff.; 8:32ff.; 10:14–15). They can only progress on their pilgrimage as they fulfill the responsibility of living as children of light. This understanding supports the case made that Paul constructed his letter to the Romans around Israel's experience of coming out of bondage and shame. This type—this visual

---

[687] Käsemann, *Romans*, 362, considers that the passage reflects the exhortations given at baptism.

Romans 13

aid from the history of Israel—is fulfilled in the church, the true inheritor of the promises of God (Gal 6:16).

The exhortation to put on the armor of God was originally spoken to Israel; while the individual Christian applies it to himself, it is, nevertheless, an exhortation to the community.

Isa 59:9–10 speaks of captive Israel being in darkness and knowing nothing of justice. Paul follows this theme in Rom 13:12–13. He urges his readers not to fall into the same sins that Israel fell into on her pilgrimage (Isa 59:2–8, 12–15; cf. 1 Cor 10:1–13), when she involved herself in orgies, drunkenness, sexual immorality, debauchery, dissension and jealousy. Paul used very similar language in 1 Cor 10:6ff., when he warned the Corinthians that God could act to discipline them as he had disciplined the children of Israel. The setting of the exhortation in the Corinthian letter was the wilderness wanderings. We have seen that Paul is able to use material from the Egyptian and Babylonian exoduses to illustrate what God has done for his people through the death of Christ, "our Passover." Typology continues to be the key to interpreting Paul.

13:13 Let us behave decently, as in the daytime, not in orgies and drunkenness, not in sexual immorality and debauchery, not in dissension and jealousy.

When Paul writes "Let us behave decently, as in the daytime," he is saying that he and the Roman believers must be open to public scrutiny. He identifies with them, saying that he and they should live transparent lives, doing nothing of which they would be ashamed. For example, the Roman Christians should not be involved in "orgies." The term refers to secret rites and rituals in the worship of pagan gods, especially Bacchus.

Repeated "drunkenness" is also forbidden (cf. 1 Cor 5:11). In 1 Cor 6:10, Paul lists drunkards as people who will not inherit the kingdom of God. This is a warning to believers in an age when alcohol is readily available and much consumed. While it cannot be denied that wine was the accepted refreshment of the NT world, we must recognize Scripture's warning of its misuse; it can bring the strongest man to destruction (Gen 9:21; Prov 20:1; 1 Tim 3:3; Titus 2:3). In the Greek text, the phrase translated "orgies and drunkenness" may suggest an act of drunken revelry rather than two distinct practices.

Paul urges the Roman believers not to be involved in sexual immorality. Again, this is a sin that is as prevalent in modern society as it was in the ancient world. Sex, which is powerful and beautiful, is God's gift to mankind. It brings incredible joy and comfort when contained within the realm of a true and permanent relationship between a man and a woman. We live in an age when traditional forms of morality have largely been abandoned. Indeed, the pain from broken relationships with the psychological and emotional damage they wreak has not yet reached its high water mark. This is not how God intended it to be as he wants sex to be the evidence of genuine love and total trust. If these are present in a relationship, it is difficult to see why anyone should deny the partner the protection that the legal status of marriage gives.

"Debauchery" refers to perverted virtue or morality, and extends the bounds of sexual immorality. As with orgies and drunkenness, the use of the phrase "sexual immorality and debauchery" may be intended to suggest one composite idea or practice. The nouns are plural, suggesting frequent repetition.

"Dissension" refers to attempts to overthrow the prevailing opinion. There are times when it is right to question the status quo; indeed, it is essential for this to take place if there is going to be reform. Paul is not against such freedom. He was, after all, guilty of dissention when he proclaimed the Gospel of Christ in the synagogues. When people embraced "the Way," it meant a shift of power from Jewish leaders to those who were often Gentile (i.e., the God-fearing) and with little official training.

Paul is not concerned in this particular passage about attempts to bring down corrupt leaders. He is concerned, rather, with the overthrow of a person who was disliked because of differences over legitimate alternative policies. Sadly, we find dissension in churches when people think the pastor's ministry is over and they seek to influence others in support of his removal. This has happened throughout history, and no less in biblical history. It is even more tragic when people who were once used by God become the center of dissension. Such examples are Miriam and Aaron, who tried to replace—or, at the very least, share leadership with—Moses, their brother (Num 12). Whether in a civil or a church context, believers should not be involved in dissension unless it is to remove corrupt officials.

"Jealousy" is a state of heart and mind that causes much suffering. It is often hidden under a veneer of respectability. It ruins relationships, twists truth, and excuses gross injustices. To succumb to jealousy's enticements is to be a prisoner of a ruthless mistress. "Dissension and jealousy" is the third pair of nouns in the list and is often the result of drunken revelry and debauchery.

Romans 13

13:14 Rather, clothe yourselves with the Lord Jesus Christ, and do not think about how to gratify the sinful nature.

The lifestyle of the people of God is to be different from that of the world. While there are notable exceptions, the sins Paul has listed, which gratify the "sinful nature," are typical of unredeemed humankind. If their application to twenty-first century Western society is denied, the huge sale of news stand and video shop material—pandering to basic instincts and values—stands as witness. Paul gives explicit instructions as to how to deal with such temptations when they attack the believer (1 Cor 10:1–13; Gal 5:16–26; Phil 4:8–9). He should give them no place in his thinking. Appetites must not become the stooges of Satan, who seeks to control people by intoxicating their lives with base passions.

When Paul speaks about gratifying the "sinful nature," he uses the term σαρξ (*sarx*) "flesh." In using *sarx*, Paul has not necessarily referred to the sinful nature of people as the NIV suggests. As we have seen, *sarx* "flesh" has a range of meanings reflecting the weakness of humanity.[688] Paul refers to Christians as continuing in their fallen creaturely weakness. While this does not necessarily equate to sinning, it probably does in this verse. Paul is exhorting the Roman Christians not to gratify the *sarx* as they wait for the completion of their redemption when Christ returns.

In exhorting the Roman believers to "clothe" themselves (ἀλλὰ ἐνδύσασθε τὸν κύριον Ἰησοῦν Χριστὸν), Paul appeals to the church community to live a Christ-like life. This is always corporate language (see Eph 4:24; Col 3:10). The language of clothing is found throughout the OT. It refers to preparation for doing evil (Ps 73:6) or good (Ps 45:3; Isa 51:9) as well as the transformation of people through life events (Job 8:22; Ps 30:11; 35:26; 109:29; 132:16; Isa 52:1; 61:10).

CONCLUSION OF ROMANS CHAPTER THIRTEEN

Paul continues his exhortation that the church should live a holy life. This is not a call to mysticism but to practical godly living where truth is upheld and ruling authorities are honored.

God's people are to clothe themselves with Christ Jesus. The scriptural basis of this appeal is taken from Isa 60:1, where Israel was commanded to awake from her sleep and prepare for her second exodus. This OT text echoes

---

[688] See Excursus F: Sin in the Theology of Paul, p. 271.

in the background as Paul warns the church to awake from slumber because her salvation is nearer now than when she first believed (v. 11). Thus, New Exodus imagery continues to drive the argument and appeal. The church is to live in such a way to be fit for the coming of the divine bridegroom—an event that Isa 62:1–5 foretold.

Romans 14

THE MESSIAH KING AND HIS PEOPLE'S DIFFERENCES (14:1–23)

Accept him whose faith is weak, without passing judgment on disputable matters. One man's faith allows him to eat everything, but another man, whose faith is weak, eats only vegetables. The man who eats everything must not look down on him who does not, and the man who does not eat everything must not condemn the man who does, for God has accepted him. Who are you to judge someone else's servant? To his own master he stands or falls. And he will stand, for the Lord is able to make him stand.

One man considers one day more sacred than another; another man considers every day alike. Each one should be fully convinced in his own mind. He who regards one day as special, does so to the Lord. He who eats meat, eats to the Lord, for he gives thanks to God; and he who abstains, does so to the Lord and gives thanks to God. For none of us lives to himself alone and none of us dies to himself alone. If we live, we live to the Lord; and if we die, we die to the Lord. So, whether we live or die, we belong to the Lord. For this very reason, Christ died and returned to life so that he might be the Lord of both the dead and the living.

You, then, why do you judge your brother? Or why do you look down on your brother? For we will all stand before God's judgment seat. It is written: "'As surely as I live,' says the Lord, 'every knee will bow before me; every tongue will confess to God.'" So then, each of us will give an account of himself to God.

Therefore let us stop passing judgment on one another. Instead, make up your mind not to put any stumbling block or obstacle in your brother's way. As one who is in the Lord Jesus, I am fully convinced that no food is unclean in itself. But if anyone regards something as unclean, then for him it is unclean. If your brother is distressed because of what you eat, you are no longer acting in love. Do not by your eating destroy your brother for whom Christ died. Do not allow what you consider good to be spoken of as evil. For the kingdom of God is not a matter of eating and drinking, but of righteousness, peace and joy in the Holy Spirit, because anyone who serves Christ in this way is pleasing to God and approved by men.

Let us therefore make every effort to do what leads to peace and to mutual edification. Do not destroy the work of God for the sake of food. All food is clean, but it is wrong for a man to eat anything that causes someone else to stumble. It is better not to eat meat or drink wine or to do anything else that will cause your brother to fall.

So whatever you believe about these things keep between yourself and God. Blessed is the man who does not condemn himself by what he approves. But the man who has doubts is condemned if he eats, because his eating is not from faith; and everything that does not come from faith is sin. (Romans 14:1–23)

INTRODUCTION

Paul begins this section in appealing for the weak and the strong to accept each other. In view of the discussion he had earlier of the division between Jews and Gentiles in chapter 9–11, it is likely that this is the division that is referred to in this section. This is made even more likely by the mention of difficulty of making allowance for food and holy days, the very issues that supported the two sectors of the church that was represented by Jewish and Gentile interests.

Paul stresses that we are all accepted because Christ has died (Rom 14:9, 15) and that no one should be quick to judge because we are yet to be judged by God (Rom 14:10–12). Paul makes the startling claim that if one causes another to stumble because of his attitude, he sins against Christ himself (Rom 14:20). The principle that Paul says must be applied is whether a person does not condemn him/herself in what they do. If they don't, and it is not clearly forbidden nor harming other believers, they are free to continue their chosen course. Thus Paul put down a mark for the importance of Christian freedom.

14:1 Accept him whose faith is weak, without passing judgment on disputable matters.

In Christian congregations there are people from different backgrounds and with different experiences. At this point in the letter, Paul writes to the Roman believers about his concern for their differences in faith and the attitudes they adopt towards each other as a result. Exactly who Paul has in mind when addressing this exhortation is not clear[689] as the definition of those with weak faith (or, by implication, strong faith) does not necessarily fall along ethnic lines.[690] He clearly sees himself as one of the strong,[691] but argues that such as he must follow the example of Jesus (Rom1:3; cf. Phil 2:5–9).

In any community there are those who are full of confidence and opinion. Others are far less robust and hesitant to the point of causing themselves pain in their uncertainties. The "weak" are not necessarily ignorant of Christian doctrine but struggle to work out its consequences and implications.[692] It is all too easy for those who are "strong" to become frustrated with those who do not share their self-confidence. In a community where all must be taken seriously and their opinions respected, there is always tension. Paul speaks into such a situation, for differences of opinion and conviction can cause rift and division.

He urges those who are strong in faith to make sure their confidence does not damage weak believers. They are to do this by not passing judgment on them. Paul is anxious that respect for the consciences of other Christians is given and that things are not pressed on them of which they are unsure. What a model Paul is presenting! God does not want a church full of successful and confident people. He wants a church to be full of believers with different natures and characters so that, as they care for each other's needs, the world sees how they love one another. This love is not to be like that of the tax collectors (Matt 5:46) but like the love of God who, in his infinite power and

---

[689] For a detailed discussion, see Reasoner, *Strong*. Nanos, *Mystery*, argues that the weak are non-Christian Jews, while Gagnon, "Weak," 64–82, argues that the term refers to Gentile Christians. Käsemann, *Romans*, 374, thinks that the strong are Gentile believers who think the Jews are over scrupulous. See also Fitzmyer, *Romans*, 687, and Witherington, *Romans*, 395. Keck, "What," 18, notes: "It is no less obscure why, if the (Jewish) 'root' supports the (Gentile) graftee, it is the strong Gentile who is urged to 'bear with the failings of the weak' (Jewish Christian). Does one not expect Paul to ask the scrupulous 'root' to be patient with the freewheeling Gentile until the graft is 'set'?"

[690] See also Wright, *Romans*, 731, who says: "The best reading of this problem, I think, is that the divisions Paul knew to exist within the Roman church have at least a strong element about them of the Jew/Gentile tension that has been underneath so much of the letter. This is by no means to say that 'the weak' are Jewish Christians and 'the strong' are Gentile Christians. Paul is himself a Jewish Christian who sees himself as one of the 'strong.'" Moo, *Romans*, 837, thinks that the term "the strong" suggests dominance and poses questions as to the examples that Paul gives, for they represent both groups.

[691] See Rom 15:1.

[692] See Fitzmyer, *Romans*, 689; Cranfield, *Romans*, 698, 700.

wisdom, comes alongside frail and uncertain believers, working to help them grow and embrace certainties. Imposing stronger "faith" on a weak believer results in a false discipleship where the belief system of others are held without understanding their foundations. The divine example must be the guide as the letter to the Philippians demonstrates. In that letter, Paul used a beautiful piece of poetry—probably adapted as a hymn—to speak of the example of Christ (Phil 2:6–11). This understanding of who the strong are is contrary to what most scholars hold, seeing the description as a reference to numerical superiority. However Paul will go on to say:

> Accept one another, then, just as Christ accepted you, in order to bring praise to God. For I tell you that Christ has become a servant of the Jews on behalf of God's truth, to confirm the promises made to the patriarchs so that the Gentiles may glorify God for his mercy, as it is written: "Therefore I will praise you among the Gentiles; I will sing hymns to your name." Again, it says, "Rejoice, O Gentiles, with his people." And again, "Praise the Lord, all you Gentiles, and sing praises to him, all you peoples." And again, Isaiah says, "The Root of Jesse will spring up, one who will arise to rule over the nations; the Gentiles will hope in him."

> May the God of hope fill you with all joy and peace as you trust in him, so that you may overflow with hope by the power of the Holy Spirit. I myself am convinced, my brothers, that you yourselves are full of goodness, complete in knowledge and competent to instruct one another. I have written you quite boldly on some points, as if to remind you of them again, because of the grace God gave me to be a minister of Christ Jesus to the Gentiles with the priestly duty of proclaiming the gospel of God, so that the Gentiles might become an offering acceptable to God, sanctified by the Holy Spirit (Rom 15:7–16)

Clearly the exhortation is that the Jewish believers welcome the Gentile believers who Christ himself has welcomed and whose welcome has been made possible by the ministry that Paul has fulfilled. Paul has written to the Gentiles to assure them that they are "full of goodness, complete in knowledge and competent to instruct one another,"[693] and that they should be full of joy and peace because God has welcomed them.

---

[693] Particularly relevant for a Gentile community in danger of succumbing to the claim that they are not holy if they refuse to become Jews.

14:2 One man's faith allows him to eat everything, but another man, whose faith is weak, eats only vegetables.

Paul presents two extremes of faith. One is of a Christian who has no conscience about what he eats. The other belongs to one who is deeply distressed over issues relating to meat and who, therefore, is vegetarian. There is no suggestion in the Scripture that vegetarianism was an issue, so it is probable that Paul has believers in mind, like the ones in Corinth, who are deeply concerned with the meat's origin (1 Cor 10:23–32). In Rome, it appears that some of the believers are taking the rather extreme measure of only eating vegetables in order to ensure that they do not unknowingly eat meat that had been offered to idols.

14:3 The man who eats everything must not look down on him who does not, and the man who does not eat everything must not condemn the man who does, for God has accepted him.

Paul raises an issue that was a common problem in the early church. The Christians lived in societies where pagan gods were worshiped daily, the meat of the sacrificed animals being sold on to market traders. Consequently, it was almost impossible to be certain that meat bought in the marketplace was free from association with idol worship. Those who converted to Christ from idolatry knew the significance of such offerings. They were the means of celebrating fellowship with the forces of darkness and the meat of such sacrificed animals was the property of the deities who had been worshiped. "How," such Christians asked, "could any believer eat such food?" They reasoned that it could only be by sinful compromise, offending God and rupturing fellowship with him.

While Paul believes that idols have no objective reality or existence (1 Cor 8:1–8), he realizes, nevertheless, that eating meat sacrificed to them is a cause of great difficulty for some. He explains that there is a reality of demons exploiting idols and enslaving those who worship them.

Here, in Rom 14:3, Paul lays down an important principle of Christian tolerance. It is all too easy to see one's own position as superior. The matter under consideration was the eating of or abstaining from certain meats. Those who ate them saw themselves as more robust and stronger in faith than those who abstained; those who abstained saw themselves as more spiritual and sensitive to the will of God than those who ate. Both believed that they were the ones concerned for the glory of God.

14:4 Who are you to judge someone else's servant? To his own master he stands or falls. And he will stand, for the Lord is able to make him stand.

Paul stresses the inappropriateness of intruding into somebody else's relationship with God. His argument is clear: "What right have you got to judge someone whom God has accepted?" If some of the Roman believers were to claim that they knew things about another believer of which God was ignorant, it would be the height of arrogance in the face of his omniscience, for he knows all things. Paul's point is that when God accepts a believer, he becomes God's responsibility.[694] Judgment in such matters is not for his fellow believers to exercise—for God has never assigned such authority to them. A pressing reason for Paul writing this letter was because such a presumption was in danger of ripping the church apart.

14:5 One man considers one day more sacred than another; another man considers every day alike. Each one should be fully convinced in his own mind.

Paul moves from the issue of meat-eating and applies the same principle to another matter that was straining the relationship between Jewish and Gentile believers in Rome. Some believed that certain days were more holy than others and ought to be observed by following rules that had developed around them. Others did not see any intrinsic sacredness in these days, for God was with them in all their affairs of life and not just in "holy affairs." Such Christians could not see why they should be forced to keep days as holy when the whole of life was holy.

The subtle thing about the choice Paul made in raising these examples is that the eating of meat distressed the Gentile believers[695] but the non-

---

[694] Käsemann, *Romans*, 370, says: "Paul is announcing his confidence that the Lord of the community, having once received a member, can cause him to stand again when he falls. Grace is stronger than human frailty."

[695] Snodgrass "Kingdom," 521–25, argues that the weak are Jewish believers who consider that the food laws of the OT continue to apply. See also Witherington, *Romans*, 330–37, who confuses numerical strength with theological strength., see also Käsemann, *Romans*, 366, who considers the reference to "the strong" to be about numerical strength and sees it to be the Christian Gentile majority. The different opinions on the identity of the weak and the strong reflect how each group viewed itself and its behavior. Both groups were convinced that their attitude and behavior was what God wanted, and saw themselves as strong. It is true that the Gentiles had the numerical strength in the Roman church, but minorities are often stronger in their convictions—especially if driven by an orthodoxy that sustains their sense of superiority.

observance of certain days distressed the Jewish believers. He carefully selected issues that gave both parties an insight into the pain of being abused, misunderstood, or rejected. It is this contrast of experiences—highlighted in the following verse—that suggests it is the Gentile believers who are referred to as the weaker in the matter of the eating of meat. If this is not so, then both examples would be about Jewish offense, and this would not serve the greater purpose of both parties learning to accept each other.

14:6 *He who regards one day as special, does so to the Lord. He who eats meat, eats to the Lord, for he gives thanks to God; and he who abstains, does so to the Lord and gives thanks to God.*

As is Paul's practice, he restates the essence of the argument. The attitude of the believers' hearts is the real issue. The argument Paul is making is similar to that found in 1 Cor 8–10, but there are significant differences between the two situations and their associated problems.

In Corinth, some were exercising their freedom by eating idol meat in the pagan temple itself. To "weaker brethren," this suggested a participation in fellowship with the demons that hid behind the idols. However, in Rome the issue does not appear as complicated. Possibly the situation is different because, with a strong Jewish community (estimated between 20,000 and 50,000 at the time of Claudius' edict[696]), kosher butchers were well established and provided the assurance that the meat on sale had not had contact with temple worship. Obviously, we have no idea how many such butchers survived the edict—possibly the majority were expelled. Nevertheless, it is reasonable to suggest that if there was ongoing trade from Gentile converts who preferred kosher meat because of its unpolluted source, some businesses would have been taken over to meet the demand.

---

[696] In ca. AD 49, Emperor Claudius expelled Jews from Rome (probably because Christianity had caused unrest within the Jewish community). There is some debate about what actually happened. It is reported by Suetonius that it was a result of some disturbances "at the instigation of Chrestos." This was probably due to some Jewish-Christian missionaries encountering opposition from Jews in Rome when they preached that Jesus was the Christ (see also Acts 18:2). Cassius Dio minimizes the event, and Josephus—who was reporting on Jewish events—does not mention it at all. Some scholars hold that the expulsion did not happen, while others have only a few missionaries expelled for the short term. The silence about the edict in official records is hardly surprising as Claudius was obsessed with making edicts, and this one was minor compared to others he had made.

14:7 For none of us lives to himself alone and none of us dies to himself alone.

Paul stresses that no one is a free agent. We all have responsibilities to someone else—a husband has responsibilities to his wife and the wife has responsibilities to her husband, a father to his children and the children to their father, an employee to his employer and the employer to his employee, etc. This said, all are responsible to God, and their lives and deaths are significant to him. Christ has died to save us, and our death is the means by which we enter into his immediate presence. Both life and death serve the purposes of God for his children. We are, therefore, responsible to him in both life and death. To use the psalmist's words: "Where shall I flee from your presence?" (Ps 139:7).

14:8 If we live, we live to the Lord; and if we die, we die to the Lord. So, whether we live or die, we belong to the Lord.

No matter what experiences life brings to Paul and the believers in Rome, he reminds them that they are kept by Christ. There may be things that happen that are the opposite of what they want, but Paul encourages them that their status cannot be threatened for they "belong to the Lord."

Paul is saying that God uses the whole range of human experience to teach us about his faithfulness and bring believers to maturity in Christ (see comments on Rom 5:1–8; 8:35ff.). In viewing life from this perspective, distressing experiences become part of the teaching process by means of which God prepares his people for heaven.

The experience of the community is prominent in Paul's thinking– evidenced by the repeated use of the pronoun "we." Theirs is a corporate experience that comes from sharing in the death of Christ (see comments on Rom 6:1–5), and exists because of membership of the covenant community. It is essentially covenantal and corporate, flowing from the work of the Messiah and his Spirit.[697]

14:9 For this very reason, Christ died and returned to life so that he might be the Lord of both the dead and the living.

The reason for Christ's death, resurrection, and ascension was the restoration of creation—especially humankind—to its original position of subjection to his Lordship. Through Adam's sin, the cosmos had not merely

---

[697] Contra Jewett, *Romans*, 848, who says: "This passage is a clear example of collective mysticism." It is, rather, a clear example of covenantal oneness.

come under the curse of God's judgment but had passed into the "control" of Satan. However, the death and resurrection of Jesus terminated that relationship just as Adam's disobedience had ruptured the relationship between creation and God.

The restoration of all things to their pre-fallen condition is known by theologians as "recapitulation," when the control of all things—created and uncreated—will be handed back to Christ. Sadly, not all people will know this return to blessedness. Humankind, made in the image of God, has been given extraordinary dignity in that God's salvation is not forced upon it; salvation is offered but not imposed. Humankind is invited to exercise their right to respond. Without that right and responsibility being exercised they remain in the kingdom of darkness and outside of the transformation, i.e., outside of the recapitulation. They have denied salvation for one simple reason: they have chosen to remain in the kingdom of darkness—the body of sin. They remain in Adam, and they are responsible for the consequences that flow from the state of alienation.[698]

The declaration that Jesus is Lord would have been seen as an affront to the Emperor. Caesar not only claimed absolute rights over his subjects, he claimed to be the son of God. This claim of divinity impacted many in the empire, especially those in the state's direct employment. They demonstrated their allegiance to him by offering sacrifices. There were times that this practice of honoring Caesar as the incarnate god was demanded of all citizens of the empire. Consequently, submission to the Lordship of Christ placed the Roman Christians in real danger of rousing the state's anger and experiencing its punishment.

Paul is not declaring a political manifesto in this statement—he is declaring a theological truth. Nevertheless, such truth inevitably has implications in many aspects of life including its political dimension.

---

[698] Käsemann, *Romans*, 372, says: "Christ has gone through life and death and now has power over both. The contour of the cosmocreator becomes visible, who leaves no one in a private sphere and who orients all things to himself. Belonging to him or not becomes the eschatological criterion of all humanity and thus characterizes all activity, transcending our criteria."

14:10 You, then, why do you judge your brother? Or why do you look down on your brother? For we will all stand before God's judgment seat.

Paul introduces his question to the believers with the words "You, then," making the charge personal. He does not write a generalization such as "we ought not to judge," but addresses the conscience of the believers who gathered to hear the letter read to them.

The issues raised are the judging of and the looking down on brothers. Paul stresses that they are not only undesirable actions, they are sinful. Judgment usurps God's authority. This will become clear on the day of judgment when all will stand before him—not only those who have been condemned by judgmental spirits[699] but also those who have exercised such judgment. The implication seems to be that the one who was unjustly judged will become the accuser and the one who was the self-righteous accuser will be the one charged.

Of course, in writing this, Paul would not want to imply that Christians should not express concern when people are behaving badly but that concern should be expressed in a spirit of love. Christ made it clear that, when believers sin, those in close contact ought to encourage them to repent (Matt 18:15). When this fails, it is the church's responsibility to bring discipline (Matt 18:16–17; 1 Cor 5:2–5). What is different in these cases from the ones dealt with in Rom 14 is that Paul is dealing with matters of conscience regarding ceremonial law. The discipline of believers takes place when the moral law has been broken.

14:11 It is written: "'As surely as I live' says the Lord, 'Every knee will bow before me; every tongue will confess to God.'"

Paul concludes his argument with a quotation from Isa 45:23. The way he uses this Scripture to support his argument demonstrates how the Scripture determined his worldview. Isaiah had said these words in Yahweh's name and Paul was able to bring the principles behind them to bear on the problems that existed in the Roman church. Paul is anxious that his converts develop this biblical mindset, and that they learn to put all of the issues of life—whether personal and trivial, or international and crucial—into the framework of biblical revelation and thinking (cf. Rom 12:1–2). When Israel failed to do this in the OT (negotiating her place among the nations instead) she was swallowed

---

[699] Some Greek MSS (ℵ^c, C^2, Ψ, 048, 0209, and the *Koinē* text-tradition) read *Chrisou* instead of *theou*, which is the reading of the majority of the best MSS (ℵ*, A, B, C*, D, F, G, 630, 1506, 1739).

up with compromise (Isa 31:1–3). However, when she embraced the worldview proclaimed by the prophets, she triumphed and God's name was glorified (Isa 66:10–22).

Paul has also used Isa 45:23 in Phil 2:1–12, where he applied it to all bowing before Christ. However, here in Romans he retains the original Isaianic context of bowing before Yahweh. This ability to move between "God" and "Christ" (i.e., applying the Scripture about Yahweh to Christ) is strong evidence that Paul understood and taught that Jesus is God (this would be developed by the fathers into Trinitarianism). Here, Paul supports his contention by blending Isa 49:18 and Isa 45:23, quoting the latter with minor changes to the word order. The use of Isa 49:18 is of interest to our theme, for the remnant benefits from the subjection of the nations. They are provided as an inheritance and become the attire for the remnant's marriage to Yahweh: "'As surely as I live,' declares the LORD, 'you will wear them all as ornaments; you will put them on, like a bride'" (Isa 49:18).[700]

14:12 So then, each of us will give an account of himself to God.

At this point, Paul stresses personal responsibility. As we have seen earlier, we have to be careful not to apply to the individual what is only true of the church. However, while it is true that the church has a corporate responsibility, Paul unequivocally speaks to the individual members of the Roman congregation. He makes it clear that each believer has to put into action what he has been taught. If he fails to do so, he will bear his own guilt on the day of judgment. This shows that Paul expects a judgment for the believer (2 Cor 5:10). This does not relate to salvation but to his life following conversion to Christ. The particular case Paul has in mind at this point is the damage done to other believers.

This is not an isolated passage. It is clear that there was an ongoing concern in church leadership over this issue (Acts 15:5–21; 21:20–21). The church of the twenty-first century also needs to heed this warning. All too often, sensitive believers avoid fellowship with professing local churches because they, or others they know, have been dealt with harshly and uncaringly within them. Christ does not deal with them in such a way. He is the good shepherd who gives his life for his sheep (John 10:11). When church ideals are in conflict with the compassion and love of Christ, they must be questioned. This is not suggesting that churches abandon standards but that they must hold them in the

---

[700] See Käsemann, *Romans*, 372–73.

context of Christ's compelling love rather than destructive legalism which promotes self-righteousness and self-satisfaction.

14:13 Therefore let us stop passing judgment on one another. Instead, make up your mind not to put any stumbling block or obstacle in your brother's way.

We should not pass judgment on others over matters that are not crucial to our relationship with God. Not only is judgment negative but it puts a stumbling block in the way of those who are being criticized. Such hindrance to their progress is no small thing as the Christian life is likened to a pilgrimage towards our spiritual home. Such criticism discourages others on their pilgrimage, deflecting them from the road that Christ has called them to walk along. For that reason it is sin.

14:14 As one who is in the Lord Jesus, I am fully convinced that no food is unclean in itself. But if anyone regards something as unclean, then for him it is unclean.

Paul states his position clearly. He describes himself as one who is "in the Lord Jesus." In doing this, he identifies himself with the status of every other believer.[701] He is not seeking to lord it over the believers, but appeals to them on equal terms.

This conciliatory posture was not always adopted by Paul. When the objective truth of the Gospel was at stake, he was very assertive (Gal 2:14). However, he does not take this confrontational position with the Roman believers for good reason. This was not an issue of Gospel truth or apostolic authority.

Paul's position remains true to the one taken in the earlier part of the chapter. No food is intrinsically unclean. God has given all food as a gift—even food offered in sacrifice to demons is intrinsically clean. However, if a believer is unable to thank God for providing such food—believing it to be unclean—he ought not to eat it. In writing this, Paul was handling the "weaker" believers in Rome with great sensitivity. The eating of meat was a serious issue for them, causing them (they thought) to become psychologically and spiritually "unclean."

---

[701] Contra Morris, *Romans*, 486, who understands the statement to be based on Paul's union with Christ, citing the GNB: "My union with the Lord Jesus makes me certain."

In this example, Paul demonstrates his love for Christ and the people of God. He not only tells the weaker in faith not to eat meat but, in his letter to the Corinthians, he says that if in the eating of meat a brother is offended, the stronger in faith should stop eating, even though it was his God-given right to enjoy (1 Cor 8:13). Here is a demonstration of the pastoral heart. In his tenderness, Paul thinks of others above himself. He stands with the weaker brothers, and even though his theological reasoning dismisses their arguments, his love and respect for them does not allow him to march away from the argument as the victor and indulge himself in his legitimate freedoms.

How different churches would be if they recognized the legitimate diversity of views as well as the folly of imposing their views on others who have not been persuaded of their perspective. When people are pressurized to conform to expressions of personal preferences rather than the clear directives of Scripture, their growth is inevitably stunted. There are many things that are good but are not the essence of the Gospel—such practices as keeping certain days as holy, upholding good and sensible health principles, and other social norms that societies throw up as "best practice." It is amazing how Christians can confuse their cultural heritage with "Christian norms" and assume that it is an essential non-negotiable part of the Gospel.

14:15 *If your brother is distressed because of what you eat, you are no longer acting in love. Do not by your eating destroy your brother for whom Christ died.*

Paul takes his advice a step further. Earlier, he had been concerned about the weaker brother and his difficulty in eating meat previously offered to idols. Now he widens the issue. He tells those with robust consciences that if their eating of meat causes others to stumble, they affect the faith of those who see danger and defilement in eating in such a way.[702] Paul writes that they are no longer acting in love for, in insisting on their rights, they are in danger of destroying the ones for whom Christ has died.

This is an amazing assertion. These "stronger" believers had seen themselves as mature and liberated members of the church. Paul is effectively saying "If you are mature, then behave as such. Put the needs of the weaker brother as a priority in your lives. It has cost Christ his life to bring this brother into fellowship with himself. Do you dare drive him away as a consequence of

---

[702] Murray, *Romans*, vol. 2:190, points out that more than grief is involved as there is hurt from the violation of a religious principle.

demanding your right to practice your freedom?" Such a perspective seriously challenges what most of us understand as Christian maturity. Rather than being strong and arguing for one's own point of view, Christian maturity is about servanthood and following Christ in his self-denial (Phil 2:1–15).

14:16 Do not allow what you consider good to be spoken of as evil.

What does Paul refer to when he writes that they should not let what they "consider as good to be spoken of as evil?"[703] It could be argued that it refers to their freedom to eat meat. That certainly has been the flow of the argument. However, it could also be argued that it is a preparatory statement, for in the following verse, he pleads that the members of the church recognize that there is something much bigger than their own interests—the kingdom of God. Indeed, he goes on to show how these contentious issues fall into their proper place when seen in the context of the reign of God.

This exhortation needs to be heard and obeyed by the people of God in the twenty-first century. Christian communities can be divided over matters that are of little significance when seen in light of the issues about which God is concerned. Personal preferences and prejudices can be dressed up as the most spiritual of arguments to justify pressurizing others into accepting them. Such attempts to "defend the truth" demonstrate a lack of spirituality, for the love that pervaded Paul's appeal is missing. The absence of love is not rectified by blind devotion to a doctrinal system, no matter how correct and orthodox it might be (1 Cor 13:1–13).

14:17 For the kingdom of God is not a matter of eating and drinking, but of righteousness, peace and joy in the Holy Spirit.

The kingdom of God has not been explicitly mentioned until now,[704] despite the fact that the whole of the letter has been dealing with the subject. The Son of David was predicted to be the inaugurator of the kingdom, and he had come in the person of Jesus (Rom 1:3). The letter is centered on the

---

[703] Gagnon, "Meaning," 675–89 argues that, despite the widespread disagreement over the meaning of "your good (thing)" in Rom 14:16, the "charism" interpretation of this phrase as "the faith of you, the strong, to eat all things" should be regarded as secure.

[704] See Jewett, *Romans*, 863, who points out that while the kingdom of God is rare in Paul's letters, the way it is used here suggests he assumes that the church in Rome has a clear understanding of its theological significance.

ethnicity of the kingdom.[705] It is composed of Jews and Gentiles, and the letter deals with the problems that this "new man" experiences. Paul is clearly distressed that the church is caught up with matters that divide. The apostles met to give authoritative guidance to the Gentiles (Acts 15:6–29), but the evidence suggests that the instructions fell on many Jewish believers' deaf ears (Acts 21:20–21).

14:18 Because anyone who serves Christ in this way is pleasing to God and approved by men.

The definite article with "Christ" indicates that the term is being used titularly. This confirms that Paul's use has this Messianic significance and that it had not been lost in the Gentile mission. This confirms the correctness of reading the letter in light of the OT expectations regarding Israel's long promised Messiah king, who is the Christ. Thus references throughout the letter to the term "Christ" are correctly read as Messianic in meaning and significance.

It is typical of Paul to write that serving the preference of others serves Christ. It is pleasing to God (Phil 2:1–15) as Christian living should not fight for rights but strive for unity. It respects the uncertainties and fears of others, and is concerned to see them grow into Christ. It is all too easy to think we are serving Christ when motivated by the prejudices of our own hearts and not by his Spirit. How easy it is to confuse the two. How many dreadful mistakes have been made by people who have claimed they were doing God's will while causing the name of Christ to be brought into disrepute? When we serve Christ out of the motive of caring for others, we bring delight to the heart of God and an acknowledgment by others that we are not motivated by bigotry or the like.

14:19 Let us therefore make every effort to do what leads to peace and to mutual edification.

The term εἰρήνης "peace" is used earlier in the letter where Paul refers to "peace with God" (Rom 5:1; 8:6). Those who are at peace with him are obliged

---

[705] While some commentators (See Turner, S., "Interim," 323–42) say that the "kingdom of God" refers to a future kingdom, the following statement clearly presents the kingdom as present in the church.

to be at peace with other believers as this promotes "mutual edification."[706] This clearly suggests that imposing one's view on another is not to be tolerated.

Great effort is needed to enter into the thinking and fears of other people. If we do not take the trouble to appreciate where they come from in terms of the experiences and traditions that mold their understanding, we have little hope of treating them with respect. Without such effort, we are effectively saying that others have to be made in our image—something that is not only dangerous but blasphemous. The only one who has the right to someone in his own image is God himself.

Without understanding how our differences have come into existence, we can never be instruments of peace and attain mutual edification. Demanding conformity to our own particular understanding of secondary issues divides rather than unites. Indeed, it is important that we understand why we hold *our* own views lest we canonize the tradition into which we were converted or which we have adopted.

14:20 Do not destroy the work of God for the sake of food. All food is clean, but it is wrong for a man to eat anything that causes someone else to stumble.

Paul returns to the issue of eating meats. He has no difficulty in upholding the Jewish view that all prescribed food is clean, for it is the provision of the gracious Creator God. However, he is not limiting himself to prescribed food. Paul is saying that all food is clean—something with which Peter had to come to terms (Acts 9:9–16). But Paul is equally clear that what God has declared clean can easily become the instrument of Satan, for the insistence of "true understanding" and the practice of one's own rights can lead to the destruction of a weaker brother's faith.[707]

What is sinful is not the eating of meat but the arrogant manner in which it is eaten. It reveals that the freedom demonstrated is irresponsible and nothing to do with the truth and love of God but rather the arrogant rights of the

---

[706]The uses of οἰκοδομή for congregational edification are found elsewhere in Paul (1 Cor 3:9–10; 14:3, 5, 12, 26; 2 Cor 10:8; 12:19; 13:10), and they are used in the LXX as a metaphor to describe the work of God in building Israel as a congregation for himself (Jer 12:16; 38:4, 28; 40:7; 49:10; 45:4; 51:34).

[707] The Greek leaves it unclear who the person is that is eating. In v. 14, the reference was to the "weaker" brother and the same argument may continue. However, the grammar and immediate context suggest that the reference is to the "stronger" brother. For support, Moo, *Application*, 462; Käsemann, *Romans*, 378; Cranfield, *Romans*, 723–24.

offender. How easily that which is good divides and offends, causing the work of God to be destroyed in a sensitive soul. No amount of arguing about the lack of "spirituality" or about the sovereign grace of God to care for his own will diminish the responsibility that we carry for causing others to stumble. No one defended such doctrines more than the Apostle Paul; yet here he is, pleading for the unity that Christ prayed for, and making it clear that there is no compromise in the giving of high regard and attention to those who are in need of sympathy and support.

14:21 It is better not to eat meat or drink wine or to do anything else that will cause your brother to fall.

Not only is it better but it is necessary! The motive of love for fellow believers makes abstinence from what is legitimate something that is God-honoring and glorifying. It is not the other way around as is often argued by advocates of so-called biblical freedom. Freedom is not given so that we may suit ourselves; rather, freedom is given so that we can share in the immense privilege of advancing the kingdom of God—making his love known to his people and to those who are outside of the covenants of promise. It is to be used so that it reveals the tenderness of the one who is the good shepherd. Freedom is to be restrained for the sake of those who would feel trampled upon and despised by those who consider themselves to be the stronger. By forgoing their freedom to eat meat, the Roman believers will show how much they love their brothers and sisters.

Unexpectedly, Paul raises the issue of drinking wine. In light of the fact that drinking wine was widespread and only drunkenness is condemned in the Scriptures, many assume that the reference points to a pagan ritual that took place in the temple.[708] However, in light of what Paul has written to the believers, it seems probable that he was advising the believers to consider the effect of wine on fellow believers. As today, some will have enjoyed drinking to excess and will have tried to curb their dependence on wine since their conversion. Paul's advice is to abstain from drinking wine lest others, who struggle with a history of personal abuse, hear about or see your enjoyment of it.

---

[708] See Morris, *Romans*, 491; Moo, *Romans*, 861.

14:22 So whatever you believe about these things keep between yourself and God. Blessed is the man who does not condemn himself by what he approves.

Paul clearly sees that theological correctness can be morally deficient if it is used to score points. However, there are issues that a believer can keep in his heart. According to the text, certain things can be pondered without being published.

There is clearly a pastoral dimension to teaching. One of the elements is the ability to judge how different Christian truths should be presented and when their implications, as far as Christian living is concerned, should be pressed. Just as there are stages in human development from infancy to adulthood, so there is progression for the Christian. This does not deny that some people develop more rapidly than others, but it does mean that a wise believer should take this into account when dealing with a young Christian.

Does the phrase "Blessed is the man" refer to God's blessing on those who behave in accordance with their conscience, or is it merely Paul's approval of those who act in such a way? Its close proximity to the statement about keeping truth private ought to guide our understanding. It would seem that Paul is saying that the ones who are blessed are those who know that they have struck the right balance. They know that they are not condemned by their conscience. It would, therefore, seem that the blessedness is that of a clear conscience.[709]

14:23 But the man who has doubts is condemned if he eats, because his eating is not from faith; and everything that does not come from faith is sin.

In contrast to the man who has a clear conscience and is blessed, the one who goes against his conscience is condemned. It follows that in this case, being condemned is not referring to God's condemnation but the condemnation of the conscience.[710] However, such self-condemnation leads to God's condemnation, for action "that does not come from faith is sin."

CONCLUSION OF ROMANS CHAPTER FOURTEEN

The new community in Rome is in danger of division—worse than that, it is in danger of civil war. The issue centers on the observance of the law and the

---

[709] Jewett, *Romans*, 871, says: "The blessing in this case comes to everyone who maintains integrity with the faith as they have received it from God, whether it is consistent with the preferences of other groups or not."

[710] There is possibly an echo of the argument in Rom 4, where Paul wrote about Abraham not wavering through unbelief. See Wright, *Romans*, 742.

keeping of its ceremonial requirements. Paul is concerned that this division between Jew and Gentile believers could be the bridgehead that Satan will use to destroy this "new creation" in the capital city.

The key to the whole issue is that Christ is the Lord. It is not for others to judge; rather, they should recognize that Christ has called believers from different backgrounds and with these backgrounds come problems that the Gospel has to address. Paul quotes from the writing of Isaiah to support his argument: Every knee will bow and every tongue will confess the Lordship of Christ [God] (Isa 45:23). Once again, Second Exodus material is used to make the case for the New Exodus. In considering how people are accepted into the kingdom of God, Paul makes it clear that it is not about eating or drinking but righteousness, peace and joy in the Holy Spirit.

Romans 15

THE MESSIAH KING AND HIS SERVANT'S WORK (15:1–33)

We who are strong ought to bear with the failings of the weak and not to please ourselves. Each of us should please his neighbor for his good, to build him up. For even Christ did not please himself but, as it is written: "The insults of those who insult you have fallen on me." For everything that was written in the past was written to teach us, so that through endurance and the encouragement of the Scriptures we might have hope.

May the God who gives endurance and encouragement give you a spirit of unity among yourselves as you follow Christ Jesus, so that with one heart and mouth you may glorify the God and Father of our Lord Jesus Christ.

Accept one another, then, just as Christ accepted you, in order to bring praise to God. For I tell you that Christ has become a servant of the Jews on behalf of God's truth, to confirm the promises made to the patriarchs so that the Gentiles may glorify God for his mercy, as it is written: "Therefore I will praise you among the Gentiles; I will sing hymns to your name."

Again, it says, "Rejoice, O Gentiles, with his people." And again, "Praise the Lord, all you Gentiles, and sing praises to him, all you peoples." And again, Isaiah says, "The Root of Jesse will spring up, one who will arise to rule over the nations; the Gentiles will hope in him." May the God of hope fill you with all joy and peace as you trust in him, so that you may overflow with hope by the power of the Holy Spirit.

I myself am convinced, my brothers, that you yourselves are full of goodness, complete in knowledge and competent to instruct one another. I have written to you quite boldly on some points, as if to remind you of them again, because of the grace God gave me to be a minister of Christ Jesus to the Gentiles with the priestly duty of proclaiming the gospel of God, so that the Gentiles might become an offering acceptable to God, sanctified by the Holy Spirit.

Therefore I glory in Christ Jesus in my service to God. I will not venture to speak of anything except what Christ has accomplished through me in leading the Gentiles to obey God by what I have said and done—by the power of signs and miracles, through the power of the Spirit. So from Jerusalem all the way around to Illyricum, I have fully proclaimed the gospel of Christ. It has always been my ambition to preach the gospel where Christ was not known, so that I would not be building on someone else's foundation. Rather, as it is written: "Those who were not told about him will see, and those who have not heard will understand." This is why I have often been hindered from coming to you.

But now that there is no more place for me to work in these regions, and since I have been longing for many years to see you, I plan to do so when I go to Spain. I hope to visit you while passing through and to have you assist me on my journey there, after I have enjoyed your company for a while. Now, however, I am on my way to Jerusalem in the service of the saints there. For Macedonia and Achaia were pleased to make a contribution for the poor among the saints in Jerusalem. They were pleased to do it, and indeed they owe it to them. For if the Gentiles have shared in the Jews' spiritual blessings, they owe it to the Jews to share with them their material blessings. So after I have completed this task and have made sure that they have received this fruit, I will go to Spain and visit you on the way. I know that when I come to you, I will come in the full measure of the blessing of Christ.

I urge you, brothers, by our Lord Jesus Christ and by the love of the Spirit, to join me in my struggle by praying to God for me. Pray that I may be rescued from the unbelievers in Judea and that my service in Jerusalem may be acceptable to the saints there, so that by God's will I may come to you with joy and together with you be refreshed. The God of peace be with you all. Amen. (Romans 15:1–33)

INTRODUCTION

The chapter continues the theme followed in the preceding chapter. Believers should not fight for their rights but consider the needs of others, especially the needs of those who are weak in their faith. In doing this they are following the example of the one they say they serve (Rom 15:3–4).

Paul goes on to show that this acceptance was foretold by the prophets, a fact that suggests that those who are the strong, who need to be urged to accept the weaker brethren, are the Jews, for such a citation is especially suited to them in their reluctance to give up their Jewish understanding of what God requires, which tended to be mostly about ritual participation. Their mutual acceptance was to be of the same kind as they have received from Christ who had every right to reject us all because of our uncleanness.

Paul reflects on his ministry, which is not one of salvage to a second rate status but of the restoration of humanity to the privileged position of being priests unto God. He sees his own ministry to be priestly (Rom 15:16) and it is into this ministry that the Gentiles have been brought.

Paul expresses the desire that he will be able to visit them on his way to Spain where he desires to plan the church of Christ (Rom 15:28). He tells of his plans to visit Jerusalem with the gift provided by the Gentile churches. He solicits prayer for this endeavor that he knows is dangerous because of the hatred some hold towards him for defending Gentile freedom (15:31).

15:1 We who are strong ought to bear with the failings of the weak and not to please ourselves.

Most scholars consider that Paul is now making an appeal to the Jewish believers for they know there is only one God and that idols are nothing.[711] But has Paul swung from appealing to the Gentiles in chapter 14 to appealing to the Jews in this chapter? I have argued that Paul was addressing the Jewish believers in Rom 14:22–23; therefore, this verse is not a change of argument but an application of what he was saying. If this is so, then the one who is not eating out of faith is not the Gentile who is going beyond what his conscience allows, but the Jew who is going beyond what love allows.

15:2 Each of us should please his neighbor for his good, to build him up.

The pastoral heart of Paul shines through again as he appeals to the believers. He is anxious that they learn to be more concerned for the needs of others rather than their own rights and freedoms.

The respect and love believers give each other complement the teaching ministry of the church in strengthening them in their faith. Indeed, formal

---

[711] "Under the gospel, the strong—those who, because of the inner freedom which has been given to them, have plenty of room in which to maneuver, have an inescapable obligation to help carry the infirmities, disabilities, embarrassments and encumbrances of their brothers who are having to live without that inner freedom which they themselves enjoy." Cranfield, *Shorter*, 353. Cranfield also suggests the strong are the believing Gentile majority, 341. See also, Fitzmyer, *Romans*, 687.

teaching can be undone if the members of the congregation do not live out the realities to which they have been exposed, grieving the Holy Spirit as well as "weaker" brethren. While the translators of the NRSV and the NIV understand "building up" in v.2 to apply to the individual, the term regularly refers to the community in Paul's other writings (1 Cor 14:5; Eph 4:12, 29).

In the introduction to the commentary, I suggested Paul's reason for writing the letter was to give the Romans guidance over the issues that were causing divisions in other churches. The Jewish-Gentile relationship was at the center of most of the early church's problems. This suggestion seems to be confirmed in this penultimate chapter. Paul is constantly appealing to his countrymen to accept the Gentiles, showing the Jews that, as the Lord's servant, they have been appointed to bring the light of the good news to the nations. They are to be servants to the Gentiles–not preferring themselves over the ones they serve (Phil 2:2–4).

15:3 *For even Christ did not please himself but, as it is written: "The insults of those who insult you have fallen on me."*

Paul appeals to the great example of Christ in accordance with the apostles' teaching (2 Cor 8:9–15; Phil 2:1–11; Heb 12:1–3; 1 Pet 2:21–25), for when arguments fail, examples often triumph. The example of the Son of God, who offered up his life for those who hated and killed him, has transformed more lives than arguments have ever done. Christ was not only an example because he relinquished his own will but because he subjected himself to the violence and rejection of humankind in all of its ugly brutality. Very soon, those authorities that crucified Jesus would turn on the Roman believers themselves. They will become another example of a vessel chosen for privilege becoming a vessel fitted for wrath.

Paul's point is clear—we have an obligation to follow Christ's example if we dare to call ourselves his disciples. He put others before himself. The citation from the OT is Ps 69:9 (LXX) and it is used elsewhere in the NT (Mark 15:36; Luke 23:36; John 19:29; Rev 13:8). It is significant that, rather than alluding to the actual events in the life of Christ that demonstrate his self-giving, Paul goes back to the OT Scriptures for his support. There can be little doubt that the suffering referred to in the psalm is seen by Paul to speak prophetically of the passion of Christ. We can only speculate about why he avoided making direct reference to the life of Jesus. It is not that he rejected any desire to know anything about the earthly Jesus (as some have argued from 2 Cor 5:16). The reference to not wanting to know Christ after the flesh probably means that he did not want to interpret his life from any nationalistic Messianic perspective as he would have done before his conversion.

15:4 For everything that was written in the past was written to teach us, so that through endurance and the encouragement of the Scriptures we might have hope.

The importance of the Jewish Scriptures for the fledgling church cannot be exaggerated. The Jewish believers and the God-fearers were saturated with them because they had no other sacred writings (the NT only existed as an emerging collection). The OT gave them the theological framework by which they interpreted the significance of the life, death and resurrection of Jesus. However, it was not only the life of Jesus that was interpreted through the lens of OT expectation, their experiences were as well.

We have seen in the introduction to the commentary how widespread Paul's use of the Scriptures was in his thinking and writing. He was not unique. The same OT perspective permeated the thinking of the entire church. This is evident from the argument being presented as his readers were expected to understand the context of references and significance of echoes. If our presentation of Romans has been correct, the whole of this Epistle exemplifies this undergirding dependence.

The reference to having hope is significant, for Paul has written in Rom 5:1–5 that hope is the fruit of the gift of the Spirit to the church. Without the outworking of the Word and Spirit, the early church's living hope cannot be experienced. It was the Spirit who applied the promise of the OT to the fledgling church and it is he who continues to apply the same, with its NT fulfillment, to the church of today. Any Christian community which does not keep the Word and the Spirit in balance is in danger of having a deficient understanding and experience of God's grace.

15:5 May the God who gives endurance and encouragement give you a spirit of unity among yourselves as you follow Christ Jesus,

Paul prays out of personal experience (2 Cor 1:3–11). The prayer is not a platitude uttered from the safety of a distant administrative center. It was written by a man who is in the heat of battle and desires for the church in Rome to share in what he knows of God's sustaining grace and encouragement.

He prays not only for endurance but also for God's encouragement. As these two blessings flow into the believers' lives, they become united in heart and mind and together gladly submit to Christ. This unity will lead them to serve one another as Paul has encouraged them to do in Rom 15:1.

15:6 So that with one heart and mouth you may glorify the God and Father of our Lord Jesus Christ.

This is the goal of the Gospel. The ultimate purpose of God in saving people for himself is that they might corporately demonstrate the character and wisdom of their Savior (Eph 3:10–13). It is no more wrong of God to desire to be acknowledged by those he has saved than for parents to want to hear expressions of love and joy from the children they bore. It is not a selfish obsession, because God is the God of love who rejoices in the overthrow of evil and the recovery of his creation from Sin's captivity. According to the Westminster Catechism, man's chief end is to love God and enjoy him forever.

15:7 Accept one another, then, just as Christ accepted you, in order to bring praise to God.

The statement in the Greek begins with the conjunction Διὸ (*dio*) "wherefore." Paul's appeal is based on the preceding verses where he explained the goal and effects of the Gospel and the example set by Christ.

Christian relationships are not an optional extra to discipleship. They are an essential part of the Christian life for, when lived out as God intends, they bring him praise. For the believer, there can be no greater reason for pursuing Christian reconciliation and mutual encouragement than this. As this reason was given in the previous verse, its repetition indicates the importance of accepting one another.

I have claimed that the letter to the Romans is a pastoral letter about Jewish/Gentile relationships. Here, in this verse, Paul makes his final appeal for the acceptance of the Jew by the Gentile community and the Gentile by the Jewish Christian community.[712] His appeal sums up his plea made since Rom 14:1 and has been based on the theological argument of Jewish and Gentile equality as discussed in chapters 1–12. This understanding is endorsed by the next verse, which emphasizes the Gentiles' acceptance into the new covenant community.

However, it must be noted that it is wrong to consider Paul's appeal as a demand to overlook sinful actions in the quest for peace. When a man took his

---

[712] Sass, "Römerbriefs," 510–27, argues that vv.7–13 are a summary of the whole letter. In Rom 15:9b–12, Paul uses OT quotations as evidence for his Gospel.

father's wife in the Corinthian church (1 Cor 5:1–13), Paul did not urge the congregation to accept him–he threatened that he would discipline any who behaved in such a way. He made it clear that such behavior violated the commands of God; even the pagans drew the line at such behavior. Respecting the weak did not mean tolerating issues that violated the moral law of the Torah. Roman believers are to accept one another in the way that Christ accepted them, i.e., with no reservation and out of immeasurable grace. The example of Christ is a far greater influence than a theoretical discussion of acceptance and has inspired the reconciliation of people over the centuries who would never have known the restoration of relationship.

15:8 For I tell you that Christ has become a servant of the Jews on behalf of God's truth, to confirm the promises made to the patriarchs,

The phrase "I tell you," introduces a solemn doctrinal pronouncement.[713] In this verse, there is an echo of Isa 42:1–9, where the servant establishes justice on the earth (v.4) and is made a light for the Gentiles (v.6). As a result, the blind are given their sight, captives are delivered (v.7), and idols are exposed as valueless (v.8).

Servanthood had been Israel's calling, but she failed to fulfill her role.[714] Now the servant church has been called to fulfill the task that Israel refused to do by bringing good news to those in darkness. Paul clearly sees Jesus, the Christ, to be the one who would bless the Gentiles, fulfilling the promise made to Abraham, Isaac, and Jacob (Gen 22:18; 26:4; 28:14).[715]

---

[713] Cranfield, *Shorter*, 356.

[714] Williams, "Righteousness," 288, says that Rom 15:8–9a should be translated: "Christ has become a servant from the Jews for the sake of God's truthfulness." If this is correct, then the idea is that God has stayed faithful to his original promise and blessed the Gentiles through the seed of Abraham.

[715] See Keck, "Soteriology," 86. Wagner, "Servant," 475, points out that Paul clinches his argument concerning Gentiles' acceptance by appealing to the Torah (Deut 32:43), the Prophets (Isa 11:10), and the Psalms (Ps 17:50; 116:1 [LXX]) as witnesses that the divine goal of the Messiah's ministry is the creation of a community of Jews and Gentiles glorifying God together. Wagner, op. cit., 477, says that: "Christ is envisioned as God's servant, ministering on behalf of God's faithfulness to his promises."

15:9 So that the Gentiles may glorify God for his mercy, as it is written: "Therefore I will praise you among the Gentiles; I will sing hymns to your name."

The reason for the Gentiles being evangelized is that God will be glorified as a result of his saving mercy towards them. In other words, the whole of creation is to acknowledge that God is a merciful and gracious God.[716] Man, who had long been in the clutches of Satan and deceived regarding God's nature, will see that he had believed the lie.

While the purpose of the Gospel is to bring salvation and not judgment, those who reject its message will suffer the consequence of turning away from the Savior. Those who welcome the news of God's grace will be transformed, becoming the instruments by which his grace is magnified. Paul demonstrates this has been God's purpose throughout history and cites Ps 18:49 to illustrate its biblical basis.

15:10 Again, it says, "Rejoice, O Gentiles, with his people."

Further evidence is given for the welcome the Gentiles are to receive. Paul quotes from the song of Moses (Deut 32:43), which was composed in the closing days of his life as he prepared to bless the tribes of Israel. The song warned the Jews of the character of God—he would punish their rebellion and be vindicated among the nations. The passage Paul quotes is a call to the nations to recognize that Yahweh is just and righteous in all his dealings, not allowing even his elect to be excused for their wrongdoing.

Although the original song did not explicitly state that the Gentiles would be brought into the covenant community, this is the logical deduction. Moses' song does not finish with the judgment of the Jews and the praise of the Gentiles but with the promise that Yahweh will take vengeance on his enemies and make atonement for his land and his people. Yahweh's call to the nations to rejoice suggests they are going to share in the blessing of Israel's restoration. Those who oppose his people, however, will come under judgment: "Rejoice, O ye nations, with his people; for he will avenge the blood of his servants, and will render vengeance to his adversaries, and will be merciful unto his land, *and* to his people (Deut 32:43). The song is, in effect, a summary of the history that

---

[716] Du Toit, "Römerbrief," 69–77, notes that the beginning of the letter has the Gentiles turning from God, refusing to acknowledge him, and coming under his judgment. By the conclusion of the letter, all this has changed as a result of the Gospel. Out of those who were "by nature children of wrath," God has brought into existence a new humanity—made up of Jews and Gentiles—which loves and serves him.

Paul has been outlining in the letter, showing how Israel missed the purpose of her calling and how the Gentiles have been brought in to bring glory to God. The choice of the text is clearly no coincidence, especially as its conclusion is that Israel will be saved.

15:11 And again, "Praise the Lord, all you Gentiles, and sing praises to him, all you peoples."

Paul adds a further OT text to his catena. This time it is Ps 117:1. The two-verse psalm is a summons to the nations to worship the Lord in praise of his love and faithfulness. At face value, it is a plea from the Jewish community to the Gentiles to join in the worship of Yahweh. It presupposes—in line with Paul's reasoning—that there is no priority among them: "Praise the Lord . . . all you people."

15:12 And again, Isaiah says, "The Root of Jesse will spring up, one who will arise to rule over the nations; the Gentiles will hope in him."

Most modern scholars divide the prophecy of Isaiah into sections composed by different authors. However, as far as NT authors were concerned the prophecy had only one author, and they developed their arguments from that perspective.

Paul quotes from Isa 11:1, 10, which predicts the conversion of the Gentiles. This text was understood by the early church to anticipate the later Second Exodus texts, which are prolific in the book of Isaiah. So, once again, we find Paul's use of the OT has strict regard for the original setting of the texts. His use of the OT is mostly confined to demonstrating how they have been spiritually fulfilled through the exodus that Christ has achieved for his people.[717] In saying that Jesus was to rule over the nations, Paul is making a significant political statement. Many in Rome must have hoped desperately that no representative of the Imperial household was present when this statement was read out. It was a direct challenge to the power of the state to say that God

---

[717] Cranfield, *Shorter*, 358, says: "In the quotation of the promise that the Gentiles shall hope in the coming scion of Jesse, the Messiah of the Jews, a promise now already being fulfilled in the lives of the Gentile Christians in Rome, there is an implicit appeal to the strong (many of them Gentile Christians) to receive (compare v. 7) and show consideration to those weak brothers (most, if not all of them, Jewish Christians), according them special honour for the sake of their Kinsman, the Messiah of the Jews, who is the Gentiles' only true hope." This interpretation of the "strong" has been challenged by this commentary. It finds the "strong" to refer always to the Jews.

would raise his Christ above the nations and all would bow to him. The verse illustrates how the Gospel can clash with the political realm because what fallen leaders seek can be diametrically opposed to what God desires—the establishment of righteousness.

15:13 May the God of hope fill you with all joy and peace as you trust in him, so that you may overflow with hope by the power of the Holy Spirit.

Paul adds his own prayer to the Scriptures that he has quoted. It is a beautifully crafted prayer that expresses the most important need of the believers in Rome. He calls God the "God of hope," echoing the previous verse. He does not change the prospects of life so that they become less gloomy but giving hope to man in Sin when, humanly speaking, there is no hope (Eph 2:14–18).

When Paul asks God to fill believers with "all joy and peace" as they trust in him, there is no doubt that he saw emotion to be a key factor in Christian experience and development. He was not looking to produce intellectual know-it-alls in Rome but a community of believers with a loving heartfelt appreciation of the God who had saved them. Unless our intellectual understanding is transformed into overwhelming joy and peace, we must question the nature of our spiritual understanding. Joy and peace are not the products of intellectual attainment but come from trusting in God. Here is the beautiful simplicity and profoundness of the Gospel. While it has engaged some of the finest minds in attempts to penetrate its truths, its treasures and benefits are offered even to children—for God is a God who meets all who respond to him in simple faith.

Paul desires for the believers to overflow with hope by the power of the Holy Spirit, reflecting the hope of the Gentiles (v. 12). Its abundance in their lives will be the result of the Spirit's work. Already he has written to them about the Holy Spirit pouring love into their hearts (Rom 5:5), inspiring a hope which does not disappoint. Because of this powerful work of God by his Spirit, Paul dares to pray that they will overflow with hope.

Since hope affects the way they live and confront the problems of life, they will need an abundance of it in the years ahead, for Nero—driven by his evil and deranged mind—will turn the capital into a burning inferno. He will blame the city's destruction on the infant church, and the believers—the scapegoat of a madman—will suffer unspeakable cruelty for their faith in Christ.

15:14 I myself am convinced, my brothers, that you yourselves are full of goodness, complete in knowledge and competent to instruct one another.

Some see vv.14–16 as key to the exhortatory discourse of Romans.[718] Paul encourages the members of the church by praising the quality of their lives. His praise of the Roman church is not with an ulterior motive. He is not like those public speakers of the ancient world who praised their audience with an eye on the rewards they would receive for their flattery. Paul is realistic about their moral achievements and knows that they are far from perfect. The point is that he sees that the Romans would allow the Spirit to fulfill his ministry in their lives. If they are full of goodness, they will behave towards each other with love and respect. If they have true knowledge, they will understand how knowledge without love counts for nothing (1 Cor 13:2).

The believers in Rome were equipped to instruct each other; this would mean that Gentiles would teach Jews as well as vice versa. It was this ministry of teaching that the Jews believed was their unique calling, but it had led to pride and arrogance. The Gentiles were not as competent in teaching as their Jewish brethren because they had less knowledge of the OT promises. However, well-instructed Gentiles would acquire this theological perspective and would be competent to address Jewish pride. Gentiles would exhort Jewish believers, and this would not be because they had usurped the Jew's historic role but because they had been called to such a ministry by Abraham's God.

15:15 I have written to you quite boldly on some points, as if to remind you of them again, because of the grace God gave me

The apostles believed their responsibility was to keep reminding the church of her inheritance in Christ (2 Pet 3:2; 1 John 5:13; Heb 12:1–3) and Paul acknowledges that he has written "quite boldly on some points." This may indicate his awareness of the sensitive nature of the issues he has raised. He is certain that problems will not go away unless they are confronted and resolved by a clear understanding of the history of salvation. By making a comparison between the ways God has accepted the Jews he has been able to demonstrate that the calling of the Gentiles is not a distortion of the law but its very principle.[719]

---

[718] See Longacre and Wallis, "Eschatology," 367–82.

[719] Bryne, "Boldly," 83–96, thinks that Paul is seeking to bring the Roman church under his apostolic authority and into a place where it accepts that the law could not

15:16 To be a minister of Christ Jesus to the Gentiles with the priestly duty of proclaiming the gospel of God, so that the Gentiles might become an offering acceptable to God, sanctified by the Holy Spirit.

Paul describes his ministry in terms of it being a priestly duty. We have noted in Rom 12:1 that the priests in the OT were appointed to represent the firstborn, taking their place in the ministry based on the tabernacle. Yahweh claimed all of Israel's firstborn for himself, the sons being designated to be Yahweh's priests. The term λειτουργὸς (*leitourgos*) "minister"[720] is often used of the Levite in the LXX. Paul has not been released from the obligation to serve God; rather he, like all other redeemed people, is obliged to serve God with his whole life. Indeed, it is because Jesus–God's firstborn–has been delivered up to death that Paul is required to serve as a priest. It is the only response he can make to the God who has spared him through the giving up of his own Son as the Passover sacrifice (1 Cor 5:7b: "For Christ, our Passover lamb, has been sacrificed").[721]

The Jewish nation's priestly duty had been to bring the light of the knowledge of God to the nations, but she failed miserably. Paul sees himself as called to fulfill this work so that the Gentiles are brought into the blessings of the covenant. Their conversion is, therefore, the goal of his ministry. He knew it would happen because the Scriptures predicted it (Gen 12:3; Isa 2:2–3; 11:10; 19:21–25) and he had been commissioned to the task by the risen Christ (Acts 26:17–18).

The Holy Spirit must sanctify the Gentiles to make them acceptable. Paul is not speaking of individual Gentiles being brought into the covenant through personal response and faith; he is viewing them as an entity (προσφορὰ [*prosphora*)] "sacrifice" is singular). This parallels Israel's sanctification when she was brought out of bondage (Isa 50:8; 53:11).

While this New Exodus of God's people has been achieved through the cross, it is the Holy Spirit who brought about their unity with Christ.[722] The

---

bring justification at the coming judgment. Thus, Paul seeks to fulfill his apostolic calling to the Gentiles, endeavoring to help them understand the wider vision of God's eschatological people.

[720] Fitzmyer, *Romans*, 711, acknowledges the term can have a secular meaning but argues that it takes a religious nuance from the context in which Paul has used it.

[721] The Greek does not have "lamb." Christ is the firstborn sacrifice in Paul's understanding, see Holland, *Contours*, 237–74.

[722] See notes on introduction to Rom 6.

same Spirit applies this saving work to individuals as he circumcises their hearts and gives them the existential status required for membership in the new covenant community. By this circumcision they are brought into their already-secured inheritance, and can make offerings that are acceptable to God.

The phrase "the Gentiles might become an offering acceptable to God," suggests they are being brought into the same ministry as the believing Jews. They are also part of the holy nation, the NT priesthood, and it is their responsibility to share the good news with those they meet. In the NT, all those who have been redeemed through Christ, their Passover, are priests unto their God.[723]

It has been pointed out that, while Paul uses priestly terminology for his work of evangelism,[724] he never uses this terminology when speaking of those who preside in worship or lead in the celebration of the Eucharist (the Lord's Table). It was later generations of Christians who reintroduced the OT order, despite the fact that the NT had clearly seen this to have been fulfilled in Christ (Heb 10:11–18). Indeed, the institution of the "Lord's Supper" was nothing more than the Christian version of the Passover, when "Christ, our Passover lamb, has been sacrificed" (1 Cor 5:7).[725] Any later developments of "real presence" or other "sacramental significance" would not have been in the minds of Jesus or the apostles. This is made clear when we question the widely-held view of Hellenism as a key for interpreting the NT, and read, instead, the NT out of the OT. As there is *no* evidence of sacramentalism in the OT sacrificial system, we need to question claims to its presence in the NT. Once the inauguration of the Lord's Supper was removed from its original setting of the Passover, the parameters of its significance were lost and the door was opened to an understanding that was not part of the original celebration.

---

[723] Cranfield, *Romans*, 755, has shown that Paul's frame of reference for designating himself as a priest is the Levites. This observation supports the claim that the ministry of Paul and the believers is rooted in their redemption through the death of their firstborn–Christ, our Passover (1 Cor 5:7). See Holland, *Contours*, Chaps 11 and 12.

[724] Dillon, "Priesthood" 156–68.

[725] For a discussion on the significance of John 6:54, "unless you eat the flesh of the Son of Man . . .," see Excursus F: Sin in the Theology of Paul p. 271. Note that the discussion is in the context of the Passover, which both OT and NT see to be the occasion of Yahweh's marriage to his people. The imagery is matrimonial, i.e., covenantal, not sacramental or mystical.

15:17 Therefore I glory in Christ Jesus in my service to God.

For Paul, there could be no greater privilege than being a servant of God. He glorified God for the honor of being called into his service. This was not being said by a man who had lived a life of ease because of privilege, but by one who had experienced immense suffering because of his loyalty to Jesus Christ.

15:18 I will not venture to speak of anything except what Christ has accomplished through me in leading the Gentiles to obey God by what I have said and done—

In saying that he "will not venture to speak," Paul can be understood in one of two ways. He may be saying that he is not competent to speak beyond his own experience of ministry, so purposely limiting himself to this. Alternatively, he might be stressing that he has nothing about which to boast. It is God alone who can take glory for what has been achieved. In light of the context, it is probably the latter interpretation that expresses Paul's intention.

15:19 By the power of signs and miracles, through the power of the Spirit. So from Jerusalem all the way around to Illyricum, I have fully proclaimed the gospel of Christ.

While Paul rarely speaks of involvement in miraculous ministry (2 Cor 12:12), his companion, Luke, reported on it more freely (Acts 13:4–12; 14:8–10; 16:16–18, 25–34; 19:11–20). It is much wiser to let others report on the blessings God has given to our service rather than getting caught up in the cult of self-promotion. Such a cult robs Christ of his glory.

Paul writes: "So from Jerusalem all the way around to Illyricum." Illyricum is part of the Balkan region, which was known as Yugoslavia. This statement creates a problem because there is no record of Paul ministering in this region. Some have concluded that Illyricum is intended to represent the western limit of the eastern part of the Roman Empire. If this is so, then Paul is claiming that he has evangelized the whole of the empire apart from Italy and the west. This interpretation, however, presents its own problem. It was not physically possible for Paul to have preached everywhere in such a vast area. The most plausible understanding is that Paul has preached in its chief centers, confident in the knowledge that others have radiated out from them with the Gospel message.

A better translation of the phrase τὸ εὐαγγέλιον τοῦ Χριστοῦ (*to euangelion tou Christou*) "the gospel of Christ" is "the gospel about Christ."

This has been the thrust of exposition throughout this commentary, for the letter is about Jesus, the Son of David (Rom 1:3) who is the Christ.[726]

15:20 *It has always been my ambition to preach the gospel where Christ was not known, so that I would not be building on someone else's foundation.*

Paul sought to evangelize regions where no one had gone. One such region was to the west of Italy, i.e., Spain. While his intended visit to Italy would serve to strengthen the church in Rome as he shared fellowship with them (Rom 1:11–12), his main purpose was to make the visit a stepping-stone to the west (cf. Rom 15:24). Even though he avoided building on other people's foundations, it would seem that he saw no reason not to exercise an evangelistic ministry while passing through regions on his way to his intended field of ministry (Rom 1:15).

15:21 *Rather, as it is written: "Those who were not told about him will see, and those who have not heard will understand."*

In citing Isa 52:15 (LXX), Paul is not justifying his efforts to take the Gospel to the unreached but his view of himself as part of the servant ministry.[727] Here, it is sufficient to note that he deliberately applies a text that speaks of the suffering Servant to Jesus. For Paul, there is no doubt that Christ fulfills this ministry to the nations, bringing about their forgiveness and reconciliation to God.

Nevertheless, as comments on Rom 1:1 suggest, the application of Servant passages was not limited to Christ by the early church. She saw herself as continuing this ministry—overwhelmed with the privilege and responsibility of making the Gospel known.

15:22 *This is why I have often been hindered from coming to you.*

If we go outside Paul's letter to the Romans, we find examples of him acknowledging how Satan hindered him at times (e.g., 1 Thess 2:18). However, in this verse, Paul is not suggesting that Satan had prevented him from visiting Rome. The reasons for the delay must have been the various ministries in which he was involved (vv. 19–20) for he was constantly stretched. In light of his principles and goals, it was vital for him to identify his priorities (Rom 1:14–

---

[726] Fitzmyer, *Romans*, 714.

[727] See Holland, *Contours*, chapter 4, for a more detailed discussion.

16; 15:23–33). He had to be sensible and plan his work ahead, endeavoring (though not always succeeding) to keep to time schedules (cf. Acts 20:16; 2 Cor 1:15ff.; Titus 1:5). Thus, "This is why" indicates that Paul has given an account of the Gentile mission (see Rom 15:1–22) he has been involved in so that those in Rome could understand what had occupied his time and energies. It was these noble activities that had delayed his long desired visit to Rome

15:23 But now that there is no more place for me to work in these regions, and since I have been longing for many years to see you,

It is evident Paul had not evangelized all the regions of Asia, so what does he mean by such a statement? It can only be that he saw his ministry to be pioneering–preparing ground and establishing congregations that would take the Gospel to the unevangelized regions of Asia. As a result of this strategy, there were no more places for him to go.

Paul wants to move into Spain and employ the same "relay" strategy there, setting up congregations with the expectation that the Gospel would diffuse throughout the nation by means of the believers' testimonies. With this strategy, the infant church expanded rapidly—and it still does where such a plan of action is implemented! Too often in the West, we lack Paul's missionary vision—we major on his doctrine but ignore his practice. As a result, the transforming gospel is not heard and people are left in darkness. The church cannot call herself apostolic if she does not practice the actions of the apostles. Upholding the apostles' doctrine is essential, but it's equally important to follow their practice too.

15:24 I plan to do so when I go to Spain. I hope to visit you while passing through and to have you assist me on my journey there, after I have enjoyed your company for a while.

It is unlikely that Paul was able to achieve his goal of ministering in Spain as we know he was arrested in Jerusalem after writing this letter (Rom 15:25). From Jerusalem, he was taken to Rome at his insistence that he be tried under Roman law in front of Caesar (Acts 25:11; 28:16). He chose this in order to thwart the malicious intentions of the Jews who plotted his death (Acts 23:12–30).

While there is no evidence that Paul fulfilled his plan to evangelize Spain, some argue that he was released from house-arrest in Rome and continued on to Spain, being rearrested sometime later. Subsequently, he was brought back to Rome where, according to Christian tradition, he was beheaded at Tre

Fontane Abbey (i.e., Three Fountains Abbey), during the reign of Nero (about 65 AD).

When Paul writes: "to have you assist me on my journey," he uses the verb προπεμφθῆναι (*propemphthēnai*, aorist passive infin.), which is often translated "escorted by." It has been suggested that he is looking for more than financial or material support; Paul hopes the Roman believers will share with him in the mission he plans in Spain by sending representatives to work with him. This was not so that he would have company on the journey but that his practice of involving established churches in reaching unevangelized areas could be put into action (Acts 13:1–3; 2 Cor 8:22ff.; Phil 2:25–30; 2 Tim 4:9–13). By this strategy, Paul gives us the model for training Christian workers. Like Jesus, he discipled them by means of his own example (1 Tim 1:15–16; 2 Tim 2:2–3; 3:10–4:2).

15:25 Now, however, I am on my way to Jerusalem in the service of the saints there.

Some say Paul does not appeal to the believers in Rome for funds to support the suffering believers in Jerusalem because he wished the gift to be from churches he had established. This is hardly likely to be the reason as, at the time of writing, he was traveling in the opposite direction to Rome, en route for Jerusalem. It would have been unrealistic for Paul to invite the Roman believers to contribute to the gift. His letter—written in Corinth—would have to be delivered speedily to Rome in order for a collection to be made. This would then have be transported quickly across or around the Mediterranean and given to Paul and his party who were on their way to Jerusalem. It is more realistic to think that Paul was asking the Roman believers to pray that the gift would be acceptable to the Jews. This was important because of the strain between the Jewish and Gentile sections of the Jerusalem church for, despite the immense suffering of their brethren, the Judaizers would be tempted to press for the gift to be rejected, fearing it would defile the community.

The suggestion that Paul sought to "buy" legitimacy for his Gentile mission through the presentation of the gift is not acceptable. The proposal misses the fact that the Jerusalem Council had already endorsed his mission (Acts 15). What Paul's action does is to remind us of the practical ways in which the unity of the church can be promoted. His theological knowledge was being given expression; by means of this tangible display of concern Paul was able to underscore the unity that Christ had brought about through his death.[728]

The gift for the poor saints in Jerusalem was a priority for Paul. This was no ordinary gift. If it had been, he would have entrusted it to others and made his way to Rome and then Spain without such a detour. Paul saw the gift as a vital expression of the unity of Jews and Gentiles in the Gospel. Establishing this principle was so important that it took priority over his consuming passion of making Christ known in regions beyond.

Some have seen the delegation that Paul led to Jerusalem to be an expression of the prophetic promise that the nations would come to Jerusalem to worship the Lord (Isa 2:1–5).[729]

15:26 For Macedonia and Achaia were pleased to make a contribution for the poor among the saints in Jerusalem.

The term οἱ πτωχοι (*hoī ptōchoi*) "the poor" [ὁι πτωχός (*ho ptōchoi*)] became a technical term for the pious who were often oppressed and economically deprived (1 Cor 16:3; 2 Cor 8:19). However, there is no reason to see it being used here in this technical sense as Paul says that the contribution is for the poor *among* the saints.

Some believe the Jerusalem church was vulnerable to famine conditions. It has been argued that its members had used their resources to support those believers who had stayed on in Jerusalem after Pentecost. They remained in the city in order to take advantage of apostolic instruction before returning to their homes throughout the empire. While there was clearly great generosity, it is probably claiming too much to say that it left the church members impoverished and without the means of coping with famine. The poor are found in every society, and the church in Jerusalem would not have been exempt.

Following the council of Jerusalem (Acts 15), the apostles urged Paul not to forget the poor, and this request brought ready agreement (Gal 2:10). 2 Cor 8:8–15—a passage referring to the same collection as mentioned in Galatians—shows his ability to manage this important project and his lack of

---

[728] See also Wright, *Romans*, 756, who says: "For Gentiles to give money for Jewish Christians was a sign that the Gentiles regarded them as members of the same family; for Jewish Christians to accept it would be a sign that they in turn accepted the Gentiles as part of their family. The collection was designed to accomplish, mutatis mutandis, the same thing that Paul had been urging in 14:1–15:3."

[729] See Munck, *Salvation*.

embarrassment in asking for money in order to care for those in need. (While he was unabashed in seeking support for others, he was reluctant to seek it for himself [Phil 4:10–20], preferring to make tents rather than be misunderstood [1 Cor 9:1–18]). The mention of Macedonia and Achaia indicates how far from Jerusalem the contributors lived and how Paul taught the Gentile churches of their debt to the Jewish believers as the ones who brought them the good news.

It is clear from the request made by the apostles at Jerusalem and the willing practice of Paul that caring for the physical needs of people is not to be seen as a deviation from Gospel ministry but a vital expression of it. It is a sad situation when professing Christians are reluctant to support the practical relief of the destitute while priding themselves on being disciples of Christ. It should be noted that Paul's efforts are directed toward the poor among the saints. That does not exclude compassion toward the unbelieving poor, but it is nevertheless a priority toward the believing poor who are often suffering because they are believers.

15:27 *They were pleased to do it, and indeed they owe it to them. For if the Gentiles have shared in the Jews' spiritual blessings, they owe it to the Jews to share with them their material blessings.*

The willing response of the Gentile churches must have been a great encouragement to Paul in his desire to see the two sections of the church learn to respect and accept each other. Their response flowed from the sense of debt they had to the Jewish believing community.[730] Paul spells out what that debt is: they have shared in the spiritual blessings of the old covenant community. This is not to say, of course, that the Jewish nation had, in turn, delighted in the way God had blessed the Gentiles through the Gospel of Christ–most Jews deeply resented them for claiming to be the true inheritors of the Abrahamic blessings.

The name "the Jews" could refer to the nation of Israel or to the remnant community (the Jewish church). The nation had been given the promises and borne the hope of their fulfillment throughout long years of suffering. Tragically, she had rejected the one to whom these promises pointed. The remnant, however, recognized and welcomed the bringer of salvation (Luke 2:25–38) and accepted its mission to make his salvation known to the nations.

---

[730] Contra Munck, *Mankind*, who claims that the reason for the gift was to provoke the Jews to jealousy (Rom 10:19; 11:13–14). Munck's view has been embraced and modified by others.

However, while the Gentiles owed a great debt to the Jewish remnant there are good grounds for saying they also owed one to the entire Jewish nation for it was used by God as an "incubator" for the Gospel promises. Without Jewish history and the theology that grew out of it, it is impossible to understand the message of Yahweh's redeeming activity for his creation.

15:28 So after I have completed this task and have made sure that they have received this fruit, I will go to Spain and visit you on the way.

The language of receiving the fruit is unusual, some suggesting that it had ceremonial roots. If this is correct, it suggests that Paul anticipated a formal handing over of the gift for the poor in Jerusalem. This fulfilled the promise he had made to the Jerusalem Council as recorded in Gal 2:10. No doubt Paul hoped the gift would be presented in a community setting, with the consequent public recognition in Jerusalem of the care and concern of distant Gentile brethren. Paul was prepared to use every means to get across the message of unity between believing Jews and Gentiles. This gave the gift a higher priority, which is probably why he wanted to take it himself rather than send it with an embassy.

As we have seen, Paul expected to follow the visit to Jerusalem with a visit to Rome on his way to Spain, where he planned to start church-planting. We know from the Acts of the Apostles that his pathway was going to be anything but straightforward. (In Jerusalem, he was beaten and almost lynched, then put on trial before the high priest and successive Roman governors. He endured a dangerous and eventful voyage to Rome where he was detained under house-arrest for two years, awaiting his appeal to Caesar.) Did Paul have any inkling of what was going to happen to him as he approached Jerusalem? Certainly he was aware of dangers facing him there (Rom 15:31), and would soon be warned by Agabus of his impending imprisonment (Acts 20–21). How different the cause of the Gospel would have been if the early believers had risk-assessed their missionary endeavors and not accepted the challenge to take the Gospel to the furthest corners of the earth.

15:29 I know that when I come to you, I will come in the full measure of the blessing of Christ.

Paul's assurance that he would visit the Roman church in the full measure of the blessing of Christ could express one of the following understandings.

First, Paul did not consider himself to be unique, bringing to the believers something they did not already have. He anticipated he would receive from them the same Gospel fellowship he would bring. He expresses his confidence that believers experience the presence of Christ when they meet together (Matt 18:20). He had verbalized the same expectation of Christ's presence in another setting when he instructed the Corinthians to gather in the name of Jesus in order to deliver one of their members over to Satan (1 Cor 5:4). As Paul would not be with them, it is clear that he did not see his presence to be necessary for Christ to be with them. The heritage of believers meeting together with their Lord is still the privilege and inheritance of the church today.

A second possible understanding of the verse is that Paul thought he was bringing blessings that only an apostle could impart. Clearly, the apostles had a unique authority in the early church, and the visit from such a representative of Christ would inevitably be anticipated with excitement over the blessing that would accompany such a visit.

15:30 I urge you, brothers, by our Lord Jesus Christ and by the love of the Spirit, to join me in my struggle by praying to God for me.

Here, we have mention of the three members of the Godhead who the church would later describe as "The Trinity." Just how Paul intended this statement to be understood is not clear. What is generally agreed by scholars is that the understanding of God as triune developed slowly in the thinking of the early church and that too much weight must not be placed on early texts.

However, despite the prevailing opinion, a case can be made that the church used Trinitarian language earlier than is supposed. It has been argued that the Christology of the NT is not titular (understanding who Christ is by analyzing his titles such as Son of Man, Last Adam, Messiah, etc.) as previous generations had supposed, but functional (understanding Christ's person by focusing on what he has achieved).[731] If this is correct, there is reason to believe the church grasped the uniqueness of Christ early in her existence. She certainly recognized his death as the means by which Yahweh had redeemed his creation which is something no creature could do! (Rom 8:18–25).

Paul's request for prayer gives some insight into the agony he went through in his attempts to reconcile the two wings of the church. His appeal to συναγωνίσασθαί (*sunagonisasthai*) "strive together" indicates his concern. He knew his life was in constant danger because of the intense hatred some Jews had towards him. He covets the prayers of the Roman believers that the visit he

---

[731] See Holland, *Contours*, chaps 11 and 12 .

is about to make might achieve the goal for which he longed. The danger Paul was willing to face in going up to Jerusalem shows his concern for the Jewish believers and the unity of the church. This concern, no doubt, expresses his knowledge that Christ had specifically prayed for the unity of his people (John 17:11). Divisions amongst believers ought to be the very last option, not the first knee-jerk reaction, to disagreements.

15:31 Pray that I may be rescued from the unbelievers in Judea and that my service in Jerusalem may be acceptable to the saints there.

We can only imagine the intensity of feeling that built up as Paul approached Jerusalem. He was urged by Christians on his journey not to put himself in danger (Acts 21:7–14). The prophecy given by Agabus (Acts 21:10–11) would have taken all hope of a peaceful outcome from his heart, but he still continued with his visit. Paul was putting his life on the line for the sake of achieving a better understanding and acceptance of the Gentile believers by the Jewish church. There can only be one reason for such commitment: Paul believed that what he was doing was of vital importance for the work of the Gospel. Such an example must surely condemn us for taking our unity in Christ so lightly!

Despite the fact that this was such an important issue for Paul, the book of Acts says very little about whether he achieved his goal. He appears to have presented the collection, or been in the act of presenting it, when Jews from Asia caused a riot and dragged him from the temple (Acts 24:17; 21:27). The relative silence on this point in Acts suggests this aspect of the visit was not successful (possibly Luke chose to avoid mentioning it in case it caused distress).[732] If this is so, Paul had again experienced what many pastors repeatedly encounter: God's people, while claiming to have the highest ideals as their motives, undo the work of the God they say they love by showing intolerance to other believers. Of course Paul also expresses the opposite concern. He is aware how leaders can become dictatorial and harsh in their role as leaders (Acts 20:26–27).

15:32 So that by God's will I may come to you with joy and together with you be refreshed.

Paul was to visit them soon but in circumstances he did not envisage when writing these words. A short time later, he was arrested (Acts 24–27), detained

---

[732]See Dunn, *Diversity*, 256ff.

in prison and went through several trials in Judea and Caesarea. Having asserted his legal rights as a Roman citizen, Paul was taken to Rome under escort. Here, he was given great opportunities to witness while under house arrest, awaiting Caesar's pleasure to try him (Acts 28:16–31).

15:33 The God of peace be with you all. Amen.

The simplicity of the words do not relate the profoundness of the reality. Paul prays for the Roman believers to share in what he has experienced for himself (Phil 4:9). Soon, these very people were going to need to know the God of peace as a living reality. Some would be burned to death as human torches in the gardens of Nero for his amusement, while others were to entertain the depraved Roman crowds by having their limbs ripped apart by lions in the Coliseum. This small Christian community had no idea that its testimony would inspire countless millions of Christians to be faithful to Christ, some even unto death.

There has been ongoing debate among scholars as to whether Paul actually concluded his letter at this point—they see chapter 16 as not being part of the original letter to the Romans but added at a later date.[733] Those who favor this displacement theory claim the doxology at the end of chapter 16 was originally at the end of chapter 15. This is supported by a manuscript dated around 200 AD. Other MSS have the doxology after Rom 15:33 and Rom 14:23, while two ninth century MSS and a derivative one from the fourteenth century omit it entirely. One of these MSS does, however, leave a space at the end of chapter 14, suggesting there may have been something that the copyist intended to insert. However, not all scholars accept this interpretation. Indeed, there is a growing minority that accepts the location of chapter 16 as it is in most manuscripts.[734]

---

[733] Manson, "Others," 225–41, suggested that Rom 16 was added as a cover letter to make it easy for a copy of the letter to be sent to Ephesus where Paul knew many people. Witherington, *Romans*, 351, sees the chapter to be part of the original letter and argues that its purpose was to encourage the Gentile majority—the "strong" in Witherington's understanding—to accept the returning Jews (the "weak") who Paul met during their Diaspora from the capital. This, in Witherington's thinking, explains why so many are mentioned at the conclusion of this letter in comparison to other letters.

[734] See Wright, *Romans*, 758.

CONCLUSION OF ROMANS CHAPTER FIFTEEN

Paul urges unity, and refers to himself and Christ as examples of those who did not pass judgment on non-essentials. He has shown how Christ has fulfilled the promises made to Abraham and how they intrinsically included the Gentiles. He has also demonstrated how Jesus was fulfilling the mission Israel had failed to perform. Paul, using a series of OT citations which predicted the outcome of the New Exodus, demonstrates that believing Gentiles have the right to be within the new covenant community. He showed the believing Jewish community how they were obliged to welcome them.

Paul describes his own ministry in priestly terms. His ministry fulfills what Israel failed to achieve, for she was called to be a priestly people who would take the knowledge of God to the nations. Paul is living in the way he has exhorted others to live in chapter 12, and that includes accepting one another and putting aside any concept of national superiority.

Paul's account of the signs which have accompanied the preaching of the Gospel is further evidence that he sees his ministry in terms of the New Exodus (Rom 15:19). They are the same signs that marked the Exodus from Egypt and the same ones Scripture also said would take place under the leadership of David's descendant. Christ, the true Son of David, has secured the New Exodus of his people.

Romans 16

THE MESSIAH KING AND HIS PEOPLE IN ROME (16:1–27)

I commend to you our sister Phoebe, a servant of the church in Cenchrea. I ask you to receive her in the Lord in a way worthy of the saints and to give her any help she may need from you, for she has been a great help to many people, including me.

Greet Priscilla and Aquila, my fellow-workers in Christ Jesus. They risked their lives for me. Not only I but all the churches of the Gentiles are grateful to them. Greet also the church that meets at their house. Greet my dear friend Epenetus, who was the first convert to Christ in the province of Asia.

Greet Mary, who worked very hard for you. Greet Andronicus and Junias, my relatives who have been in prison with me. They are outstanding among the apostles, and they were in Christ before I was. Greet Ampliatus, whom I love in the Lord. Greet Urbanus, our fellow worker in Christ, and my dear friend Stachys. Greet Apelles, tested and approved in Christ. Greet those who belong to the household of Aristobulus. Greet Herodion, my relative. Greet those in the household of Narcissus who are in the Lord. Greet Tryphena and Tryphosa, those women who work hard in the Lord. Greet my dear friend Persis, another woman who has worked very hard in the Lord. Greet Rufus, chosen in the Lord, and his mother, who has been a mother to me, too. Greet Asyncritus, Phlegon, Hermes, Patrobas, Hermas and the brothers with them. Greet Philologus, Julia, Nereus and his sister, and Olympas and all the saints with them. Greet one another with a holy kiss. All the churches of Christ send greetings.

I urge you, brothers, to watch out for those who cause divisions and put obstacles in your way that are contrary to the teaching you have learned. Keep away from them. For such people are not serving our Lord Christ, but their own appetites. By smooth talk and flattery they deceive the minds of naive people. Everyone has heard about your obedience, so I am full of joy over you; but I want you to be wise about what is good, and innocent about what is evil.

The God of peace will soon crush Satan under your feet. The grace of our Lord Jesus be with you. Timothy, my fellow-worker, sends his greetings to you, as do Lucius, Jason and Sosipater, my relatives. I, Tertius, who wrote down this letter, greet you in the Lord. Gaius, whose hospitality I and the whole church here enjoy, sends you his greetings. Erastus, who is the city's director of public works, and our brother Quartus send you their greetings.

Now to him who is able to establish you by my gospel and the proclamation of Jesus Christ, according to the revelation of the mystery hidden for long ages past, but now revealed and made known through the prophetic writings by the command of the eternal God, so that all nations might believe and obey him—to the only wise God be glory forever through Jesus Christ! Amen. (Romans 16:1–27)

INTRODUCTION

The problems posed by chapter 16 have been discussed elsewhere.[735] They include a list of Roman believers to whom Paul wishes to send greetings. As it is thought by most that he had not founded or visited the church in Rome, there are many who doubt that this chapter concluded the letter. Some have suggested the chapter belongs to another letter that had been sent to a church whose members were well known to Paul.[736] There is, however, evidence suggesting that its location is misplaced.

When writing to churches he had founded, it was unusual for Paul to mention people by name. For example, there is a notable absence of names in letters to the Corinthian, Galatian, Philippian, and Thessalonian churches, ones which Paul had planted on his missionary journeys. The nearest passage that is similar to the ending of the letter to the Romans is Col 4:15, 17. These are verses in the concluding chapter of a letter written to a church Paul had not founded (Col 1:6–8). A possible pattern Paul adopts is that he does not give personalized greetings to churches he planted but gives them to churches founded by others. If this evidence is reliable, it would be fair to conclude that Paul did not found the church in Rome because he greeted almost thirty named believers at the close of his letter.

---

[735] See Donfried, "Romans," 44–52.

[736] Jewett, "Ecumenical," 93, previously treated chapter 16 as belonging to a letter written to Ephesus. He came to reject this, accepting that it was part of the original letter to the Romans.

What does he hope to achieve with this familiarity? Perhaps he wants to establish a relationship with them that would profit his mission to Spain, or perhaps he has the well-being of the congregation in mind. The names suggest that most of the believers greeted by Paul are Jews. Indeed, some of them have been key workers with him in past missionary endeavors. In writing to a church which was in danger of rejecting its Jewish roots, Paul may be anxious for the Gentile believers to welcome and honor his kinsmen; after all, some of them had come to Christ before him and had ministered to his needs with dedication and kindness (one is described as "a mother" to him). A positive response to the commendations would help to prevent the threatened rift between the two sections of the Roman congregation.

His appeal is similar to the one made to the Gentile churches to provide for the needs of the saints in Jerusalem. In Rome, however, the need among the Jews is not merely practical but emotional, social, and spiritual. The Roman Gentiles are to care for these worthy representatives of the Jewish believing community, and, as an expression of their compassion, they are to share their material prosperity with those who had shared their spiritual heritage (hinted at in Rom 15:26–27).

Since it is acknowledged by most that Paul had yet to visit Rome, how did he know the people he greeted in Rom 16:3–16? We know that Claudius, the Roman Emperor, had expelled the Jews from the city in 49 or 50 AD. This was the reason Priscilla and Aquila were absent from Rome and for meeting Paul in Corinth (Acts 18:1–3). They were able to go back to Rome after the death of Claudius. No doubt before their return, Priscilla and Aquila would have talked with Paul about the key believers in Rome as well as the problems they faced within and outside their congregations.

If we accept this reasoning about Priscilla and Aquila, we must accept the possibility that Paul met other believing Jews from Rome in his travels, drawing close to many of them. Many of these would have returned to Rome—along with Priscilla and Aquila—when the way became clear.

Others known by Paul would have gone to Rome for different reasons. Phoebe, from the church in Cenchrea, seems to have had financial independence and was able to travel for personal or business reasons. It is possible that she was the one entrusted to deliver Paul's letter to the Roman believers.

Another possible explanation for Paul's knowledge of the congregation is that his parents lived in Rome before moving to Tarsus, leaving behind family in the city.⁷³⁷ If this is what happened, Paul's wider family would be a source of information about the church in Rome.

16:1 I commend to you our sister Phoebe, a servant of the church in Cenchrea.

Phoebe is from Cenchrea.⁷³⁸ This is one of the two ports of Corinth, the capital city of Southern Greece (the Roman province of Achaia). As Corinth is thought by many to be the place where Paul wrote his letter (see commentary on Rom 16:23), it is likely that Phoebe is its bearer. The following verse suggests she was a wealthy woman, so it is possible that she was visiting Rome for business reasons and agreed to carry the letter for him. Her background—indicated by her pagan name—was not Jewish. Possibly, she was one of those converted through Paul's Corinthian mission.

While some translate διάκονος ς(*diakonos*) as "deaconess," many doubt Paul intended to suggest that Phoebe held an office in the Cenchrean church. It is possible the term was used to denote a function rather than an office. If this is correct, then the term indicates that she functioned as a servant of the church, giving support to those in need. Such a functional significance of *diakonon* must equally apply to male deacons, their description not being that of an office they hold but a ministry they exercise.

16:2 I ask you to receive her in the Lord in a way worthy of the saints and to give her any help she may need from you, for she has been a great help to many people, including me.

Paul's commendation of Phoebe is a model of diplomacy. He reminds the Romans of their status. They are saints, i.e., people of God. Just as God welcomes people into his family, they are to welcome Phoebe. Paul asks them to help her in whatever way she needs while she fulfills the reason for her visit to Rome. This could be by giving spiritual support as well as the practical help of hospitality—something Paul has already exhorted the believers to do (Rom 12:13).

---

⁷³⁷ See Little, *Mission*.

⁷³⁸ There are six places known in antiquity with the name of Cenchrea. The most likely home of Phoebe is the one near Corinth, which was one of the city's two ports. It was situated seven kilometers southeast of Corinth on the Saronic Gulf. It served the trade route with Asia and was an important commercial center.

The affection shown to Phoebe by her home church in Cenchrea is obvious from Paul's commendation. She had helped many, including Paul himself.[739] Such selfless people are vital for the life of the church for they exercise an essential pastoral gift for the Christian community. Pastoral ministry is not the exclusive ministry of the "pastor" as the Spirit gives this gift more widely in the church for the blessing of God's people.

16:3 Greet Priscilla and Aquila, my fellow workers in Christ Jesus.

Like Paul, Priscilla and Aquila were Jews with Roman names. They had settled in Corinth after being expelled from Rome under the edict made by the Emperor Claudius. This affected all the resident Jews in the city.[740] In Corinth, Priscilla and Aquila met Paul, who worked with them for eighteen months. It was during this time that he established the Corinthian church (Acts 18:1–3).

After this, Priscilla and Aquila moved with Paul to Ephesus (Acts 18:18). Here, they used their gift of hospitality in opening up their home to Apollos, who had come to the city. They exercised a pastoral gift too, taking time to help him have a clearer understanding of the way of God (Acts 18:24–26).

In time, they returned to Rome where they opened up their home to believers again. If it is true that Paul had never visited the city, Priscilla and Aquila would have been incredibly important to him as ambassadors, telling of

---

[739] Whelan, "Phoebe," 67–85, points out that under Roman law, women could acquire wealth and freely dispose of it. He says there is evidence in voluntary associations—especially religious ones—that women served as patrons and gained positions of leadership. Whelan suggests this was Phoebe's status, and that Paul, in introducing her, was returning favor to her in response for all that she had done for him and his co-workers. This is, of course, highly speculative. However, whatever Phoebe's role in her church, there have been godly women of other generations who have used their resources for the sake of the Gospel. In England, a notable example was the Countess of Huntingdon, who supported many of the leading preachers of the eighteenth-century revival. Witherington, *Romans*, 383, suggests that Phoebe was Paul's benefactor, and had been sent ahead of him to Rome—as his representative—to prepare for his coming.

[740] Acts 18:2 records the event. There is some debate about what actually happened. It is reported by Suetonius, and Cassius Dio minimizes the event. Josephus, who was reporting on Jewish events, does not mention it at all. Some scholars hold that it didn't happen; others record that only a few missionaries were expelled for the short term.

all they had observed of the apostle as they worked alongside him. No doubt, having returned to Rome, they continued in their trade of tentmaking.[741]

(After living in Rome for a period of time, the couple traveled back to Ephesus, opening up their home to all the believers. The Ephesian church met there under the oversight of Timothy [1 Cor 16:19; 2 Tim 4:19].)

Whenever the couple are named, Priscilla is often mentioned before her husband (Acts 18:18, 26; 2 Tim 4:19 [for reverse order, see Acts 18:2; 1 Cor 16:19]). This order is unusual in ancient writings, perhaps implying her greater contribution to Christian work or her higher social status.

16:4 They risked their lives for me. Not only I but all the churches of the Gentiles are grateful to them.

We have partial knowledge of the sufferings Paul experienced in Corinth and Ephesus—the two cities where we know he worked alongside Priscilla and Aquila. Indeed, most of them are mentioned incidentally when Paul felt the need to give his credentials as an apostle (Acts 19:29–40; 1 Cor 15:30; 2 Cor 11:23b–33). We have no details of how Priscilla and Aquila risked their lives, but it is evident from what Paul writes that their devotion to him and to other believers was widely known and highly valued.

The reference to "the churches of the Gentiles" has been seen to suggest that there were Gentile churches meeting separately from Jewish churches.[742] However, in the light of Paul's insistence on the acceptance of each group by the other, it does not seem likely that he would encourage separate congregations.

16:5 Greet also the church that meets at their house. Greet my dear friend Epenetus, who was the first convert to Christ in the province of Asia.

Again, we find Priscilla and Aquila giving hospitality, for a church meets in their home in Rome as it will in Ephesus (1 Cor 16:19). There was probably a number of "house churches" scattered throughout Rome (Rom 16:14–15), in keeping with the common practice of the early church (Col 4:15; Philemon 2).

---

[741] Barr, "Tentmakers," 98–113, claims that Priscilla and Aquila were involved in the importation of cilicium (haircloth) to Rome and the manufacture of tents for the Roman army. Barr argues that Paul knows so many people in the city he has yet to visit because of the many contacts he had through the tentmaking trade. Such people were highly mobile.

[742] Oster, "Congregations," 39–52.

Church buildings did not become common until the fourth century. It is quite possible that the believers in Rome continued to meet in the synagogue as well, but their unique identity as followers of Christ would eventually bring this relationship to an end.[743]

Epenetus is greeted with warm affection. Paul describes him literally as "the firstfruits of Asia." Again, Paul uses Paschal (Passover) imagery—the firstfruits being brought from the fields three days after the sacrifice of the Passover lamb (Lev 23:11). It was not the harvest crop that Paul had in mind but the Levitical priesthood (evidenced by references to priestly ministry [Rom 12:1–2; 15:16]), which was given as a token that Yahweh claimed not only the firstborn but the whole nation. Epenetus was the first from that region who had become a priest of the new covenant.

16:6 Greet Mary, who worked very hard for you.

Mary is an unknown member of the Roman church. We don't know if she was Jewish or Gentile, for her name was common in both communities. She is representative of the millions whose devotion and service are the backbones of the churches to which they belong. The reference to her having worked very hard for the Roman believers suggests she had labored with Paul and had rendered a service to the apostolic team on behalf of the Roman church (cf. Phil 2:25–30).

16:6 Greet Andronicus and Junia, my relatives who have been in prison with me. They are outstanding among the apostles, and they were in Christ before I was.

Andronicus and Junia appear to have been a married couple, the latter name being a common Roman name for women.[744] The term συγγενεῖς (*sungeneis*) "relatives" can be translated "kinsmen," so the couple were either part of Paul's extended family or unrelated fellow Jews whom he knew well.

While it is normally accepted that the "relatives" mentioned in chapter 16 (vv. 7, 11, 21) are Paul's kinsmen or countrymen, it is of interest to see how the

---

[743] Nanos, *Mystery*; Dunn, *Parting*.

[744] Cervin, "Note," 464–70, has established that Junia is a feminine name by studying the method of transcribing Latin names into Greek. Cervin closes the discussion in his article "A proper examination of the linguistic evidence regarding the name "Junia" show that the name is feminine not masculine." Its accusative form in the Greek is VIounia/n. This solution removes ambiguity as to the gender implied.

term is used in the rest of the NT. Its plural form is used in Mark 6:4; Luke 1:58, 61; 2:44; 14:12; 21:16 and Acts 10:24, most translators giving "relatives." When Paul uses the plural form of the term in his letter to the Romans, however, the translation "kindred" is favored (except NIV).

The singular form of the term is found in Luke 1:36 and John 18:26. In most cases, it is translated "relative." However, when it appears in Rom 16:11, the same Greek word is translated "kinsman" or "countryman" (except NIV). Translators appear to be reluctant to concede that Paul may have had relatives in Rome, possibly due to the prevailing opinion that Paul had neither visited nor founded its church. He certainly had family who were sympathetic to him as a Christian (Acts 23:12–22), and while it is true that he was from Tarsus (in modern Turkey), there is no reason why Christian members of his family could not have traveled west to settle in Rome. Indeed, as has been mentioned, his immediate family may well have been citizens of the city of Rome, leaving the wider family in order to settle in Tarsus where Paul was raised.

Andronicus and Junia are referred to as "outstanding among the apostles." This use of the term "apostles" does not mean they were among the twelve, for the term was used in a wider sense in the early church (Acts 14:4, 14; 2 Cor 11:13–15; 12:11ff.). The term ἀποστολος (*apostolos*) "apostle" means "sent." The writer to the Hebrews describes Jesus as an apostle because he was sent by God the Father, to make known the good news. In his letter to the Galatians, Paul wrote that he was sent by "Jesus Christ and God the Father" (Gal 1:1) by the will and command of God (1 Cor 1:1). This is a description that Andronicus and Junia could apply to themselves. As apostles, their ministry would have been accompanied by supernatural events (2 Cor 12:12) as Christ's, Paul's and the other apostles' had been; and their role would have been to encourage faith in God's elect, imparting knowledge (teaching) that would lead to Godliness (Titus 1:1).

It is of interest that Junia was called an apostle. This begs the question as to whether apostles' wives who believed and accompanied their husbands on their missions were apostles by dint of their marriage (1 Cor 9:5). Alternatively, it may be that Junia was an apostle in her own right. Of course, if this is so, then God's calling, equipping and use of married women in the church may need to be revisited by some.

Andronicus and Junia were "in Christ" before Paul. They were part of the original Jewish church, taking the Gospel to the Gentiles as they worked and suffered alongside him.⁷⁴⁵ We have seen throughout the letter that Paul regularly uses the expressions "in the Lord" or "in Christ." These phrases speak of membership of the Messianic community, which exists because the Spirit has united believers with Christ in his death.⁷⁴⁶

The mention of a second couple to whom Paul sends greetings hints at the importance of married couples to the early church's missionary endeavors. It was not only that they gave each other support (1 Cor 9:5)—no doubt compensating for each other's weaknesses—but they were able to work in situations where a single person, such as Paul, could not operate or would have difficulty.⁷⁴⁷ Of course there are also ministries that single people can do that married people would find equally very difficult. Sadly, some married believers neglect what they are commanded first to give, i.e., themselves to their family responsibilities. In failing to do this they dishonor Christ rather than glorify him. Single people don't have this particular restriction and distraction and are able to engage in work that married people should not even consider (1 Cor 7:32–35). Thus both the married and the single have their own special gifting that expresses the will of the same Lord who gives gifts to his people as he wills.

16:8 Greet Ampliatus, whom I love in the Lord.

Ampliatus is a slave name. We can only guess how Paul knew a slave living in Rome. It is possible that his master, along with his household, had moved to Rome, or that his freedom had been gained through a process of manumission, leaving him free to travel. Paul's affection for Ampliatus is unashamedly expressed! It must have been a great encouragement to slaves in the early church to know they were valued by their Christian brothers and sisters. Loving people for their own sakes rather than for their status or influence is an important testimony to the power of the Gospel and the love of Christ.

---

⁷⁴⁵ Of course, Peter had "opened the door to the Gentiles" (Acts 15:7), but that had not been the result of a planned mission to them. It was imposed by the Spirit and was a mission with which the church had to come to terms.

⁷⁴⁶ See commentary on Rom 6:1ff.

⁷⁴⁷ For a discussion on the various ministries women might have exercised in the early church, see Witherington, *Romans*, 390–93.

16:9 Greet Urbanus, our fellow-worker in Christ, and my dear friend Stachys.

Urbanus is another member of the Roman congregation with a slave name. The status of being a fellow-worker in Christ must have given dignity and self-respect to one who Virgil referred to as nothing other than a talking tool. It would seem that Urbanus worked alongside Paul in his missionary endeavors.

We know nothing of Stachys other than that Paul regarded him with affection. Indeed, Paul describes him as "beloved" (translated "dear friend" by the NIV), suggesting that he knows Stachys very well.

16:10 Greet Apelles, tested and approved in Christ. Greet those who belong to the household of Aristobulus.

The reference to Apelles's testing suggests that he has endured something beyond the normal. We have no other reference to him, but no doubt such a commendation must have encouraged him greatly. Aristobulus might be the grandson of Herod the Great, who was a friend of the Emperor, Claudius. While Paul makes no mention that Aristobolus had become a Christian, the reference suggests that a number of his household had become believers.

16:11 Greet Herodion, my relative. Greet those in the household of Narcissus who are in the Lord.

Again, we have Paul referring to a relative or kinsman (see comment on v. 7). The greeting gives little away about Herodion. Indeed, the virtual silence supports the view that he was a blood relative as there seems little point in Paul isolating one of his many countrymen in Rome in order to send such a brief greeting.

Narcissus is not greeted personally, so he is probably head of a household with believing members. It is of interest that Narcissus was the name of a famous person in Rome in the middle of first century CE. He was a freed man who had risen to an exalted position under Claudius. This aroused great jealousy in many Romans citizens, to the point that, after Claudius' death, he was provoked to commit suicide. If this Narcissus is the man referred to in this verse (and many assume he is), his untimely death would have put the Christians in his household in a very dangerous position through association.

16:12 Greet Tryphena and Tryphosa, those women who work hard in the Lord. Greet my dear friend Persis, another woman who has worked very hard in the Lord.

The warmth and appreciation of these greetings cannot be ignored by those who claim that Paul was a misogynist. Whatever one thinks about Paul's statements concerning the subjection of women to their husbands, it is clear that he had a high regard for his female colleagues. Sadly, many women carry far too many responsibilities in churches and the mission field because men have not been willing to respond to the challenge.

16:13 Greet Rufus, chosen in the Lord, and his mother, who has been a mother to me, too.

Rufus is a Latin name. Since it is possible that the Gospel of Mark was written for the Roman church, the Rufus mentioned in Mark 15:21—a son of Simon of Cyrene—may be the same person.[748] Simon was clearly a Jew, visiting Jerusalem for the Passover.

The greeting gives us an insight into the support that Paul received from the mother of Rufus. Possibly, his recollection goes back to when Rufus and his mother joined his apostolic band. Perhaps she met his needs as a mother would have done, caring for her own son at the same time. This would have been very important to Paul as, unlike other apostles, he did not have a wife to help him. Being welcomed into a Christian family is the source of joy and comfort for thousands of unmarried Christian workers. Such hospitality is a ministry that enriches many single people (Acts 18:1–3).

If the identification of Rufus as a son of Simon of Cyrene is correct, it follows that his mother was from Cyrene. It seems likely that, following the death of Simon, Rufus and his mother left Cyrene and served Paul's apostolic band in its missionary work. (Notice the presence of Lucius from Cyrene in the fledgling church in Antioch [Acts 13:1]). At some point after the death of Claudius, Rufus and his mother (who were Jews) moved to Rome, where they became part of the body of believers.

---

[748] See Witherington, *Romans*, 394.

16:14 Greet Asyncritus, Phlegon, Hermes, Patrobas, Hermas and the brothers with them.

Again, we have a list of unknown acquaintances. Both Origen[749] and Eusebius[750] link Hermes with the early Christian writing, "The Shepherd." This identification has been contested by modern scholarship.[751]

16:15 Greet Philologus, Julia, Nereus and his sister, and Olympas and all the saints with them.

Extending the greeting to "all the saints with them" suggests that the named believers are the heads of Christian households. Perhaps they are the leaders of house-church groups in Rome.[752]

16:16 Greet one another with a holy kiss. All the churches of Christ send greetings.

A kiss had long been a form of greeting by men in the ancient world (Luke 7:45). Paul's exhortation to the believers in Rome was that it should be a holy kiss. This probably means that they should greet one another as holy in the Lord, as fellow members of the new covenant community. They were to welcome one another, extending the acceptance that Christ had given them. When Paul wrote to believers in Corinth and Thessalonica, he exhorted the believers similarly (1 Cor 16:20; 2 Cor 13:12; 1 Thess 5:26), while Peter urged the Jews of the dispersion to greet each other with a kiss of love (1 Pet 5:14).

Paul sends the greetings of the churches to the believers. As the recognized apostle to the Gentiles, he was able to represent churches even though he had not founded or had contact with them all.

---

[749] Comm. *In. ep. ad Romanos,* 10.31 (PG 14.1282).

[750] Historia *Ecclesiastica,* 3.3.6.

[751] See Fitzmyer, *Romans,* 742, for details.

[752] Finger, "Julia," 36–39, strains the text to suggest that Julia was a racist, Paul urging her to put away her prejudices and welcome others of different ethnic backgrounds.

Romans 16

16:17 I urge you, brothers, to watch out for those who cause divisions and put obstacles in your way that are contrary to the teaching you have learned. Keep away from them.

This sudden denunciation of some of the congregation seems odd in view of the appeal Paul has made in chapter 14 that the Roman believers accept one another. As a result, some have claimed the chapter does not belong to the original Roman letter but is part of another letter written by Paul.

However, such a closing exhortation to believers to be on their guard is found in some of Paul's other letters (cf. 1 Cor 16:22; Gal 6:12ff.; Phil 3:18ff.), suggesting that contention for the Gospel went on within congregations as well as outside. It is not clear what specific problem among the Roman believers Paul had in mind—perhaps he was thinking of Jews who were trying to persuade the Gentiles the needed to be circumcised or of other groups who were rejecting his exhortation to accept one another. If the latter case is true, Paul urges the church to reject those who are jeopardizing the unity of the believing community. A similar exhortation is found in 2 Cor 6:14–18. Traditionally, this passage has been seen to instruct believers not to marry unbelievers. However, in recent years it has been recognized that Paul is telling the Roman Christians to keep separate from those who seek to usurp authority in the church and nullify his influence.

16:18 For such people are not serving our Lord Christ, but their own appetites. By smooth talk and flattery they deceive the minds of naive people.

It is better to translate κοιλία (*koilia*) as "bellies" rather than "appetites." It would seem from such a direct reference to food that the agitators are those who are contending for their right to eat what they wish. If this is correct, they could be the Jews who see no harm in eating meat sacrificed to idols, or in putting their freedom ahead of serving the weaker brethren. Their teaching is right theologically, but it has been taken outside of the dimension of love and it has become motivated by a desire to exercise rights.

The problem with identifying "such people" as Judaizers is there is no suggestion they used flattery. Their belief that they conformed to the law would suggest that their argument would be direct and confrontational. However, it might be that they had developed a more tactful approach to win over the Gentiles—this seems to have been happening in Colossae (Col 2:8, 16–18). The identification of the various groups that Paul contended with is an ongoing problem for scholarship.[753]

16:19 Everyone has heard about your obedience, so I am full of joy over you; but I want you to be wise about what is good, and innocent about what is evil.

The news of the Roman believers' obedience was spoken of in other churches. It must have been a real encouragement to others to know there was such a congregation of believers in the capital city of the empire.

The response of the faithful in Rome is not described as belief but obedience (Rom 1:5). This does not deny that the message received was about faith in God, but obedience to the message believed was considered by Paul to be a hallmark of faith. As a result of their response, Paul experienced overflowing joy that God's word was transforming lives in Rome.

However, despite his joy, Paul writes that he wants the believers to be spiritually mature, i.e., wise and innocent. He wants them to recognize instinctively what God is doing; in other words, he wants them to be wise about what is good. Rather than having personal experience of evil, he wants them to be ignorant of it. (Paul writes a similar thing to the Philippians in Phil 4:8.) This desired innocence is underlined in the next verse, where reference is made to the serpent who beguiled Adam and Eve. Paul is concerned that the innocence of the Roman believers might leave them vulnerable to smooth talkers. Being taken in by such people can be disastrous.

16:20 The God of peace will soon crush Satan under your feet. The grace of our Lord Jesus be with you.

The use of the definite article with Satan τὸν σατανᾶν (*ton satanan*) found elsewhere in the NT (Matt 12:26; Luke 10:18), suggests this is a description or title rather than a name. It is "the Satan." But what does Paul mean by this? He could be referring to those he sees as the servants of Satan, who seek to undermine the work of God among the Romans. If this is correct, then Paul expects these troublemakers to come under some form of judgment.

---

[753] North, "Words," 600–614, argues that *eulogia* and *chresto logia* are used disparagingly to describe a means of deception; *chresto logia* is an unusual word and includes an allusion to the plant chreston ("wild endive") that some charlatans used to ensure their popularity and success. Paul presents his opponents as being no better than those who used magic to woo those who had responded to Paul's Gospel from their faith in Christ.

In Rev 3:9, the apostle John records the words of Jesus to the church in Philadelphia: "I will make those who are of the synagogue of Satan, who claim to be Jews though they are not, but are liars—I will make them come and fall down at your feet and acknowledge that I have loved you." Paul has already compared the unbelieving Jewish community with Pharaoh (Rom 9:17–18). The picture given in Revelation is of the apostate Jewish nation serving the will of the state as it persecuted the church.[754] This situation could be reflected here, and if so, then the fall of Jerusalem in AD 70 would have been a significant blow to this unholy alliance.

The expression: "the grace of our Lord Jesus Christ" is used regularly by Paul. It denotes the outpouring of God's free love through his Son upon his people. Grace is more than love. It speaks of the love between those in a covenant relationship—one in which they have vowed to protect and care for each other. It is best illustrated by the love between a husband and wife, which excludes all others and sacrificially strives for each other's blessing and happiness. Paul is praying the Roman believers will be conscious of this unconditional love with which God has blessed them. It is a love that burns in a believer's heart, transforming everything.

16:21 Timothy, my fellow-worker, sends his greetings to you, as do Lucius, Jason and Sosipater, my relatives.

Paul concludes his own greetings so that he might convey those of his companions. Timothy had worked with Paul from his earliest days in the faith (Acts 16:1–4; 17:14ff.; 18:5; 19:22; 20:4ff.; 1 Cor 16:10ff.; Phil 2:19–24; 1 Thess 3:2, 6). He was clearly a key worker and is regularly mentioned by Paul in his letters.

For comment on Paul's "relatives," see the discussion on Rom 16:7. While Lucius may be a variant of Luke, the name does not refer to the Gentile physician as Lucius was a Jew, being a kinsman or relative of Paul. It is possible that he is Lucius of Cyrene, who worked alongside Paul as one of the band of prophets and teachers in the church in Antioch (Acts 13:1). This Lucius had come to Antioch as a result of the persecution following Stephen's death, and had spoken to the Jews and Greeks in the city about the Lord Jesus. Despite this serious situation, Lucius and those with him knew great blessing on their

---

[754] See Smolarz, *Covenant;* and Wright, *Perspectives.*

ministries and the church expanded significantly; as a result, Paul was brought to Antioch to help Barnabas teach the new believers (Acts 11:19–26).

Jason may be the resident of Thessalonica who gave hospitality to Paul when he stayed there for three weeks. Because Paul took the opportunity each Sabbath day to explain the Scriptures regarding Jesus in the synagogue, jealous Jews precipitated a riot, subjecting Jason to frightening harassment (Acts 17:1–9).

16:22 I, Tertius, who wrote down this letter, greet you in the Lord.

It appears that at this point in the dictation of the letter, Paul allowed Tertius to send his own greeting to the believers in Rome. He regularly used a secretary like Tertius, or even an amanuensis.[755] While this may have been necessitated by failing eyesight or another condition that made writing difficult (Gal 6:11; Phlm 19), this may not have been the case, for many in Paul's day commonly enjoyed the support of a secretary or an amanuensis.

16:23–24 Gaius, whose hospitality I and the whole church here enjoy, sends you his greetings. Erastus, who is the city's director of public works, and our brother Quartus send you their greetings.

Not only did Gaius give hospitality to Paul but his home seems to have been used by the church for its gatherings. His name was Roman and he was obviously wealthy, having a home large enough for the "whole church" to meet in and "enjoy."

As it is normally accepted that Paul's letter was written in Corinth, it is assumed this was Gaius's home city. It is of interest that, in the letter to Timothy, the writer mentions "Erastus stayed (or remained) in Corinth" (2 Tim 4:22). This lends support to the idea that the letter to the Romans was written there as greetings were sent from Erastus to the Roman believers (Rom 16:24). Since Gaius is named alongside him, it would be fair to conclude that Gaius was living in Corinth also.

While there is no mention of him in the account of the Corinthian church's founding in Acts 18, Paul does record that he baptized a Gaius from the congregation (1 Cor 1:14) and he is assumed to be the Gaius of Rom 16:23 LXX. If he is the same man, it is possible he was converted as a result of Paul's

---

[755] Such a person was given a high degree of freedom to write on behalf of the person who engaged him. (The modern equivalent would be a ghost writer.) A secretary would not have that liberty but would take a letter down verbatim.

ministry in Corinth (Acts 18:8), being baptized by him along with Crispus, the synagogue ruler, and the household of Stephanus (1 Cor 1:14,16). As has been mentioned, Gaius was clearly a man of means, being able to purchase a property large enough to comfortably house the Corinthian congregation. He was also hospitable, extending his kindness to Paul during his time in Corinth.

(There is a reference to a Gaius in Acts 20:4. He was from Derbe, which is about 100 miles from Paul's birthplace in Tarsus. Paul and Barnabas visited Derbe early in their missionary endeavors [Acts 14:6–7, 20b–21a] and a large number of people from the city became disciples–indeed, Gaius of Derbe became one of Paul's traveling companions [Acts 20:4]. It is not known if he is the same Gaius who lived in Corinth, having moved there to further his business interests. Finally, the Apostle John wrote to a church elder called Gaius, commending him for his adherence to the truth as well as his hospitality and support to traveling Christian workers [3 John 1:1–6]. This is of interest as the Gaius of Corinth gave hospitality to the Apostle Paul and supported the work of the Gospel by allowing the church to meet in his home. These similarities open up the interesting possibility that Gaius of Rom 16 became an elder of a church and the Apostle John's "dear friend.")

Erastus, the city's treasurer or steward, also sends greetings to the Roman church. His position as the city's treasurer ("director of public works") suggests that he enjoyed a comfortable standard of living.[756] Clearly, there were some in the Corinthian church who were among the "elite" of society (implied by 1 Cor 1:26).

There is another reference to an Erastus. He is described as one of Paul's helpers who was sent by Paul to Macedonia with Timothy (Acts 19:22). These two helpers were sent ahead to prepare the churches' collections for the needy saints in Jerusalem. If this Erastus is the Erastus of Rom 16, he would fulfill this role superbly, being the treasurer of Corinth!

Quartus is someone about whom we have no other information. One can assume he was a believer, perhaps known to the Roman believers.

Having greeted those he knows or has heard of in Rome, Paul concludes his letter by reminding his readers that the message keeping them is the same

---

[756] Disputed by Meggitt, "Erastus," 218–23, who argues that his socioeconomic situation was most likely indistinguishable from that of his fellow believers. If correct, his conversion, therefore, is not evidence of the spread of the Gospel among the powerful of the city.

as that preached to the Old Testament covenant community. It has, at last, been brought to completion, for the message of God's grace is being preached to all nations. This was Israel's calling and service. She was to bring the nations into the community that was set apart to be the bride of Yahweh.

16:25 Now to him who is able to establish you by my gospel and the proclamation of Jesus Christ, according to the revelation of the mystery hidden for long ages past,

This verse begins with what is known as the closing formula. The conclusions found throughout Paul's letters have been carefully studied and found to reflect the theology found earlier in the letter.[757] In this conclusion, Paul speaks of the Gospel having gone to the nations. This is a clear reflection of the theme is argued for in chapter 4—that Abraham is the father of many nations.[758]

Since the Gospel is not only about saving people from God's judgment but also about making them into the people God wants them to be, the term στηρίξω (*stērixō*) "establish" is used. The goal of the Gospel is to bring people into the kingdom of God where they will love and serve him as they live holy lives. Just as the Jews were to be established in their inheritance, so Paul wants the Roman believers to be established in theirs.

When Paul says, "by my Gospel," he is not suggesting that his Gospel is any different from that of the other apostles. All of the indications are that he received the content of his gospel from those who had gone before. He was never hesitant to acknowledge his dependency. By referring to "my Gospel," he echoes his calling to apply the good news to the Gentiles. Paul had worked hard to keep them from having to accept the normal Jewish initiation rites of circumcision and dietary laws, etc. In doing this, he had insisted the Gentiles were not obliged to become Jews in order to be reconciled with God. This defense of Gentile liberty made many Jews—even believers—suspicious of him. Some hated Paul so much for what they considered was betrayal of true faith that they sought to kill him. It is this distinctive application of the good news that enables Paul to speak of "my Gospel." Thus his reference to not having received his Gospel from men (Gal 1:12) probably means that he came to see, without any human aid, that the Gentile believers were not to be

---

[757] Weima, "Closings," 177–97.

[758] Not all think the doxology is Pauline or part of the original letter. For discussion, see Elliott, "Language," 124–30; Wright, "Romans," 758.

circumcised and that on this issue hung the essence of the Gospel, i.e., it is acceptance without the works of the law.

The proclamation of the Gospel revealed the "mystery." This technical term denotes that the purposes of God cannot be known other than when God reveals them. God's purpose is to bring his creation back under his control, having redeemed it through the death of his Son. In this new creation there is no longer a division between Jew and Gentile as both are united in Christ to form one new man. This act of redemption glorifies God before the whole of his creation, and extends his honor. In turn, this leads to the chief end of man—the worship of his Creator.

16:26 But now revealed and made known through the prophetic writings by the command of the eternal God, so that all nations might believe and obey him—

Paul cannot separate the preaching of the Gospel and, by implication, its content from the prophetic writings. This was not the result of man's planning but of the command of God. It is no wonder that the Gospel is sometimes called "the Gospel of God."

16:27 To the only wise God be glory forever through Jesus Christ! Amen.

It is fitting that Paul finishes his letter in this way, for it was the purpose of his life. He sought through everything he did to honor God and bring others to love and serve him. This is what the letter to the Roman believers is about. He has shown them they are a redeemed people with an obligation to live no longer for their own pleasure or enjoyment. Indeed, they were not even to live as model citizens of the Roman Empire but as members of the kingdom of God. Their calling was to submit themselves to what God required and to seek his glory.

Paul says that God is glorified through Christ Jesus. This is not only saying that Christ has glorified God, but that God is honored and glorified as we embrace what he has done through Christ's death and resurrection and to live in light of the claims made by his Son.

CONCLUSION TO CHAPTER SIXTEEN

This closing section gathers together the themes from the earlier part of the letter and brings them to a glorious conclusion.

Paul's purposes have been to encourage the Roman church and to persuade her believers of the certainty concerning their future. This will prove to be essential, for days will soon unfold when the might and pride of the Roman Empire will be unleashed against her in an attempt to wipe the Christian community from the face of the earth. Recalling Paul's words will bring unspeakable comfort to thousands of Christians in the city and empire of Rome. Yet, while many will lose their lives, others will be attracted to the Christ as a result of witnessing willing deaths. Instead of the church dying, it will grow, and eventually see the demise of the decadent state.

The historic realities of suffering and the seemingly meaningless triumph of evil over good must make us wary of interpreting Paul's statements about suffering in too simplistic a way. It is easy for those who have had few knocks in life to speak of "proving the promises to be true," but Paul did not write these words to assure those who are at ease in this life that God would look after their interests. He wrote to those who were about to be deprived of the most basic human rights and who knew they could lose everything they owned, including life itself. For these Roman believers—whose testimony in the face of appalling suffering will win the admiration of the most skeptical of historians—Paul's words will prove to be the comfort that enables them to see a far greater treasure and to strive for a far more glorious citizenship. They will, indeed, prove the promise that God has given them "all things" (Rom 9:28–39).

EXCURSUS K: CONCERNING METHODOLOGY

My exegesis of Paul has been on the basis that he was a Jewish teacher who was committed to the theology of the Old Testament. I made my case for this understanding in my recent book *Tom Wright and the Search for Truth (Search for Truth)* where I presented the evidence to support such an understanding. There I showed that contrary to widespread thinking Paul engaged with neither Hellenism or the Jewish Intertestamental Literature. Several scholars have responded to this accusing me of producing a Gnostic version of Paul, someone who could not exist as a real person (i.e. a person who has no historical substance) in the first century church.

This is such a serious charge, which if true, invalidates all that I am arguing for in this commentary on Paul's greatest letter. I have investigated the charge and found it to be groundless. I answered the accusation with a second edition of the *Search for Truth* which has a chapter added in which I specifically deal with one scholars' detailed critique.[759] I will not repeat the argument I presented, important though I believe it is. Here I wish to demonstrate that the Paul I am advocating was far from a Jewish oddity but was, in fact, part of a huge movement that spanned the first and second century CE. My argument is that Paul was not alone in using this theological method of limiting himself to the Jewish scriptures as his interpretive grid. It was the practice of the early church, and its origin was in Jesus himself.

Throughout the gospels we find that Jesus repeatedly exegeted Old Testament texts in an authoritative manner where he asks in various forms, 'What does the scripture say'. Jesus never once sought to address the arguments of the teachers of the Law by engaging with their exegetical methods. He simply went directly to the text and appealed to what it clearly stated. His authority was clear to all (Matt 4:7, 4:10, 21:13; Mark 1:22, 27).

Earlier scholarship thought that Paul used his training as a rabbi to argue for the gospel. Books were written to demonstrate this[760] and it was argued that the difficult-to-interpret passage in Galatians 4:24–27 was an example of him using this rabbinic method. However, in more recent scholarship it has been

---

[759] Garlington, D. B., 'Review Essay of *"Tom Wright and the Search for Truth: A Theological Evaluation* by Tom Holland", *The Paul Page* (August 20, 2018), http://www.thepaulpage.com/review-essay-of-tom-wright-and-the-search-for-truth-a-theological-evaluation-by-tom-holland/.

[760] Davies, W. D. *Paul and Rabbinic Judaism*, London, 1955

recognized and generally accepted that this text is not a rabbinical exegesis of the Old Testament basis of the passage but an example of 'intertextual exegesis' which is found extensively throughout the New Testament.[761]

In this method of reading the New Testament, it has been realized that a writer engages with a text from the Old Testament to support an argument that he is making. His own solution to the problem he is trying to solve is then read back into the original 'borrowed' text from the Old Testament to give that ancient text a greater clarity and meaning not hitherto appreciated but which is consistent with the overall newly discovered understanding.

So, with this new insight as to what Paul was saying in Galatians 4, which is now widely accepted as an example of intertextual reading the meaning of Paul's argument, any claim that Paul relied on or used in anyway his massive rabbinical learning cannot be upheld. In this particular case, Paul in Galatians 4:27 is using Isaiah 54:1 to unpack his Old Testament credentials for welcoming the Gentile believers into the New Covenant community. He believed that through appealing to this Isaianic text he was able to demonstrate that the believing Gentiles were accepted as his people on an equal status with the believing Jews.

What is important about this method of reading is that it is not haphazard. Whatever argument he is making he turns to an appropriate text from an Old Testament. He normally cites the verse within the argument he is making in his letter or, if not a citation, then he gives a clear allusion to the OT passage he wants to use as he teaches his readers to understand where his argument is rooted.

What is also important is that the text cited or alluded to is not abused, but it's clear meaning in the context of the passage it belongs to is what the apostle has picked up and used to build his argument. This type of reading is not specifically rabbinic. Indeed, Richard Hays has shown that it is a feature found in other religious writings as well as in the New Testament.[762]

In other words, Paul, when he became a disciple of Jesus, really did know the renewing of his mind. He followed the exact same method that his new master used, of dealing with the Old Testament text in its immediate context to

---

[761] Jobs, K. H., 'Jerusalem, Our Mother: Metalepsis and Intertextuality in Galatians 4:21-31' *WTJ* 55 (1993) 299–320, Harmo, M. S., *She Must and Shall Go Free: Paul's Isaianic Gospel in Galatians*, BZNW 168. New York: de Gruyter, 2010.

[762] Hays, R. B., *Echoes of Scripture in the Letters of Paul*, New Haven/London, 1989.

establish its meaning. He had clearly put aside his previous training as a rabbi, despite the years he had invested in gaining the high esteem it had brought him. And just as any student would have to do if they changed mentorship from one rabbinic master to another, he followed his new teacher's method of exegeting scripture. No doubt this is behind his statement 'we have the mind of Christ'.

Now can it really be claimed that having gone through such a radical transformation that Paul would surrender this newly accepted exegetical method and put himself under the influence of Greek or even Intertestamental texts? I would suggest that such an argument is preposterous.

In the book *Search for Truth* I have considered the passages in Paul's letters which have traditionally been understood to show that Paul used these Greek and Jewish texts or their cultures to illustrate his message. While Wright disagrees with some of these uses, he happily follows them in a number of cases. I found in my research that rather than helping Paul's argument, these extra biblical texts in fact confuse it.

However, when an Old Testament model for the argument is sought, i.e. passages which deal with the same theme that fits the argument, then Paul's argument becomes gloriously clear and with no exegetical or doctrinal problems having to be explained away. I have demonstrated this *Search for Truth* where I dealt with the issue and what I find truly comforting is that no reviewer has challenged the arguments I have made, even those who object to my understanding of Paul's exegetical method. All that is argued to support their opposition, as Garlington and others have, is to say that *Search for Truth* cannot be trusted because it presents a Docetic version of Paul, i.e. one that had no historic existence.

Despite making these firm rejections of my work because of this perceived Docetic version, none of the reviewers have supported their understanding of Paul with any hard evidence to vindicate their case. Indeed, it is clear that they make their claims not because they have studied the evidence but because they hold it as self-evident, i.e. that Paul was Hellenized and as a consequence he used Hellenism as a tool to promote his message. In comparison, I have considered this crucial hermeneutical issue during fifty-five years of study, bible teaching and research in which I have successfully supervised over twenty students for their PhD and each one used the insights I am discussing as the hermeneutic for their research. All but one who completed and submitted their work received the award they had worked for. It was by adopting this exegetical method that they opened doors to new understandings and were awarded their PhD for what was often described by their examiners as ground breaking work that deserved the award. The scrutiny of world-leading examiners in their field of specialization has indirectly supported my claim that Paul did not engage with Hellenism.[763]

Now, I know that I stand outside the prevailing academic understanding and I am more than happy that others engage and critique my arguments. But what is not fair is to take a stance without a proper discussion of the evidence, which means that my case has been dismissed as groundless by a method that is itself groundless.

I acknowledge that to follow the clear exegetical methods of Jesus and Paul will demand a massive change of mind and the surrender of numerous engrained assumptions that have never been properly tested, so I more than understand the backlash these scholars are making. Indeed, they encourage me, for they have clearly seen the issue that I have raised, and I wrote *Search for Truth* to invite this response. But I believe that, rather than having created a Docetic version of Paul, I have in fact identified the mindset not of Jesus and Paul, and this was the one that was followed by the entire apostolic community. When the modern reader follows the same method of reading, incredible light is shed on the passages that for far too long have been hidden by the fog of Hellenism.

The most influential advocate for the method of interpretation I am critiquing is Tom Wright. I have answered his claims in *Search for Truth* where

---

[763] Indeed, the following world leading scholars have added their endorsement to the proposals I am making.

"Dr Holland has produced a stimulating volume which deserves the most careful scrutiny from New Testament students. It is a remarkably fresh and creative study which makes one re-think familiar passages in new ways." - Prof H I Marshal, Aberdeen University, *Evangelical Quarterly*

"A fresh and useful treatment of Pauline theology, and many of its arguments offer corrections to widespread misunderstandings of Paul", Prof Anthony C. Thiselton, Nottingham University, *Expository Times*

"This is a fascinating work that definitely requires thorough study and it will certainly lead to serious debate regarding many aspects of Paul's theology. The author however time and again pre-empts us herein by engaging other important points in discussion. This discussion will definitely (have to) be continued," Prof HJB Combrink, University of Stellenbosch.

"No one has helped me read & understand St. Paul more than Tom Holland. I find his work to be the near perfect balance of creative yet careful, original yet faithful. While many talk about theological exegesis—Dr. Holland actually does it, and he does it well, Dustin Messer (www.kuyperian.com)

Romans 16

I have shown that he repeatedly appeals to Hellenistic sources and Intertestamental literature to make and support his arguments. Because most have not done the research that he has done, his handling of this material and his statements concerning their application and significance have been taken as authoritative. However, in the volume just mentioned, I have gone through his claims with care and shown repeatedly how his confidence should be weighed and his contribution to the arguments made should be questioned. Although he disputes that the sources he uses have any influence on his theology, my research has shown that this is clearly not so.

Wright begins his reinterpretation of Paul by claiming that before his conversion he was a Zealot. In this movement he acquainted himself with the key figures of Zealot history and strove to follow their examples. When Paul became a follower of Christ he withdrew from the movement and became a proclaimer of the gospel of peace. To answer the conundrum of how Saul could at the same time, be both a Zealot and a disciple of Gamaliel, a highly respected teacher who was a pacifist, Wright appeals to Rabbi Akiba. He does this despite Akiba's dates (50–135 CE) mean that he could have not influenced Paul. Wright nevertheless claims that because Akiba was a pacifist who later became a Zealot, this was something that demonstrates that Paul could have also done as well. The weakness of this argument is that it depends on demonstrating that this is what Akiba actually did, and as I have shown, it does not stand scrutiny.

I have carefully studied Wright's argument on this now widely-accepted position concerning Paul having been a Zealot and I have found it has no foundation at all.[764] Despite Akiba providing nothing to support Wright's argument that others were able to be under two masters who differed radically

---

[764] Wright was clearly aware of the weakness of his evidence for he wrote

'True, Akiba is credited with this only one passage, which has sometimes been regarded as suspect, but again, the rejection of rabbinic thinking makes it all the more likely that the rejection of Messianism in post—135 rabbinic thinking makes it all the more likely that this reference, preserved against the tendency of this tradition (to exonerate a hero like Akiba from complicity in the failed revolt), is historically well founded.'

But in this construction Wright ignores the fact that it was far from unusual to attach arguments to key figures in Judaism and certainly zealots who needed a leader they could identify with that would give them a kudos that would impress other Jews and possibly be more inclined to give them support. The zealots would not care that they had damaged Akiba's reputation, especially if he had not been part of their movement. For a detailed analysis see Holland, *Search for Truth*, 419-435.

from each other in doctrine and practice at the same time, which Wright and others have claimed, I found evidence that showed that Akiba was exactly the evidence I needed to support my contention that the Paul I have described is far from being a Docetic myth.

Apart from the hugely different messages both men preached, Akiba took the very same position I am suggesting Paul himself held. He rejected Hellenism and was ultra-conservative in his commitment to the Old Testament scriptures—a position that was clearly appealing to his contemporaries because he drew tens of thousands of followers. Those who have objected to my construction of Paul's biography and the teaching it has spawned have accused me of describing a Paul who never existed. Their claim is that the man I have described could not possibly have lived in the first century. Their argument is that the traditional conservative Jewish identity could have no longer existed in the first century because the Jewish mindset had absorbed Hellenism. For this reason, they argue, Paul would have been unable to avoid being a man of his age and therefore his teaching would have been influenced by Hellenism. Paul's message, they argue, could not be of a Jewish origin alone.[765]

So Akiba turns out to have had the same outlook that I have claimed Paul had; he kept himself apart from Hellenism. This did not nullify his ministry, rather, it promoted it, for Akiba had between 12,000 to 48,000 disciples.[766]

---

[765] 5 So for example, Chadwick, H., "All Things to All Men (1 Cor.1X.22)" *NTS* 1 (54-55) 261-275.273 says: "The eschatological and apocalyptic character of the primitive Palestinian Gospel was a grave liability in preaching the Gospel of Christ to an audience of Hellenistic intellectuals, he boldly reinterpreted the Gospel so as to put into the background the concept of the end of the world, and interpreted the supremacy of Jesus Christ in terms of Cosmic Wisdom, the agent of God in creation. Boers, H., "Jesus and the Christian Faith : New Testament Christology since Bousset's Kyrios Christos" *JBL* 89 (1970) 450-6.435 says: "Hellenistic Jewish Christianity may ease the transition from Palestinian Jewish to Hellenistic Christianity, but this does not alter the fact that it was a transition into ‚something new." Kee, H. C., "Christology and Ecclesiology. Titles of Christ and Models of Community" *SBL 1982 Seminar Paper* pp 227-242.232 says: "From Jew to Gentile, from Palestine to the Diaspora, from an apocalyptic to a Gnostic environment, from the social and political role of a Jewish sect to that of a world religion - all these contextual alterations necessitated a rapid series of translations of the kerygma". Kummel, W. G., *The Theology of the New Testament According to its Major Witnesses. Jesus-Paul-John*, London, 1974., 105f and 118f says that it is impossible to distinguish between the thought of the earliest church and that of the Hellenists.

[766] A figure ranging from 12,000 to 48,000 disciples is given by Lois Ginzberg, 'Akiba Ben Joseph', *Jewish Encyclopedia*, Vol 1 P 306.

Clearly his 'narrowness' was not a problem for drawing followers. In fact, it seems to have been his greatest asset.

The following is an extract of an article written by the esteemed Jewish scholar Louis Ginzberg:

If the older Halacha is to be considered as the product of the internal struggle between Phariseeism and Sadduceeism, the Halacha of Akiva [Akiba] must be conceived as the result of an external contest between Judaism on the one hand and Hellenism and Hellenistic Christianity on the other. Akiva no doubt perceived that the intellectual bond uniting the Jews—far from being allowed to disappear with the destruction of the Jewish state—must be made to draw them closer together than before. He pondered also the nature of that bond. The Bible could never again fill the place alone; for the Christians also regarded it as a divine revelation. Still less could dogma serve the purpose, for dogmas were always repellent to rabbinical Judaism, whose very essence is development and the susceptibility to development. *Mention has already been made of the fact that Akiva was the creator of a rabbinical Bible version elaborated with the aid of his pupil, Aquila (though this is traditionally debated), and designed to become the common property of all Jews. But this was not sufficient to obviate all threatening danger. It was to be feared that the Jews, by their facility in accommodating themselves to surrounding circumstances—even then a marked characteristic—might become entangled in the net of Grecian philosophy, and even in that of Gnosticism. The example of his colleagues and friends, Elisha ben Abuyah, Ben 'Azzai, and Ben Zoma strengthened him still more in his conviction of the necessity of providing some counterpoise to the intellectual influence of the non-Jewish world.*[767]

Ginzberg could not be clearer. Akiba [Akiva] accepted that the Jewish people had to accommodate themselves to the Roman occupation, but it was quite another thing to accept its alien philosophy. Thus Paul was not the only rabbi of the first century who avoided engaging with Hellenism. Indeed, Hengel who is regarded as the most authoritative writer on the history of the Zealots has pointed out that many first century Palestinian Jew rejected the culture that their occupiers brought with them.[768]

---

[767] Lois Ginzberg, 'Akiba Ben Joseph', *Jewish Encyclopedia*, Vol 1 P 306. Italics added.

[768] Hengel, Martin, *The Zealots: Investigations into The Jewish Freedom Movement In The Period From Herod I Until 70 A.D*, tr. by David Smith, Edinburgh: T. & T. Clark, 1989, 180,

So we know that Akiba had tens of thousands of students who followed his example and who, as his disciples, were vocal advocates of his views. This fact alone demonstrates that there was a clear hunger for a strong commitment to the teaching of the Jewish scriptures and this movement was far from insignificant.

If we explore the influence of Akiba's disciples, we will gain a much clearer understanding of how widespread this reading of scripture that I am describing was followed.

The disciples of Akiba were rabbis who had their own congregations. The minimum size of a congregation to maintain a rabbi was ten families based on the principle of each family contributing a tenth of their income to pay a salary to for his service. If we take Ginzberg's lower figure of the number of Akiba's disciples, then 12,000 Jewish leaders were directly under Akiba's teaching and they in turn were committed to repeating what they learned. This was not an option to consider, it was a condition of being part of the movement he led.

If each man had two children, a low figure for Jewish families of that time, then the total number of people being instructed in their families numbered 48,000 people. These teachers would have had at least 10 families under their care. So if they also had two children each then the number indirectly under the influence Akiba's teaching is 480,000. This does not take into account that the number of children was probably considerably larger based on the size of families at that time and that it uses the lower figure of disciples that Ginzberg has given. If we had gone with larger number of disciples cited by Ginzberg, then the 480,000 number would be 1,920,000 people! This is clearly a huge number and I am happy to use the much lower figure to avoid exaggeration.

Now, the actual population of the Jewish nation pre 70 CE has been cited as 4 million by some authorities and 5 million by others.[769] If we take the higher 5 million figure, then one person in ten was significantly influenced by Akiba, and if the lower figure of 4 million, then one in eight was significantly influenced by him. Now, these population figures relate to the population before the 70 CE war that brought about the conquest of Jerusalem. So, after that momentous event the percentage of Jews significantly influenced by Akiba, taking that the pre-Jerusalem fall had a populations of 4.2 million, the

---

[769] Harnack, Adolf, *Die Mission und Ausbreitung Des Christentums In Den Ersten Drei Jahrhunderten*, [1st ed.], Leipzig: J. C. Hinrichs, 1902, cited by Joseph Jacobs *Jewish Encyclopedia,* 1902.

ratio could be as low as one in six, as some suggest a million people died in the slaughter of that war.⁷⁷⁰

These numbers relate to the influence that Akiba had on the Jewish community. Added to this number, if my claim that Paul did not Hellenize the Christian gospel is true, then the members of the fledgling first century church which preceded Akiba must be added. Obviously, these were ahead of the game as far as Akiba and his followers were concerned by about 70 years. We know that 3,000 were converted on the Day of Pentecost, and in a very short time the number had reached 5,000 (Acts 4:4). The sudden explosion of this 'Jewish sect' was disrupting Judaism as its message about Jesus spread like wildfire. News of this movement reached the synagogues throughout the Roman world. There was clearly a lot of confusion in, as well as outside, of this movement, but the apostles travelled far and wide to explain the significance of the teaching, death and resurrection of Jesus.

Often Paul attended synagogues and was urged by the people to tell them about the message he was preaching concerning Jesus and the Way. These enquirers had no problem in the way Paul was expounding the Jewish scriptures which was identical to the 'primitive gospel' message preached by Peter on the Day of Pentecost. Thus, the early churches were established in the gospel that was first preached immediately after the resurrection of Jesus. There had been no adaption or development of the message and it was the foundation of the numerous congregations being formed. Indeed, the only debate concerning interpretation was over the Law and how it applied to the Gentile converts.

We also ought to note that when Paul eventually returned to Jerusalem after his third missionary journey as recorded in Acts 20:10, he was greeted with the statement, 'You see, brother, how many thousands of Jews have believed, and all are zealous for the law.'

There are two things that we should note from this statement.

First, despite the scattering of the believers through the earlier persecution and the fact that thousands of pilgrims present on the Day of Pentecost who had

---

⁷⁷⁰ Tacitus writes that that the population of Jerusalem at its fall was 600,000 while Josephus, states that there were 1,100,000 slain when the city fell in CE 70, with 97,000 being sold as slaves. Josephus says that there were as many as 1,100,000 slain in the slaughter that took place but qualifies this figure by noting that Jerusalem was besieged during the Passover. Thus, the majority of the 1,197,000 would have been visiting the city for the festival. Information provided by Joseph Jacobs in *Jewish Encyclopedia* 1902.

become followers of Jesus as the Christ had returned to their homes scattered throughout the Roman empire, massive church growth had still continued in Jerusalem.

And second, clearly these new believers saw that a right understanding and application of the law was critical for them to accept the message of the apostles and receive a welcome into the believing community. The way the apostles exemplify this reading is given throughout the book of Acts where a typological exegesis was clearly taken as the given method so, Acts 2:25, 29, 34; 4:25; 7:45; 13:22, 34, 36. In each of these statements the Old Testament texts are exegeted typologically. The gist of the statements is that David said this or experienced this, so how much more greater is the fulfilment in the Greater Son of David. Such typological exegesis was not new to the apostle's audiences, for it is found throughout the Old Testament.[771]

We can draw from this that whatever the apostles taught, it had satisfied the zeal that these converts had for the law. This in turn points to how we should challenge any hermeneutical proposals for anything that violated this respect for the law. These people must have seen how right it was to say that Christ has fulfilled the law in a way that did not demand that they disrespected the law. There could be no slipshod exegesis of their ancient texts and, like Akiba was to strive for, they would have smelt a rat if anyone sought to allow Hellenism to intrude into their sacred traditions.

This large number of people who became followers of Christ in Jerusalem were all part of families, so through their witness the apostolic teaching which focused on interpreting the Old Testament in light of the Christ event was brought to their families. So, the numbers of people in Jerusalem who came under the influence of the apostles teaching was huge.

Antioch soon challenged Jerusalem as the primary Christian base followed by the establishing of other communities such as those in Corinth, Ephesus, Thessalonica and others. Substantial numbers attended their meetings in order to worship and be taught, and they went on to spawn other congregations in their own localities (Acts 19:26; Col 1:5–6; 1 Thess 1:7–10). These are just the

---

[771] Goppelt L., *Typos: TheTypological Interpretation of the Old Testament in the New*, trans. D. H. Madvig (Grand Rapids, MI: Eerdmans, 1982). Davidson, Richard M., "Typological Structures in the Old and New Testaments," *Andrews University Seminary Studies 20.1* (Spring 1982), 61-62. Ninow, F., Indicators of Typology within the Old Testament: *The Exodus Motif*, Friedensauer Schriftenreihe: Reihe I, Theologie, Band 4 (Berlin: Peter Lang, 2001), 24n34. Ribbens, B. J.. "Typology of Types: Typology in Dialogue", *Journal of Theological Interpretation* Vol. 5, No. 1 (Spring, 2011), pp. 81-95. Wood, J. E., "Isaac Typology in the New Testament", *New Testament Studies* 14 (1967-68) 583-589. For Paul's use of typology see Holland, *Search for Truth*, 247-401.

congregations that Paul and his converts founded and don't include the churches in Philippi or Rome. Clearly there was an explosion of Christian presence throughout the Roman empire with the teaching that accompanied the emergence of these congregations.

Added to these numbers of course is the unrecorded church planting activities of other Christian workers which took the message to other parts of the world. We know little about the work of these evangelists but for the evidence of the fruit of their activities. The churches planted in India by Thomas come into this category of unrecorded expansion and are examples of this hidden history. In each of these new congregations the message of the apostles took root, and this was founded on a correct reading of the Old Testament scriptures. Even though no firm numbers can be given to the membership of these new vibrant communities that where reproducing themselves throughout the Roman empire and beyond, it is reasonable to assume that it was at least the same numbers as those Jews who were to eventually come under the teaching of Akiba. So, by the early years of the second century this method of reading the Jewish scriptures and their interpretation of them was a very significant hermeneutic both within the Christian/Jewish communities and then the Jewish communities themselves.

Thus, the evidence shows that there was a very large number of Christians and Jews following the sort of interpretation of Israel's scriptures that I have described. Akiba had mystical leanings and happily embraced an allegorical reading of the Song of Solomon, while there is very little reference, if any at all, to this text in the New Testament. The apostle's method was essentially a typological reading of their scriptures in light of the Christ event. A characteristic of this interpretation is that the apostles kept to the Jewish traditions and history which focused on the Fall, Redemption from Egypt and then from Babylon with recognition of the key figures and covenants made with Israel through them that were part of these events. This fact becomes clear when we read Romans and Galatians, two letters to mainly Gentile churches. Paul expected them to understand the details of Jewish salvation history, so clearly their teachers were committed to sharing these details as part of their instruction.

In all of Paul's recorded sermons there is but one very brief mention of a Hellenistic source. This was when he cited one of their poets at Mars Hill (Acts 17:22–23). He drew nothing from the poet to make a theological point. Indeed, he immediately challenged the understanding of the widely held Greek belief in dualism by declaring that Jesus had been raised from the dead. This immediately caused the crowd to turn from him to go and see what other 'strange' teachings they could learn discover.

Important evidence that the apostles did not adapt their presentation to its audience but stayed faithful to the methodology given to them by Jesus is found in the way Paul answered both Felix and Agrippa (Acts 24:10–22; 26:1–32). Before two important local officials who had the power to either free him or to sentence him to death, Paul explained his position and his message. In neither presentation Paul made is there a hint of him appealing to the Hellenism which Felix and Agrippa would have been trained in as a requirement for the office they both held. So, at the most critical moment, when he is arguing for his acquittal before thoroughly Hellenized men who had the power to sentence him to death, not once did Paul refer to anything they would have been conversant with. Instead, his presentation was a carbon copy of the message preached on the Day of Pentecost which took place weeks after Jesus's death and resurrection. Such a fact is surely hugely telling.

Now we have seen that for whatever reason, Akiba adopted the same method as his Christian opponents in distancing himself from Hellenism for fear that its influence would damage the faith of the people he taught.

As a young Rabbi, Akiba committed himself to oppose the Messianic claims of Jesus.[772] To do this he had read all the Christian writings of which he could avail himself. This collection must have included copies of Paul's letters for he was the most prolific writer in the apostolic community. This may well answer the question of how Akiba came to have this aversion to engaging with the texts of Hellenism So, in this way, there is possibly an unexpected link between the two teachers.

Now, we are never told that Paul feared this pollution of his Jewish heritage. He is silent on his exegetical method. He just does it, and he seems to assume that he did not need to explain it to either his listeners or his readers. This suggests that his way of exegesis was widely followed in the all churches. Even when he spoke in the synagogue he used the same method and did not think he had to explain how he reached the conclusions he did.

In contrast, from what Ginzberg tells us, Akiba was very clear about his method. He no doubt debated this with other rabbis, so his method would have no doubt been discussed throughout the Jewish communities for he was so famous and clearly making a stand that everyone had to take a position on. If

---

[772] Levey, Samson H., "Akiba in Search of the Messiah; a Closer Look" *Judaism* 41 no. 4, Fall 1992, p 334-345.

any of his followers became a follower of Jesus they would have had no problem with the way they read and expounded the scriptures

It also must be appreciated that we are not engaging with an insignificant rabbi who would have had limited influence. Akiba became the head of the largest rabbinic school in Jewish history so it is likely that his influence would not be limited to the teaching he gave his own disciples. Just as he read the Christian writings in order to engage in debate with their claims, so other rabbis, if they were worthy of their teaching role, would have had to engage with his teaching.

It was probably this huge rabbinic block that influenced Rome when, after the war, they looked for the most reliable community they could trust to steer the nation in a peaceful path. And they chose the rabbinic movement.[773] This

---

[773] The following extract from the article on Judaism in Encyclopedia Britannica explains how Judaism became the preferred agent for Rome to deal with the Jewish people, 'After the defeat of Bar Kokhba and the ensuing collapse of active Jewish resistance to Roman rule (135–136), politically moderate and quietist rabbinic elements remained the only cohesive group in Jewish society. With Jerusalem off-limits to the Jews, rabbinic ideology and practice, which were not dependent on the Temple, priesthood, or political independence for their vitality, provided a viable program for autonomous community life and thus filled the vacuum created by the suppression of all other Jewish leadership. The Romans, confident that the will for insurrection had been shattered, soon relaxed the Hadrianic prohibitions of Jewish ordination, public assembly, and regulation of the calendar and permitted rabbis who had fled the country to return and re-establish an academy in the town of Usha in Galilee.

The strength of the rabbinate lay in its ability to represent simultaneously the interests of the Jews and the Romans, whose religious and political needs, respectively, now chanced to coincide. The rabbis were regarded favorably by the Romans as a politically submissive class, which, with its wide influence over the Jewish masses, could translate the Pax Romana (the peace imposed by Roman rule) into Jewish religious precepts. To the Jews, on the other hand, the rabbinic ideology gave the appearance of continuity to Jewish self-rule and freedom from alien interference. The rabbinic program fashioned by Johanan ben Zakkai and his circle replaced sacrifice and pilgrimage to the Temple with the study of Scripture, prayer, and works of piety, thus eliminating the need for a central sanctuary (in Jerusalem) and making Judaism a religion capable of practice anywhere. Judaism was now, for all intents and purposes, a Diaspora religion, even on its home soil. Any sense of real break with the past was mitigated by continued adherence to purity laws (dietary and bodily) and by assiduous study of Scripture, including the legal elements that historical developments had now made inoperable. The reward held out for scrupulous study and fulfillment was the promise of messianic deliverance—i.e., the divine restoration of all those institutions that had become central in Jewish notions of national independence, including the Davidic monarchy, Temple service, and the ingathering of Diaspora Jewry. Above all these rewards were the assurance of personal resurrection and participation in the national rebirth. Encyclopedia

was done because they had not taken part in the Zealot movement, which caused Rome to conclude that they were not interested in politics but in the study of their religious texts. This fact alone casts serious doubt on Wright's claim that all first century Jews had a political position and that many of the rabbinics were part of the Zealot movement.[774] It was because of this momentous appointment by Rome, to be the official representatives of the Jewish people, that they were catapulted to a status that no other grouping, even though more politically powerful, had. The rabbinical movement continues to exert influence up to this present day. It was a position given to them by Rome who saw them as the only grouping they could trust!

Another point in which we see the shadow of Paul in the thinking of Akiba is his liturgical thinking and practice. He wrote the liturgy for celebrating the Passover, a liturgy used annually to this day. And into that liturgy he introduced the reading of the Song of Solomon, commonly known as the Canticles. He was not the first rabbi to see how this could be interpreted as being applied to the love that Yahweh had for Israel, His bride![775] However this understanding was not widely followed as it was argued that the Song was not a suitable picture to represent the divine marriage because its intimate details were seen as sordid and unfitting to speak of Yahweh's love for Israel. It was Akiba who described the book as the Holy of Holies and drove through this rabbinic squabbling to insert the reading into the celebration of the annual Passover.

How did this connection come about? No other Jewish teacher seems to have been prepared to take the step that Akiba took. But for a Jewish teacher who had read the letters of Paul, he could not miss how the church was claiming the Old Testament teaching of the divine marriage and the love that God has for his New Covenant people. Akiba would, I suggest, have seen the need to use the Song to repeatedly remind Israel that she alone was the true divine bride and the delight of Yahweh's heart. He took a step that even the apostles with their strong doctrine of the divine marriage never dared to make; of speaking of this relationship is terms of such intimate language.

So, reviewing the argument developed in this chapter, the prevailing view that it was the apostles themselves who adapted their message to communicate

---

Britannica, *Rabbinic Judaism (2nd–18th century)*, https://www.britannica.com/topic/Judaism/Rabbinic-Judaism-2nd-18th-century. Emphasis added

[774] A view that Hengel firmly challenged, see his *The Zealots*, 180.

[775] Of course, the theme was well known through the teaching of the prophets. There was nevertheless a widespread reluctance to link the Song to Yahweh's love for Israel.

with the gentiles in imagery and illustrations they were familiar with has been challenged. By this adaptation, it is claimed, the Christian message evolved and eventually lost connection with its deep roots in the Jewish faith and importantly in the way its scriptures were now being valued and expounded.

Now the 'parting of the ways' between the early church and Judaism certainly began in the first century but it was driven by the persecution that the church prompted by Jewish leaders who sought to stop the spread of their message in the Jewish community. To facilitate this opposition, the Jewish leaders aligned themselves with the interests of Rome and brought to the attention of its officials that the Christian sect had effectively surrendered its legal status given by Rome for being a part of Judaism. She was thereby deprived of the licensed religion status that Rome had given the Jewish nation, a license that allowed her freedom to follow her own religion. Judaism officially expelled the Christian community from its ranks and it was put outside of the status it had previously enjoyed. Because of this separation, the church became a target by Rome and its servants when her followers refused to take part in the emperor worship Rome required of all it ruled over. Naturally this division was not one the church sought for. She benefited from the status of being a part of the Jewish community and recognized the debt she owed the Jewish people for giving them the scriptures that had taught them about God and his mercy in Christ. Their one desire was to share how the promises of the scriptures had been fulfilled In Christ, but this was the very position the Jewish leaders were anxious to nullify. The division of the church and the Jewish state was therefore not driven by the church adopting a Hellenistic stance, but rather for insisting that her interpretation was perfectly orthodox. The church exegeted the scriptures in a normal way but claimed that her interpretation was the only correct reading, which was an afront to the Jewish religious leadership. In the first century the church affirmed her rightful position in the Jewish community believing she had done nothing to deserve expulsion contending her message was about how God had fulfilled the scriptures and nothing more.

The doctrinal division of the parting of the ways came in the second century as leaders who had come from Greek backgrounds trained through Greek institutions understandably read the New Testament as Greek text, and read their Hellenistic perspectives into the texts. The Septuagint, the widely used Greek text of the Old Testament, was read by the new generation of Gentile leaders without appreciating the background and culture from which it had emerged. The translators, who had provided this collection of the Hebrew scriptures in a language Greek-speaking Jews could understand, have been shown by scholarship to have struggled to keep the meaning of the Hebrew texts in the Greek terms they carefully selected in order to emphasize what the Greek terms should convey of the original Hebrew meaning that Hebrew-speaking Jews would understand.[776] But the Church Fathers failed to grasp this and read the Geek meaning of the gentile world which the new believing community was rooted in. They inevitably drifted from the Hebraic apostolic understanding as other paradigms moved into the vacuum their absence produced. These leaders had no hesitancy in appealing to familiar illustrations drawn from Greek culture. Thus, the Jewish church was better prepared for the inevitable challenge that Hellenism would bring, while the Gentile church in contrast fell to the dangers of the assimilation of Hellenism that Akiba was fighting to resist.

It was in this period of church history that the 'dividing of the ways' took place. It was not the break with Judaism that many think took place in the first century, but a division within the Christian community when parts of the church embraced Hellenism. It was not a visible or violent division and probably not even recognized by most, but while almost undetected it was nevertheless hugely significant.

It can be said that there were three main divisions in the first hundred years of the churches life. The apostles had urged the Jewish church to welcome Gentile believers in Jesus as brethren and as equals. It was this policy that deeply offended the unbelieving Jewish community (as well as some of the believing community!). It was not because of a wholesale embracing of Hellenism as has often been held. There were those who called themselves followers of Jesus but who separated themselves from the teaching of the apostles because they thought their position had abandoned the law by accepting Gentiles without requiring circumcision

Then there was the growing separation from Judaism as her hostility to the message of the believing community in her ranks provoked the Jewish leaders to deep resentment. This resulted in her using all her links with the Roman state to encourage it to turn on the witnessing church. This second separation resulted in the believing community being forced out of Judaism to make its own stand,

---

[776] See Hill, D., *Greek Words and Hebrew Meanings. Studies in the Semantics of Soteriological Terms*, London, 1967 and Ziesler, J., *The Meaning of Righteousness in Paul*, Cambridge, 1972. These studies demonstrate that the LXX, rather than abandoning the Hebrew text in favor of a Greek reading, the translators sought to be faithful to the original meaning of the Hebrew scriptures. It was this meaning that the early church fathers lost.

one that was deprived protection from Roman law which it had exploited under the guise of being a sect within Judaism and its licensed religion status.

Then there was the Hellenization of the church, which did not take place in the first century as many have supposed but in the second century when two sections of the church holding to the need to stay within Old Testament/apostolic teaching strove in different ways for the truth of the Gospel. One presented it as the fulfilment of the Old Testament while the other increasingly leaned to the Greek world's thirst for wisdom and intellectual completion. One was based on the message from Jerusalem and the other on the message devised by Athens.

This point is confirmed by Clement who records how, through a visit to Palestine, he learned things which he had previously not known about and felt compelled to record this information for the sake of Gentile believers. By this visit he came into direct contact with a body of material and a way of understanding of which he had previously been unaware. A comparison between Clement and the epistle of Barnabas shows that parallels exist which would suggest that either one borrowed from the other, or more likely, that they used a common midrash. What is important about this material is that it is characteristic of a very archaic period of Christianity'.

Clement's testimony is clear evidence of an ancient tradition of understanding he had not had in his earlier teaching ministry that he was so impressed he wanted to share it. It also shows there was more than one understanding of how to read the Jewish scriptures. One followed the teaching of Jesus and his example of not engaging with rabbinic traditions or other extra biblical materials. The second, followed by Gentile churches taught by second century leaders, while faithfully and sincerely held was not the same as the churches which retained their thinking and understanding in line with what they had received from the preaching and teaching of the apostles. As all churches ultimately had their roots in apostolic evangelism and teaching, something had caused them to adopt a different tradition. It was, I suggest, created by the new emerging leadership that had its training not in 'the school of the prophets' but in the school of Philo and similar places of learning. This new stream of understanding soon robbed the church of her most important heritage. Thus, contrary to popular scholarly opinion, the Hellenization of the church did not take place in the first century. This widely held theory is the result of reading the New Testament from the presumption that the New Testament writings were Greek in thought as well as in language. This is the reading that prevails to this day, and with this fixed position most scholars have failed to examine the evidence fairly. This prevailing reading unintentionally reads Greek thought and concepts into the teaching of the New Testament documents. I have undertaken this examination elsewhere[777] and discovered that passages normally appealed to as evidence of Hellenization have their own problems and these are only removed when alternative readings that come from the Old Testament are identified. When this is done there is a massive transformation of thinking and understanding for the reader and the depths and unity of the two testaments becomes gloriously obvious.

It is my contention that to recover the apostolic message we must read the Old Testament in the way that the apostles read it and read the New Testament as the final chapter of the Old. By doing this we are reading Old Testament theology as the ground for our understanding of the New Testament. By such a reading, we enter into the understanding and teaching of the apostolic church and do not engage ourselves with the Hellenism that robbed the second century church of her heritage. The documents of the New Testament were not written in the context of the Hellenized second century church but in the context of the first century church which still had its roots firmly fixed in its Old Testament Jewish heritage.

The ultimate evidence that this is the intended way of reading the books of the New Testament is what happens to our understanding when we read it in such a way. The book you have in your hands is part of that evidence for you to consider.

---

[777] See Holland, *Tom Wright and the Search for Truth*, second edition revised and extended, Apiary Publishing, London, 2019.

Conclusion to the Letter

Like many other commentators, I have sought to follow the teaching of Paul, the apostle to the Gentiles. Some have come to recognize the weight of OT evidence that Paul carried with his arguments, causing a range of scholars to seek to identify the scope of its influence on his theology. However, it has been my contention that, despite moving towards a reading of Paul that takes his Jewishness seriously, many have not appreciated how much Hellenistic baggage they carry, depositing it unconsciously into Paul's arguments. It is my contention that until the OT heritage is properly identified and evaluated; we will not get to the heart of what Paul has said to the church. In trying to accomplish this, much has had to be examined.

We have found that Paul rarely spoke to individuals in his letters; rather, he addressed churches. At all points, his theology was affected by the corporate perspective. This is not only important for a correct understanding of Paul but of the entire NT. As reading corporately was natural Jewish people, converts from among them who were appointed to teach the Gentiles would have been able to expound the apostles' letters correctly. It must be remembered that the Hellenistic individualism of the early Gentile converts was light years away from the extreme forms spawned by the Enlightenment. As a result, even without Jewish help, Gentile believers in the first century would have had far less difficulty in embracing a corporate reading than members of our extremely individualistic western societies of today, including, sadly, our Christian churches. Tragically, these churches are mostly taught by leaders who have unwittingly read the NT through a predominantly individualistic lens and who have made no serious attempt to recover the lost heritage.

In the first chapter, we saw how Paul rooted his gospel in the promises God had made, particularly to David. So we read that Jesus is of the seed of David (Rom 1:3) and the one who brings the righteousness of God to completion (Rom 1:16–18). This saving activity is desperately needed because of the rebellion of humanity towards its Creator (Rom 1:19–32).

In chapter 2, Paul remonstrated with those who thought they were excluded from the just condemnation that he said, in chapter1, would come upon the ungodly (the Gentiles). In chapter 3, he explained that circumcision was not a guarantee that Jews will be saved—what mattered was the circumcision of their hearts. We noted in Rom 2 that Paul's reference to justification in this particular text is limited to the Jewish understanding of being included in the eschatological community. Paul was saying that only those who strive after righteousness will qualify for this limited experience of justification. This matches the requirements of the Baptist, to repent and be baptized. It is unwise and problematic to read Paul's fully developed Christian theology into this discussion with the representative of the Children of Abraham.

The opening of chapter 3 is made up of a citation of OT texts, all of which have links with the Exodus theme. The accumulative force of these texts–that man is in exile from God–results in the incredible statement of Rom 3:21–26, in which Paul described the death of Christ. The exilic theme of the previous verses continued as Paul built his argument on a possible earlier confession of the church that represented Christ as the atoning Passover sacrifice. In Rom 3:27–32, he stressed that, in this new covenant arrangement the eschatological Passover inaugurated, there was no special status for Jews or Gentiles. Both call on the same Creator, who is faithful to his covenant promises.

Chapter 4 focused on the issues of justification and membership of the new covenant community. Abraham's justification was considered in terms of the requirements God made upon him. Paul demonstrated that they had nothing to do with Abraham's circumcision, for he was uncircumcised when justified. By contrast, David—another key figure in Jewish history—was circumcised but not justified. By means of this evidence, Paul established that the Jewish community, whose members had undergone circumcision, could not assume covenant membership. They stood in the same state of need as the Gentiles, who they so often despised.

The discussion on justification in chapter 4 established there has been a failure in understanding aspects of Pauline theology. Justification as covenant-making is the primary meaning behind the statement that "Abraham believed God, and it was counted to him as righteousness." We also found that, for Paul, the event that showed Abraham as a justified man was his obedience to Yahweh, when he went to offer his son as a sacrifice on Mount Moriah. It was not the act that justified him, but the faith that made his obedience possible. He knew that Yahweh would keep his promise to give seed through Isaac, and would, therefore, raise his son from the dead. Paul's point was that this is the same faith NT believers exercise, for they believe God has raised Jesus from the dead and has raised up a spiritual family as a result.

Conclusion to the Letter

In chapter 5, we found that Paul continued the theme of the New Exodus through his use of pilgrim and Paschal language. The discourse on the fall of man in Adam explained humankind's plight, which had previously been discussed in terms of its consequences rather than its origin. By explaining the cause of humanity's predicament, Paul offset the stage for his subsequent discussion of how God brought about a new humanity through the representative death of his Son. Paul's analysis of the consequence of the fall was that it was devastating; all, without exception, could only be saved by participation in the death of Christ.

In chapter 6, Paul expanded the theme of man's solidarity in Adam, which he introduced in chapter 5 (though it is implicitly present in the earlier chapters). His case was that Adam's disastrous representative role can be compensated for by the last Adam. Like the Adam of Genesis, the last Adam's actions will have far-reaching consequences for those who are part of the people he represents. While Adam's sin in the garden brought all under condemnation, Christ's death on the cross brought many into and under righteousness. Throughout chapter 6, Paul continued to use exodus language. He paralleled the baptism into Christ with the baptism into Moses (1 Cor 10:1–4), and so his understanding of baptism into Christ is found to be corporate. The glory of God being displayed in the New Exodus is with a far-greater intensity than in the original Exodus. The believers are freed from slavery to Sin in order to be servants (not slaves) of righteousness–a title that carries all of the OT connotations of Israel's call to be the servant of the Lord.

We found that chapter 7 exhibited all the signs of a typical piece of Jewish literature, with Paul reviewing the history of the human family. He used many pictures in his collage: Adam, Abraham, Moses, the Gentiles, himself, and the rest of the believing community. Paul began this part of his letter with a reference to marriage. This is the key to the corporate dimension of his argument since divine marriage symbolism is never used in scripture to describe an individual's relationship with God. This appreciation enabled us to see that the passage was not an illustration but an actual description of covenantal reality. The point that Paul established was that salvation depends on Christ; for through his death, the covenantal relationship binding humanity to Satan was cancelled. Christ severed Satan's authority, which had been given to him by the law. (The law was obliged, because of its covenantal nature [i.e., expressing the will of the covenantal God] to respect relationships which were entered into freely and, therefore, had to respect the right of the husband, in this case Satan.) Now, the believing community was in a position to marry another. She was pledged to Christ, her redeemer, whose death delivered her from Sin.

Chapter 8 continued the theme of the Exodus, with Paul drawing from its imagery. He described the believing community as the son of God who is led by the Spirit. This leading is reminiscent of the cloud and pillar of fire—symbols of the Spirit—that lead the children of Israel to the promised land. He picked up on the promise of the new creation, which was predicted by the prophets, saying that the church, along with creation, groan for this fulfillment. He said that this will be accomplished when the "birth pangs" have been completed. The final display of the sons of God (the ones redeemed by their firstborn brother [Rom 8:29]) will bring to completion the redemption of creation.

Throughout the chapter, Paul used pilgrimage language. This was especially true in the "who shall separate us" acclamation, for no forces that Satan can array will separate the covenant community from the love of God. Its members are assured of their eventual safe arrival in Zion.

In chapter 9, Paul highlighted the tension that implicitly existed in his letter thus far. The question had to be asked, "Where are the Jewish people in this New Exodus salvation?" Paul began by asserting that he valued the blessed heritage that he share with every other Jew, reiterating the key features of those blessings.

In order to explain the status of the Jewish people, Paul reviewed salvation history. He showed that God often bypassed lawful inheritance rights to favor people with no rights. Paul discussed these matters at a corporate level, for when individuals were referred to, it was in relation to the people they represented.

Paul's discussion on the hardening of Pharaoh's heart was explored in some detail, my conclusion being that the passage was not about election to salvation but Yahweh's right to elect to privilege and service. Paul's warning was that those who turn from this high calling will become vessels of wrath and come under God's judgment. His lesson was that the hardening (i.e., judgment) of Israel was not an exception—it reflected the pattern of God's dealings with the nations. Disobedient Israel had no divine right to avoid this consequence, even though she had been the one chosen above all other nations to be the instrument of their blessing.

In chapter 10, Paul sought to show his kinsfolk that the gospel is not a departure from the law but what the law pointed to and was intended to serve.

Drawing on a familiar passage in Deut 30:11–14, he showed Moses was anxious that the people understood the law to be the benchmark for revelation. It was by this code that all claims to represent God were to be judged. He also showed that Christ is the end of the law for all who believe. I challenged the widespread reliance on intertestamental literature to unlock Paul's teaching and hopefully demonstrated that his discussion is not about the incarnation of Christ but about his ascension and his sending of the Spirit to dwell among his people. Paul saturated his passage with New Exodus imagery and OT quotes (as he did with chapters 9 and 11), framing his argument with them.

In the eleventh chapter, Paul discussed the status of his people, the nation of Israel. He reviewed salvation history and recalled the times when it seemed that Yahweh had abandoned his people. He was able to show through the experience of Elijah that Yahweh had always been faithful to the remnant, even when apostate.

However, what was different in the period of apostasy when Paul lived was the fulfillment of the promise that the Gentiles would be brought into the blessings of Israel. Paul explained the Jewish root still remained, but the Gentiles have been grafted into this root (which is the covenant Yahweh made with Abraham). As a result, this hardening was like no other hardening in redemptive history. It changed the "game plan" once and for all. Israel can no longer claim her unique status.

Despite this major shift away from exclusivity, Paul insisted that Yahweh did not cast Israel off. He prophesied that Israel will be saved (i.e., people who have the faith of Abraham), sharing with the Gentiles in the covenant blessings promised to their father, Abraham.

At this point in his letter (chapter 12), Paul turned to apply his teaching to the life of the believing community in Rome. He reminded the Christians that, together, they were called to a priestly ministry, to be holy and pleasing to God and transformed in its thinking so that his will could be discerned. Because of their interdependence, they were to recognize that their gifting was not haphazard but the result of God's will and, as such, their gifts were to be exercised for the sake of the entire community.

Paul exhorted the community to be characterized by sincere and devoted love, a hatred of evil, and humility. The church was to be zealous in service, joyful in hope, patient in affliction, prayerful, and generous. Her members were to live in harmony, and to resist snobbishness. The church also had to resist taking revenge against those who had wronged her, confident that God would eventually settle all accounts.

In chapter 13, Paul discussed the role of authorities and the respect and support the believers were to give them because they served the purposes of God. The believers were to display the character of God by loving their fellowmen and by keeping the commandments–indeed, by going beyond them in living their spirit. He instructed the church to recognize the urgency of the times they lived in and to be fully committed to the Lord.

Paul urged the church to care for the weak (chapter 14)—the "weak" being those believers who were did not have strong faith. She was to do this without passing judgment upon them in any way. Although they confused peripheral matters of faith with ones that were more essential, Paul appealed to the church to love and respect rather than reject such people.. Paul's case was clear, these were men and women for whom Christ had died; they had value and worth, and any type of judgment of them would be wrong. The "strong" were exhorted to go out of their way not to cause these believers to stumble. Issues related to eating and drinking were not at the heart of the message of the kingdom of God, and, therefore, were not at the forefront of the church's concerns but weak brothers and sisters were!

In chapter 15, we find that Paul continued his discussion on the relationship between strong and weak believers, for accepting one another was essential if the Roman church was to be healthy. The importance of this matter was demonstrated by Christ, who became a servant of the Jews on behalf of God's truth. His servanthood confirmed the promises made to the patriarchs, resulting in the Gentiles glorifying God for his mercy. Paul supported his argument with an array of OT texts which show that the Gentiles are to be accepted. The acceptance of one another is the evidence of the work of God and this openness brings them joy and peace along with the overflow of hope given by the Holy Spirit.

Finally, in the closing section of his letter, Paul sought to give his understanding of his own ministry—a service in which he gloried. He was "a minister of Christ Jesus to the Gentiles, with the priestly duty of proclaiming the gospel of God." His goal was that the Gentiles would live holy lives, offering themselves to God as an acceptable sacrifice. In recalling the signs and miracles, through the power of the Spirit, that accompanied his preaching, Paul described his ministry as fulfilling the long-anticipated New Exodus, and cited a New Exodus text from Isaiah (Isa 52:15).

Conclusion to the Letter

Paul saw his ministry in the east to be complete; after visiting Jerusalem with the collection for the poor, he planned to travel to Rome in preparation for his ministry in Spain. He was aware of the dangers that faced him in returning to Jerusalem and Judea, and elicited the prayers of the Roman believers for his acceptance and protection while he was there.

In closing his letter, which he had dictated to Tertius and, likely, entrusted to Phoebe as its carrier, Paul wrote a series of greetings to people he knew (chapter 16). These greetings were often accompanied by warm commendations. He concluded with a warning to the church—to beware of those who would cause divisions—and a summary of all that he had sought to impart to the believers in Rome:

> Now to him who is able to establish you by my gospel and the proclamation of Jesus Christ, according to the revelation of the mystery hidden for long ages past, but now revealed and made known through the prophetic writings by the command of the eternal God, so that all nations might believe and obey him— to the only wise God be glory forever through Jesus Christ! Amen.

And so we come to an end of commenting on the letter to the Romans. While it is a letter to a particular church, written two thousand years ago, the church of today needs its message no less. May we be helped to live it out in the twenty first century, for God's honor and his glory

BIBLIOGRAPHY

Agersnap, S. *Baptism and the New Life. A Study of Romans 6.1-14*. Oakville, CT: Aarhus University Press, 1999.

Albright, W. F., and C. S. Mann. *Matthew*. Garden City, NY: Doubleday, 1971.

Aletti, J. N. "L'argumentation Paulinienne en Rm. 9." *Bib* 68 (1987) 41-56.

———. "Rm. 7:7-25 encore une fois: enjeux et propositions." *NTS* 48:3 (2002) 358-76.

Allison, D. C., Jr. "Jesus and the Covenant." *JSNT* 29 (1987) 57-78.

Anderson, B. W. *The Eighth Century Prophets: Amos, Hosea, Isaiah, Micah, Proclamation Commentaries*. Philadelphia: Fortress Press, 1978

Anderson, C. "Romans 1:1-4 and the Occasion of the Letter: The Solution to the Two Congregation Problem in Rome." *TJ* 14 (1993) 2-40.

Ashton, J. *The Religion of Paul the Apostle*. New Haven; London: Yale University Press, 2000.

Aune, D. "Human Nature and Ethics in Hellenistic Philosophical Traditions and Paul: Some Issues and Problems." In *Paul in His Hellenistic Context*, edited by T. E. Pedersen, 291-312. Minneapolis: Fortress, 1995.

Badke, W. B. "Baptised into Moses—Baptised into Christ: A Study in Doctrinal Development." *EvQ* 60 (1988) 23-29.

Bailey, K. E. "St Paul's Understanding of the Territorial Promise of God to Abraham. Romans 4:13 in its Historical and Theological Context." *NESTTheolRev* 15 (1994) 59-69.

Balsdon, J. P. V. D. *Roman Women: their History and Habits*. London: Bodley Head, 1963.

Barclay, J. M. G. "Paul and Philo on Circumcision: Romans 2:25-29 in Social and Cultural Context." *NTS* 44:4 (1998) 536-56.

Barr, G. K. "Romans 16 and the Tentmakers." *IBS* 20:3 (1998) 98-113.

Barrett, C. K. *A Commentary on the Epistle to the Romans*. London: A. & C. Black, 1957.

———. *From First Adam to Last: a study in Pauline theology*. London: A. & C. Black, 1962.

Barth, Markus. *Colossians : A New Translation with Introduction and Commentary*, The Anchor Bible Series, 34B. New York, N.Y.: Doubleday, 1994.

Bauckham, R. *The Climax of Prophecy*, Edinburgh: T. & T. Clark, 2000.

Baxter, A. G., and J. A. Ziesler. "Paul and Arboriculture: Romans 11:17–24." *JSNT* 24 (1985) 25-32.

Beale, G. K. *The Book of Revelation: A Commentary on the Greek Text: The New International Greek Testament Commentary.* Grand Rapids: Eerdmans, 1999.

———. "Did Jesus and His Followers Preach the Right Doctrine from the Wrong Texts?: An Examination of the Presuppositions of Jesus' and the Apostles' Exegetical Method." *Them* 14:3 (1989) 89-96.

Bechtler, S. R. "Christ, the *Telos* of the Law: The Goal of Romans 10:4." *CBQ* 56:2 (1994) 288-308.

Beet, J. A. *Commentary on St. Paul's Epistles to the Corinthians.* New York: Macmillan, *1882*.

Bekken, P. J. "The Word is Near You: A Study of Deuteronomy 30:12–14." In *Paul's Letter to the Romans in a Jewish Context.* Beihefte Zur Zeitschrift Für Die Neutestamentliche. Berlin: New York: Walter de Gruyter, 2007.

Bell, R. H. "Rom. 5:18-19 and Universal Salvation." *NTS* 48:3 (2002) 417-32.

Belli, F. "Un'allusione a Is. 50:8-9 in Rm. 8:31-39." *RBB* 50:2 (2002) 153-84.

Ballentine, G. L. "Death of Jesus as a New Exodus." *RevExp* 30 (1962) 27-41.

Berkley, T. W. *From a Broken Covenant to Circumcision of the Heart. Pauline Intertextual Exegesis in Romans 2:17-29.* SBL Dissertation Series 175. Atlanta: Society of Biblical Literature, 2000.

Best, E. *A Commentary on the First and Second Epistles to the Thessalonians.* London: Black. 1977.

———. *A Critical and Exegetical Commentary on Ephesians, The International Critical Commentary.* Edinburgh: T. & T. Clark, 1998.

———. *The Letter of Paul to the Romans.* The Cambridge Bible Commentary: New English Bible. Cambridge: Cambridge University Press, 1967.

———. *One Body in Christ: A Study in the Relationship of the Church to Christ in the Epistles of the Apostle Paul.* London: SPCK, 1955.

Betz, H. D. *Galatians: A Commentary on Paul's Letter to the Churches in Galatia.* Philadelphia: Fortress, 1979.

———. "Transferring a Ritual: Paul's Interpretation of Baptism in Romans 6." In *Paul in His Hellenistic Context*, edited by Troels Engberg-Pedersen, 84-118. Minneapolis: Fortress, 1995.

Bird, M. F. *The Saving Righteousness of God: Studies on Paul, Justification and the New Perspective.* Paternoster Biblical Monographs. Eugene, OR: Wipf & Stock, 2007.

Bird, M. F., and M. P. Preston. *The Faith of Jesus Christ: Exegetical, Biblical, and Theological Studies.* Peabody: Hendrickson, 2009.

Black, M. "The Pauline Doctrine of the Second Adam." *SJT* 7 (1954) 170-79.

———. *Romans, New Century Bible.* London: Oliphants, 1973.

———. "The 'Son of Man' in the Old Biblical Literature." *ExpTim* 60 (1948-1949) 11-15.

Blauw, J. "Paul as a Pioneer of Inter-Religious Thinking." *Studies in SID* [Kampen] 7 (1997) 66-75.

Bligh, J. "Baptismal Transformation of the Gentile World." *HeyJ* 37:3 (1996) 371-81.

Blocher, Henri. *Original Sin : Illuminating the Riddle,* New Studies in Biblical Theology, 5. Leicester: Inter-Varsity Press, 1997.

Bockmuehl, M. "1QS and Salvation in Qumran." In *Justification and Variegated Nomism,* vol. 2. Wissenschaftliche Untersuchungen Zum Neuen Testament, edited by D. A. Carson, P. T. O'Brien, and M. A. Seifrid, 343-59. Grand Rapids: Baker Academic, 2001.

Boers, H. "Jesus and the Christian Faith: New Testament Christology since Bousset's Kyrios Christos." *JBL* 89 (1970) 450-56.

———. "The Structure and Meaning of Romans 6:1-14." *CBQ* 63:4 (2001) 664-82.

Bornkamm, G. *Paul.* Trans. by D. M. G. Stalker. London: Hodder & Stoughton, 1971.

———. "The Revelation of Christ to Paul on the Damascus Road and Paul's Doctrine of Justification and Reconciliation: A Study in Galatians 1." In *Reconciliation and Hope: New Testament Essays on Atonement and Eschatology Presented to L. L. Morris on His 60th Birthday,* edited by R. Banks, 90-103. Exeter: Paternoster, 1974.

Bowker, J. "The Son of Man." *JTS* 28 (1977) 19-48.

Braaten, C. E. "Romans 12:14-21." *Int* 38:3 (1984) 291-96.

Brewer, D. I. "The Use of Rabbinic Sources in Gospel Studies." *TynBul* 50 (1999) 281-98.

Broyles, C. C. *Psalms.* Peabody: Hendrickson, 1999.

Bruce, F. F. *The Epistle of Paul to the Romans: An Introduction and Commentary.* London: Tyndale, 1963.

Büchsel, F. "θυμός." In *TDNT* 3:168.

———. "λύω." In *TDNT* 4:335-56.

Budd, P. *Numbers*, Word Biblical Commentary, 5 (-Waco: Word Books Ltd, 1984).
Bultmann, R. *Neueste Paulusforschung. Tru* (1936) Tübingen.
———. *Theology of the New Testament.* London: SCM, 1952.
———."Ursprung und Sinn der Typologie als hermeneutischer Methode." *TLZ* 75 (1950) 205-12.
Burke, T. J. *Adopted into God's family: Exploring a Pauline Metaphor.* Downers Grove, IL: InterVarsity, 2006.
Byrne, B. "Rather Boldly (Rom 15:15): Paul's Prophetic Bid to Win the Allegiance of the Christians in Rome." *Biblica* 74 (1993) 83-96.
———. *Sons of God—Seed of Abraham: A Study of the idea of the Sonship of God of all Christians in Paul against the Jewish Background.* Ana Bib 83. Rome: Biblical Institute, 1979.
Caird, G. F. B. "The Descent of Christ in Ephesians 4:7-11." *SE* 2. Berlin: Akademia (1964) 535-45.
———. *New Testament Theology.* Oxford: Oxford University Press, 1994.
Calvin, J. *Romans.* Edinburgh: The Calvin Society, 1850.
Campbell, D. A. "The Atonement in Paul." *Anvil* 11:3 (1994) 237-50.
———. *The Deliverance of God: An Apocalyptic Rereading of Justification in Paul.* Grand Rapids: Eerdmans, 2009.
———. "Romans 1:17—A Crux Interpretation for the ΠΙΣΤΙΣ ΧΡΙΤΟΥ Debate." *JBL* 113:2 (1994) 265-85.
Campbell, W. S. "The Freedom and Faithfulness of God in Relation to Israel." *JSNT* 13 (1981) 27-45.
———. *Paul and the Creation of Christian Identity* (Library of New Testament Studies). Edinburgh: T. & T. Clark, 2006.
———. "The Rule of Faith in Romans 12:1-15:13." In *Pauline Theology Vol. 3 Romans*, 259-86. Minneapolis: Fortress, 1995.
Carbone, S. "Israele nella Lettera ai Romanai." *RivistBib* 41:2 (1993) 139-70.
Carson, D. A. "Christological Ambiguities in the Gospel of Matthew." In *Christ the Lord: Studies in Christology presented to Donald Guthrie*, edited by H. H. Rowdon, 97-114. Leicester: InterVarsity, 1982.
———. *The Gospel According to John.* Downers Grove, IL: InterVarsity, 1991.
Casey, M. *From Jewish Prophet to Gentile God: The Origins and Development of New Testament Christology.* Cambridge: Clarke, 1991.
Casey, R. P. "The Earliest Christologies." *JTS* 9 (1958) 253-77.

Cervin, R. S. "A Note Regarding the Name 'Junia(s)' in Romans 16:7." *NTS* 40:3 (1994) 464-70.
Chadwick, H. "All Things to All Men (1 Cor. IX:22)." *NTS* 1 (1955) 261-75.
Charlesworth, J. H. "A Caveat on Textual Transmission and the Meaning of Abba: A Study of the Lord's Prayer." In *The Lord's Prayer and Other Prayer Texts from the Greco-Roman Era*, edited by J. H. Charlesworth, M. Harding, and M. Kiley, 1-14. Valley Forge, PA: Trinity, 1994.
Chilton, B. "Romans 9-11 as Scriptural Interpretation and Dialogue with Judaism." *ExAud* 4 (1988) 27-37.
Chilton, B., and P. Davies. "The Aqedah: A Revised Tradition History." *CBQ* 40 (1978) 514-46.
Coleman, T. M. "Binding Obligations in Romans 13:7: A Semantic Field and Social Context." *TynBul* 48 (1997) 307-27.
Colpe, G. "Ὁ υἱός του ἀνθρώπου." In *TDNT* 8:400-477.
Court, J. M. "Paul and the Apocalyptic Pattern." In *Paul and Paulinism: Essays in Honour of C. K. Barrett*, edited by M. D. Hooker and S. G. Wilson, 57-66. London: SPCK, 1982.
Cousar, C. P. "Paul and the Death of Jesus." *Int* 52 (1998) 38-52.
Coxon. P. "The Paschal New Exodus in John: An Interpretive Key with Particular Reference to John 5-10." Unpublished PhD thesis submitted to the University of Wales, St. David's College, 2010.
Cranfield, C. E. B. *The Epistle to the Romans*, vols. 1 & 2. ICC Series. Edinburgh: T. & T. Clark, 1975, 1979.

———. "Has the Old Testament Law a Place in the Christian Life? A Response to Professor Westerholm." *IBS* 15:2 (1993) 50-64.

———. *Romans: A Shorter Commentary*. Grand Rapids: Eerdmans, 1985.

———. "Some Observations on Romans 8:19-21." In *Reconciliation and Hope*, edited by R. Banks, 224-30. Exeter: Paternoster, 1974.

Cullmann, O. *Baptism in the New Testament*. Translated by J. K. S. Reid. London: SCM, 1950.

———. *The Christology of the New Testament*. Translated by S. C. Guthrie and A. N. Hall. London: SCM, 1959.

———. The State in the New Testament. London: SCM, 1957.

Dahl, N. *The Crucified Messiah, and Other Essays*. Minneapolis: Augsburg Publishing House, 1974.

Davidson, Richard M., "Typological Structures in the Old and New Testaments," *Andrews University Seminary Studies 20.1* (Spring 1982)

Davies, R. E. "Christ in Our Place: The Contribution of the Prepositions." *TynBul* 21 (1970) 71-91.

Davies, R. P. "Passover and the Dating of the Aqedah." *JJS* 30 (1979) 59-67.

Davies, W. D. *Jewish and Pauline Studies*. Philadelphia: Fortress, 1955.

———. "Paul and the People of Israel." *NTS* 24 (1977) 4-39.

———. *Paul and Rabbinic Judaism*. 2nd ed. London: SPCK, 1955.

Davila, J. R. "The Old Testament as Background to the New Testament." *ExpTimes* 117:2 (2005) 53-57.

———. *The Provenance of the Pseudepigrapha: Jewish, Christian, or Other?* Supplements to the Journal for the Study of Judaism. Leiden: Brill, 2005.

De Jonge, M. "The Earliest Christian Use of Christos: Some Suggestions." *NTS* 32:3 (1986) 321-43.

De Lacey, D. R. "Image and Incarnation in Pauline Christology: A Search for Origins." *TynBul* 30 (1979) 3-28.

DeMaris, R. E. "Funerals and Baptisms, Ordinary and Otherwise: Ritual Criticism and Corinthian Rites." *BibToday* 29 (1999) 23-34.

Denova, R. I. "Paul's Letter to the Romans 13:1-7: The Gentile-Christian Response to Civil Authority." *Enc* 53:3 (1992) 201-29.

Derrett, J. D. M. *Law in the New Testament*. London: Darton, Longman & Todd, 1970.

———. "You Abominate False Gods; But Do You Rob Shrines? (Rom. 2:22b)." *NTS* 40:4 (1994) 558-71.

Dillon, J. R. "The Priesthood of St Paul, Romans 15:15-16." *Worship* 74:2 (2000) 156-68.

Dodd, C. H. *According to the Scriptures: The Substructure of New Testament Theology*. London: Nisbet, 1952.

———. *Essays in New Testament Studies*. Manchester: Manchester University Press, 1953.

———. *The Interpretation of the Fourth Gospel*. Cambridge: Cambridge University Press, 1953.

Donaldson, T. L. "The Curse of the Law and the Inclusion of the Gentiles: Galatians 3:13-14." *NTS* 32 (1986) 94-112.

———. Paul and the Gentiles: Remapping the Apostle's Convictional World. Minneapolis: Fortress, 1997.

———. "Riches for the Gentiles (Rom. 11:12): Israel's Rejection and Paul's Gentile Mission." *JBL* 112 (1993) 81-98.

Donfried, K. P. "A Short Note on Romans 16." In *The Romans Debate*, edited by K. P. Donfried, 44-52. Edinburgh: T. & T. Clark, 1991.

Donne, B. K. *Christ Ascended.* Exeter: Paternoster, 1983.

Downing, J. "Jesus and Martyrdom." *JTS* 14 (1963) 279-93.

Dozeman, T. *God at War : Power in the Exodus Tradition.* New York, N.Y.: OUP, 1996.

Driver, J. *Understanding the Atonement for the Mission of the Church.* Scottdale, PA: Herald, 1986.

Dunn, J. D. G. "1 Corinthians 15.45. Last Adam, Life Giving Spirit." In *Christ and Spirit in the NT, Studies in honour of C. F. D. Moule*, edited by Lindars. B. and Smalley SS, 127-46. Cambridge: Cambridge University Press, 1973.

———. *Baptism in the Holy Spirit.* London: SCM, 1970.

———. *Christology in the Making. An Inquiry into the Origins of the Doctrine of the Incarnation.* 2nd ed. London: SCM, 1989.

———. *The Epistle to the Galatians*, Black's New Testament Commentary Series. Peabody: Hendrickson,1993.

———. *Jesus and the Spirit: A Study of the Religious and Charismatic Experience of Jesus and the First Christians as Reflected in the New Testament.* London: SCM,1975.

———, editor. Jews and Christians: The Parting of the Ways, AD70 to 135; the Second Durham Tübingen Research Symposium on Earliest Christianity and Judaism (September 1989), Wissenschaftliche Untersuchungen Zum Neuen Testament: Vol. 66, Tübingen: Mohr,1992.

———. *The New Perspective on Paul: Collected Essays.* Wissenschaftliche Untersuchungen Zum Neuen Testament. Tübingen: Mohr Siebeck, 2005.

———. "Paul's Understanding of the Death of Jesus." In *Reconciliation and Hope*, essays presented to L. L. Morris on his 60th birthday, edited by R. Banks, 125-41. Exeter: Paternoster Press, 1974.

———. *Romans 916.* Waco: Word, 1988.

———. *The Theology of Paul the Apostle.* Edinburgh: T. & T. Clark, 1998.

———. *Unity and Diversity in the New Testament: An Inquiry into the Character of Earliest Christianity.* 2nd ed. London: SCM, 1990.

———. "Who Did Paul Think He Was? A Study of Jewish-Christian Identity." *NTS* 45:2 (1999) 174-93.

Durham, J. I. *Exodus*. Waco: Word Books, 1987.

Du Toit, A. B. "Die Kirche als doxologische Gemeinschaft im Römerbrief." *Neot* 27 (1993) 69-77.

Earnshaw, J. D. "Reconsidering Paul's Marriage Analogy in Romans 7:1-4," *NTS* 40 (1994) 68-88.

Edwards, J. R. *Romans*. Peabody: Hendrickson, 1992.

Elliott, J. K. "The Language and Style of the Concluding Doxology to the Epistle to the Romans." *ZNW* 72 (1981) 124-30.

Ellis, E. E. "11 Cor V.1-10 in Pauline Eschatology." *JNTS* 111 (1959) 211-24.

———. "A note on 1 Cor. 10:4." *JBL* 76 (1957) 53-56.

———. *Paul and His Recent Interpreters*, Grand Rapids: Eerdmans, 1967.

———. *Paul's Use of the Old Testament*, Edinburgh: Oliver & Boyd, 1957.

———. *Prophecy and Hermeneutic in Early Christianity*. Grand Rapids: Eerdmans, 1978.

———. "Traditions in 1 Corinthians." *NTS* 32:4 (1986) 481-502.

Emerton, J. A. "The Origin of the Son of Man Imagery." *JTS* 9 (1958) 225-42.

Engberg-Pedersen, T. *Paul and the Stoics*. Louisville, KY: Westminster John Knox, 2000.

Eskola, T. "Paul, Predestination and 'Covenantal Nomism'—Re-assessing Paul and Palestinian Judaism." *JSJ* 28 (1997) 390-412.

Esler, P. "Ancient Oleiculture and Ethnic Differentiation: the Meaning of the Olive-Tree Image in Romans 11." *JSNT* 26 (2003) 103-24.

Espy, J. M. "Paul's 'Robust Conscience' Re-Examined." *NTS* 31 (1985) 161-88.

Fee, G. D. "Christology and Pneumatology in Romans 8:9-11." In *Jesus of Nazareth, Lord and Christ: Essays on the Historical Jesus and New Testament Christology,* edited by J. B. Green and M. Turner, 312-31. Grand Rapids: Eerdmans, 1994.

———. *God's Empowering Presence: The Holy Spirit in the Letters of Paul.* Peabody: Hendrickson, 1994.

Finger, R. H. "Was Julia a Racist? Cultural Diversity in the Book of Romans." *DS* Chicago 19:3 (1993) 36-39.

Fitzmyer, J. A. "The Consecutive Meaning of ΕΦ' Ω in Romans 5:12." *NTS* Vol. 39:3 (1993) 321-39.

―――. *Romans: A New Translation with Introduction and Commentary.* Anchor Bible. New York: Chapman, 1993.

Foerster, W. "εἰρήνη," *TDNT* 2:400-420.

Ford, D. "What about the Trinity?" In *Meaning and Truth in 2 Corinthians,* edited by F. Young and D. Ford, 255-60. Grand Rapids: Eerdmans, 1987.

Ford, J. M. "The Son of Man Euphemism?" *JBL* 87 (1969) 189-96.

Friesen, G., and J. R. Maxson. *Decision Making and the Will of God: A Biblical Alternative to the Traditional View.* Portland, OR: Multnomah, 1980.

Fretheim, T. E. *Exodus*, Louisville: Westminster John Knox, 1991.

Fuller, R. H. *The Foundations of New Testament Christology.* London: Lutterworth, 1965.

Furnish, V. P. *The Moral Teaching of Paul*, Nashville: Abingdon, 1979.

Gager, J. G. "Functional Diversity in Paul's Use of End Time Language." *JBL* 84 (1970) 325-37.

Gagnon, R. A. J. "The Meaning of ὑμῶν τὸ ἀγαθόν in Romans 14:16." *JBL* 117:4 (1998) 675-89.

―――. "Why the 'Weak' at Rome Cannot be Non-Christian Jews." *CBQ* 62 (2000) 64-82.

Garlington, D. B. "The Obedience of Faith in the Letter to the Romans. Part III: The Obedience of Christ and the Obedience of the Christian." *WTJ* 55 (1993) 87-112.

―――. "Review Essay of "Tom Wright and the Search for Truth: A Theological Evaluation by Tom Holland", *The Paul Page* (August 20, 2018), http://www.thepaulpage.com/review-essay-of-tom-wright-and-the-search-for-truth-a-theological-evaluation-by-tom-holland/.

―――. "Romans 7:14-25 and the Creation Theology of Paul." *TJ* 11:2 (1990) 197-235.

Garnet, P. *Salvation and Atonement in the Qumran Scrolls*, Wissenschaftliche Untersuchungen Zum Neuen Testament. 2. Reihe (Wunt II), 3. Tübingen: Mohr, 1977.

Gaston, L. "Israel's Enemies in Pauline Theology." *NTS* 28:3 (1982) 400-423.

Gathercole, S. J. "A Law unto Themselves: The Gentiles in Romans 2:14-15 Revisited." *JSNT* 23:3 (2002) 27-49.

―――. *Where is Boasting? Early Jewish Soteriology and Paul's Response in Romans 1 – 5.* Grand Rapids: Eerdmans, 2002.

Getty, M. A. "Paul and the Salvation of Israel: A Perspective on Romans 9-11." *CBQ* 50:3 (1988) 456-69.

Giblin, C. H. "Three Monotheistic Texts in Paul." *CBQ* (1975) 527-47.

Ginzberg, L. *The Legends of the Jews*, Philadelphia: Jewish Publication Society of America,1925.

Given, M. D. "Restoring the Inheritance in Romans 11:1." *JBL* 118 (1999) 89-96.

Glancy, J. "Israel vs. Israel in Romans 11:25-32" *USQR* 45:3/4 (1991) 191-203.

Goldingay, J. *Psalms vol 2:42-89*. Grand Rapids: Baker Academic, 2007.

Goppelt, L. *Typos. The Typological Interpretation of The Old Testament in the New*. Translated by D. H. Madvig. Grand Rapids: Eerdmans, 1982.

Goulder, M. *The Psalms of the Return (Book 5, Psalms 107-150)*, Journal for the Study of the Old Testament. Supplement Series; Studies in the Psalter, 258; 4. Sheffield: Sheffield Academic Press, 1998.

Gray, G. *A Critical and Exegetical Commentary on Numbers*. Edinburgh: T. & T. Clark, 1903.

Grech, P. "The Old Testament as a Christological Source in the Apostolic Age." *BibToday* 2 (1975) 127-45.

Greek-English Lexicon of the New Testament and Other Early Christian Literature (BDAG). 3rd ed. Chicago: University of Chicago Press, 2001.

Green, G. L. *The Letters to the Thessalonians*. Grand Rapids: Eerdmans. 2002.

Gulley, N. R. "Ascension of Christ." In *ABD* 1:472-74.

Gundry, R. H. *Sōma in Biblical Theology: With Emphasis on Pauline Anthropology*, (Monograph Series). Cambridge: Cambridge University Press, 1976.

Hahn, F. *The Titles of Jesus in Christology, their History in Early Christianity*. New York: World Publishing,1969.

Hall, D. R. "Romans 3:1-8 Reconsidered." *NTS* 29 (1983) 183-97.

Hamerton-Kelly, R. G. "Sacred Violence and the Curse of the Law (Galatians 3.13). The Death of Christ as a Sacrificial Travesty." *NTS* 36 (1990) 98-116.

Hanson, A. T. *New Testament Interpretation of Scripture*. London: SPCK, 1980.

Harman, A. *Psalms*. Fearn: Christian Focus, 1998.

Harmo, M. S., *She Must and Shall Go Free: Paul's Isaianic Gospel in Galatians. BZNW*. New York: de Gruyter, 2010.

Bibliography

Harnack, Adolf, *Die Mission und Ausbreitung Des Christentums In Den Ersten Drei Jahrhunderten,* [1st ed.]. (Leipzig: J. C. Hinrichs, 1902). cited by Joseph Jacobs Jewish Encyclopedia 1902.

Harris, W. H, III. *The Descent of Christ: Ephesians 4:7-11 and Traditional Hebrew Imagery,* Arbeiten Zur Geschichte Des Antiken Judentums Und. Leiden: E. J. Brill, 1996.

Harris, M. J. *Jesus as God: the New Testament use of Theos in Reference to Jesus.* Grand Rapids: Baker, 1992.

Hays, R. B. "Adam, Israel, Christ." In *Pauline Theology, Vol. III, Romans,* Edited by Hay, D. M. and Johnson, E. E. Minneapolis, MN: Fortress, 1995.

———. *The Conversion of the Imagination: Paul as Interpreter of Israel's Scripture.* Grand Rapids: Eerdmans, 2005.

———. *Echoes of Scripture in the Letters of Paul.* New Haven, CT: Yale University Press. 1989.

———. "Have we found Abraham to be our Father According to the Flesh? A Reconsideration of Rom 4:1." *Nov T* (1985) 76-98.

———. "ΠΙΣΙΣ and Pauline Christology: What is at Stake?" in SBL Seminar Papers, edited by E. H. Lovering Jr., 714-29. Atlanta: Scholars Press, (1991).

———. "'Who Has Believed Our Message': Paul's Reading of Isaiah" In *New Testament Writers and the Old Testament: An Introduction,* edited by J. M. Court. London: SPCK, 2002.

Hellholm, D. "Die argumentative Funktion von Römer 7:1-6." *NTS* 43:3 (1997) 385-411.

Hendriksen, W. *Exposition of Paul's Epistle to the Romans: Vol.1: Chapters 1-8,* Grand Rapids: Baker, 1981.

Hengel, M. *The Atonement: The Origins of the Doctrine in the New Testament.* Philadelphia: Fortress, 1981.

———. *The Son of God, The Origin of Christology and the History of Jewish-Hellenistic Religion.* Translated by J. Bowden. London: SCM, 1976.

———. *The Zealots: Investigations into The Jewish Freedom Movement In The Period From Herod I Until 70 A.D,* tr. by David Smith, Edinburgh: T. & T. Clark, 1989.

Hester, J. D. *Paul's Concept of Inheritance: A Contribution to the Understanding of Heilsgeschichte*. Scottish Journal of Theology, occasional papers: 14. London: Oliver & Boyd, 1968.

Hill, D. *Greek Words and Hebrew Meanings. Studies in the Semantics of Soteriological Terms*. London: Cambridge University Press, 1967.

Hills, J. V. "Christ was the Goal of the Law: Romans 10:4." *JTS* 44:2 (1993) 585-92.

Hoehner, H. W. *Ephesians: An Exegetical Commentary*. Grand Rapids: Baker Academic, 2002.

Hodge, C. *A Commentary on Romans*. Grand Rapids: Eerdmans, 1886.

Holland, T. "A Case of Mistaken Identity: The Harlot and the Church (1 Corinthians 5-6)." *ATI* 1 (2008) 56-68. Online: http://atijournal.org/ATI_Vol1_No1.pdf.

———. *Contours of Pauline Theology*. Fearn, Scotland: Christian Focus, 2004.

Hooker, M. D. "Adam in Romans 1." *NTS* 6:3 (1960) 297-306.

———. "Further Notes on Romans 1." *NTS* 13 (1967) 297-306.

———. "Interchange in Christ." *JTS* 22:2 (1971) 349-61.

———. *Paul: Apostle to the Gentiles,* St Paul's Lecture given at St Botolph's, Aldgate on November 16th, 1989.

———. "Paul and 'Covenantal Nomism.'" In *Paul and Paulinism: Essays in Honour of C. K. Barrett*, edited by M. D. Hooker and S. G. Wilson, 47-56. London: SPCK, 1982.

Horst, J. "μελη." *TDNT* 4:555-68.

Howard, J. K. "Into Christ: a Study of the Pauline Concept of Baptismal Union." *ExpTim* 79 (1968) 147-51.

———. "Passover and Eucharist in the Fourth Gospel." *SJT* 20 (1967) 329-37.

Jansen, F. J. "The Ascension, the Church and Theology." *TToday* 16 (1959) 17-29.

Jeremias, J. *New Testament Theology*. London: SCM, 1971.

———. *The Prayers of Jesus*. Philadelphia: Fortress, 1967.

Jewett, R. "Ecumenical Theology For the Sake of Mission." In *Pauline Theology*, vol. 3, edited by D. M Hay and E. E. Johnson, 80-108. Minneapolis: Fortress, 1995.

———. *Paul's Anthropological Terms: A Study of their Use in Conflict Settings*. Arbeiten Zur Geschichte Des Antiken Judentums Und. Leiden: Brill, 1971.

Bibliography

———. *Romans: A Commentary.* A Critical and Historical Commentary. Minneapolis: Fortress, 2006.

Jobs, K. H., 'Jerusalem, Our Mother: Metalepsis and Intertextuality in Galatians 4:21-31' *WTJ* 55 (1993).

Johnson, A. R. *Sacral Kingship in Ancient Israel.* Cardiff: University of Wales Press, 1967.

Johnson, D. G. "The Structure and Meaning of Romans 11." *CBQ* 46 (1984) 91-103.

Johnson, B. C. "Tongues: A Sign for Unbelievers?—a Structural and Exegetical Study of 1 Corinthians XIV 20-25." *NTS* 25 (1978/79) 180-203.

Johnson, L. T. *Reading Romans: A Literary and Theological Commentary.* New York: Crossroads, 1997.

Karlberg, M. W. "Israel's History Personified: Romans 7:7-13 in Relation to Paul's Teaching on the Old Man." *TrinJ* 7 (1986) 68-69.

Karris, R. J. "Romans 14:1-15.13 and the Occasion of Romans." In *The Romans Debate*, edited by K. P. Donfried, 65-84. Peabody: Hendriksen, 1991.

Käsemann, E. *Exegetische Versuche und Besinnungen I.* Gottingen: Vandenhoeck & Ruprecht, 1965.

———. *Romans.* Grand Rapids: Eerdmans, 1980.

Kay, B. N. *The Thought Structure of Romans with Special Reference to Chapter 6.* Austin, TX: Scholar Press, 1979.

Keck, L. E. "Christology, Soteriology, and the Praise of God (Romans 15:7-13)." In *The Conversation Continues: Studies in Paul and John in Honour of J. Louis Martyn*, edited by R. T. Fortna and B. R. Gaventa, 85-97. Nashville: Abingdon, 1990.

———. "Towards the Renewal of New Testament Christology." *NTS* 32 (1986) 362-77.

———. (1995) "What Makes Romans Tick?" In *Pauline Theology*, vol. 3, edited by D. M. Hay and E. E. Johnson, 3-29. Minneapolis: Fortress, 1995.

Kee, H. C. "Christology and Ecclesiology. Titles of Christ and Models of Community." *SBL* Seminar Papers, 227-42.

Keesmaat, S. C. "Exodus and the Intertextual Transformation of Traditions in Romans 8:14-30." *JSNT* 54 (1994) 29-56.

———. "*Paul and His Story: Exodus and Tradition in Galatians.*" Horizons in Biblical Theology 18.2 (*1996*) *133-68.*

Kennedy, A. A. *Saint Paul's Conception of the Last Things*. London: Hodder and Stoughton, 1904.

Kidner, D. *Genesis*. Leicester: InterVarsity, 1967.

———. "Sacrifice—Metaphors and Meaning." *TynB* (1982) 119-36.

Kim, S. "The Mystery of Rom. 11:25-26 Once More." *NTS* 43:3 (1997) 412-29.

Kirby, J. C. *Ephesians: Baptism and Pentecost—An Inquiry into the Structure and Purpose of the Epistle to the Ephesians*. London: SPCK, 1968.

Klijn, A. F. J. "The Study of Jewish Christianity." *NTS* 20 (1974) 119-31.

Kline, M. G. "The Old Testament Origins of the Gospel Genre." *WTJ* 1.38 (1975) 1-27.

Klein, W. W. *The New Chosen People: A Corporate View of Election*. Eugene: Wipf & Stock, 2001.

Kirkpatrick, A. F. *The Book of Psalms*. Cambridge: Cambridge University Press, 1910

Knox, J. *Life in Christ: Reflections on Romans 5-8*. Greenwich: Seabury, 1961.

Knox, W. L. *St. Paul and the Church of the Gentiles*. Cambridge: Cambridge University Press, 1939.

Kosmala, H. "The Bloody Husband." *VT* 12 (1962) 14-28.

Kramer, W. *Christ, Lord, Son of God*, London: SCM. 1966.

Kraus, Hans-Joachim. *Psalms 60-150*. Minneapolis: Fortress, 1993.

Kreuzer, S. "Der den Gotlosen rechtfertigt (Röm. 4:5). Die frü hjü dische Einordnung von Gen. 15 als Hintergrund für das Abrahambild und die Rechtfertgungslehre des Paulus." *TheolBeitr* 33:4 (2002) 208-19.

Krimmer, H. *Römer-Brief*. Stuttgart: Hänssler, 1983.

Kroger, D. "Paul and the Civil Authorities: An Exegesis of Romans 13:1-7." *AsiaJournTheol* 7:2 (1993) 344-66.

Kummel, W. G. *The Theology of the New Testament according to its Major Witnesses: Jesus—Paul—John.* London: SCM, 1974.

Kuss, Otto, *Der Römerbrief*. Regensburg: F. Pustet, 1963-1978.

Laato, T. "Paul's Anthropological Considerations: Two Problems." In *Justification and Variegated Nomism,* vol. 2. Wissenschaftliche Untersuchungen Zum Neuen Testament, edited by D. A. Carson, P. T. O'Brien, and M. A Seifrid, 343-59. Grand Rapids: Baker Academic, 2001.

Lagrange, M. J. *Saint Paul. Épître aux Romains*. Paris: Gabalda, 1950.

Lambrecht, J. "Paul's Christological Use of Scripture in 1 Cor. 15:20-28." *NTS* 28:4 (1982) 502-27.

Lamp, G. W. H. *The Seal of the Spirit. A Study in the Doctrine of Baptism and Confirmation in the New Testament and the Fathers*. London: Longmans, Green & Co., 1951.

Landy, F. *Hosea* (Sheffield: Sheffield Academic Press, 1995).

Lane, W. L. "Covenant, the Key to Paul's Conflict with Corinth." *TB* 33 (1982) 3-29.

Laurer, S. "Traces of a Gospel Writing in 1 Corinthians 1 to 7: Rediscovery and Development of Origen's Understanding of 1 Corinthians 4:6b." PhD diss., University of Wales, 2010.

Leaney, A. R. C. "1 Peter and the Passover: An Interpretation." *NTS* 10 (1963/64) 238-51.

Lee, Y. L. *Pilgrimage and the Knowledge of God*. Unpublished PhD diss., University of Wales, Lampeter, 2007.

Leenhardt, F. J. *L'epitre de Saint Paul aux Romains*. Geneva: Labor et Fides, 1981.

Lemico, E. "The Unifying Kerygma of the New Testament." *JSNT* 33 (1998) 3-17.

Levenson, J. D. *The Death and Resurrection of the Beloved Son. The Transformation of Child Sacrifice in Judaism and Christianity*. New Haven: Yale University Press, 1993.

Levey, Samson H., "Akiba in Search of the Messiah; a Closer Look", *Judaism* 41 no. 4, Fall 1992.

Lincoln, A. *Ephesians*. Dallas: Word, 1990.

———. "From Wrath to Justification" In *Pauline Theology*, vol. 3, edited by David M. Hay and E. Elizabeth Johnson, 130-59. Minneapolis: Fortress, 1995.

Longacre, R. E., and W. B. Wallis. "Soteriology and Eschatology in Romans." *JETS* 41:3 (1998) 367-82.

Longenecker, B. W. "Pistis in Romans 3:25—Neglected Evidence for the 'Faithfulness of Christ'?" *NTS* 39:3 (1993) 478-80.

Longenecker, R. N. *Galatians*. Waco: Word, 1990.

———. "Prolegomena to Paul's Use of Scripture in Romans." *BBR* 7 (1997) 145-68.

Lyall, F. "Roman Law in the Writings of Paul—Adoption." *JBL* 88 (1969) 458-66.

Maartens, P. J. "The Relevance of 'Context' and 'Interpretation' to the Semiotic Relations of Romans 5:1-11." *Neot* 29 (1995) 75-108.

———. "The Vindication of the Righteous in Romans 8:31-39: Inference and Relevance." *HvTSt* 51:4 (1995) 1046-87.

MacGregor, G. H. C. "Principalities and Powers: The Cosmic Background of Paul's Thought." *NTS* 1:2 (1954/55) 17-28.

Macintosh, A., *A Critical and Exegetical Commentary on Hosea*. Edinburgh: T&T Clark, 1997.

Mackay, J. L. *Exodus: A Mentor Commentary*. Fearn, UK: Christian Focus, 2001.

Maddox, R. "The Function of the Son of Man in the Gospel of John." In *Reconciliation and Hope, New Testament Essays on Atonement and Eschatology, Presented to L. L. Morris on His 60th Birthday*, edited by R. Banks, 186-204. Exeter: Paternoster, 1974.

Maile, J. F. "The Ascension in Luke-Acts." *TynB* 37 (1986) 29-59.

Maillot, A. L´épître aux Romains: épître de l´oecuménisme et théologie de l´histoire. Paris: Centurion, 1984.

Malherbe, A. J. *The Letters to the Thessalonians*. New York: Doubleday, 2000.

Malick, D. E. "The Condemnation of Homosexuality in Romans 1:26-27." *BibSac* 150:599 (1993) 327-40.

Mánek, J. "The New Exodus in the Book of Luke." *NovT* (1955) 8-23.

Manson, T. W. "Romans," *PCB*, 940-53.

———. "St. Paul's Letter to the Romans—and Others." In *The Romans Debate*, edited by K. Donfried, 1-16. Minneapolis: Augsburg, 1977.

———. *The Teaching of Jesus: Studies of Its Form and Content*. 2nd ed. Cambridge: Cambridge University Press, 1935.

Marsh, J. *The Fullness of Time*. London: No Publisher, 1952.

Marshall, I. H. "Living in the 'Flesh.'" *BibSac* 159:636 (2002) 387-403.

———. The Origins of New Testament Christology. Leicester: InterVarsity, 1976.

———. "Palestinian and Hellenistic Christianity: Some Critical Comments." *NTS* 19:2 (1973) 271-87.

Martin, J. P. "Kerygma of Romans." *Int* 25:2 (1971) 308-28.

Martin, R. P. Colossians: The Church's Lord and the Christian's Liberty. Exeter: Paternoster, 1972.

Mays, J. L. *Psalms: Interpretation: A Bible Commentary for Teaching and Preaching.* (Louisville, Ky.: Westminster John Knox, 1994).

McKay, C. "Ezekiel in the NT." *CQR* 162 (1961) 4-16.

McKelvey, R. T. The New Temple: The Church in the New Testament. London: Oxford, 1969.

McKnight, S. A. New Vision for Israel: The Teachings of Jesus in National Context. Grand Rapids: Eerdmans, 1999.

McWhirter, J. *The Bridegroom Messiah and the People of God: Marriage in the Fourth Gospel.* Society for New Testament Studies Monograph Series. Cambridge: Cambridge University Press, 2006.

Meggitt, J. J. "The Social Status of Erastus (Rom. 16:23)." *Nov Test* 38:3 (1996) 218-23.

Meissner, S. "Paulinischer Soteriologie und die 'Aqedat Jitzchaq." *Jud* 51 (1995) 33-49.

Metzger, B. M. "The Punctuation of Rom. 9:5." In *Christ and Spirit in the New Testament: In Honour of Charles Francis Digby Moule,* editors B. Lindars and S. Smalley, 95-112. Cambridge: Cambridge University Press, 1973.

———. *The Text of the New Testament.* 3rd ed. New York: Oxford University Press, 1992.

Meyer, B. F. "The Pre-Pauline Formula in Rom. 3:25-26a." *NTS* 29 (1983) 198-208.

Michael, O. *KEK.* Göttingen: Vandenhoeck & Ruprecht, 1957.

Millard, A. R. "Covenant and Communion in First Corinthians." In *Apostolic History and the Gospel: Essays Presented to F. F. Bruce on His Sixtieth Birthday,* edited by W. Gasque and R. P. Martin, 242-48. Exeter: Paternoster, 1970.

Miller, J. C. *The Obedience of Faith, the Eschatological People of God, and the Purpose of Romans.* SBL Dissertation Series, 177. Atlanta: SBL, 2000.

Molland, E. *Das Paulinische Euangelion: Das Wort und die Sache.* Oslo: Jacob Dybwad, 1934.

Monte, W. D. "The Place of Jesus' Death and Resurrection in Pauline Soteriology." *SBT* 16 (1988) 39-97.

Moo, D. J. *The Epistle to the Romans.* Grand Rapids: Eerdmans, 1996.

———. "'Law,' 'Works of the Law' and legalism in Paul." *WTJ* 45 (1983) 73-100.

Morris, L. L. *The Apostolic Preaching of the Cross*. London: Tyndale, 1955.

———. The Atonement: Its Meaning and Significance. Leicester: InterVarsity, 1963.

———. *The Epistle to the Romans*. Leicester: InterVarsity, 1988.

———. "The Meaning of *Hilasterion* in Romans 3:25." *NTS* 2 (1955) 33-43.

———. "The Passover in Rabbinic Literature." *AusBR* 4 (1954/55) 57-76.

Moule, H. C. G. The Epistle of Paul the Apostle to the Romans with Introduction and Notes. Cambridge: Cambridge University Press, 1903.

Moule, C. F. D. *An Idiom Book of New Testament Greek*. Cambridge: Cambridge University Press, 1979.

———. "The Influence of Circumstances on the use of Christological Terms." *JTS* 10 (1960) 247-64.

———. *The Origin of Christology*. Cambridge: Cambridge University Press, 1977.

———. *The Sacrifice of Christ*. London: Hodder & Stoughton, 1956.

Muddiman, J. *A Commentary on the Epistle to the Ephesians*. London: Continuum, 2001.

Muilenburg, J. "The Son of Man in Daniel and the Ethiopic Apocalypse of Enoch." *JBL* 79 (1960) 197-209.

Munck, J. *Christ and Israel: An Interpretation of Romans 9-11*. Philadelphia: Fortress, 1967.

———. "Jewish Christianity in Post-Apostolic Times." *NTS* 6:2 (1959) 103-16.

———. Paul and the Salvation of Mankind. London: SCM, 1959.

Murray, J. *The Collected Writings of John Murray, Vol 2: Lectures in Systematic Theology*. Edinburgh: Banner of Truth, 1977.

———. *The Epistle to the Romans*, vols. 1 & 2. London: Marshall, Morgan & Scott, 1967.

Nanos, M. D. "The Jewish Context of the Gentile Audience Addressed in Paul's Letter to the Romans." *CBQ* 61:2 (1999) 283-304.

———. The Mystery of Romans: the Jewish Context of Paul's Letter. Minneapolis: Fortress, 1996.

Nida, E. A., and J. P. Louw. *Lexical Semantics of the Greek New Testament: A Supplement to the Greek-English Lexicon of the New Testament Based on Semantic Domains*. Atlanta: Scholars, 1992.

Ninow, F. *Indicators of Typology within the Old Testament: The Exodus Motif.* Friedensauer Schriftenreihe, Reihe A Theolgie. Frankfurt-am-Main; New York: Peter Lang, 2001.

Nixon, R. E. *The Exodus in the New Testament.* London: Tyndale, 1963.

Noordtzij, A. *Numbers.* Grand Rapids: Zondervan Pub. House, 1983.

North, J. L. "'Good Words and Faire Speeches' (Rom. 16:18 AV): More Materials and a Pauline Pun." *NTS* 42:4 (1996) 600-614.

Nwachukwu, M. S. C. *Creation-Covenant Scheme and Justification by Faith: A Canonical Study of the God-Human Drama in the Pen uch and the Letter to the Romans.* Rome: Editrice Pontifica Universita Gregoriana, 2002.

Nygren, A. *Commentary on Romans.* London: SCM, 1958.

Olyott, S. The Gospel as It Really Is: Paul's Epistle to the Romans Simply Explained. Darlington: Evangelical, 1979.

O'Neill, J. C. *Paul's Letter to the Romans.* Harmondsworth: Penguin, 1975.

Oster, R. E. "Congregations of the Gentiles (Rom 16:4): A Culture-Based Ecclesiology in the Letters of Paul." *ResQuar* 40 (1998) 39-52.

Otto, K. *Der Römerbrief. Übersetzt und erklärt.* 3 vols. Regensburg, Pustet, 1963/ 1978.

Pamment, M. "The Kingdom of Heaven according to the First Gospel." *NTS* 27 (1981) 211-32.

Pao, D. W. *Acts and the Isaianic New Exodus.* Grand Rapids: Baker, 2002.

Pate, C. M. *Adam Christology as Exegetical and Theological Substructure of II Corinthians 4:7-5:21.* Lanham, MD: University Press of America, 1991.

Perrin, N. *A Modern Pilgrimage in New Testament Christology.* Philadelphia: Fortress, 1974.

Peterson, A. K. "Shedding new light on Paul's Understanding of Baptism: A Ritual-Theological Approach to Romans 6." *StudTheol* 52 (1998) 3-28.

Peterson, D. "Worship and Ethics in Romans 12." *TynBul* 44:2 (1993) 271-88.

Petersen, N. R. *Rediscovering Paul: Philemon and the Sociology of Paul's Narrative World.* Philadelphia: Fortress, 1985.

Pierce, C. A. *Conscience in the New Testament.* London: SCM, 1955.

Piper, J. *The Future of Justification: A Response to N. T. Wright.* Nottingham: InterVarsity, 2008.

Powers, D. G. *Salvation through Participation. An Examination of the Notion of the Believers' Corporate Unity with Christ in Early Christian Soteriology.* Leuven: Peeters, 2001.

Powys, D. *"Hell": A Hard Look at A Hard Question.* Carlisle: Paternoster, 1998.

Punt, J. P. "Hermeneutics and the Scriptures of Israel." *Neot* 30:2 (1996) 377-426.

Qualls, P., and J. D. Watts. "Isaiah in Ephesians." *RevExp* 93:2 (1996) 249-59.

Ra, K. U. "An Investigation of the Influence of the Paschal—New Exodus Motif on the Description of Christ and His Work in the Gospel of John (chapters One to Four)." Unpublished PhD thesis submitted to the University of Wales, St. David's College, 2009.

Räisänen, H. "Paul's Conversion and the Development of His View of the Law." *NTS* 33 (1987) 404-19.

Rancine, J. F. "Romains 13:1-7: Simple Preservation de l'ordre Social?" *EstBib* 51:2 (1993) 187-205.

Rapinchuk, M. "Universal Sin and Salvation in Romans 5:12-21." *JETS* 42:3 (1999) 427-41.

Reasoner, M. *The Strong and the Weak: Romans 14:1-15:13 in Context.* Cambridge: Cambridge University Press, 1999.

Reumann, J. "The Gospel of the Righteousness of God: Pauline Reinterpretation in Rom. 3:21-31." *Int* 20 (1966) 432-52.

Ribbens, B. J.. "Typology of Types: Typology in Dialogue", *Journal of Theological Interpretation* Vol. 5, No. 1 (Spring, 2011)

Richardson, A. *An Introduction to the Theology of the New Testament.* London: SCM, 1958.

Ridderbos, H. "The Earliest Confession of the Atonement in Paul (1 Cor. 15:3)." In *Reconciliation and Hope: Essays Presented to L. L. Morris on His Sixtieth Birthday*, edited by R. Banks, 76-89. Exeter: Paternoster, 1974.

———. *Paul: An Outline of His Theology.* Grand Rapids: Eerdmans, 1975.

———. "ὑπερ." In *TDNT* 8:507-16.

Robichaux, K. S. "Christ the Firstborn." *AffCr* 2 (1997) 30-38.

Robinson, D. W. B. "Towards a Definition of Baptism." *RTR* 34 (1975) 1-15.

Robinson, J. A. T. *Wrestling with Romans.* London: SCM, 1979.

Rogerson, J. W. "Corporate Personality." In *ADB* 1:1156-157.

———. "The Hebrew Conception of Corporate Personality: A Re-examination." *JTS* 21 (1970) 1-16.

Rosenberg, R. A. "Jesus, Isaac and the Suffering Servant." *JBL* 84:4 (1965) 381-88.

Rosner, R. S. *Paul, Scripture & Ethics: A Study of 1 Cor. 5-7.* Leiden: Brill, 1994.

Ross, A. *A Commentary on the Psalms : Volume 1 (1-41).* Grand Rapids: Kregel Academic & Professional, 2011.

Russell, W. "The Apostle Paul's Redemptive-Historical Argumentation in Galatians 5:13-26." *WTJ* 57:2 (1995) 333-57.

Ryan, J. M. "God's Fidelity to Israel and Mercy to All." *TBT* 35:2 (1997) 89-93.

Sahlin, H. "The New Exodus of Salvation according to St. Paul." In *The Root of the Vine: Essays in Biblical Theology*, edited by A. Fridrichsen, 81-95. Westminster: Dacre, 1953.

———. "Adam-Christologie im Neuen Testament." *ST* 41 (1987) 11-32.

Sampley, J. P. *Paul in the Greco-Romans World.* Harrisburg: Trinity, 2003.

Sanders, E. P. *Paul.* Oxford: Oxford University Press, 1991.

———. Paul and Palestinian Judaism. London: SCM, 1977.

Sandmel, S. "Parallelomania." *JBL* 81 (1962) 1-13

Sandnes, K. O. "'Justification by Faith'—An Outdated Doctrine? The 'New Perspective' on Paul—A Presentation and Appraisal." *Theology & Life* 17-19 (1996) 127-46.

Sandy, W. and A. Headlam. *A Critical and Exegetical Commentary of the Epistle to the Romans.* Edinburgh: T. & T. Clark, 1902.

Sass, G. "Röm 15:7-13—als Summe des Römerbriefs gelesen." *EvT* 53 (1993) 510-27.

Schaefer, J. R. "The Relationship between Priestly and Servant Messianism in the Epistle to the Hebrews." *CBQ* 30 (1968) 359-85.

Schillebeeckx, E. *Jesus: An Experiment in Christology.* Translated by H. Hoskins. New York: Seabury, 1979.

Schnackenburg, R. *Baptism in the Thought of St. Paul: A Study in Pauline Theology.* Translated by G. R. Beasley-Murray. Oxford: Basil Blackwell, 1964.

Schneider, B. "The Corporate Meaning and Background of 1 Cor. 15:45b—O Eschatos Adam eis Pneuma Zōiopoioun." *CBQ* 29 (1967) 450-67.

Schoeps, H. J. *Paul: The Theology of the Apostle Paul in the Light of Jewish Religious History.* London: Lutterworth, 1961.

———. "The Sacrifice of Jesus in Paul's Theology." *JBL* 65 (1946) 385-92.

Schrange, W. *Der erste Brief an die Korinthens 1.* Teilband, 1 Kor. 1:1-6:11. Benziger: Neukirchener, 1991.

———. *Der erste Brief an die Korinthens 2.* Teilband, 1 Kor. 6:12-11: 16. Benziger: Neukirchener, 1995.

Schreiner, T. R. *Circumcision: An Entrée into 'Newness' in Pauline Thought.* PhD diss., Fuller Theological Seminary, 1983.

———. "Did Paul Believe in Justification by Works?: Another Look at Romans 2." *BullBibRes* 3 (1993) 131-55.

———. "Does Romans 9 Teach Individual Election unto Salvation? Some Exegetical and Theological Reflections." *JETS* 36 (1993) 25-40.

———. "Paul's View of the Law in Romans 10:4-5." *WTJ* 55 (1993) 113-35.

———. *Romans*, Grand Rapids: Baker, 1998.

Schweizer, E. *Lordship and Discipleship.* Naperville: Allenson, 1960.

———. "πνεῦμα." *TDNT* 4, 435.

———. "The Son of Man." *JBL* 79 (1960) 119-29.

Scott, J. M. "Adoption, Sonship." In *DPL*, 15-18.

———. *Adoption as Sons of God: An Exegetical Investigation into the Background of ΥΙΟΘΕΣΙΑ in the Pauline Corpus.* Tübigen: Mohr-Siebeck, 1992.

Scroggs, R. *The Last Adam: A Study in Pauline Anthropology.* Oxford: Blackwell, 1966.

Seifrid, M. "Romans." In *Commentary on the New Testament Use of the Old Testament,* edited by G. K. Beale and D. A. Carson, 607-94. Grand Rapids: Baker Academic, 2007.

Shepherd, M. H. *The Paschal Liturgy and the Apocalypse.* London: Lutterworth, 1960.

Shin, C. S. "New Exodus Motif in the Letter to the Hebrews." PhD diss., University of Wales, Lampeter, 2007.

Shogren, G. S. "Presently Entering the Kingdom of Christ: the Background and Purpose of Col. 1:12-14." *JETS* 31 (1988) 173-80.

Shum, Shiu-Lun. *Paul's Use of Isaiah in Romans: A Comparative Study of Paul's Letter to the Romans and the Sibylline and Qumran Sectarian Texts.* Wissenschaftliche Untersuchungen Zum Neuen Testament. Tübingen: Mohr Siebeck, 2002.

Siegert, F. *Argumentation Bei Paulus, Gezeigt an Röm. 9-11*. Wissenschaftliche Untersuchungen Zum Neuen Testament 34. Tübingen: Mohr, 1985.

Skehan, P. W. *Studies in Israelite Wisdom and Poetry*. Washington, DC: Catholic Biblical Association, 1971.

Smiles, V. M. "The Concept of 'Zeal' in Second Temple Judaism and Paul's Critique of it in Romans 10:2." *CBQ* 64:2 (2002) 282-99.

Smith, G. "The Function of 'Likewise' (Ὡσαύτως) Romans 8:26." *TynBul* 49 (1998) 29-38.

Smolarz, S. R. *Covenant and the Metaphor of Divine Marriage in Biblical Thought: A Study with Special Reference to the Book of Revelation*. Eugene, OR: Wipf & Stock, 2010.

Snodgrass, S. G. "Is the Kingdom of God about Eating and Drinking or Isn't It? Romans 14:17." *NovTest* 42:3 (2000) 521-25.

Song, Y. M., and J. S. Du Rand. "The Story of the Red Sea as a Theological Framework of Interpretation." *VE* 30(2), Art. 337, 5 pages. DOI: 10.4102/ve.v30i2.337.

Stählin, G. "απαξ." *TDNT* 1:381-84.

Stanley, C. D. *Arguing with Scripture: The Rhetoric of Quotations in the Letters of Paul*. London: T. & T. Clark, 2004.

Stanton, G. H. *A Gospel for a New People: Studies in Matthew*. Edinburgh: T. & T. Clark, 1992.

Stendahl, K. "The Apostle Paul and the Introspective Conscience of the West." *HTR* (1963) 199-215.

Stott, J. R. W. *The Message of Ephesians: God's New Society*. Leicester: InterVarsity, 1979.

Stowers, S. K. "Paul's Dialogue with a Fellow Jew in Romans 3:1-9." *CBQ* 46 (1984) 707-22.

———. *A Rereading of Romans*. New Haven: Yale University Press, 1994.

Strickland, W., Jr., W. C. Kaiser, D. J. Moo, W. A. Van Gemeren, and S. N. Grundy. *Five Views on Law and Gospel*. Grand Rapids: Zondervan, 1996.

Strom, M. *Reframing Paul: Conversations in Grace and Community*. Downers Grove, IL: InterVarsity, 2000.

Stuhlmacher, P. *Paul's Letter to the Romans: A Commentary*. Louisville, KY: Westminster John Knox, 1994.

———. "The Theme of Romans." *ABR* 36 (1988) 31-44.

Stuhlmacher, P., and E. R. Kalin. *Reconciliation Law and Righteousness: Essays in Biblical Theology.* Philadelphia: Fortress, 1986.

Talbert, C. H. "Non-Pauline fragment at Romans 3:24-26." *JBL* 85:3 (1966) 287-96.

———. *Romans.* Macon, GA: Smyth & Helwys, 2002.

Taylor, V. *The Atonement in the New Testament Teaching.* 2nd ed. London: Epworth, 1954.

———. *The Epistle to the Romans.* London: Epworth, 1955.

Thielman, F. "The Story of Israel and the Theology of Romans 5-8." In *Pauline Theology*, vol. 3, editor by David M. Hay and E. Elizabeth Johnson, 169-96. Minneapolis: Fortress, 1995.

Thiselton, A. T. *Hermeneutics: An Introduction.* Grand Rapids: Eerdmans, 2009.

———. *The Hermeneutics of Christian Doctrine.* Grand Rapids: Eerdmans, 2007.

———. *The Living Paul: An Introduction to the Apostles Life and Thought.* Downers Grove, IL: InterVarsity, 2009.

Theron, D. J. "Adoption in the Pauline Corpus." *EvQ* 28 (1956) 6-14.

Tobin, T. H. "What Shall We Say That Abraham Found?: The Controversy behind Romans 4." *Dia* 35:3 (1996) 193-98.

Torrance, T. F., *Theology in Reconstruction.* London: SCM, 1965.

Trumper, T. J. R. "From Slaves to Sons!" *Foundations* 55 (2006) 17-19.

Tsumura, D. T. "An OT Background to Romans 8:22." *NTS* 40:4 (1994) 620-21.

Turner, M. *The Holy Spirit and Spiritual Gifts Then and Now.* Carlisle: Paternoster, 1996.

Turner, N. *Grammatical Insights into the New Testament.* Edinburgh: T. & T. Clark, 1965.

Turner, S. "The Interim, Earthly Messianic Kingdom in Paul." *JSNT* 25:3 (2003) 323-42.

Udoeyop, E. A. "The New People of God and Kingdom Fruitfulness: An Exegetical and Theological Study of the Parable of the Wicked Tenants in Matthew 21:33-46 and its Significance for a Corporate Hermeneutic." PhD diss., Queen's University Belfast, 2006.

Van der Horst, P. W. "Only then will All Israel be Saved: A Short Note on the Meaning of καὶ οὕτως in Romans 11:26." *JBL* 119:3 (2006) 521-25.

Vaughan, C. J. *St Paul's Epistle to the Romans.* London, 1885.

Vermes, G. "Redemption & Genesis XXII. The Binding of Isaac and the Sacrifice of Jesus." In *Scripture and Tradition in Judaism*, 193-227. Leiden: Brill, 1961.

Vleugels, G. "The Jewish Scriptures in Galatians and Romans." Brussels: *Analecta Bruxellensia*, vol. 7 (2002) 156-63.

Wagner, J. R. "The Christ, Servant of the Jews and Gentiles: A Fresh Approach to Romans 15:8-9." *JBL* 116:3 (1997) 473-85.

———. *Heralds of the Good News: Isaiah and Paul "in Concert" in the Letter to the Romans, Mitchell.* Supplements to Novum Testamentum, vol. 101. Leiden: Brill, 2003.

Wanamaker, C. A. *The Epistle to the Thessalonians: A Commentary on the Greek Text.* Grand Rapids: Eerdmans. 1990.

Warnack, V. "Taufe und Heilsgeschehen Nach Röm. 6." *ALW* 111:2 (1954) 259.

———. "Die Tauflehre des Römerbriefes in der Neueren Theologischen Diskussion." *ALW* 2 (1958) 274-332.

Watts, R. E. "For I Am Not Ashamed of the Gospel: Romans 1:16-17 and Habakkuk 2:4." In *Romans and the People of God: Essays in Honor of Gordon D. Fee on the Occasion of His 65th Birthday*, edited by Sven K. Soderlund and N. T. Wright, 3-25. Grand Rapids: Eerdmans, 1999.

Webb, W. J. *Returning Home; New Covenant and Second Exodus as the Context for 2 Corinthians 6:14-7:1.* JSNTSupp 85. Sheffield: JSOT Press, 1993.

Wedderburn, A. J. M. "Adam and Christ: An Investigation into the Background of 1 Corinthians XV and Romans V:12-21." PhD diss., Cambridge University, 1970.

———. "The Theological Structure of Romans 5:12." *NTS* 19 (1973) 339-54.

Weima, J. A. D. "The Pauline Letter Closings: Analysis and Hermeneutical Significance." *BullBibRes* 5 (1995) 177-97.

Wenham, D. *Paul: Follower of Jesus or Founder of Christianity?* Grand Rapids: Eerdmans, 1995.

Westerholm, S. *Israel's Law and the Church's Faith.* Grand Rapids: Eerdmans, 1988.

———. *Perspectives Old and New on Paul: The "Lutheran Paul" and his Critics.* Grand Rapids: Eerdmans, 2004.

Whelan, C. F. "Amica Pauli: The Role of Phoebe in the Early Church." *JSNT* 49 (1993) 67-85.

Whiteley, D. E. H. "St. Paul's Thought on the Atonement." *JTS* 8 (1957) 240-55.

———. *The Theology of St. Paul.* Oxford: Oxford University Press, 1964.

Whitsett, C. G. "Son of God, Seed of David: Paul's Messianic Exegesis on Romans 1:3-4." *JBL* 119:4 (2000) 661-81.

Wilckens, U. *Der Brief an die Römer*, 3 vols. Benziger/Neukirchenes, 1978, 1980, 1982.

Williams, S. M. "The 'Righteousness of God' in Romans." *JBL* 99 (1980) 241-90.

Winger, M. "The Law of Christ." *NTS* 46:4 (2000) 537-46.

Winter, B. *Seek the Welfare of the City: Christians as Benefactors and Citizens.* Grand Rapids: Eerdmans, 1994.

Witherington, B., III. *Grace in Galatia: A Commentary on St. Paul's Letter to the Galatians.* Grand Rapids: Eerdmans, 1998.

———. *Paul's Letter to the Romans: A Socio-Rhetorical Commentary.* Grand Rapids: Eerdmans, 2004.

Wood, J. "Isaac Typology in the New Testament", *New Testament Studies* 14 (1967-68)

———. "The Purpose of Romans." *EvQ* 40:4 (1968) 211-19.

———.

Wright, N. T. "Adam in Pauline Christology." In *SBL Seminar Papers*, edited by K. H. Richards. Chico, CA (1983) 359-89.

———. *The Climax of the Covenant: Christ and the Law in Pauline Theology.* Edinburgh: T. & T. Clark, 1991.

———. *The Epistles of Paul to Colossians and Philemon: An Introduction and Commentary.* Leicester: InterVarsity, 1986.

———. *Jesus and the Victory of God.* London: SPCK, 1996.

———. "The Letter to the Romans: Introduction, Commentary, and Reflections." In *The New Interpreter's Bible, Volume X, Acts–1 Corinthians*, edited by L. E. Keck, 359-770. Nashville: Abingdon, 2002.

———. "The Messiah and the People of God." PhD diss., Oxford University, 1980.

———. *The New Testament and the People of God.* London: SPCK, 1992.

———. "The Paul of History and the Apostle of Faith." *TB* 29 (1978) 61-88.

———. "Redemption from the New Perspective? Towards a Multi-Layered Pauline Theology of the Cross." In *Redemption*, edited by S. T. Davies, D. Kendall, and G. O. O'Collins, 69-100. Oxford: Oxford University Press, 2006.

———. "Romans and the Theology of Paul." In *Pauline Theology*, vol. 3, edited by David M. Hay and E. Elizabeth Johnson, 30-67. Minneapolis: Fortress, 1995.

———. *What Saint Paul Really Said.* Oxford: Lion, 1997.

Wright, S. "Regeneration and Redemptive History." PhD diss., Westminster Theological Seminary, 1999.

Wu, J. L. "The Spirit's Intercession in Romans 8:26-27: An Exegetical Note." *ExpTimes* 105 (1993) 13.

Yinger, K. L. "Romans 12:14-21 and Nonretaliation in Second Temple Judaism: addressing persecution within the community." *CBQ* 60 (1998) 74-96.

Young, N. H. "C. H. Dodd, 'Hilaskesthai' and His Critics." *EQ* Vol. 48:2 (1976) 67-78.

———. "Did St. Paul Compose Romans 3:24f." *ABR* 22 (1974) 23-32.

Zeller, D. *Der Brief an die Römer*. Regensburg: Friedrich Pustet, 1985.

Ziesler, J. A. *The Meaning of Righteousness in Paul: A Linguistic and Theological Enquiry.* London: Cambridge University Press, 1972.

———. *Paul's Letter to the Romans.* London: SCM, 1989.

Zorn, W. D. "The Messianic Use of Habakkuk 2:4a in Romans." *Stone-Campbell Journal* 1:2 (1998) 213-30.

Zwiep, A. W. *The Ascension of the Messiah in Lukan Christology.* Leiden: Brill, 1997.

INDEX OF AUTHORS

Agersnap, S. 225, 673
Albright, W. F. 78, 673
Aletti, J. N 320, 399, 673
Allison, D. C., Jr. 313, 519, 673
Anderson, B. W. 284
Ashton, J. 3, 673
Aune, D. 86, 269, 673
Badke, W. B. 229, 673
Bailey, K. E. 153, 673
Ballentine, G. L. 12, 674
Balsdon, J. P. V. D. 319, 673
Barclay, J. M. G. 95, 673
Barr, G. K. 632, 673
Barrett, C. K. 36, 64, 92, 116, 384, 417, 549, 673, 677, 684
Barth, Markus 277, 465, 673
Bauckham, R. 415, 673
Baxter, A. G. 509, 674
Beale, G. K. 7, 415, 430, 674, 695
Bechtler, S. R. 456, 674
Beet, J. A. 211, 674
Bekken, P. J. 461, 674
Bell, R. H. 222, 674
Belli, F. 383, 674
Berkley, T. W. 87, 674
Best, E. 86, 127, 234, 250, 379, 674
Betz, H. D. 189, 226, 674

Bird, M. F. 131, 675
Black, M. 115, 120, 218, 378, 673, 674, 675, 679
Blauw, J. 4, 675
Bligh, J. 227, 675
Blocher, Henri 282, 675
Bockmuehl, M. 305, 675
Boers, H. 3, 225, 652, 675
Bornkamm, G. ... 19, 41, 124, 477, 675
Bowker, J. 120, 675
Braaten, C. E. 560, 675
Brewer, D. I. 30, 675
Broyles, C. C. 272, 675
Bruce, F. F. 19, 46, 354, 361, 365, 505, 532, 676, 689
Büchsel, F. 79, 378, 676
Budd, P. 130, 676
Bultmann, R. 112, 120, 218, 676
Burke, T. J. 361, 403, 676
Byrne, B. 345, 362, 676
Caird, G. F. B. ..41, 359, 417, 465, 676
Calvin, J. 1 88, 515, 516, 517, 520, 676
Campbell, D. A. 59, 114, 131, 132, 254, 529
Campbell, W. S. 23, 401, 437, 528
Carbone, S. 515, 676

Carson, D. A. .. 41, 120, 172, 675, 676, 687, 695

Casey, M. 5, 277, 677

Casey, R. P. 41, 120, 124

Cervin, R. S. 633, 677

Chadwick, H. 2, 368, 652, 677

Charlesworth, J. H. 359, 677

Chilton, B. 677

Coleman, T. M. 574, 677

Colpe, G. 218, 677

Court, J. M. 37, 91, 677, 683

Cousar, C. P. 120, 677

Coxon, P. 13, 113, 677

Cranfield, C. E. B. ... 85, 92, 113, 121, 138, 142, 267, 364, 365, 372, 380, 411, 417, 456, 515, 585, 598, 605, 609, 611, 615, 677

Cullmann, O. . . 41, 218, 227, 406, 569, 677

Dahl, N. 164, 678

Davidson, Richard M. 656, 678

Davies, P. 30

Davies, R. E. 120

Davies, W. D. 3, 41, 121, 208, 218, 242, 250, 287, 345, 401, 462, 516, 519

Davila, J. R. 31, 678

De Jonge, M. 41, 678

De Lacey, D. R. 41, 678

DeMaris, R. E. 226, 678

Denova, R. I. 569, 678

Derrett, J. D. M. 91, 301, 678

Dillon, J. R. 615, 678

Dodd, C. H. 49, 115, 122, 193, 215, 378, 430, 678, 699

Donaldson, T. L. ... 157, 327, 502, 679

Donfried, K. P. 628, 679, 685, 688

Donne, B. K. 463, 679

Downing, J. 116, 679

Dozeman, T. 435, 679

Driver, J. 120, 679

Du Rand, J. S. 695

Du Toit, A. B. 610, 680

Dunn, J. D. G. .. 1, 3, 4, 15, 41, 59, 64, 67, 116, 120, 122, 127, 130, 155, 166, 170, 175, 182, 189, 218, 286, 288, 304, 310, 313, 342, 350, 357, 359, 373, 375, 378, 418, 465, 517, 624, 633, 679

Durham, J. I. 192, 679, 680

Earnshaw, J. D. 302, 680

Edwards, J. R. 83, 680

Elliott, J. K. 644, 680

Ellis, E. E. 350, 680

Emerton, J. A. 120, 680

Engberg-Pedersen, T. 3, 674, 680

Eskola, T. 314, 680

Esler, P. 508, 680

Espy, J. M. 313, 327, 680

Fee, G. D. 218, 349, 351, 354, 372, 375, 680, 697

Finger, R. H. 638, 681

Fitzmyer, J. A. 1, 20, 68, 142, 145, 215, 375, 418, 448, 549, 559, 585, 605, 614, 617, 638, 681

Index of Authors

Foerster, W. 203, 681
Ford, D. 681
Ford, J. M. 313
Fretheim, T. E. 192, 681
Friesen, G. 535, 681
Fuller, R. H. 19, 681, 694
Furnish, V. P. 572, 681
Gager, J. G. 342, 364, 681
Gagnon, R. A. J. 585, 596, 681
Garlington, D. B. ... 135, 325, 647, 649, 681
Garnet, P. 130, 682
Gaston, L. 395, 682
Gathercole, S. J. 85, 172, 189, 682
Getty, M. A. 436, 682
Giblin, C. H. 301, 682
Ginzberg, L. . . 130, 529, 653, 654, 659, 682
Given, M. D. 117, 496, 682
Glancy, J. 514, 682
Goldingay, J. 272, 682
Goppelt, L. 194, 460, 656, 682
Goulder, M. 471, 682
Gray, G. 130, 682
Grech, P. 41, 682
Green, G. L. ..... xvii, 86, 289, 681, 682, 687
Grundy, S. N. 696
Gulley, N. R. 463, 466, 682
Gundry, R. H. 682

Hahn, F. 379, 682
Hall, D. R. 100, 678, 683
Hamerton-Kelly, R. G. 379, 683
Hanson, A. T. 287, 345, 683
Harman, A. 471, 683
Harmo, M. S. 648, 683
Harnack, Adolf 654, 683
Harris, M. J. 406
Hays, R. B. 7, 19, 37, 39, 55, 131, 135, 144, 215, 308, 328, 345, 430, 437, 471, 517, 648, 683
Headlam, A. 286, 313, 365, 378, 693
Hellholm, D. 299, 683
Hendriksen, W. 415, 683, 685
Hengel, M. ... 2, 41, 653, 654, 660, 684
Hester, J. D. 356, 684
Hill, D. 7, 115, 147, 173, 288, 658, 662, 684
Hills, J. V. 456, 684
Hodge, C. 156, 413, 437, 684
Hoehner, H. W. 127, 684
Holland, T. ... i, iii, vii, viii, ix, xvii, 12, 18, 31, 37, 44, 116, 119, 125, 127, 134, 139, 153, 162, 166, 167, 168, 180, 194, 206, 218, 226, 233, 244, 247, 248, 252, 257, 258, 260, 264, 266, 276, 279, 281, 284, 288, 310, 314, 317, 319, 327, 337, 340, 342, 344, 345, 347, 348, 351, 352, 355, 376, 379, 383, 401, 402, 403, 406, 407, 421, 430, 448, 449, 458, 462, 476, 479, 480, 496, 505, 512, 518, 524, 529, 530, 572, 614, 615, 617, 623, 647, 650, 652, 656, 664, 681, 684

Hooker, M. D... 64, 65, 208, 215, 314, 342, 677, 684

Horst, J. 260, 684

Howard, J. K. .... vii, xvii, 122, 684

Jansen, F. J. 466, 684

Jeremias, J. 359, 684

Jewett, R. ... 26, 44, 69, 142, 269, 282, 288, 298, 460, 461, 470, 523, 525, 590, 596, 600, 628, 685

Jobs, K. H. 648, 685

Johnson, A. R. 118

Johnson, B. C. 516

Johnson, D. G. 495

Johnson, L. T. 566

Kaiser, W. C. 696

Kalin, E. R. 696

Karlberg, M. W. 310, 685

Karris, R. J. 20, 685

Käsemann, E.. 19, 46, 67, 85, 90, 112, 118, 119, 124, 130, 134, 142, 153, 167, 203, 254, 258, 300, 303, 310, 353, 364, 365, 372, 380, 411, 437, 501, 515, 578, 585, 588, 591, 593, 598, 685

Kay, B. N. 36, 685

Keck, L. E. 41, 232, 585, 609, 685, 699

Kee, H. C. 3, 652, 686

Keesmaat, S. C. 113, 351, 378, 686

Kennedy, A. A. 286, 686

Kidner, D. 115, 130, 178, 532, 686

Kim, S. 514, 686

Kirby, J. C. 465, 489, 686

Kirkpatrick, A. F. 110, 686

Klein, W. W. 376, 686

Klijn, A. F. J. 3, 208, 686

Kline, M. G. 686

Knox, J. 131, 686

Knox, W. L. 227

Kosmala, H. 319, 686

Kramer, W. 379, 686

Kraus, Hans-Joachim ... 272, 460, 471, 686

Kreuzer, S 147, 686

Krimmer, H. 379, 686

Kroger, D. 573, 686

Kummel, W. G. 3, 652, 687

Kuss, Otto 301, 687

Laato, T. 18, 687

Lagrange, M. J. 249, 687

Lambrecht, J. 218, 687

Lamp, G. W. H. 687

Landy, F. 284, 687

Lane, W. L. 37, 345, 687

Laurer, S. 77, 92, 549, 687

Leaney, A. R. C. 228, 229, 687

Lee, Y. L. 201, 687

Leenhardt, F. J. 249, 365, 437, 687

Lemico, E. 21, 687

Levenson, J. D. 428, 432, 436, 687

Levey, Samson H. 658, 687

Lincoln, A. ... 288, 460, 464, 465, 489, 687

Index of Authors

Longacre, R. E. 613, 688
Longenecker, B. W. 135
Longenecker, R. N. 21
Louw, J. P. 112, 150, 313, 691
Lyall, F. 356, 688
Maartens, P. J. 206, 384, 688
MacGregor, G. H. C. 313, 688
Macintosh, A. 214, 284, 688
Mackay, J. L. 192, 688
Maddox, R. 120, 688
Maile, J. F. 463, 465, 688
Maillot, A. 249, 688
Malherbe, A. J. 86, 688
Malick, D. E. 68, 688
Mánek, J. 113, 688
Mann, C. S. 78, 673
Manson, T. W. 218, 625, 688
Marsh, J. 228, 689
Marshall, I. H. ...... vii, xvii, 3, 41, 689, 691
Martin, J. P. 397
Martin, R. P. 313
Maxson, J. R. 535, 681
Mays, J. L. 272, 471, 689
McKay, C. 120, 689
McKelvey, R. T. 120, 122, 689
McKnight, S. A. 359, 689
McWhirter, J. 276, 689
Meggitt, J. J. 643, 689
Meissner, S. 162, 689

Metzger, B. M. 406, 556, 689
Meyer, B. F. .... xx, 130, 689
Michael, O. .... viii, 689
Millard, A. R. 689
Miller, J. C. 20, 690
Molland, E. 19, 690
Monte, W. D. 167, 228, 690
Moo, D. J. .... vii, 68, 121, 123, 131, 142, 160, 313, 373, 402, 414, 422, 457, 461, 465, 480, 515, 585, 598, 599, 690, 696
Morris, L. L. .41, 76, 79, 82, 104, 115, 116, 122, 142, 151, 160, 210, 228, 255, 366, 384, 390, 418, 532, 594, 599, 675, 680, 688, 690, 693
Moule, C. F. D. 41, 115, 120, 406
Moule, H. C. G. 342
Muddiman, J. 465, 690
Muilenburg, J. 218, 690
Munck, J. ...3, 401, 437, 444, 480, 620, 621, 690
Murray, J. 159, 173, 290, 365, 437, 516, 595, 691, 694
Nanos, M. D. 3, 21, 569, 570, 585, 633, 691
Nida, E. A. 112, 150, 313, 691
Ninow, F. 194, 656, 691
Nixon, R. E. 227, 691
Noordtzij, A. 130, 691
North, J. L. 130, 640, 691
Nwachukwu, M. S. C. 364, 691
Nygren, A. 36, 691

705

Olyott, S. 373, 691
Oster, R. E. 632, 691
Otto, K. 687, 691
Pamment, M. 78, 691
Pao, D. W. 691
Pate, C. M. 185, 215, 691
Perrin, N. 167, 692
Petersen, N. R. 36, 692
Peterson, A. K. 225, 226, 244
Peterson, D. 534, 692
Pierce, C. A. 85, 692
Piper, J. ... 32, 172, 414, 417, 421, 423, 424, 425, 430, 432, 692
Powers, D. G. 230, 688, 692
Powys, D. 287, 692
Preston, M. P. 675
Punt, J. P. 18, 692
Qualls, P. 692
Ra, K. U. 13, 113, 435, 692
Räisänen, H. 395, 692
Rancine, J. F. 573, 692
Rapinchuk, M. 213, 692
Reasoner, M. 585, 692
Reumann, J. 124, 692
Ribbens, B. J. 656, 692
Richardson, A. 120, 692
Ridderbos, H. 112, 167, 218, 229, 252, 287, 297, 357, 426, 438, 693
Robichaux, K. S. 378, 693
Robinson, J. A. T. 365

Rogerson, J. W. 306, 693
Rosenberg, R. A. 211, 693
Rosner, R. S. 574, 693
Ross, A. 693
Russell, W. 338, 693
Ryan, J. M. 481, 693
Sahlin, H. 215, 228, 693
Sampley, J. P. 3, 693
Sanders, E. P. 3, 169, 282, 284, 286, 305, 314, 352, 448, 519, 693
Sandmel, S. 31, 32, 693
Sandnes, K. O. 206, 693
Sandy, W. 286, 693
Sass, G. 608, 694
Schaefer, J. R. 19, 694
Schillebeeckx, E. 167, 694
Schnackenburg, R. 232, 465, 694
Schneider, B. 121, 694
Schoeps, H. J. 167, 211, 694
Schrange, W. 249, 694
Schreiner, T. R. 83, 93, 247, 253, 312, 350, 351, 357, 397, 414, 417, 421, 424, 425, 430, 437, 442, 456, 694
Schweizer, E. 86, 120, 218, 694
Scott, J. M. 357, 362, 403, 691, 694
Scroggs, R. 215, 250, 694
Seifrid, M. 116, 225, 442, 517, 675, 687, 695
Shepherd, M. H. 123, 638, 695
Shin, C. S. 13, 488, 695
Shogren, G. S. 351, 695

Index of Authors

Shum, Shiu-Lun. 31, 695
Siegert, F. 401, 695
Skehan, P...............................120, 695
Smiles, V. M. 454, 695
Smith, G. 370, 654, 684, 695
Smolarz, S. R.206, 251, 415, 641, 695
Snodgrass, S. G. 588, 695
Song, Y. M. 12, 127, 481, 482, 657, 660, 661, 695
Stählin, G. 256, 695
Stanley, C. D. 18, 695
Stanton, G. H............................... 695
Stendahl, K....................327, 395, 696
Stott, J. R. W. 356, 696
Stowers, S. K.100, 142, 220, 265, 696
Strickland, W., Jr...................456, 696
Strom, M. 3, 696
Stuhlmacher, P. 120, 124, 342, 516, 530, 696
Talbert, C. H..................112, 570, 696
Taylor, V. 167, 379, 696
Theron, D. J............................... 696
Thielman, F. ...208, 228, 378, 403, 696
Thiselton, A. T. ...... vii, viii, 226, 414, 650, 696
Tobin, T. H..........................144, 696
Torrance, T. F............................ 696
Trumper, T. J. R. 362, 696
Tsumura, D. T. 367, 697
Turner, M. 350, 406, 697

Turner, N. 697
Turner, S.............................. 597, 697
Udoeyop, E. A. 78, 697
Van der Horst, P. W. 515, 697
Van Gemeren, W. A. 696
Vaughan, C. J. 697
Vermes, G............................ 211, 697
Vleugels, G............................ 19, 697
Wagner, J. R. 18, 609, 697
Wallis, W. B. 613, 688
Wanamaker, C. A. 86, 697
Warnack, V........................... 227, 697
Webb, W. J. 185, 698
Wedderburn, A. J. M. ... 215, 286, 313, 698
Weima, J. A. D. 644, 698
Wenham, D.................................. 698
Westerholm, S. 172, 456, 677, 698
Whelan, C. F........................ 631, 698
Whiteley, D. E. H. 125, 211, 310, 342, 698
Whitsett, C. G. 41, 698
Wilckens, U. ..130, 167, 342, 364, 379, 411, 437, 698
Williams, S. M...... xvii, 395, 609, 698
Winger, M. 303, 698
Winter, B. 571, 698
Witherington, B., III. 1, 125, 189, 374, 376, 535, 569, 576, 585, 588, 625, 631, 635, 637, 698
Wood, J........................... 23, 656, 698

Wright, S. 699

Wu, J. L. 699

Yinger, K. L. 561, 699

Young, N. H. 112, 115, 253, 349, 681, 699

Zeller, D. 211, 379, 699

Ziesler, J. A. 7, 46, 85, 91, 112, 135, 147, 173, 203, 239, 254, 288, 349, 352, 358, 375, 378, 509, 515, 662, 674, 699

Zorn, W. D. 59, 700

Zwiep, A. W. 465, 466, 700

INDEX OF TOPICS

Aaron.... 128, 195, 265, 434, 487, 555, 580

Abrahamic...... 27, 155, 156, 181, 183, 366, 444, 621

Abram/Abraham.xv, 8, 18, 21, 27, 28, 38, 54, 58, 79, 80, 85, 104, 105, 127, 139, 141, 142, 143, 144, 145, 146, 147, 148, 149, 150, 151, 152, 153, 154, 155, 156, 157, 158, 159, 160, 161, 162, 163, 164, 165, 166, 167, 168, 173, 174, 175, 176, 177, 178, 179, 180, 181, 182, 183, 185, 186, 192, 195, 196, 197, 198, 199, 201, 203, 205, 223, 225, 232, 236, 242, 262, 268, 271, 319, 336, 346, 356, 362, 363, 366, 375, 378, 380, 386, 393, 396, 402, 403, 404, 408, 409, 410, 411, 413, 415, 416, 417, 422, 425, 426, 428, 434, 440, 444, 445, 448, 485, 486, 493, 495, 496, 497, 498, 500, 503, 504, 505, 506, 507, 508, 510, 513, 515, 517, 518, 520, 521, 522, 526, 531, 548, 600, 609, 613, 626, 644, 666, 667, 669, 673, 676, 683, 696

accounting.... 145, 169, 170, 172, 173, 175, 183, 184, 197, 258

acquit/acquittal97, 145, 146, 169, 170, 171, 173, 174, 175, 176, 182, 183, 184, 185, 195, 196, 197, 198, 219, 254, 335, 658

Adam.... 25, 29, 40, 61, 64, 65, 69, 80, 83, 102, 107, 112, 120, 125, 133, 137, 147, 190, 193, 194, 199, 202, 207, 212, 213, 214, 215, 216, 217, 218, 219, 221, 222, 223, 224, 225, 226, 230, 238, 239, 240, 241, 242, 243, 244, 247, 248, 249, 250, 251, 252, 267, 270, 272, 277, 278, 279, 282, 283, 284, 286, 290, 291, 295, 296, 297, 298, 299, 301, 304, 306, 307, 309, 310, 314, 315, 316, 317, 318, 319, 320, 321, 322, 325, 326, 328, 331, 332, 335, 337, 338, 339, 340, 341, 342, 343, 344, 345, 346, 350, 353, 354, 356, 364, 365, 370, 378, 379, 382, 398, 404, 436, 442, 444, 445, 449, 450, 502, 503, 522, 534, 591, 623, 640, 667, 673, 675, 679, 683, 684, 691, 693, 694, 698, 699

Adamic .120, 125, 185, 216, 218, 222, 248, 366, 378

adopt/adoption..4, 101, 146, 184, 236, 334, 336, 356, 358, 360, 361, 362, 367, 370, 393, 402, 403, 416, 557, 573, 584, 664

adultery/adulterous/adulteress . 10, 57, 72, 90, 149, 160, 215, 240, 241, 242, 252, 255, 261, 272, 285, 286, 291, 298, 300, 302, 318, 342, 343, 482, 552, 567, 575

alienation ..39, 90, 109, 111, 202, 217, 395, 398, 591

allegiance..8, 229, 265, 268, 288, 346, 410, 474, 498, 534, 552, 553, 591

Althaus 134

Amos 24, 42, 74, 81, 153, 221, 238, 243, 313, 366, 437, 500, 541, 552, 673

ancestry................. 393, 405, 485, 513

anointed 9, 10, 14, 419, 420, 425, 433, 440, 569

anthropology 86, 270, 283, 320

apocalyptic 2, 350, 366, 368, 652

apostate 641, 669

apostolic ... 3, 5, 26, 39, 176, 274, 328, 421, 492, 514, 536, 550, 594, 613, 618, 620, 633, 637, 650, 656, 658, 662, 663, 664

Aqedah..116, 162, 164, 211, 305, 380, 677, 678

ascend/ascended/ascension 16, 97, 451, 457, 459, 460, 462, 463, 464, 465, 466, 467, 468, 469, 488, 489, 491, 492, 590, 669

ascent 463, 464, 466, 469, 483, 492

atone/atonement/atoning 19, 112, 113, 115, 116, 117, 118, 119, 121, 122, 123, 124, 125, 126, 128, 129, 130, 134, 135, 136, 139, 163, 164, 168, 185, 195, 199, 220, 258, 331, 342, 444, 479, 529, 610, 666

authority. 19, 61, 67, 76, 88, 107, 111, 216, 236, 244, 250, 252, 256, 265, 286, 287, 298, 300, 301, 302, 303, 304, 307, 313, 316, 322, 327, 337, 339, 340, 342, 343, 344, 353, 367, 374, 432, 439, 442, 471, 489, 503, 525, 541, 556, 565, 567, 568, 569, 570, 571, 572, 574, 588, 592, 594, 613, 623, 639, 647, 667

Baal 493, 497, 498, 506, 510

Babylon/Babylonian 11, 12, 39, 41, 43, 46, 56, 59, 92, 96, 101, 109, 111, 113, 114, 117, 124, 131, 132, 133, 134, 136, 140, 165, 173, 179, 194, 202, 203, 205, 208, 209, 228, 243, 246, 250, 290, 330, 331, 332, 340, 357, 364, 369, 371, 377, 378, 383, 384, 389, 398, 404, 442, 443, 446, 452, 453, 455, 456, 471, 472, 478, 495, 519, 524, 539, 554, 579, 657

baptism 31, 45, 118, 127, 153, 187, 194, 225, 226, 227, 228, 229, 230, 232, 233, 234, 235, 236, 237, 239, 244, 245, 246, 259, 269, 299, 303, 332, 339, 347, 359, 475, 578, 667

baptismal 125, 226, 227, 231, 232, 237, 244, 380, 475

Baptist 12, 16, 31, 119, 122, 127, 261, 276, 340, 666

Baptists 33

baptize/baptized/baptizing 29, 96, 227, 228, 229, 230, 232, 233, 234, 235, 237, 239, 244, 264, 303, 307, 332, 475, 642, 666

barbarian 248, 352

believer/believers 6, 13, 14, 20, 21, 22, 24, 25, 26, 27, 35, 39, 49, 50, 51, 52, 53, 56, 59, 65, 74, 76, 77, 80, 82, 83, 84, 85, 87, 91, 93, 95, 96, 105, 107, 115, 116, 126, 137, 139, 147, 155, 156, 164, 166, 167, 169, 180, 181, 184, 187, 188, 191, 194, 197, 202, 204, 207, 208, 209, 210, 211, 212, 213, 219, 221, 224, 226, 227, 230, 233, 234, 235, 236, 238, 242, 243, 244, 246, 247, 250, 252, 253, 254, 255, 256, 257, 258, 259, 260, 261, 262, 263, 264, 265, 266, 267, 269, 276, 279, 280, 282, 283, 289, 291, 295, 296, 302, 304, 309, 311, 315, 316, 317, 325, 332, 336, 341, 344, 345, 346, 347, 348, 349, 350, 352, 353, 354, 355, 356, 357, 358, 360, 362, 363, 366, 367, 368, 369, 370, 371, 372, 373, 374, 376, 377, 379, 380, 381, 384, 386, 387, 388, 389, 390, 395, 399, 400,

Index of Topics

403, 408, 412, 413, 426, 430, 440, 441, 444, 450, 452, 457, 458, 460, 462, 471, 473, 477, 479, 481, 491, 495, 496, 497, 498, 499, 501, 504, 505, 507, 508, 509, 511, 513, 514, 515, 517, 518, 521, 526, 528, 529, 530, 531, 532, 533, 534, 535, 536, 537, 538, 539, 540, 541, 542, 543, 544, 545, 546, 547, 549, 551, 552, 553, 554, 555, 556, 557, 558, 559, 560, 561, 562, 563, 564, 565, 566, 568, 569, 570, 571, 572, 574, 575, 577, 578, 579, 580, 581, 584, 585, 586, 587, 588, 589, 590, 592, 593, 594, 595, 597, 598, 599, 600, 601, 605, 606, 607, 608, 609, 612, 613, 615, 618, 619, 620, 621, 622, 623, 624, 625, 628, 629, 630, 631, 632, 633, 635, 636, 637, 638, 639, 640, 641, 642, 643, 644, 645, 646, 648, 656, 662, 663, 665, 666, 667, 670, 671

betrothed....... 261, 301, 303, 332, 355, 386, 391, 566

binding . 116, 162, 164, 165, 168, 199, 202, 322, 380, 534, 667

birth .. 8, 12, 16, 32, 85, 142, 143, 145, 159, 160, 161, 162, 163, 167, 177, 181, 230, 231, 235, 266, 272, 275, 280, 285, 329, 338, 366, 367, 409, 410, 411, 420, 422, 429, 436, 511, 537, 546, 668

birthright 347, 397, 411, 413, 425, 432

blaspheme/blasphemed 17, 72, 92, 329

blessing/blessings ... 14, 18, 24, 28, 29, 50, 51, 53, 67, 81, 100, 110, 111, 147, 149, 156, 157, 170, 176, 177, 181, 190, 193, 195, 197, 198, 210, 223, 234, 237, 253, 264, 271, 291, 294, 316, 321, 339, 344, 347, 363, 386, 388, 395, 396, 397, 401, 402,

404, 405, 408, 409, 413, 416, 417, 425, 428, 430, 434, 438, 440, 441, 449, 454, 458, 460, 469, 481, 482, 483, 485, 495, 501, 502, 504, 507, 509, 511, 513, 515, 521, 522, 526, 539, 541, 546, 553, 576, 600, 604, 607, 610, 614, 616, 621, 622, 623, 631, 641, 668, 669

blood. 8, 9, 17, 99, 101, 109, 113, 115, 118, 124, 125, 126, 127, 133, 134, 135, 163, 186, 188, 197, 201, 204, 210, 211, 220, 231, 275, 291, 331, 337, 366, 380, 434, 490, 519, 610, 636

bodies ... 60, 62, 66, 67, 159, 162, 260, 271, 278, 280, 283, 298, 309, 310, 329, 331, 333, 334, 337, 350, 353, 354, 355, 360, 367, 376, 379, 389, 527, 528, 530, 535, 557

body of Christ....... 226, 233, 241, 249, 250, 252, 261, 298, 303, 353, 357, 367, 538, 539, 542, 546, 548

bondage .. 12, 40, 47, 56, 66, 107, 111, 114, 120, 125, 132, 133, 139, 165, 179, 186, 203, 223, 230, 239, 253, 254, 264, 268, 296, 299, 300, 315, 318, 319, 327, 331, 334, 335, 339, 353, 360, 365, 370, 381, 442, 447, 452, 455, 476, 479, 482, 517, 524, 529, 531, 578, 614

branch............506, 508, 510, 511, 514

bride of Christ....... 231, 239, 240, 251, 255, 328, 482, 538

bride/bridal ... viii, xv, 10, 45, 97, 119, 127, 140, 187, 188, 198, 205, 206, 231, 235, 236, 239, 240, 241, 251, 254, 255, 262, 276, 284, 299, 300, 302, 303, 307, 318, 319, 325, 327, 328, 330, 332, 340, 341, 343, 355, 359, 368, 381, 382, 386, 390, 396,

450, 453, 474, 482, 484, 491, 526, 529, 532, 538, 562, 593, 644, 660, 661

bridegroom .. 186, 276, 284, 328, 330, 382, 391, 474, 483, 484, 526, 529, 582

bride-purchase 303, 319

captive/captives/captivity .. 10, 13, 14, 16, 56, 69, 111, 124, 176, 186, 191, 197, 198, 203, 204, 211, 259, 286, 297, 329, 369, 380, 416, 443, 455, 464, 472, 476, 488, 579, 608, 609

ceremony/ceremonial. 6, 93, 103, 128, 178, 179, 191, 192, 230, 242, 271, 327, 331, 453, 592, 601, 622

chastening 204, 384, 500, 509

chiasm 44, 45

Christology/Christological/ Christologies . 3, 16, 41, 43, 44, 45, 46, 120, 185, 216, 218, 222, 288, 349, 351, 406, 407, 461, 462, 465, 469, 471, 479, 623, 652, 675, 676, 677, 678, 679, 680, 681, 682, 683, 684, 685, 686, 687, 689, 690, 691, 692, 694, 699, 700

circumcise/circumcision 6, 15, 20, 21, 28, 49, 50, 72, 85, 93, 94, 95, 96, 97, 99, 103, 105, 119, 140, 141, 144, 147, 151, 152, 153, 154, 155, 158, 161, 169, 171, 181, 183, 186, 187, 188, 190, 194, 198, 199, 223, 236, 237, 277, 281, 292, 319, 395, 412, 449, 490, 497, 507, 515, 560, 615, 644, 663, 665, 666

community/communities .. vii, ix, 4, 6, 7, 16, 18, 20, 23, 24, 25, 27, 28, 29, 30, 31, 32, 33, 35, 37, 38, 51, 54, 55, 57, 58, 66, 69, 72, 76, 81, 84, 86, 88, 89, 91, 93, 96, 97, 101, 103, 104, 109, 114, 117, 123, 126, 129,

132, 133, 138, 140, 146, 148, 153, 163, 171, 176, 181, 185, 186, 187, 188, 190, 194, 197, 198, 199, 202, 205, 207, 208, 209, 210, 213, 217, 219, 223, 224, 225, 226, 227, 229, 233, 234, 235, 236, 237, 238, 239, 240, 242, 243, 246, 248, 249, 250, 252, 255, 259, 260, 261, 264, 267, 269, 272, 273, 274, 278, 291, 294, 299, 301, 305, 306, 307, 308, 310, 311, 314, 323, 325, 326, 327, 332, 336, 343, 344, 345, 346, 347, 348, 351, 352, 354, 355, 356, 357, 358, 359, 360, 363, 366, 367, 369, 370, 374, 375, 376, 377, 379, 380, 383, 384, 385, 389, 390, 395, 396, 397, 398, 400, 405, 408, 409, 412, 416, 428, 430, 432, 437, 443, 444, 445, 446, 447, 453, 460, 467, 468, 471, 472, 473, 476, 477, 479, 482, 488, 489, 491, 495, 496, 497, 504, 506, 507, 509, 510, 512, 513, 514, 515, 522, 528, 529, 530, 532, 534, 535, 537, 538, 539, 543, 549, 551, 559, 561, 563, 564, 570, 572, 576, 579, 581, 585, 586, 588, 589, 590, 596, 601, 606, 607, 608, 609, 610, 611, 612, 615, 619, 621, 622, 625, 626, 629, 631, 633, 635, 638, 639, 641, 644, 646, 648, 650, 655, 656, 657, 658, 659, 661, 662, 663, 666, 667, 668, 669, 699

condemn/condemnation 52, 70, 72, 84, 87, 94, 99, 105, 106, 107, 149, 189, 190, 191, 194, 198, 205, 212, 219, 221, 224, 238, 243, 265, 315, 323, 332, 333, 335, 337, 338, 339, 341, 386, 390, 401, 402, 404, 407, 448, 525, 527, 583, 584, 587, 600, 624, 665, 667

corporate/corporately/corporateness .. vii, viii, 23, 24, 25, 26, 28, 68, 69, 72, 75, 84, 96, 112, 127, 147, 169,

Index of Topics

174, 182, 187, 189, 190, 194, 195, 196, 197, 198, 206, 208, 210, 213, 215, 217, 224, 226, 228, 230, 231, 232, 233, 234, 236, 237, 245, 246, 248, 249, 250, 252, 255, 259, 260, 261, 262, 280, 281, 288, 297, 299, 302, 306, 307, 308, 310, 317, 320, 321, 324, 325, 326, 327, 339, 341, 343, 344, 345, 349, 350, 351, 352, 353, 354, 356, 357, 358, 359, 360, 368, 374, 375, 376, 378, 396, 397, 398, 400, 412, 414, 416, 417, 421, 422, 425, 430, 433, 435, 439, 442, 445, 475, 480, 488, 531, 532, 534, 535, 537, 538, 539, 540, 543, 549, 558, 581, 590, 593, 608, 665, 667, 668

corruption 6, 67, 81, 289, 309, 321, 573

cosmic 11, 107, 134, 366, 367, 476, 490

Cosmic 2, 368, 652, 688

covenant/covenantal .. vii, 8, 9, 10, 14, 16, 18, 19, 20, 21, 23, 24, 25, 28, 29, 37, 49, 50, 54, 55, 57, 58, 59, 66, 74, 76, 85, 87, 89, 90, 93, 94, 95, 96, 97, 100, 101, 102, 104, 110, 112, 114, 117, 119, 120, 121, 124, 125, 127, 131, 133, 135, 136, 138, 139, 143, 144, 145, 146, 147, 148, 149, 150, 151, 152, 154, 155, 156, 157, 158, 161, 162, 164, 165, 166, 167, 169, 170, 171, 172, 174, 175, 176, 177, 178, 179, 180, 181, 182, 183, 184, 185, 186, 187, 188, 189, 190, 191, 192, 193, 194, 195, 196, 197, 198, 199, 202, 203, 204, 205, 208, 209, 210, 213, 214, 215, 216, 219, 220, 221, 228, 229, 235, 236, 237, 240, 241, 242, 243, 249, 250, 251, 252, 254, 255, 258, 259, 262, 270, 276, 277, 278, 279, 283, 284, 285, 286, 288, 290, 292, 294, 295, 296, 297, 299, 300, 301, 302, 303, 304, 306, 307, 309, 310, 313, 314, 316, 318, 325, 327, 329, 330, 331, 332, 337, 339, 340, 341, 342, 343, 345, 350, 351, 353, 357, 359, 360, 362, 366, 369, 370, 375, 376, 384, 385, 386, 387, 395, 396, 397, 398, 402, 403, 404, 410, 412, 413, 414, 415, 416, 419, 428, 430, 434, 436, 442, 443, 444, 445, 446, 447, 448, 453, 454, 456, 458, 459, 466, 467, 469, 475, 476, 478, 479, 480, 484, 486, 487, 488, 494, 496, 497, 500, 501, 502, 504, 505, 506, 507, 508, 509, 510, 511, 512, 513, 514, 518, 519, 520, 521, 522, 525, 534, 541, 552, 553, 558, 570, 590, 610, 614, 615, 621, 641, 644, 666, 667, 668, 669

covenant-breaking 284

covenanted 267

covenant-keeping.. 124, 137, 430, 505

covenant-making . 154, 158, 167, 176, 196, 327, 666

creation ... 2, 11, 16, 25, 40, 43, 44, 45, 46, 60, 63, 64, 67, 70, 80, 89, 109, 126, 133, 182, 185, 191, 192, 195, 196, 197, 205, 207, 219, 229, 231, 233, 269, 277, 282, 304, 307, 308, 318, 320, 325, 326, 334, 335, 337, 346, 350, 353, 360, 361, 364, 365, 366, 367, 368, 375, 377, 378, 390, 391, 404, 407, 436, 441, 443, 469, 480, 490, 495, 505, 525, 529, 533, 590, 601, 608, 609, 610, 622, 623, 645, 652, 668

credit/credited/crediting 138, 141, 142, 143, 145, 146, 147, 148, 151, 152, 154, 161, 164, 165, 166, 167, 169, 172, 173, 174, 175, 176, 177,

178, 179, 180, 181, 182, 184, 195, 196, 198, 258, 298, 418, 506, 508, 651

creditor.. 30

crucified..... 37, 44, 63, 155, 191, 217, 238, 247, 249, 280, 395, 455, 570, 606

curse 92, 179, 190, 192, 198, 218, 299, 364, 365, 378, 415, 549, 550, 560, 591

Cyrus 419, 420, 425, 426, 433, 436, 439, 440, 450, 569

darkness 43, 56, 59, 61, 64, 65, 66, 67, 69, 70, 73, 79, 88, 90, 92, 96, 105, 110, 111, 126, 132, 133, 140, 147, 163, 168, 172, 178, 179, 197, 203, 206, 209, 213, 219, 226, 234, 240, 244, 245, 248, 252, 258, 261, 262, 265, 267, 268, 269, 279, 290, 295, 296, 299, 313, 325, 326, 338, 341, 346, 355, 370, 376, 382, 384, 387, 388, 389, 390, 403, 418, 419, 454, 455, 476, 477, 490, 499, 535, 559, 567, 575, 578, 579, 587, 591, 609, 618

David/Davidic.... 9, 10, 11, 13, 14, 15, 16, 18, 19, 28, 32, 35, 36, 38, 39, 40, 41, 42, 44, 45, 47, 56, 70, 77, 100, 101, 104, 108, 110, 111, 117, 118, 119, 120, 121, 124, 132, 141, 148, 149, 150, 151, 154, 163, 164, 173, 174, 175, 182, 183, 185, 198, 199, 203, 206, 207, 209, 223, 261, 262, 264, 271, 272, 273, 281, 292, 308, 336, 337, 338, 343, 346, 370, 383, 386, 388, 400, 402, 404, 405, 410, 443, 449, 452, 453, 463, 464, 467, 468, 469, 471, 472, 476, 478, 479, 483, 486, 489, 490, 491, 493, 499, 500, 501, 519, 521, 528, 552, 569, 596, 617, 626, 654, 656, 660,

665, 666, 677, 684, 688, 692, 696, 698, 699

death. 8, 10, 12, 16, 26, 29, 41, 42, 43, 45, 46, 49, 52, 58, 60, 65, 69, 80, 82, 83, 96, 101, 102, 104, 105, 109, 112, 114, 115, 116, 117, 118, 119, 120, 121, 122, 124, 125, 126, 128, 129, 130, 131, 132, 133, 134, 135, 136, 138, 139, 140, 142, 149, 152, 153, 157, 159, 161, 162, 163, 164, 165, 166, 167, 168, 169, 179, 181, 184, 185, 188, 190, 191, 193, 194, 199, 201, 202, 203, 204, 205, 209, 210, 211, 212, 213, 214, 215, 216, 217, 218, 219, 220, 221, 222, 223, 225, 226, 227, 228, 230, 231, 232, 233, 234, 235, 237, 238, 239, 241, 242, 243, 244, 245, 246, 248, 249, 250, 251, 252, 254, 255, 256, 257, 258, 259, 262, 263, 264, 267, 268, 269, 278, 295, 296, 297, 298, 299, 300, 301, 302, 303, 304, 307, 309, 311, 312, 314, 315, 316, 317, 319, 322, 323, 325, 326, 327, 328, 329, 330, 332, 333, 334, 335, 336, 338, 339, 340, 342, 343, 344, 345, 347, 349, 350, 352, 353, 354, 355, 361, 364, 366, 367, 369, 370, 373, 374, 377, 378, 380, 382, 384, 385, 386, 387, 388, 389, 390, 405, 414, 419, 434, 442, 447, 453, 454, 455, 456, 458, 465, 466, 469, 470, 471, 474, 475, 476, 478, 479, 489, 490, 491, 492, 501, 502, 504, 505, 507, 511, 513, 518, 520, 523, 527, 528, 529, 531, 533, 534, 536, 554, 555, 556, 557, 559, 560, 570, 576, 579, 590, 591, 607, 614, 615, 618, 620, 623, 625, 629, 635, 636, 637, 641, 645, 655, 658, 666, 667

deliverance. 12, 14, 39, 40, 46, 47, 58, 70, 100, 111, 115, 124, 126, 131, 133, 137, 138, 165, 166, 179, 183,

Index of Topics

201, 202, 203, 205, 209, 241, 242, 244, 252, 254, 264, 265, 267, 269, 325, 329, 330, 331, 332, 335, 338, 340, 343, 355, 356, 370, 371, 422, 442, 455, 458, 459, 467, 476, 478, 483, 525, 660

depravity 60, 64, 65, 66, 68, 69, 73, 109, 272, 290, 294

descend/decent 151, 217, 297, 451, 463, 466, 467, 468, 470, 471

descendant .. 10, 11, 13, 16, 35, 39, 40, 41, 42, 44, 45, 47, 77, 118, 281, 338, 383, 386, 400, 405, 409, 469, 476, 493, 496, 626

diatribe 72, 87, 97, 100

discipline/disciplined .. 7, 74, 259, 261, 295, 325, 328, 511, 512, 513, 547, 555, 561, 572, 579, 592, 609

disobedience ... 56, 58, 64, 80, 97, 111, 150, 202, 212, 214, 216, 219, 222, 238, 240, 242, 273, 283, 284, 295, 306, 314, 316, 328, 356, 365, 378, 398, 419, 427, 436, 437, 442, 446, 472, 494, 521, 522, 526, 534, 591

divorce ... 192, 286, 315, 322, 382, 575

domain .. 138, 146, 150, 169, 175, 197, 258, 274, 275, 335, 356, 398

doulos 36, 37, 167, 263, 264, 265, 288, 318

dualism .. 248, 281, 283, 295, 321, 658

ebed 36

ecclesiology 172, 197

elected .. 104, 164, 252, 376, 403, 412, 416, 428, 431, 432, 437, 441, 482

election. 152, 264, 376, 386, 393, 394, 397, 398, 411, 413, 414, 415, 416, 417, 421, 422, 423, 424, 425, 426, 427, 428, 430, 431, 432, 433, 436, 437, 442, 444, 447, 450, 479, 494, 520, 521, 668

epistemological 244

eschatology/eschatological .. 2, 12, 15, 18, 23, 45, 46, 55, 59, 77, 78, 101, 117, 118, 121, 122, 123, 124, 125, 127, 134, 138, 168, 187, 202, 205, 223, 234, 235, 236, 237, 252, 254, 301, 336, 337, 340, 343, 344, 347, 348, 350, 358, 364, 368, 370, 374, 377, 401, 415, 424, 430, 437, 443, 453, 466, 469, 495, 504, 505, 514, 517, 518, 528, 591, 614, 652, 666

Eucharist/Eucharistic ... 122, 125, 275, 380, 615, 684

evangelism/evangelize 3, 4, 23, 53, 54, 57, 91, 412, 542, 615, 617, 619, 664

excommunication 401

excursus 297, 298

exegetical .... viii, 8, 72, 149, 241, 415, 647, 649, 650, 658

exile/exiles/exilic ... 10, 11, 18, 39, 40, 43, 46, 47, 49, 55, 56, 58, 59, 61, 66, 70, 74, 76, 92, 96, 97, 100, 101, 102, 107, 108, 109, 111, 113, 114, 120, 124, 126, 131, 132, 133, 134, 136, 137, 139, 147, 179, 193, 194, 196, 198, 202, 203, 205, 206, 208, 219, 222, 228, 243, 264, 268, 303, 336, 357, 370, 371, 377, 379, 382, 384, 385, 386, 389, 395, 398, 404, 435, 437, 440, 443, 445, 446, 449, 452, 453, 455, 456, 459, 460, 463, 471, 472, 476, 477, 478, 479, 482, 484, 495, 504, 513, 517, 519, 520, 524, 525, 539, 666 exodus..... ix, 8, 10, 47, 125, 127, 139, 140, 168, 192, 198, 205, 226, 227, 228, 229, 230, 232, 233, 234, 235, 241, 246, 247, 254, 259, 269, 278, 329, 330, 331, 332, 335, 337, 347, 356, 364, 366, 378, 396, 399, 434, 442, 453, 463, 483, 484, 487, 495, 511, 517, 519, 528, 581, 611, 667

extra-biblical................ 417, 488, 491

firstborn 8, 43, 45, 123, 124, 125, 126, 127, 128, 129, 130, 133, 163, 168, 188, 202, 211, 269, 288, 331, 334, 336, 337, 342, 355, 361, 364, 365, 366, 367, 375, 377, 378, 380, 409, 411, 413, 416, 423, 424, 425, 431, 432, 434, 436, 476, 490, 505, 526, 528, 529, 534, 614, 615, 633, 668

firstfruit/firstfruits 334, 347, 353, 360, 367, 368, 369, 434, 493, 495, 505, 557, 633

flesh iii, 11, 27, 28, 30, 40, 41, 88, 96, 112, 151, 198, 208, 252, 260, 270, 271, 273, 274, 275, 276, 277, 278, 279, 280, 281, 282, 283, 286, 288, 291, 294, 295, 296, 297, 310, 321, 326, 335, 338, 339, 342, 344, 346, 348, 353, 355, 390, 398, 406, 410, 430, 489, 490, 503, 534, 535, 553, 581, 606, 615

foreknew....... 244, 334, 361, 375, 493, 497, 526

foreknowledge 136, 299, 374, 375, 376, 397

forensic .. vii, 112, 114, 138, 145, 148, 170, 184, 286, 458

forgiven 80, 82, 84, 141, 148, 149, 150, 190, 197, 198, 337, 359, 456, 519

forgiveness. 58, 82, 84, 109, 114, 115, 149, 150, 175, 177, 178, 181, 183, 189, 195, 209, 223, 291, 336, 397, 458, 490, 512, 513, 519, 530, 548, 561, 578, 617

fullness..... 59, 94, 208, 209, 257, 307, 348, 354, 368, 369, 458, 489, 490, 493, 501, 502, 526, 546

Gamaliel................ 234, 246, 287, 651

glorification................... 374, 386, 463

gracious 150, 199, 219, 224, 425, 526, 598, 610

grafted.... 27, 402, 403, 436, 493, 494, 495, 506, 507, 508, 509, 510, 513, 526, 669

grafting................. 495, 506, 509, 510

Greco-Roman 2, 3, 288, 402, 403, 574, 677, 693

Greek . 1, 2, 3, 4, 5, 6, 7, 8, 14, 29, 33, 36, 37, 51, 56, 76, 79, 86, 91, 104, 106, 111, 112, 126, 135, 138, 150, 203, 208, 213, 223, 229, 232, 234, 236, 248, 253, 263, 267, 270, 271, 274, 276, 277, 278, 282, 288, 289, 295, 320, 321, 341, 344, 345, 350, 352, 354, 374, 381, 406, 407, 454, 459, 474, 481, 497, 503, 515, 516, 544, 545, 579, 592, 598, 608, 614, 633, 634, 649, 658, 662, 663, 664, 674, 682, 684, 690, 691, 697

guilty 69, 78, 101, 119, 146, 150, 165, 169, 170, 259, 272, 306, 346, 384, 502, 525, 577, 580

harden 85, 393, 431, 433, 436

hardening 75, 156, 398, 415, 420, 422, 423, 425, 426, 427, 431, 433, 434, 437, 439, 441, 494, 500, 514, 668, 669

harlot............. 110, 191, 273, 302, 443

Index of Topics

headship ... 29, 91, 146, 202, 213, 217, 218, 222, 229, 291, 297, 339, 344, 478

heart 15, 27, 28, 34, 43, 51, 52, 53, 65, 66, 67, 69, 71, 72, 73, 75, 81, 83, 86, 87, 88, 90, 93, 95, 96, 100, 101, 102, 105, 112, 113, 119, 145, 150, 153, 157, 160, 165, 166, 174, 179, 180, 182, 183, 185, 188, 192, 196, 198, 206, 208, 210, 221, 222, 237, 244, 258, 259, 266, 268, 270, 271, 275, 279, 290, 291, 292, 293, 294, 297, 300, 302, 313, 315, 316, 318, 319, 323, 324, 326, 331, 341, 350, 361, 375, 387, 393, 395, 398, 400, 401, 413, 420, 422, 423, 425, 427, 431, 433, 434, 435, 437, 439, 440, 442, 451, 452, 453, 454, 457, 459, 463, 468, 473, 474, 475, 476, 477, 491, 499, 500, 503, 508, 519, 523, 525, 533, 536, 542, 548, 550, 563, 574, 575, 580, 595, 597, 600, 603, 605, 607, 608, 624, 641, 661, 665, 668, 670

heaven 59, 60, 61, 77, 78, 126, 202, 206, 210, 225, 243, 257, 275, 295, 345, 346, 347, 348, 350, 365, 366, 369, 386, 451, 452, 457, 459, 460, 462, 463, 464, 468, 469, 470, 474, 488, 489, 490, 492, 550, 555, 557, 577, 590

Heaven 691

hell 61, 512, 548

Hellenism 5, 6, 7, 34, 86, 270, 274, 282, 283, 287, 295, 296, 566, 615, 647, 649, 651, 652, 653, 656, 658, 662, 663, 664

Hellenistic 2, 3, 5, 6, 7, 15, 33, 36, 44, 86, 119, 167, 184, 279, 281, 282, 283, 287, 288, 289, 297, 298, 319, 320, 321, 324, 368, 447, 651, 652, 653, 658, 661, 662, 665, 673, 674, 689

Hellenization 2, 4, 5, 663, 664

heresy 53

hermeneutic 19, 33, 95, 245, 433, 649, 657

holy/holiness......35, 46, 57, 60, 61, 82, 100, 111, 118, 131, 136, 203, 204, 212, 231, 243, 248, 258, 259, 261, 266, 267, 268, 269, 270, 280, 290, 298, 304, 311, 315, 316, 318, 324, 326, 328, 329, 338, 352, 385, 390, 427, 435, 447, 452, 489, 490, 493, 505, 506, 527, 528, 529, 530, 531, 532, 535, 549, 581, 584, 586, 588, 595, 615, 627, 638, 644, 669, 670

human body 40, 248, 260, 275, 288, 310, 539

humanity/humankind ... vii, 18, 35, 38, 54, 55, 56, 60, 63, 64, 65, 66, 68, 69, 70, 72, 83, 102, 109, 111, 112, 133, 136, 191, 194, 202, 214, 217, 218, 222, 230, 240, 241, 247, 248, 249, 251, 252, 254, 260, 262, 263, 267, 269, 280, 283, 286, 294, 298, 304, 306, 307, 309, 310, 312, 314, 315, 316, 318, 319, 320, 321, 322, 325, 326, 328, 331, 343, 350, 353, 378, 424, 475, 476, 502, 525, 533, 534, 563, 576, 578, 581, 590, 591, 605, 606, 610, 665, 667

husband... 10, 160, 187, 193, 206, 215, 239, 241, 243, 251, 252, 255, 256, 261, 273, 279, 283, 284, 285, 286, 298, 301, 302, 303, 304, 307, 314, 319, 322, 327, 328, 329, 340, 341, 353, 457, 482, 510, 538, 559, 590, 632, 641, 667

hymns .. 40, 45, 64, 222, 586, 603, 610

idolatry..... 61, 66, 103, 215, 244, 277, 286, 352, 414, 555, 587

idols 21, 66, 72, 90, 191, 265, 285, 587, 589, 595, 605, 609, 639

immortality 71, 75, 368, 387, 525

imputation.... 169, 170, 171, 173, 175, 183, 184, 185, 197

incense 116, 506, 510

incest............................ 259, 546, 554

inclusion 16, 27, 95, 112, 157, 226, 244, 245, 407, 443, 502, 506, 507, 514, 570

individual... vii, 24, 25, 36, 65, 69, 75, 84, 96, 97, 108, 146, 147, 170, 173, 182, 188, 190, 194, 198, 202, 208, 212, 217, 227, 228, 233, 237, 239, 241, 244, 245, 246, 247, 252, 253, 255, 259, 260, 261, 267, 273, 280, 295, 297, 299, 301, 302, 306, 307, 308, 309, 310, 312, 317, 320, 324, 325, 326, 327, 341, 344, 345, 347, 348, 349, 350, 351, 354, 357, 359, 360, 368, 371, 374, 376, 397, 403, 413, 414, 415, 416, 417, 420, 421, 422, 424, 428, 430, 435, 436, 445, 447, 450, 481, 511, 520, 521, 531, 535, 536, 539, 540, 551, 579, 593, 606, 614, 667

individualism ... 24, 25, 350, 351, 357, 665

individualistic .. 25, 97, 208, 212, 215, 226, 228, 234, 248, 260, 261, 278, 299, 306, 317, 322, 323, 325, 354, 414, 415, 419, 430, 445, 531, 539, 665

individualize 327, 348

individually... 224, 228, 302, 354, 416

indwelling 208, 282, 283, 317, 348, 349, 350, 354, 370, 372

inherit 62, 77, 118, 154, 194, 231, 413, 556, 579

inheritance.. 2, 77, 102, 108, 114, 137, 147, 154, 194, 195, 196, 202, 207, 219, 243, 269, 273, 336, 340, 344, 347, 351, 356, 358, 361, 363, 364, 366, 370, 374, 377, 382, 389, 390, 391, 396, 411, 413, 416, 417, 440, 446, 456, 459, 479, 490, 496, 507, 513, 520, 557, 578, 593, 613, 615, 623, 644, 668

inherited ... 16, 50, 154, 213, 320, 321, 540

inheritors 54, 416, 621

initiation..... 6, 20, 25, 26, 28, 50, 152, 153, 331, 398, 644

Jewish-Hellenistic 684

Judaizers .. 20, 22, 155, 171, 181, 183, 199, 497, 619, 639

judgment 15, 43, 57, 58, 61, 65, 68, 71, 73, 74, 75, 78, 79, 80, 81, 82, 86, 87, 92, 97, 100, 101, 105, 106, 113, 114, 122, 123, 130, 135, 136, 137, 139, 144, 150, 153, 156, 160, 168, 191, 192, 193, 199, 212, 213, 218, 219, 228, 229, 241, 244, 250, 254, 264, 271, 288, 296, 331, 337, 338, 355, 356, 382, 386, 389, 397, 398, 401, 412, 414, 415, 416, 417, 420, 421, 422, 423, 424, 426, 429, 431, 434, 435, 437, 438, 439, 441, 442, 445, 446, 447, 449, 450, 455, 459, 498, 500, 509, 511, 512, 513, 522, 525, 527, 529, 536, 537, 551, 555, 563, 565, 567, 569, 570, 571, 572, 578, 583, 584, 585, 591, 592, 593, 594, 610, 614, 626, 640, 644, 668, 670

Index of Topics

justice . 2, 58, 61, 81, 87, 88, 101, 102, 113, 129, 130, 136, 196, 267, 329, 345, 397, 399, 402, 439, 441, 561, 570, 571, 575, 577, 579, 609

justification ..... vii, 16, 28, 72, 84, 100, 109, 112, 114, 116, 124, 132, 134, 140, 142, 143, 144, 145, 146, 148, 154, 164, 166, 167, 168, 169, 170, 171, 172, 173, 174, 175, 176, 177, 179, 181, 182, 183, 184, 185, 186, 187, 188, 190, 193, 194, 195, 196, 197, 198, 199, 202, 203, 206, 212, 219, 221, 225, 253, 254, 257, 263, 268, 286, 337, 374, 379, 384, 386, 388, 398, 422, 436, 475, 614, 666

kerygma 652

kingdom 10, 13, 15, 17, 21, 27, 43, 52, 56, 59, 61, 65, 69, 76, 77, 78, 80, 92, 94, 95, 96, 105, 111, 124, 126, 132, 133, 140, 147, 150, 157, 166, 168, 179, 203, 206, 209, 214, 219, 221, 226, 231, 234, 238, 240, 244, 245, 250, 257, 258, 261, 262, 265, 267, 269, 277, 278, 279, 289, 290, 291, 295, 296, 320, 325, 326, 338, 341, 355, 359, 362, 363, 366, 376, 377, 378, 382, 385, 435, 436, 443, 448, 454, 460, 477, 480, 490, 498, 499, 520, 533, 559, 568, 579, 583, 591, 596, 597, 599, 601, 644, 645, 670

kingship 13, 15, 149, 362

kinsman 303, 634, 636, 641

kinsmen 87, 88, 97, 132, 398, 399, 401, 430, 450, 452, 453, 482, 498, 500, 501, 502, 514, 629, 633

lamb 122, 125, 126, 133, 135, 136, 211, 260, 269, 337, 340, 342, 364, 434, 527, 529, 614, 615, 633

lawbreaker 72, 94

law-court 288

law-righteousness 490

leaven 261

legalism/legalistic 156, 171, 277, 285, 286, 305, 473, 594, 690

legalistic 156, 277, 285, 286, 473

levirate 243, 355

liberated 334, 353, 357, 360, 365, 502, 595

liberation 125, 225, 263, 264, 339, 364, 365

liturgical .86, 125, 134, 227, 324, 358, 471, 660

LXX 17, 33, 36, 38, 55, 113, 115, 119, 124, 129, 145, 148, 149, 270, 274, 280, 288, 342, 379, 406, 463, 465, 470, 471, 472, 477, 516, 565, 598, 606, 609, 614, 617, 643, 662

Maccabees 11, 31, 116

mankind 25, 57, 62, 111, 123, 210, 213, 215, 218, 219, 223, 230, 252, 270, 271, 278, 286, 306, 322, 504, 580

marriage .... iii, xv, 11, 16, 34, 57, 67, 97, 114, 115, 127, 140, 161, 181, 186, 187, 188, 191, 192, 206, 221, 224, 236, 239, 241, 243, 252, 255, 276, 284, 285, 298, 299, 300, 301, 302, 306, 309, 311, 313, 314, 318, 319, 322, 325, 327, 328, 331, 332, 340, 341, 342, 355, 359, 368, 376, 381, 382, 386, 390, 391, 482, 526, 538, 553, 575, 580, 593, 615, 634, 660, 661, 667

martyr 116

martyrdom 116, 562

matrimonial 615

matrimony 381

meat .. 21, 22, 280, 416, 583, 584, 587, 588, 589, 594, 595, 596, 598, 599, 639

Melchizedek 176, 177, 206, 207, 383, 487, 491

member/members ... iii, 22, 24, 27, 28, 31, 32, 33, 37, 43, 44, 57, 76, 92, 101, 143, 147, 157, 171, 181, 186, 187, 188, 198, 208, 213, 217, 224, 225, 233, 235, 237, 243, 252, 259, 260, 261, 264, 278, 291, 299, 307, 310, 311, 323, 324, 325, 338, 344, 353, 354, 355, 356, 368, 370, 374, 377, 385, 395, 407, 445, 468, 473, 478, 480, 488, 491, 500, 511, 515, 527, 536, 538, 539, 540, 543, 544, 559, 564, 574, 576, 588, 593, 595, 596, 606, 613, 620, 623, 628, 633, 634, 636, 638, 645, 655, 665, 666, 668, 669

membership 15, 24, 28, 29, 80, 85, 97, 171, 172, 181, 187, 188, 197, 213, 237, 395, 397, 409, 430, 497, 590, 615, 635, 657, 666

mercy 42, 50, 58, 94, 114, 116, 127, 147, 149, 151, 154, 183, 193, 219, 231, 291, 326, 336, 375, 393, 394, 397, 422, 423, 425, 426, 428, 429, 431, 434, 435, 436, 437, 438, 439, 442, 443, 446, 453, 459, 471, 476, 477, 494, 496, 499, 502, 521, 522, 527, 528, 530,531, 532, 534, 544, 547, 548, 565, 577, 586, 603, 610, 661, 670

methodological 421, 461

methodology 7, 227, 348, 368, 421, 658

mindset 7, 23, 31, 32, 33, 97, 117, 143, 184, 215, 241, 268, 288, 315, 320, 321, 341, 352, 398, 448, 514, 563, 592, 650, 652

mission. 4, 19, 23, 27, 36, 50, 92, 106, 155, 202, 381, 391, 420, 536, 576, 597, 618, 619, 622, 626, 629, 630, 635, 637

monotheism 9, 21, 139, 315

mystery 188, 226, 328, 494, 514, 628, 644, 645, 671

mystic/mystical/mysticism ... 276, 367, 464, 581, 590, 615, 657

new covenant ... xv, 11, 15, 27, 29, 37, 49, 58, 96, 118, 140, 142, 153, 155, 166, 181, 185, 186, 187, 196, 197, 198, 202, 206, 224, 225, 243, 269, 270, 271, 294, 296, 307, 311, 331, 345, 347, 350, 356, 377, 385, 386, 397, 398, 409, 443, 457, 468, 469, 473, 478, 482, 487,488, 491, 495, 502, 506, 507, 509, 513, 514, 515, 518, 519, 521, 538, 541, 608, 615, 626, 633, 638, 666

New Creation 202, 325

New Exodus ... vii, viii, xii, xv, 12, 13, 15, 16, 18, 19, 28, 34, 41, 43, 45, 49, 55, 58, 66, 97, 102, 113, 114, 116, 124, 126, 140, 163, 168, 180, 185, 187, 194, 197, 198, 202, 206, 207, 227, 228, 239, 241, 264, 267, 268, 276, 301, 328, 331, 340, 342, 343, 351, 355, 357, 370, 377, 391, 395, 396, 398, 417, 450, 460, 463, 466, 468, 469, 483, 484, 485, 486, 488, 495, 499, 519, 524, 529, 538, 578, 582, 601, 615, 626, 667, 668, 669, 670, 674, 677, 688, 691, 692, 693, 695

Index of Topics

new man . 23, 197, 205, 248, 337, 339, 352, 376, 378, 396, 489, 597, 645

New Perspective... viii, 143, 166, 169, 170, 171, 172, 175, 188, 189, 190, 196, 197, 307, 412, 448, 675, 679, 693, 699

newborn 431

nomism 191, 313, 458

non-believing 364

non-canonical 492

old man 210, 247, 248, 252, 297

pagan/pagans .. 22, 68, 91, 92, 95, 144, 226, 290, 320, 415, 425, 426, 433, 479, 498, 536, 569, 579, 587, 589, 599, 609, 630

paidagogos 448

Paschal xii, 27, 96, 118, 119, 121, 122, 123, 124, 125, 126, 127, 131, 136, 180, 185, 187, 188, 196, 197, 202, 211, 229, 254, 257, 258, 259, 276, 298, 332, 342, 366, 378, 417, 488, 505, 518, 527, 529, 633, 667, 677, 692, 695

Passover xi, 9, 19, 28, 43, 45, 96, 113, 115, 117, 118, 119, 121, 122, 123, 124, 125, 126, 127, 128, 129, 130, 133, 134, 135, 136, 151, 163, 168, 186, 187, 188, 198, 203, 204, 205, 211, 223, 227, 229, 242, 246, 260, 264, 275, 288, 300, 307, 327, 331, 332, 335, 336, 337, 338, 340, 342, 354, 380, 434, 457, 482, 505, 519, 528, 529, 579, 614, 615, 633, 637, 655, 660, 666, 678, 684, 687, 690

patriarchal 142

patristic/patristics 321, 465

Pentecost 228, 235, 348, 408, 466, 476, 489, 498, 543, 620, 655, 656, 658, 686

persecution 8, 109, 155, 334, 357, 361, 373, 383, 384, 385, 387, 553, 557, 558, 560, 641, 656, 661, 699

Pharaoh 8, 75, 107, 160, 239, 260, 265, 266, 268, 269, 302, 331, 332, 337, 339, 356, 393, 397, 398, 416, 417, 420, 422, 423, 424, 425, 426, 427, 429, 431, 432, 433, 434, 435, 436, 437, 438, 439, 440, 450, 453, 485, 499, 641, 668

Phinehas 195, 196, 198, 555

pilgrim 27, 126, 201, 202, 207, 229, 238, 344, 345, 363, 377, 379, 380, 383, 385, 396, 445, 460, 472, 479, 539, 656, 667

pilgrimage 11, 15, 27, 76, 168, 197, 201, 202, 204, 205, 207, 208, 209, 210, 223, 224, 264, 269, 327, 331, 332, 336, 337, 345, 347, 348, 351, 356, 357, 362, 363, 364, 370, 377, 380, 381, 382, 384, 387, 389, 390, 396, 452, 460, 472, 473, 477, 478, 483, 499, 517, 518, 539, 540, 578, 579, 594, 659, 668

potter 394, 397, 417, 418, 419, 420, 421, 432, 433, 435, 439, 441

prayer 86, 108, 118, 192, 329, 358, 359, 373, 411, 415, 451, 453, 454, 500, 543, 549, 550, 556, 558, 605, 607, 612, 623, 660

pre-Christian 3, 304, 312, 316

predestination 374, 411, 417

predestined ... 334, 361, 375, 378, 427, 507, 526

priest/priests 14, 41, 92, 115, 118, 128, 195, 206, 207, 210, 211, 257, 261, 265, 271, 330, 353, 362, 372, 382, 408, 487, 488, 492, 526, 528, 529, 530, 531, 549, 555, 566, 568, 572, 605, 614, 615, 622, 633

priesthood 195, 383, 457, 487, 488, 491, 528, 529, 532, 615, 633, 659

priest-king 488

priestly .. 27, 39, 51, 52, 128, 176, 206, 207, 382, 457, 487, 528, 529, 531, 532, 542, 566, 568, 586, 603, 605, 614, 615, 626, 633, 669, 670

prophecy/prophecies 12, 16, 17, 18, 20, 39, 59, 113, 118, 208, 250, 351, 382, 439, 444, 475, 476, 481, 504, 518, 519, 540, 541, 611, 624

prophet/prophets .... viii, ix, 4, 5, 7, 10, 12, 13, 14, 16, 17, 18, 19, 24, 28, 29, 32, 35, 36, 38, 39, 40, 41, 42, 43, 49, 54, 55, 56, 57, 58, 59, 63, 70, 73, 81, 87, 92, 95, 96, 104, 108, 109, 110, 113, 114, 116, 117, 118, 120, 131, 134, 137, 138, 139, 140, 147, 157, 173, 179, 182, 184, 187, 189, 193, 196, 219, 231, 239, 261, 264, 270, 271, 284, 328, 331, 335, 343, 345, 350, 366, 369, 370, 382, 383, 390, 398, 404, 405, 407, 410, 443, 444, 445, 446, 450, 452, 453, 455, 456, 464, 466, 467, 472, 475, 476, 477, 478, 482, 483, 484, 493, 496, 497, 507, 519, 522, 524, 526, 528, 541, 542, 546, 548, 574, 593, 604, 641, 660, 664, 668

propitiation .. 115, 130, 135, 140, 211, 242, 258, 286

propitiatory .. 117, 129, 130, 135, 139, 185, 331, 342, 505, 555

prostitute/prostitutes 231, 283, 553

prostitution 214

reconcile/reconciled . 39, 76, 126, 185, 191, 199, 201, 211, 425, 490, 520, 522, 623, 644

reconciliation . 23, 126, 174, 183, 184, 191, 195, 196, 201, 202, 211, 212, 490, 493, 503, 561, 608, 609, 617

redeem 43, 44, 45, 119, 184, 219, 303, 377, 385, 386, 407, 524, 559

redeemed 27, 41, 92, 93, 127, 128, 132, 133, 146, 169, 179, 181, 187, 188, 204, 205, 224, 238, 239, 246, 250, 252, 262, 264, 269, 290, 299, 300, 307, 309, 318, 327, 329, 337, 344, 355, 357, 359, 364, 366, 378, 381, 386, 403, 408, 448, 453, 458, 477, 478, 517, 526,529, 530, 532, 533, 534, 566, 614, 615, 623, 645, 668

redeemer 303, 328, 337, 355, 377, 425, 432, 526, 530, 668

redeeming 43, 46, 114, 127, 198, 206, 211, 319, 447, 490, 518, 524, 622

redemption . 3, 21, 43, 45, 82, 96, 102, 113, 116, 117, 118, 119, 120, 122, 124, 125, 126, 127, 130, 132, 133, 134, 138, 139, 140, 168, 175, 185, 187, 202, 205, 207, 211, 216, 218, 221, 224, 228, 238, 239, 256, 265, 266, 282, 289, 291, 300, 302, 326, 327, 334, 336, 337, 339, 340, 353, 360, 363, 365, 366, 367, 368, 369, 377, 378, 381, 385, 390, 408, 427, 438, 442, 453, 456, 466, 490, 491, 525, 529, 557, 559, 581, 615, 645, 668

redemptive 21, 102, 119, 203, 227, 228, 247, 250, 336, 338, 378, 412, 428, 442, 447, 450, 504, 505, 507, 508, 529, 669

Index of Topics

redemptive-historical.............247, 338

Reformation 84, 169, 170, 172

reformed....................................... 432

regeneration............226, 227, 237, 350

relations/relationship ....xv, 20, 23, 25, 37, 49, 50, 55, 59, 60, 64, 67, 68, 69, 71, 74, 79, 80, 82, 87, 88, 95, 101, 104, 112, 114, 118, 133, 135, 144, 147, 148, 150, 152, 154, 155, 169, 172, 176, 179, 181, 185, 186, 192, 194, 195, 196, 197, 198, 211, 213, 214, 216, 218, 219, 220, 221, 224, 229, 235, 236, 238, 240, 241, 242, 243, 244, 248, 249, 251, 252, 253, 255, 256, 258, 259, 260, 264, 270, 272, 276, 277, 278, 279, 283, 284, 285, 286, 289, 296, 299, 300, 301, 302, 304, 305, 306, 307, 308, 309, 310, 311, 312, 313, 314, 315, 316, 318, 321, 322, 323, 325, 327, 328, 329, 335, 337, 339, 341, 342, 343, 355, 359, 362, 375, 376, 381, 382, 383, 386, 388, 396, 402, 404, 432, 448, 450, 453, 456, 475, 476, 480, 481, 490, 496, 497, 499, 502, 513, 522, 524, 525, 546, 580, 588, 591, 594, 606, 609, 629, 633, 641, 661, 667, 670

remnant ....xv, 17, 117, 196, 375, 377, 384, 385, 394, 396, 398, 403, 405, 407, 410, 430, 440, 444, 445, 446, 453, 472, 477, 486, 493, 495, 497, 498, 499, 503, 504, 516, 517, 526, 578, 593, 621, 669

repentance 26, 68, 71, 74, 183, 194, 227, 244, 261, 305, 332, 356, 413, 427, 431, 438, 439, 459, 481, 498, 512, 521, 522, 561

representative ...30, 31, 41, 43, 47, 65, 72, 83, 87, 88, 90, 101, 108, 132, 133, 186, 202, 213, 216, 217, 218, 222, 223, 229, 230, 235, 237, 241, 248, 250, 252, 255, 258, 269, 282, 299, 301, 302, 303, 307, 308, 314, 324, 328, 339, 340, 343, 364, 397, 398, 430, 437, 476, 479, 516, 611, 623, 631, 633, 666, 667

resurrected............ 351, 353, 504, 514

resurrection.16, 35, 41, 42, 43, 44, 45, 46, 47, 49, 50, 55, 56, 58, 76, 104, 112, 118, 120, 121, 136, 152, 155, 167, 168, 169, 203, 205, 210, 218, 228, 234, 238, 243, 245, 246, 247, 256, 336, 351, 354, 368, 369, 370, 386, 387, 405, 414, 452, 455, 462, 463, 464, 465, 466, 468, 469, 488, 489, 491, 492, 504, 505, 511, 518, 546, 590, 607, 645, 655, 658, 660

righteous.....43, 55, 58, 60, 68, 71, 73, 75, 82, 83, 84, 85, 87, 94, 99, 100, 105, 107, 108, 112, 113, 114, 121, 146, 151, 152, 156, 165, 171, 173, 184, 192, 193, 196, 197, 198, 199, 201, 210, 212, 218, 220, 221, 222, 278, 279, 280, 292, 294, 311, 316, 330, 333, 335, 338, 343, 346, 350, 379, 385, 447, 449, 480, 536, 592, 610

righteousness 27, 28, 39, 55, 58, 59, 70, 73, 74, 75, 78, 88, 95, 99, 100, 101, 102, 105, 111, 112, 113, 114, 115, 124, 130, 131, 141, 142, 143, 145, 146, 147, 148, 151, 152, 153, 154, 156, 161, 163, 164, 165, 166, 167, 168, 169, 172, 173, 174, 175, 176, 177, 178, 179,180, 181, 182, 183, 184, 190, 191, 193, 195, 196, 198, 212, 219, 220, 221, 223, 240, 242, 248, 257, 259, 261, 263, 265, 266, 267, 277, 286, 288, 301, 329, 330, 333, 335, 336, 337, 349, 365, 382, 386, 394, 398, 402, 404, 413,

419, 427, 435, 440, 447, 448, 451,
452, 455, 456, 457, 458, 459, 468,
475, 492, 506, 508, 526, 529, 543,
550, 584, 594, 596, 601, 612, 665,
666, 667

sacramental/sacramentalism . 276, 615

sacrifice ... 2, 27, 44, 46, 96, 102, 113,
115, 116, 118, 119, 120, 121, 122,
125, 126, 127, 133, 134, 135, 142,
143, 161, 162, 163, 164, 165, 167,
180, 185, 197, 203, 204, 206, 207,
210, 219, 223, 228, 242, 246, 256,
257, 260, 281, 286, 331, 335, 337,
338, 342, 366, 380, 382, 422, 444,
474, 479, 505, 527, 529, 531, 532,
538, 548, 549, 558, 594, 614, 633,
659, 666, 670

sacrifices 22, 116, 117, 118, 119, 120,
123, 124, 129, 130, 134, 163, 168,
223, 280, 286, 335, 337, 343, 382,
440, 457, 527, 528, 530, 531, 532,
591

sacrificial . 38, 82, 115, 118, 123, 131,
133, 150, 163, 202, 211, 223, 256,
263, 264, 501, 531, 615

sacrificially 641

salvation 11, 12, 17, 18, 21, 25, 28,
35, 37, 38, 39, 42, 45, 50, 51, 52,
54, 55, 56, 57, 59, 63, 70, 76, 79,
80, 83, 84, 90, 93, 94, 96, 97, 100,
102, 103, 108, 112, 121, 125, 131,
132, 134, 135, 137, 138, 139, 145,
147, 152, 153, 155, 157, 160, 165,
166, 167, 169, 170, 171, 173, 174,
180, 183, 184, 191, 194, 196, 198,
202, 209, 210, 215, 218, 221, 224,
225, 230, 233, 248, 253, 273, 279,
296, 298, 299, 307, 317, 327, 328,
329, 330, 332, 335, 337, 339, 345,
351, 353, 354, 367, 371, 375, 376,
377, 378, 380, 381, 382, 383, 387,

395, 397, 398, 401, 402, 406, 407,
412, 413, 414, 415, 416, 417, 419,
420, 421, 423, 424, 425, 427, 428,
430, 432, 433, 436, 437, 438, 439,
443, 444, 447, 448, 449, 452, 453,
455, 456, 458, 459, 460, 467, 476,
477, 479, 481, 485, 490, 493, 495,
496, 500, 501, 502, 504, 507, 511,
513, 514, 516, 517, 518, 523, 525,
526, 528, 529, 530, 566, 567, 577,
578, 582, 591, 593, 610, 613, 622,
657, 667, 668, 669

sanctification.. 16, 267, 316, 376, 563,
614

sanctified...... 124, 231, 252, 376, 532,
586, 603, 614

sanctify..614

sarx.... iii, 30, 112, 260, 270, 274, 296,
309, 310, 321, 338, 341, 343, 344,
346, 355, 490, 534, 581

Satan 22, 56, 61, 64, 66, 68, 69, 84,
90, 91, 107, 109, 111, 133, 138,
174, 203, 204, 205, 213, 214, 215,
216, 217, 220, 221, 222, 224, 235,
236, 239, 240, 241, 242, 243, 244,
245, 250, 251, 252, 254, 255, 256,
259, 262, 263, 264, 266, 267, 269,
278, 279, 284, 286, 288, 291, 296,
300, 301, 303, 306, 309, 310, 312,
313, 314, 315, 316, 318, 319, 320,
321, 322, 324, 325, 326, 327, 328,
332, 335, 338, 339, 340, 341, 342,
344, 346, 348, 353, 370, 381, 396,
475, 476, 479, 524, 525, 534, 535,
536, 554, 581, 591, 598, 601, 610,
617, 623, 628, 640, 641, 667, 668

savior 425, 440, 540

savior-redeemer 425

schoolmaster 139, 448

Index of Topics

seed 28, 40, 54, 62, 132, 144, 145, 163, 165, 174, 178, 179, 232, 362, 403, 405, 409, 410, 411, 416, 425, 426, 433, 434, 497, 503, 517, 520, 609, 665, 666

Septuagint 33, 208, 662

serpent 61, 101, 284, 640

servant/servants 26, 35, 36, 37, 38, 81, 95, 113, 124, 126, 152, 173, 191, 239, 241, 264, 265, 266, 267, 268, 288, 300, 307, 309, 319, 330, 345, 379, 387, 403, 419, 420, 425, 426, 428, 433, 446, 447, 450, 476, 485, 522, 527, 529, 535, 543, 548, 555, 559, 565, 567, 568, 569, 571, 572, 573, 583, 586, 588, 603, 606, 609, 610, 616, 617, 627, 630, 640, 661, 667, 670

servanthood 377, 596, 670

sin... 39, 40, 59, 60, 61, 64, 65, 66, 67, 68, 71, 82, 83, 87, 94, 99, 100, 101, 105, 106, 107, 109, 110, 111, 112, 117, 118, 122, 125, 126, 127, 129, 130, 131, 132, 133, 136, 138, 139, 140, 141, 145, 146, 148, 149, 150, 160, 169, 171, 172, 173, 174, 175, 176, 178, 180, 181, 182, 183, 184, 185, 189, 190, 191, 192, 193, 195, 196, 197, 198, 203, 204, 212, 213, 214, 215, 216, 217, 218, 219, 220, 221, 222, 223, 224, 225, 226, 227, 230, 237, 239, 240, 241, 242, 244, 247, 248, 249, 251, 252, 253, 254, 256, 257, 258, 259, 260, 262, 263, 264, 265, 266, 267, 268, 269, 270, 271, 272, 273, 278, 279, 280, 282, 283, 284, 285, 286, 287, 288, 289, 290, 291, 295, 296, 297, 298, 300, 301, 303, 304, 305, 306, 307, 310, 311, 312, 313, 314, 315, 316, 317, 318, 319, 320, 321, 322, 323, 324, 325, 326, 327, 328, 330, 331, 333, 335, 337, 338, 339, 341, 342, 346, 347, 349, 350, 353, 356, 378, 382, 388, 398, 401, 438, 446, 448, 449, 474, 478, 492, 497, 501, 502, 512, 522, 525, 526, 529, 531, 536, 538, 542, 544, 550, 551, 559, 565, 575, 577, 579, 584, 591, 592, 594, 600, 667

Sin ..xii, 40, 41, 60, 68, 79, 84, 90, 94, 111, 131, 133, 138, 139, 166, 189, 203, 205, 213, 214, 215, 216, 220, 221, 223, 235, 236, 239, 240, 241, 242, 243, 244, 247, 248, 249, 250, 252, 253, 256, 258, 259, 260, 262, 263, 264, 265, 266, 267, 268, 269, 278, 279, 283, 284, 286, 287, 295, 296, 299, 301, 302, 303, 305, 306, 307, 309, 310, 312, 313, 314, 315, 316, 317, 318, 319, 320, 321, 322, 325, 327, 328, 332, 335, 337, 338, 339, 340, 341, 342, 343, 344, 345, 346, 348, 353, 355, 356, 365, 367, 370, 376, 378, 379, 382, 398, 447, 452, 453, 473, 476, 482, 525, 531, 534, 581, 608, 612, 615, 667, 668, 675, 692

Sinai .. 57, 83, 128, 144, 151, 170, 187, 190, 192, 193, 204, 205, 211, 214, 216, 217, 223, 265, 272, 276, 302, 307, 327, 328, 331, 332, 359, 390, 455, 459, 460, 464, 483, 484, 492, 495

sin-bearer 222

sin-cursed 525

sinful 40, 41, 60, 66, 108, 111, 148, 150, 160, 187, 236, 248, 252, 254, 261, 269, 270, 271, 272, 274, 277, 278, 279, 281, 282, 283, 289, 290, 291, 293, 296, 297, 298, 309, 310, 311, 312, 317, 318, 321, 323, 326,

328, 333, 335, 338, 341, 342, 343, 344, 345, 346,355, 439, 490, 491, 567, 581, 587, 592, 598, 609

sinfulness 18, 63, 66, 83, 101, 102, 105, 106, 132, 165, 181, 272, 273, 291, 297, 298, 323, 326, 339, 345, 365, 429, 445, 498, 503

sinless 206, 220, 262, 328

sinned 80, 82, 102, 105, 113, 132, 183, 192, 212, 213, 215, 216, 238, 259, 306, 332, 342, 390, 434, 446, 502

sinner 62, 99, 106, 148, 188, 197, 210, 242, 253, 272, 295

sinning ... 80, 132, 237, 238, 261, 262, 356, 581

slave/slaves .. 3, 36, 37, 134, 178, 186, 206, 232, 233, 238, 247, 248, 253, 257, 263, 265, 266, 267, 268, 288, 293, 311, 312, 318, 319, 321, 323, 326, 333, 352, 357, 361, 367, 403, 570, 635, 636, 655, 667

slave-market 319

slavery ... 8, 12, 36, 74, 145, 174, 204, 205, 219, 225, 257, 266, 318, 319, 362, 378, 667

solidarity/solidarities 97, 109, 202, 218, 224, 225, 230, 241, 248, 249, 269, 278, 282, 298, 299, 306, 307, 310, 337, 339, 350, 352, 397, 480, 667

soma 530

sonship 19, 36, 45, 229, 236, 333, 336, 357, 361, 362, 363, 368, 370, 403

Spirit 10, 11, 14, 15, 16, 27, 29, 35, 42, 43, 45, 46, 59, 72, 85, 94, 95, 104, 118, 119, 125, 153, 156, 181, 182, 190, 194, 201, 202, 205, 208,

224, 225, 226, 227, 228, 229, 231, 232, 233, 234, 235, 237, 238, 244, 245, 252, 269, 271, 277, 278, 296, 298, 299, 304, 305, 307, 310, 311, 317, 323, 326, 330, 332, 333, 334, 335, 336, 339, 340, 343, 344, 346, 347, 348, 349, 350, 351, 353, 354, 355, 356, 357, 358, 359, 360, 361, 362, 367, 368, 370, 371, 372, 375, 376, 380, 386, 390, 393, 399, 400, 401, 402, 405, 410, 448, 452, 463, 465, 466, 467, 468, 469, 476, 481, 488, 489, 491, 492, 507, 524, 529, 531, 532, 533, 536, 540, 541, 544, 551, 552, 553, 554, 557, 563, 584, 586, 590, 596, 597, 601, 603, 604, 606, 607, 612, 613, 614, 615, 616, 623, 631, 635, 668, 669, 670, 679, 681, 687, 689, 697, 699

Spirit-indwelling 349

Spirit-indwelt 208

stone 17, 27, 33, 56, 190, 250, 270, 329, 363, 394, 449, 459, 486, 617

story ... 13, 64, 73, 116, 125, 144, 145, 149, 161, 166, 167, 180, 186, 189, 192, 202, 215, 243, 284, 287, 308, 309, 312, 315, 328, 357, 364, 365, 385, 399, 425, 433, 435, 441, 463, 491, 499, 526, 555

storyline 193

stumbling block 256, 486, 493, 500, 583, 594

stumbling stone 394, 448

sub-narratives 472

substituted 67, 90, 128, 129, 168, 211, 381, 468, 529

substitutionary 128, 342

suffering/sufferings 41, 52, 79, 92, 107, 131, 133, 152, 159, 173, 196,

201, 202, 206, 207, 222, 226, 227, 235, 237, 247, 281, 330, 334, 358, 360, 361, 362, 363, 365, 366, 367, 371, 373, 375, 379, 383, 384, 385, 387, 388, 391, 400, 444, 453, 478, 514, 525, 541, 557, 561, 562,571, 572, 580, 606, 616, 617, 619, 621, 632, 646

temple..... 9, 10, 11, 15, 22, 38, 59, 91, 114, 116, 117, 118, 120, 121, 122, 123, 135, 163, 164, 193, 205, 275, 292, 335, 348, 354, 357, 393, 402, 404, 405, 416, 426, 446, 468, 489, 507, 531, 532, 547, 589, 599, 624

temple-robber 91

tradition .. 2, 19, 79, 83, 121, 126, 127, 131, 143, 148, 167, 242, 284, 305, 309, 345, 367, 422, 432, 437, 461, 463, 464, 465, 466, 468, 469, 529, 592, 598, 619, 651, 663

transgression. 141, 155, 156, 225, 284, 493, 501, 502

transgressions 141, 149, 150, 189, 197

tribulation 377, 477, 557, 558

tribulations 385, 557, 558

type........ 19, 21, 56, 75, 111, 226, 227, 234, 236, 237, 238, 246, 259, 266, 273, 316, 328, 335, 338, 343, 347, 349, 354, 358, 370, 377, 463, 466, 483, 487, 578, 648, 670

typological....... 47, 111, 153, 194, 227, 460, 465, 466, 468, 471, 656, 657

typology .. 40, 194, 204, 218, 370, 656

uncircumcised .. 21, 88, 102, 137, 138, 141, 151, 152, 155, 182, 183, 186,

248, 329, 352, 408, 554, 563, 564, 570, 666

uncircumcision 187, 237

union........ 16, 213, 234, 235, 237, 240, 241, 245, 276, 296, 299, 302, 307, 311, 319, 341, 367, 381, 410, 489, 553, 594

universality 57, 156, 216, 477

universally 32, 124, 301, 415, 575

weakness. 41, 161, 266, 275, 279, 280, 309, 310, 322, 334, 335, 338, 342, 353, 360, 367, 370, 371, 372, 380, 381, 400, 445, 565, 572, 581, 651

wedding 57, 94, 192, 276, 311, 340, 391, 448, 453, 562

whoredom 251, 255

wisdom . 9, 87, 89, 279, 288, 315, 413, 418, 461, 462, 494, 496, 523, 525, 548, 560, 586, 608, 663

worldview 217, 266, 312, 534, 592

wrath 59, 60, 61, 62, 67, 71, 75, 78, 79, 80, 83, 99, 105, 122, 126, 129, 130, 141, 155, 156, 186, 189, 192, 201, 202, 204, 210, 211, 242, 243, 291, 331, 342, 352, 394, 395, 412, 414, 426, 434, 435, 436, 438, 441, 450, 549, 551, 555, 565, 567, 571, 606, 610, 668

Zion 17, 56, 76, 100, 108, 118, 121, 273, 308, 329, 330, 331, 391, 394, 449, 453, 460, 464, 486, 494, 496, 514, 515, 516, 517, 518, 519, 524, 526, 578, 668

INDEX OF SCRIPTURES

Old Testament

Genesis

1:1–31	157
2:7	157
2:15–17	306, 344
2:16–17	216
2:24	276
3:1–3	365
3:3–4	349
3:4	69
3:5	64
3:14–19	219
3:15	174, 176
3:17	367
3:17–19	365
3:23–24	306
6:17	271
7:21	271
8:21	272
9:16	271
9:21	579
12–25	144
12:3b	374
12:1–3	386, 444
12:1–4	378
12:1–9	8, 178
12:2	437
12:2–3	157, 268, 508
12:3	152, 417, 614
12:7	154
12:10–20	160
14:1–16	176
14:18–20	176
14:21	177
15:1–20	144
15:1–21	8, 402
15:2–4	158
15:2–6	409
15:4–5	177
15:4–6	174
15:5	158, 178, 197, 198, 444
15:6	142, 143, 146, 154, 158, 167, 173, 174, 175, 176, 177, 180, 182, 183, 184, 195, 197, 198, 508
15:6–18	177, 179
15:7	178
15:8	158
15:12–18	242
15:13–14	124, 145, 203, 434
15:13–16	147
15:18	195, 205
16:1–4a	158
16:1–16	158
16:9–11	409
17:1–8	174
17:1–14	154
17:1–27	8
17:4, 7	508
17:4–5	139, 158
17:4–5, 16	158
17:5	157
17:8	154
17:10	186
17:11	154
17:14	271
17:16	177, 437
17:16–18	158
17:17	142, 160
18:1–15	142
18:10	410
18:10, 14	485
18:16–33	192
18:18	178, 437
18:25	105
19:24–25, 28	446
20:13	160
21:1–7	142
21:1–20	158
21:6	485
22:1–2	161

22:1–19	116, 167
22:3	161
22:5	162
22:6–8	161
22:9	116
22:10	422
22:12	313
22:14	164
22:15–17	142
22:17	444, 445
22:18	139, 609
25:1–4	160, 409
25:6	409
26:4	139, 437, 609
28:3	408
28:3–4	408
28:13–14	408
28:14	609
32:26–28	408
42:13	201
49:10	405

Exodus

1:8–22	8
1:16	337
2:1–10	8
2:23	209
3:2	9
3:10	378
3:14	428
4:21–23	422, 433
4:22	319, 359, 403, 436
4:22–23	402, 423, 529
4:23	236
4:24–26	186
5:1–11	8
7:2–4	433
7:3	13
8:8, 12–13, 28, 30–31	434
8:15, 19, 32	434
8:19	434
8:32	499
9:12	499
9:12, 34	434
9:15	434
9:15–16	429, 430, 433
9:16	485
9:20	434
9:27–28, 33	434
9:34	434
10:3	434
10:16–17	434
10:20, 27–28	434
10:28	434
11:3	434
12:7	188
12:19–22	331
12:21–24	8
12:23	9, 367
12:23–24	337
12:26	230
12:27	136
12:44–48	119
12:48	186
13:1–2	128
13:2	528
13:6	246
13:8	230, 235
13:11–15	128
14:4ff.	433
14:17–18	205
14:19	9
14:31	246
15:6	228
15:11	404
15:22	201
16:7	228
16:13–16	380
18:17–26	543
19–20	216
19:6	529
19:7–9	205
20:17	307
22:20	242
22:21	127
22:21–27	577
22:28	573
22:29b	528

23:1–9	81
23:7	146
23:20	9
23:32	240, 251
24:8	10
30:13	179
31:14	179
32:1	259
32:1,8b	265
32:1, 4, 8	302
32:1–6	191
32:1–8	57
32:1–35	509
32:8	265
32:10	191
32:11	228
32:27–28	128
32:27–35	414
32:32	401, 430
32:33–34	191
32:34	191
33:12–17	191
33:18	404
33:19	428, 485
34:1–10	191
34:1–32	459
34:10	192
35:21	292
40:34	228, 402

Leviticus

5:6–7, 11	342
7:21	179
15:10	271
16:3, 5, 9	342
16:13–14	116
18:1–5	74
18:5	458
19:2	74, 447, 535
19:16	107
19:18	565
19:33–34	96
20:7	268
20:24–26	39
21:14	206
22:4	290
23:9–11	354
23:9–15	505
23:11	633
23:17	495
24:14	130
25:3–4	367
25:10–54	367
26:11–12	552
26:14–17, 30	552

Numbers

1:53	130, 211
3:5–9	128
3:12–13	528
3:12, 44–45	128
3:40–51	128
3:42–49	128
5:2	290
6:7	290
6:16	342
6:23–27	51
6:26	51
7:16	342
8:5–14	128
8:8–32	130
8:10	130
8:17–23	128
8:18	128
8:19	129
8:22	128
9:6	290
9:13–14	96
16:19, 42	228
18:1–7	129
18:5	130
18:16	130
18:24	128
19:20	179
21:29	69
25:10–11	555
25:10–13	195
25:13	195

Deuteronomy

1:35	192
4:9	292
4:29	292
4:37	228
5:9	284
6:4	208, 375
6:5	292
6:14–15	285
6:20–25	375
7:26	243
8:7	472
9:29	246
10:16	93
11:13	292
11:26	131
11:26–28	220
14:1	403
16:19	73
21:22–23	37
22:1–3	564
24	323
24:10–13	574
25:5–10	355
28:15–68	295
29–30	87
29:18–29	513
30:6	292
30:10	460
30:11–14	459, 460, 669
30:12	460, 461, 462, 463, 465, 466, 467, 468, 469, 484, 487
30:12b	459
30:12–13	452
30:13	470, 471, 472
30:14	484
30:15,19	344
30:15–16	268, 345, 355
30:17–19	10
32–33	192
32:1–35	114
32:4	105
32:6	403
32:15–18	481
32:15–19	285
32:19–25	481
32:21	472, 481, 484, 572
32:35	481
32:41	572
32:43	609, 610, 611
33:13	472

Joshua

1:2	201
5:2–9	186
5:5	186
5:7–10	186
23:1–16	268

Judges

6:23	51

Ruth

3:12	355
4:1–8	355

1 Samuel

3:4	38
9:16	569
10:20–24	9
12:20	292
16:1	569
16:12	38
18:16	516
26:9–11	149
28:4	516

2 Samuel

3:21	516
7:1–17	9
7:4–17	386
7:5–16	500
7:11–16	405
7:11–17	148
7:12–16	402
11:1–27	149
15:1–4	537
15:13–31	400

Index of Scriptures

16:5–14 400

1 Kings

8:18 292
12:1ff. 10
18:39, 45 498
19:10, 14 497
19:18 497

2 Kings

17:1–20 10
17:27 530
18:11 443
22:19 292
25:1ff. 10
25:18–20 201

1 Chronicles

6:31–34, 39 388
25:4–5 388
25:5 388

2 Chronicles

3:1 164
5:11–14 205
7:1–3 205
15:3 530
17:7 530
29:23–24 342
34:21 398

Ezra

2:1 201
5:8 547
9:7 308

Nehemiah

1:2–3 295
4:1ff. 11
9:6 154
9:8 292
9:31 528
10:33 342

Job

8:22 581
15:8 524
24:3 574
34:15 271
41:11 .... 486, 525

Psalms

1:2 404
2:7 .... 42, 134, 569
2:8 .... 42, 154
5:8–10 101
5:9 .... 100, 108
9:14 273
10:7 .... 101, 109
14:1–3 .... 100, 108
14:7 .... 100, 108
16:11 557
17:50 609
19:4 .... 480, 484
19:5 484
19:7–14, 119 316
22 388
22:14 400
22:22–23 324
24 463
24:1–2 154
27:1–3 558
30:8–12 387
30:11 581
32 174
32:1–2 149
32:2 ..148, 173, 174, 175, 176, 182, 183, 184, 197
32:3–4 149
33:12–15 87
33:13–15 74
35:24 180
35:26 581
36:1 .... 101, 110
36:5–9 102
37:4 293
37:9 62

Reference	Page
44:4–8	308
44:8–12	384
44:10–11, 22	384
44:13–16	384
44:17–19	384
44:22	384
44:23–24, 26	385
44:24–25	385
45:3	581
47	463
49:8	130
51:3–6	100, 104
51:11	42
51:18	273
53:1–3	100
57:7	293
65:5	180
68	463
68:18	464
69	321
69:13	209
69:22	486
69:22–23	500
69:23	486
69:30–31	324
71:15	114
73:6	581
76:10	106
78:42	46
79:8–9	130
80	132
80:8–18	510
81:8–12	66
82:6	41
85:8	51
85:13	114, 180
87:5	273
88	388
88:4–5, 10–12	387
88:18b	388
89	321
89:27	43, 124, 336
94:12	404
95:8–11	437
96:1–5	154
97:10	552
98:1–6	57
98:2	114, 180
100:1–5	57
101:2	293
102:23–24	387
103:6	180
103:13	359
104:30–34	208
106:20	65, 66
106:26	470, 471, 472
106:31	195, 198
107:26	470, 471
108	321
109:29	581
110	463
110:1	206
110:1–4	207, 383
114:2	507
116:1	609
116:3–4	387
117:1	611
118	463
119:7–112	536
119:16, 151–52, 158–60, 162, 167	89
119:29, 55–92	404
119:80	293
119:163	552
121:6	389
131	207
132:16	581
134:5	313
136:25	271
139:7	590
139:19–22	552
140:1–5	101
140:3	101, 108
143	272
143:2	113

Proverbs

Reference	Page
3:5	536

17:22	548
18:4	523
19:5	483
20:1	579
20:16	574

Ecclesiastes

12:13–14	512

Isaiah

1:9	486
1:18–20	331
1:21	273
1:29	56
2:1–4	444
2:1–5	11, 54, 157, 620
2:2–3	614
3:16	273
6:6–7	566
8:14	17
9:1–7	11
9:2–7	405
9:7	13, 39, 243
10:20	398, 496
10:20–22	410
10:22	445
10:22–23	486
10:27–28	407
11:1	56
11:1–5	39
11:1–10	386
11:2–4	208
11:10	609, 614
11:11–16	410
11:16	398
11:1ff.	117
19:16–25	386
19:19–25	49, 152, 438, 440, 504
19:21–25	614
19:23–25	11, 54, 139, 503
19:24–25	444
20:3	36
22:22	39
23:4	56

24:23	56
25:11	509
26:13–19	329
26:16–18	366
27:9	18
28:5	410
28:11	449
28:11–13	250, 251
28:11–16	449
28:14–15	250
28:15, 18	475
28:16	56, 250, 251, 449, 475, 486
28:16–18	329
28:17–23	366
28:18	418
29:9–10	500
29:10	18
29:13–16	418
29:14	418
29:15	418
29:15–26	421
29:16	417, 418, 419, 420, 425, 441, 484, 485
29:17	421
29:22	56, 178
30:14	441
31:1–3	593
32:1	147
32:15–18	208
32:17	180
33:9	56
34:1–17	438
35:4	438
35:6	13
37:4, 31–32	410
37:22	273
37:24	36
37:32	398
40:1	525
40:1–5	205, 541
40:2	131, 133, 196
40:3–5	364
40:5	228, 246, 404
40:6	270

40:13	18, 486	48:16–18	370
40:29	228	48:18	220
41:8	178	48:20–21	56
41:8–9	36	49:3, 6	377
41:8–16	442	49:6	56, 58, 515
41:18–20	407	49:6–7	11
42:1	36, 208, 438, 515	49:8	209
42:1–4	152, 202	49:18	593
42:1–7	507	49:20–21	303, 355
42:1–9	321, 386, 609	49:22	515
42:1–13	208	49:22–23	11
42:5–7	54	49:26	271
42:5–17	407	50:1	382
42:6–7	49	50:1–2	355
42:7	13	50:1–8	303
42:13–14	209	50:4–10	321
42:13–16	370	50:8	124, 379, 382, 614
42:14	124	50:8–9	383
43:1	318	50:9–10	203
43:7	102, 132	51:1–3	370
44:3	202, 336, 357	51:2	178
44:22	318	51:3	379
44:24–26	407	51:5	180
44:28	433	51:5–11	114
45:1	420, 425, 433, 440	51:6, 9	301
45:1–2	420	51:7	404
45:1–4	134	51:9	581
45:1–5	569	51:17	74
45:1–10	420	51:17–23	133
45:3	420	52:1	581
45:4	420	52:1–12	56
45:5	420	52:1–13	330
45:6	420	52:3–10	476
45:7	421, 425	52:5	92
45:7–8	420	52:7	17, 39, 56, 345, 377, 452, 460, 477, 484, 517
45:8	180	52:7–10	11
45:9	417, 418, 419, 420, 421, 425, 441, 485	52:9	133
45:9b	440	52:10	56
45:13	114, 440	52:11	290
45:23	593, 601	52:13–53	41, 321
45:25	173, 193, 202	52:15	18, 478, 617, 670
46:13	180, 301	53	133, 331, 379, 478
48:9	179	53:1	17, 478

Index of Scriptures

Reference	Page(s)
53:8	179
53:10–12	330
53:11	124, 173, 203, 614
53:12	383
54:1–8	355
54:5	318
54:5–6	133
54:13	345
54:14	114, 147, 193
55:1–13	124
55:3	39, 41, 243, 478
55:3–4	117
55:13	11, 43
56:1	56, 114, 180, 220, 447
56:3–8	54
56:6–7	49
56:6–8	477
56:7	515
58:8	193, 202, 205, 228
59:2–8, 12–15	579
59:7–8	17, 100, 101, 109
59:9–10	579
59:16–20	101
59:17	220
59:19	205, 209
59:20	108, 133, 486, 496, 516, 518
59:20–21	18, 330, 465
59:21	202, 208, 336, 357, 518
60:1	578, 581
60:1–2, 13	202
60:1–3	386
60:8–14	20
60:8–16	477
60:17	208
61:1	46
61:1–2	10
61:1–3	14, 336, 357, 562
61:1–11	208
61:3	114
61:10	382, 483, 529, 581
61:10–11	330
62:1	193
62:1–2	114, 147
62:1–5	582
62:2	515
62:4–5	303, 355
62:5	318, 382
62:11	273
62:11–12	378
62:12	133
63:5	108
63:9	528
63:10	356
63:11,14	339
63:11–19	208
63:16	178
63:17	437
64:4	363
64:6	108
64:8	421, 441
64:10–12	124
65:1	472, 484
65:2	481, 482, 484
65:4	202
65:13–15	36
65:17	126, 185, 364
65:17–18	350
65:23	365
65:25	364
66:1–22	365
66:10–22	593
66:18	404
66:22	364
66:23	270

Jeremiah

Reference	Page(s)
4:4	93, 187
4:31	273
5:7	273
5:11	479
5:22–25	512
7:2–1	87
9:23–24	202
9:23–26	87, 88
9:24	137
10:12	46
11:1–17	509
11:16–17	495, 505, 506

12:16	598
13:27	290
16:21	46
17:6–18	294
17:9	293
18:4–6	441
18:6–13	435
21:8	355
22:8	445
23:1–8	117
23:3	410
23:5	405
23:10	110
25:11	369
27:5	46
29:10–14	446
30:9	405
31:3	376
31:7	410
31:9	403
31:22	479
31:29	75
31:31–34	96, 187, 243, 386
31:33	96, 518
31:33–34	473, 486, 519
32:17	228
33:4–17	117
33:4–26	386
33:14–17	10, 11
33:14–18	243
33:17	405
34:1–10	541
36:8–12	407
38:4, 28	598
40:7	598
42:2	410
43:5	410
44:7	410
45:4	598
46:12–13	445
49:10	598
51:7	209
51:13	179

Lamentations

1:6	273
1:9–22	308
2:20–22	308
3:22	439

Ezekiel

5:15	445
13:19	111
16:1–14	231, 331
16:6–14	205
16:8	300
16:9	231
16:9–14	127
16:15–29	482
16:23–34	443
16:26–58	302
16:28	273
16:59–60	187
16:59–63	243
20:1–7	186
21:1–32	295
23:29–31	110
28:19	445
32:24	390
33:15	574
34:1–16	59
34:23	405
34:23–31	117
34:25	345
36:16–27	87
36:20–23	92
36:22–32	386
36:24	10
36:24–28	11, 336, 357
36:24–38	243
36:26	96
36:26–27	11, 208, 270, 271, 347
36:27	42, 181
36:35	379
37:1–4	11, 357
37:1–14	157, 504
37:10–14	42
37:11	179
37:12–13	243

37:13	228
37:24–25	117
37:26	120, 345
38:23	515
39:23	479
42:13	342
43:4	202
43:14, 17, 20	121
43:19	342
44–45	11
44:7, 9	119
44:21–23	530
45:18–25	343
45:21–25	117, 121, 127
45:25	122, 135, 457

Daniel

7:18	50
7:22	321
12:1	366
12:2	504

Hosea

1:2	273
1:10	139, 403, 437, 445, 486
2:2	300
2:4	273
2:14	10
2:14–16	284
2:14–20	205, 331
2:16, 19	11
2:23	377, 407, 436, 443, 485, 522
3:1	10, 443
4:12	479
4:15–5	302
5:3	90
5:13–15	109
6:7	283
6:7,10	214
6:10	110
7:1–2	331
11:1	42, 236, 362, 403
11:9–11	187
12:9	10

13:3	555
13:14	47, 157, 228, 243, 504
14:1–3	331, 541
14:4–6	495
14:6	505

Joel

2:1–11, 28–32	366
2:28	271, 348, 476
2:28–29	208
2:32	406, 407, 484

Amos

2:3	313
3:1	24
3:2	74, 81, 153, 221, 437, 500
5:4–5	541
5:14–15	552
5:14–27	238
5:16–20	366
6:8	552
9:11	243

Jonah

3:10	424

Micah

1:13	273
4:2	515
4:9–10	366
4:10	273
7:7–10	308
7:15	11

Habakkuk

2:4	137

Zephaniah

3:13	398

Haggai

2:3–9	11

Zechariah

3:8–9 11
4:3, 12–14 505
4:6 .... 208, 371
6:12–14 42
9:9 121
12:10 51

Malachi

1:11 515
1:23 485
3:1 11
4:1 511

New Testament

Matthew

1:1–17 405
1:6, 17, 20 14
3:6 227
3:17 45
4:7, 4 647
5–7 549
5:5 154
5:7 548
5:10–12 .... 207, 561
5:11 552
5:14 415
5:21–22 576
5:21–22, 27–28, 31–32, 33–34, 38–
    39, 43–44 287
5:27–28 575
5:29–30 260
5:44 561
5:46 585
6:9–13 358
6:23 578
7:1–5 549
7:24–27 550
7:26–27 415
7:29 287
8:12 578
9:15 340
9:27 14
10:32 474

12:23 14
12:26 640
12:28 78
13:41 150
14:23 558
15:18–20 291
15:19–20 66
15:21–28 95
15:22 14
16:16 .... 14, 42
16:23 563
17:3, 4 14
18:15 592
18:16–17 592
18:18 295
18:20 623
18:33 548
19:27–30 387
20:1–16 94
20:30, 31 14
21:1–9 121
21:12–13 92
21:18–20 92
21:18–22 415
21:28–32 94
21:31, 43 78
21:42 .... 250, 251
22:1–4 304
22:1–14 340
22:13 578
22:21b 573
22:23–33 243
22:37–38 563
22:41–45 383
24:1–2 .... 414, 415
24:32–45 92
25:1–13 304
25:14–15 81
25:24 313
26:36 558
26:41 275
27:46 388
27:54 42
28:18 375

28:18–20 377
28:19 .... 229, 424, 475
28:19–20 387

Mark

1:22, 27 647
6:4 634
7:11 559
7:20–23 552
10:12 250
10:38 227
10:45 .... 167, 256
12:10 251
12:17 571
12:25 243
12:29–30 576
12:30 293
15:21 637
15:36 606
15:44–45 388

Luke

1:46–55, 67–79 383
1:58, 61 634
2:8–38 383
2:25–38 622
2:44 634
3:4–6 12
3:7–8 194
3:16 227
3:21 558
3:23–38 405
4:5–6 250
4:18 56
4:18–19 .... 12, 16
5:16 558
6:12 558
6:22–23 561
6:24–26 81
6:45 .... 293, 552
7:1–10 .... 76, 95
7:18–23 122
7:21–22 12
7:27 12

7:45 638
8:46 313
8:51–53 399
9:28 558
9:31 .... 230, 332
9:62 194
10:18 .... 346, 640
10:31–32 104
11:1–14 377
12:21 194
12:50 227
12:58–59 415
13:34–35 415
14:12 634
14:13 56
14:15–24 304
14:26 .... 413, 520
15:11–32 95
18:18 77
18:21 297
18:31 228
19:11–27 268
20:17 .... 250, 251
21:16 634
22:20 118
23:27–31 562
23:36 606
23:38 13

John

1–10 13
1:1–14 339
1:3 338
1:10–11 275
1:12 429
1:13 153
1:23 16
1:29 .... 122, 127
2:13, 23 276
2:13–22 91
2:18–21 507
2:19 405
2:19–22 275
3:1–2 76

3:1–8	76
3:3–9	275
3:7	481
3:13	465
3:16	194, 424, 533
3:16, 36	76
3:27–30	304, 340
3:29	276
4:15	275
5:24	76
5:34	424
5:39–40	275
6:4	275, 276
6:32–70	97
6:37, 44–45, 64–65	425, 430
6:40	76, 276
6:51–56	275
6:53	275
6:62	465
8:14, 21	463
8:39–44	514
8:44	240, 476
10:11	256, 593
10:26	425, 430
10:28	76
10:33	363
10:33–39	44
11:33–36, 38	562
11:55	276
12:1	276
12:2–23	205
13:1	276
13:3, 33	463
14:4–5, 28	463
14:15–21	467
14:16	544
14:25–27	340
15:1–8	510
15:1–11	402
15:18–27	385
15:26–27	467
16:5, 10, 17, 28	463
16:20	557
17:3	76
17:11	624
19:29	606

Acts

1:14	558
2:1–4	205
2:1–5	347
2:1–12	347
2:4–8	371
2:11	372
2:15–17	348
2:21	476
2:24–36	469
2:25, 29, 34	656
2:25–36	479
2:36–41	498
2:38	227
2:38–41	167
2:38, 41, 47–48	475
2:40	445
2:40–41	194
2:41	408
2:42	543, 558
2:44–45	558
3:1	558
3:19	445
3:21	469
4:1–22	385
4:4	408, 655
4:10	256
4:11	250, 251
4:23–31	207
4:24–31	469
4:25	656
4:31	348
4:32–35	558
5:29–32	479
5:29–34	469
6:1–4	558
6:1–6	542, 548
6:1–7	498, 543
6:4	558
6:6	531
6:7	408

Index of Scriptures

Reference	Page
6:8–15	385
7:45	656
7:51–53	75, 502
7:51–58	132
7:54–60	109, 385
8:1–8	347
8:3	277, 454
8:14–17	347
8:17	348
8:26	357
8:31–35	445
8:34–38	194
8:36	227
9:1	277
9:1–2	572
9:9–16	598
9:11	558
9:15	37, 54, 568
9:15–16	503
9:16	387
9:17	348
9:24	454
9:26–27	399
9:27	544
10:1–2	297
10:1–2, 22	94
10:17–23	76
10:22	85
10:32–34	445
10:39–44	469
10:41	93
10:44–45	348
10:44–48	347, 507
10:45–46	371
11:11–18	104
11:19–26	642
11:26	544
12:1–3	109
12:5	558
13	532
13:1	637, 641
13:1–3	357, 619
13:2	536, 541
13:4–12	616
13:5, 15	569
13:14–52	544
13:22, 34, 36	656
13:24	475
13:32–34	445
13:32–39	479
13:38–39	412
13:38–41	189
13:39	317
13:40–14	6
13:48	425, 430
14:1	569
14:4, 14	634
14:8–10	616
14:19	400
14:21–22	544
14:22	76, 250, 290, 357
15:1–2	20
15:5–21	593
15:6–9	359
15:6–29	597
15:7	635
15:7–9	348
15:7–11	182
15:12–18	104
15:12–35	395
15:14–21	507
15:15–19	467
15:15–21	104
15:16–17	14
15:22–31	544
15:28	357
16:7	536
16:7–10	357
16:14	85, 93, 425, 430
16:14–15	76
16:16–18, 25–34	616
17:1–9	642
17:10–12	569
17:22–23	658
17:30–31	74
17:31	87
17:34	194
18:1–3	629, 631, 637

Reference	Page(s)
18:2	589, 632
18:4	569
18:8	643
18:9	357
18:18	631
18:18, 26	632
18:21	52
18:24–26	631
19:1–7	347
19:2	347
19:5	475
19:6	348, 371
19:8	569
19:11–20	616
19:22	643
19:23	496
19:29–40	632
20–21	622
20:4	643
20:10	655
20:16	618
20:17–19, 31	562
20:26–27	624
20:28	233, 303
20:28–31	563
20:36–38	562
21:7–14	624
21:8–9	542
21:10–11	624
21:11	541
21:17–26	20
21:20–21	593, 597
21:20–22	560
21:27	624
21:27–32	400
22:3–5	455
23:5	573
23:12–15	454
23:12–22	560, 634
23:12–30	618
24:10–22	658
24:17	624
24:23	559
25:10–11	568
25:11	618
26:1–32	658
26:12	568
26:15–18	264
26:17–18	111, 614
26:18	568, 578
28:16	618
28:16–31	625
28:25–28	75
28:30	24

Romans

Reference	Page(s)
1–8	349
1:1, 3	487
1:1–4	35
1:2	28, 113, 193, 219, 332, 335
1:3	28, 38, 118, 119, 132, 207, 281, 338, 383, 400, 405, 473, 597, 617, 665
1:3–4	118, 134, 491
1:4	55, 122, 335, 469, 488
1:5	503, 640
1:5–6	521
1:5–7	49
1:8–15	51
1:9–10	542
1:11	545
1:11–12	617
1:11–12, 15	545
1:14–16	618
1:15	617
1:16	454, 476
1:16–17	55
1:16–18	222, 665
1:16–31	325
1:17	80
1:18–32	60, 108, 215, 310, 427, 436, 441, 480
1:19–2	288
1:19–32	665
1:26	289
1:28–32	563
1:29–31	110
1:30	65

Index of Scriptures

1:30, 32	536
2	517
2:1	560
2:1–3	87
2:1–29	72
2:4	512
2:5	192
2:5, 16	61
2:5, 8	565
2:8	74
2:12–16	216
2:13	253
2:14	289
2:14–16	153
2:17	137
2:17–24	325
2:23	137
2:25–29	95, 139, 448
2:27	289
2:28	119, 281
2:28, 29	96
2:28–29	27, 28, 87
3:3	510
3:4	253
3:5–8	100
3:7	106
3:18	101
3:19–20	412
3:20	253, 279, 280
3:21	55, 101, 102, 113, 123, 180, 193, 219, 335
3:21ff.	46, 119, 122, 168, 210, 211, 337, 382, 442
3:21–22	124
3:21–25	27, 28, 196, 207, 300, 342
3:21–26	82, 113, 118, 185, 188, 223, 229, 264, 336, 342, 505
3:21–27	332, 491
3:22–24	522
3:23	80, 147, 189, 203, 332, 437, 502
3:24	76, 124, 253
3:24, 26	124
3:24–25	124
3:24–26	123
3:25	123, 124, 134, 135, 192
3:25–26	555
3:26	168, 253
3:26–28	125
3:27	509
3:27–31	137
3:27–32	144, 666
3:29–30	183
3:13b	101
3:25ff.	335
4 517	
4:1–3, 12, 13, 16, 18	508
4:1–25	142
4:3	180, 184
4:3–5	183
4:4, 16	455
4:6	183, 184
4:7	183
4:7–8	197
4:9	201
4:11–12	18
4:11b–12	506
4:12	363
4:16	163
4:16–17	448, 505
4:17	375
4:18	201
4:19	201
4:19–24	177
4:20	201, 510
4:23–24	164
4:25	132, 152, 164, 203, 205, 335, 469
5:1	120, 201, 203, 597
5:1–4	345, 348
5:1–8	332, 590
5:1–11	201, 213, 229
5:2	201
5:2–3, 9	487
5:3	358
5:3–4	264, 557
5:3–5	27
5:5	238, 344, 347, 476, 557, 612

5:5–11	335
5:6	201
5:6–8	202, 371
5:8	238, 332, 491, 552, 560
5:9	76, 168, 202
5:10	76, 126
5:12–6	181, 396
5:12–7	300
5:12–21	212, 227, 345
5:13	156, 190
5:13, 20	412
5:14	218
5:15	239
5:15–19	218, 297
5:17	316
5:17–19	154
5:18, 19	166
5:18–19	194
5:20	190, 238, 306
5:21	243
5:12ff.	137, 278, 442
5:1ff.	358, 558, 578
6:1	332
6:1ff.	229
6:1–4	168, 225, 226, 227, 234, 236, 259, 264, 335, 347, 469
6:1–5	349, 590
6:1–7	325
6:1–10	238
6:1–11	229
6:3–4	237
6:3–11	232
6:4	205, 228, 230, 469
6:5–11	278
6:6	225, 226, 252, 314, 325
6:7	194, 206, 300, 381
6:10	487
6:11–23	258
6:13–14	530, 533
6:17–18	543
6:19a	150
6:19b	150
6:23	243
7:1–2	300
7:1–4	206, 249, 337, 381, 534
7:1–5	325
7:1–6	252, 279, 298, 306, 340, 353, 355, 457
7:1–14	345
7:2	301, 316
7:2–4	241
7:4	194
7:4–6	340, 469
7:5	296
7:5, 18, 25	290
7:5–6	324
7:7–8	300
7:7–24	324
7:7–25	312
7:10	189
7:12	111
7:16	322
7:21–25	297, 563
7:24	252
7:7ff.	307
8:1	324, 527
8:1–3	556
8:1–13	279
8:1–16	xii, 333, 335
8:2	492
8:3	43, 46, 278, 279, 335, 337
8:3, 32	126
8:3, 32	207
8:3, 34	207
8:3–4	342, 488
8:3–4, 29	529
8:3–5, 8–9, 12–13	290
8:3–8	326
8:4–5, 8–9, 12–13	296
8:4–8	278
8:5	335, 338
8:5–7	335
8:6	335, 563, 597
8:6–7	563
8:8	278
8:9	42, 278, 376, 491
8:9–11	205
8:9, 12–13	554

8:10–17	467
8:11	336, 351, 356, 368, 370
8:13	336, 534
8:13–25	255
8:14	207
8:15	554
8:15–17	42, 229
8:16–17	336, 337
8:17	202, 362, 381, 403
8:17, 29	123
8:17–25	371
8:17–39	361
8:18	375, 453
8:18–25	623
8:18–39	558
8:19–22	337
8:19–25	43
8:25–39	27
8:28,30b	197
8:29	43, 336
8:29–30	374
8:30	76
8:30–39	337
8:31	374
8:31ff.	332
8:31–39	370, 377, 379, 383, 386, 469
8:32	430, 447, 463
8:32ff.	578
8:32–34	425
8:34	372, 467, 469, 487
8:34–39	207
8:35–39	229, 345, 348
8:35ff.	590
9:1–5	81, 153, 216, 397
9:1–33	394
9:2	401
9:4	112, 480
9:5	416, 485
9:6	517
9:6–12	416
9:6–13	425, 441
9:6–17	397
9:7	485
9:8	362
9:9	485
9:11	38
9:13	413, 485
9:14	485
9:14–24	397, 422
9:17	75, 485
9:17–18	398, 641
9:18	414
9:19–24	427
9:20	485
9:22–10	421
9:25	436, 485, 522
9:25–26	193
9:25–29	401
9:25–33	398
9:26	486
9:27	486
9:28	486
9:28–39	646
9:29	486
9:30–33	21
9:32–33	250
9:33	55, 56, 251, 476, 485, 486
10:1–4	335
10:1–21	452
10:1–22	279
10:2–4	452
10:4	469, 488, 492, 536
10:5–15	387
10:6	452, 457, 461, 463, 466, 471
10:6–7	483
10:7	463, 466, 472
10:8	293
10:9	26, 452, 462
10:9–11	421
10:9–15	26
10:10	293
10:11	449
10:12–13	167, 407
10:12–18	194
10:14–15	229, 377, 381, 467, 578
10:14–17	460
10:16–21	453

10:19	484, 621	12:13	630
10:20	484	12:14	561
10:21	484	12:16	537
11:1–6	495	12:19	570
11:1–36	494	12:20	520, 561
11:5–6	455	12:21	552
11:7	420	13:1–7	79
11:7–10	495	13:1–14	567
11:9	486	13:6	571
11:10	486	13:8	457
11:11–12	495	13:9–10	577
11:11–24	27	13:11	578
11:13–14	621	13:14	290, 296
11:14	430	14:1–23	584
11:16	495	14:9	245
11:17–18	436	14:9, 15	584
11:17–21	402, 495	14:10	61, 537
11:17–34	279	14:10–12	584
11:20	436	14:10–13	560
11:20, 23	510	14:11–12	254
11:21, 24	289	14:17	557
11:22–24	495	14:20	584
11:24	436	14:21	280
11:25	398	14:22–23	605
11:25–27	21	15:1–22	618
11:25–32	496	15:1–33	604
11:26	176, 401, 466, 486, 496	15:2	551
11:26–27	108	15:3–4	604
11:27	486, 488, 518	15:4	111, 536, 557
11:33–36	429	15:7–16	586
11:34	486	15:13	557
11:35	486	15:15–16	532
12:1	52	15:16	52, 530, 605, 633
12:1–2	27, 39, 377, 568, 592, 633	15:16–17	542
12:1–8	527	15:19	626
12:1–15	261	15:20	19
12:1–21	577	15:23–24	106
12:2	281	15:23–33	618
12:3	549	15:24	617
12:6–8	549	15:25	444, 541, 618
12:8	547	15:26–27	629
12:9–11	542	15:28	605
12:9–21	358, 549	15:31	622
12:11	568	15:32	52

Reference	Pages
16:1–2	560
16:1–27	628
16:5,16	233
16:14–15	632
16:17–19	543
16:23	560, 630
16:24	642
16:25–26	328

1 Corinthians

Reference	Pages
1:1	634
1:2	26, 233, 538
1:3	51
1:14	642
1:14,16	643
1:14,17	475
1:18–25	279
1:23	45, 58, 256
1:26	643
1:26–29	38, 280
1:26–31	412
1:29	280
1:30	134
1:31	87
2:6–16	387
2:9	59, 363, 557
2:10	523
2:16	524
3:8	82
3:9–10	598
4:6	112
5–6	260, 554
5:1–2	546
5:1–6	356
5:1–8	438
5:1–11	295
5:1–13	609
5:2–5	592
5:3–5	264
5:3–8	244
5:4	623
5:5	243, 259, 290, 296
5:6–8	259, 260
5:7	123, 168, 223, 229, 336, 338, 505, 519, 615
5:7–8	97, 261
5:9–11	231
5:11	579
5:7b	125, 126
6:1–2	221, 362
6:1–3	255
6:2	154, 229, 378
6:9–10	66
6:9–11	244
6:10	290
6:11	119, 229, 252
6:16	279
6:16–17	553
6:19–20	507
6:20	134, 303, 319
7:25	547
7:32–35	635
8:1–8	587
8:4	240
8:4–7	21
8:6	540
8:9–13	23
8:13	280, 595
9:5	634, 635
9:13–14	542
9:27	537
10:1–4	47, 226, 229, 230, 259, 347, 667
10:1–6	111, 335
10:1–10	238, 244, 572
10:1–11	356, 446
10:1–13	40, 229, 438, 579, 581
10:1–14	260, 264
10:1–20	193
10:1–22	295, 356, 509
10:2	227, 232, 236, 264, 339
10:4	233
10:6–13	469
10:6–14	24
10:12	511
10:16	232
10:18–22	240

Reference	Page
10:19–22	66
10:21–22	546
10:23–32	587
11:2–16	546
11:14	289, 290
11:17–34	546
11:18	546
11:23	167
11:28	260
11:29–32	260, 356
12:8–11	540
12:10, 30	371
12:12, 27	249
12:13	227, 228, 229, 233, 235, 236, 347
12:22–26	554
13:1–13	596
13:2	613
13:4–8a	552
13:13	552
14:3	544
14:3, 5, 12, 26	598
14:4	372, 541
14:4–28	371
14:5	606
14:11	251
14:22	541
14:26–28	372
14:26–33	546
14:33b–35	546
15:3	32, 244, 354, 505
15:12–18	546
15:12–34	260
15:18	400
15:20	353, 505
15:20–28	216
15:22	25
15:24	250
15:24–25	76
15:26	520
15:26, 55	475
15:26–28	43
15:30	632
15:37–58	268
15:39	280
15:42–55	205
15:45–49	297
15:52	504
15:54	202
15:55	193, 504
16:1–3	444
16:1–4	559
16:3	620
16:15–17	541
16:19	632
16:20	638
16:22	639
16:24	400
12, 14	538

2 Corinthians

Reference	Page
1:2	51
1:3–11	607
1:8–9a	384
1:15ff	618
1:20	11, 45, 50, 343
1:22	347
2:4	562
2:4, 13	345
3:1–4, 6	349
3:3	350
3:5–18	345
3:7–6	185
3:7–11	190
3:7–18	401
3:9	58
3:13–16	45
3:18	376
4:4	64
4:4–10	383
4:7–18	389
4:8	384
5:1	350
5:1–21	349
5:2	350
5:4	350
5:10	82, 254, 593
5:14–15	245

5:16	606
5:17	126, 185, 197, 364
5:17–21	185
5:18, 20	76
5:19	184, 185, 190, 199
5:19–21	190
5:21	82, 126, 190, 342
6:1–10	264
6:4–10	383
6:8–9	384
6:8–10	384
6:14–18	576
7:5–7	544
7:11	556
8–9	559
8:1	233
8:7–8	556
8:8–15	621
8:9	338, 381
8:9–15	606
8:19	620
8:22ff.	619
10:5	390
10:8	568, 598
10:12–18	538
11:1	89
11:2	303, 340
11:7–8	542
11:13–15	634
11:16–33	387
11:23b–28	383
11:23–29	374
11:23b–33	632
11:24	400
11:25	454
11:26	384
11:28–29	345, 401
11:28–33	384
11:31	400
12:7	281
12:7–10	358
12:12	616, 634
12:19	598
12:11ff.	634
13:10	598
13:12	638
13:14	540

Galatians

1:1	634
1:3	51, 126, 232, 234
1:4	111, 188, 235
1:6	555
1:6–9	53, 454
1:12	645
1:13–14	572
1:15–17	38
1:18–20	399
2:1–10	399
2:10	620
2:11–14	180
2:14	576, 594
2:15	90, 289
2:15–16	181
2:17–21	181
2:20	280
2:20–21	181
3:1–5	181
3:2	42
3:5	347
3:6	180, 181
3:6, 8, 9, 14, 16	508
3:6–9	161
3:6–9, 26–29	495
3:10ff.	278
3:10–13	190, 198
3:13	82, 119, 126, 179, 188, 196
3:13–14	96
3:14	181, 232
3:16	145, 174, 409
3:19	145, 174, 189
3:22	189
3:24	76, 151, 155, 448
3:25	469
3:25ff.	235
3:25–27	347
3:25–29	362, 378
3:26–29	51, 188, 232, 233

Reference	Pages
3:27	234, 236
3:27–28	236
4:1–7	232
4:4	126, 405
4:4–5	209
4:4–6	349
4:6	42
4:8	289
4:13, 14	281
4:16	520
4:19	159
4:21–27	467
4:21–31	158, 188
4:22	508
4:23	161
4:24–27	517
4:29	410
5:6	188
5:11	57
5:13	542
5:13, 16–17, 19	296
5:13, 16–17, 19, 24	290
5:13–26	338
5:16	96
5:16–26	554, 577, 581
5:18	278, 469
5:19–21	66, 278, 343
5:19–21a	277
5:22	552
6:5	197
6:8	290
6:10	559
6:12	560
6:14–15	188
6:15	119
6:16	28, 579
6:12ff	639

Ephesians

Reference	Pages
1:2	51
1:3b	28
1:3–14	197, 349, 375
1:4	425, 430
1:5	236
1:7	96, 119, 127, 134, 187, 291
1:11–13	507
1:13	489
1:13–14	15, 347
1:18–23	291
1:20	206
1:20–21	463
1:20–23	489
1:21	568
1:22	406
2:1–3	240
2:1–3, 11–13	57
2:1–10	231
2:2	568
2:2–8	221
2:3	222, 289, 290, 291, 296
2:4–10	234, 245, 458
2:6	168
2:8	146
2:8–9	499
2:8–18	443
2:9	412
2:9b	412
2:10	501
2:11	96, 281
2:11–3	159
2:11–13	187, 503
2:11–15	444
2:11–18	119
2:11–19	236
2:11–21	16
2:13	96, 400
2:14	23
2:14–18	612
2:14–22	187
2:15	197, 247, 248, 281, 489
2:16	249
2:18, 21	206
2:18–20	507
2:18–22	50
2:19	504
2:21	489
2:22	550, 551
3:4–6	514

Index of Scriptures

3:6 .... 16, 42, 249, 363
3:10–11 501
3:10–13 608
4:4 489
4:4–6 232
4:6 406
4:7–13 488
4:8 .... 464, 465, 489
4:8–11 463
4:11–12 542
4:11–13 546
4:11–14 543
4:12 .... 542, 546
4:12, 29 606
4:12–13 548
4:18 64
4:20–24 540
4:24 581
4:28 .... 545, 559
5:5 .... 76, 250
5:6 74
5:8 578
5:8–20 .... 290, 578
5:17 535
5:22–25 25
5:23 249
5:25 .... 119, 127, 206, 303, 538
5:25ff. 236, 239, 319, 376
5:25–26 .... 231, 232, 363
5:25–27 ...... 96, 119, 187, 206, 340, 355
5:26 127
5:32 187
6:1–9 25
6:6 293
6:10–18 389
6:11 578
6:20 42
6:21–22 .... 544, 559

Philippians

1:1 400
1:2 51
1:9 523

1:12–30 358
1:17 454
1:19–30 387
1:24 281
1:27 42
2:1–11 606
2:1–12 593
2:1–15 .... 596, 597
2:2–4 606
2:3, 5 537
2:4–11 216
2:5–9 585
2:5–11 .... 64, 376
2:6–10 222
2:6–11 .... 465, 555, 586
2:7 338
2:10–12 540
2:15 42
2:15–16 377
2:17–18 561
2:17b–18 562
2:19–24 641
2:25 559
2:25–30 .... 619, 633
2:27 547
3:1–6 57
3:2 576
3:2–14 497
3:3 .... 59, 96
3:3–6 .... 189, 190, 191
3:3–7 277
3:4–6 .... 73, 82, 89, 316
3:6 .... 93, 190, 233, 555
3:7–11 57
3:10 385
3:10–11 96
3:18 .... 520, 562
3:18ff. 639
3:18–19 520
3:20 345
3:20–21 .... 207, 247
3:21 458
4:2–3 564
4:4–7 561

4:8–9 581
4:9 625
4:10, 14–16, 18 558
4:16 533
4:21 400

Colossians

1:2 .... 51, 400
1:3–21 222
1:6–8 628
1:8 491
1:12–13 179
1:12–14 126
1:12–21 216
1:12–22 490
1:13 .... 96, 126, 234, 568, 578
1:13–1 365
1:13–12 64
1:13–14 ..... 21, 41, 49, 57, 61, 111,
    219, 235, 363, 443, 448, 469
1:13–15 .... 119, 203
1:13–20 .... 196, 290
1:13–21 378
1:13–22 381
1:14 .... 134, 240
1:15 .... 43, 126, 364, 366
1:15, 20 378
1:15–19 134
1:15–20 378
1:20 .... 126, 366
1:22 .... 76, 281
1:24 .... 281, 561
1:27 349
2:8, 16–18 639
2:10 .... 319, 406
2:11 .... 15, 96, 119, 188, 252, 490
2:11, 13 .... 290, 296
2:11–12 198
2:11–13 .... 234, 236
2:11–13a 187
2:13b–15 188
2:14 490
2:16 21
2:16–19 23

3:1 255
3:1–13 352
3:2ff. 25
3:5 .... 290, 296
3:5–17 534
3:9–12 248
3:10 .... 23, 540, 581
3:10–11 .... 58, 352
3:10–14 54
3:15 535
4:8 53
4:15 .... 233, 632
4:17 25

1 Thessalonians

1:1 .... 25, 538
1:4 425
1:5 347
1:6–8 358
1:10 565
1:12–14 25
1:3b 558
2:8, 11–12 545
2:9–16 222
2:13–16 560
2:14–16 .... 74, 159
2:16 424
2:18 617
3:2, 6 641
4:3–8 .... 259, 376
4:9–10 553
4:13–18 544
4:16 .... 25, 247
5:11 .... 544, 551
5:12–13 547
5:18 535
5:23 283
5:26 638

2 Thessalonians

1:1 27
1:4 558
1:5–10 .... 61, 74
1:6–9 415

Index of Scriptures

1 Timothy

1:5	293
1:11–12	542
1:13	510
1:15–16	619
1:20	260
2:3–4	424
2:5	372
3:1–7	546
3:3	579
3:6	536, 537
3:8	574
3:8–13	548
3:10, 13	542
3:15	547
4:13	544
4:13–14	542
5:3	559
5:4,8	559
5:8	559
5:9–10	559
5:16	559
5:17	547
5:19	547
5:22	546
6:16	75
6:18	559

2 Timothy

1:4	562
1:7	211
1:8–14	387
1:10	387, 414, 525
1:14	348, 354
2:2–3	619
2:8–13	387
2:11–13	357
2:20–21	427
3:1–8	63
3:10–4	619
3:14–17	104
4:2	544
4:5	542
4:9–13	619
4:10	555
4:22	642

Titus

1:1	634
1:5	543, 546, 618
1:6–9	546
1:7–9	544
1:9	547
1:9, 11, 13	547
2:3	579
2:11–14	75
3:6	208

Philemon

1–2	26
2	632
4–7	52, 544
19	642

Hebrews

1:1–4	472
1:1–6	222, 366
1:1–14	64
1:3	47
1:8–9	377
2:1–3	222
2:5–9	378
2:5–18	342
2:6–13	64
2:17–18	41, 207
3:7–4	15
3:12–4	207
4:14–16	207, 372
4:15b	87
5:1–5	206
5:1–10	383
5:7	562
5:7–10	207
6:10–12	556
6:20	463
7:11–12	487
7:12	488

7:16	382	2:21–23	167
7:22	375	2:23	144
7:25	207	2:26	50
8:7–13	488	3:5–6	260
8:8–12	488	4:5	221
8:8–13	15	5:4–5	574
9:1–7	257		
9:1–10	123	1 Peter	
9:5	121	1:2	347
9:9	223	1:4	202
9:11–14	206	1:4–5	557
9:11–15	382	1:6–7	207
9:12	122	1:6–9	562
9:13	223	1:22	553
9:14	207	2:4–6	250, 507
9:22	223	2:5	530
9:24–27	222	2:5, 9	529
9:24–28	256, 488	2:6–8	56
10:11–18	615	2:7	251
10:29–31	221	2:9	38, 578
10:31	62	2:21–22	339
11:2, 17–19	157	2:21–25	606
11:11	161	3:6	319
11:17–19	163	4:9	560
11:19	444	4:12–16	558, 562
11:24–29	336	4:17	221
12:1–3	606, 613	5:1–3	547
12:1–3, 18–28	15	5:5	574
12:1–17	207	5:14	638
12:18–28	467		
12:22	204, 517	2 Peter	
12:28	387	1:3	291, 526
13:1	556	1:4	289
13:7, 17	574	1:11	290
13:16	559	1:19	578
		2:4–18	74
James		2:10, 18	296
1:2	358	2:19	290
1:2–4	207	3:2	613
1:2–8	558	3:3–5	74
1:13–18	106		
1:23–25	318	1 John	
2:1–7	81	1:4	557
2:10	83	2:15	533

Index of Scriptures

3:4 150
3:16–24 50
3:17 81
4:7–19 552
4:19 239
4:20–21 552
5:13 613

3 John

3–8 559
5–8 560
9–10 564

Revelation

1:4–6 382
1:4–8 64
1:5–6 .... 223, 378
1:5–8 45
1:6 530
1:12–18 383
1:18 256
2:1–3 554
2:2, 20–22 23
2:4 555
2:4–5, 14–16, 19–23 295
2:4–6, 14–16, 21–23 438
2:5 .... 356, 513
2:9 109
2:15 438
2:16, 21–23 260
2:20–23 264
2:20–25 240
2:22–23 243
3:1–3 438
3:9 641
3:19 260
5:10 362
6:7 192

6:16 74
6:16–17 122
13:8 606
18:2–3 66
19:6–8 16
19:7 .... 340, 562
19:7–9 319
19:9 304
20:13 475
21:1–2 517
21:1–4 15
21:5 .... 364, 365
21:22–26 507

Other Sources

Apocalypse of Baruch

21:23 475
59:6 74

2 Baruch

55:6 366

Exodus (Rabbinical Text)

R. xix.5 151
R.xix.4 151

4 Ezra

7:37f 366
8:53 475

Book of Jubilees

23:11 366
24:3 366

Wisdom

15:7 421

www.ingramcontent.com/pod-product-compliance
Lightning Source LLC
Chambersburg PA
CBHW071554080526
44588CB00010B/909